World Population Projections for the 21st Century

Research Reports of the Institute for Population
Research and Social Policy (IBS),
University of Bielefeld
General Editor Herwig Birg
Volume 21

Herwig Birg is a Professor at the University of Bielefeld, where he is Director of the Institute for Population Research and Social Policy. He gained his doctorate in Economics at the Free University of Berlin and his *Habilitation* at the Faculty of Social Sciences of the Technical University of Berlin. He is a member of several national and international scientific organizations.

Herwig Birg

World Population Projections for the 21st Century

Theoretical Interpretations and Quantitative Simulations

Campus Verlag · Frankfurt
St. Martin's Press · New York

For information in the Western Hemisphere write:
Scholarly and Reference Division,
St. Martin's Press, 175 Fifth Avenue,
New York, NY 10010

Library of Congress Cataloging-in-Publication Data

Birg, Herwig.
Population projections for the 21st century: theoretical
interpretations and quantitative simulations / by Herwig Birg.
p. cm.
Includes bibliographical references and index.
ISBN 0-312-12771-5
1. Population forecasting. 2. Twenty-first century-Forecasts.
HB849.53.B57 1995
304.6'2'0112--dc20
95-16629
CIP

Die Deutsche Bibliothek – CIP-Einheitsaufnahme

Birg, Herwig:
World population projections for the 21st century: theoretical
interpretations and quantitative simulations / Herwig Birg. –
Frankfurt/Main: Campus Verlag; New York: St. Martin's
Press, 1995
(Research reports of the Institute for Population Research and Social
Policy (IBS), University of Bielefeld; Vol. 21)
ISBN 3-593-35432-2 (Campus-Verlag)
ISBN 0-312-12771-5 (St. Martin's Press)
NE: Institut für Bevölkerungsforschung und Sozialpolitik <Bielefeld>:
Forschungsberichte des Instituts für Bevölkerungsforschung und Sozialpolitik (IBS),
Universität Bielefeld

All rights reserved. No part of this book may be reproduced or transmitted in any form
or by any means, electronic or mechanical, including photocopying, recording, or by any
information storage and retrieval system, without permission in writing from the publishers.
Copyright © 1995 Campus Verlag GmbH, Frankfurt/Main
Cover Design: Atelier Warminski, Büdingen
Printed on acid free paper
Printed in Germany

To Ursula, my wife

"The Earth is known as the mother of all things, not because she bears them, but because she nurtures and feeds what she has born."
(Johann Peter Süssmilch)

"For the first time in my life, I saw the horizon in the form of an arc. The arc was more sharply outlined by a thin, dark-blue thread - our atmosphere. Evidently, this was not a great ocean of air as I had often been told. The fragility of what I saw filled me with horror."
(Ulf Mehrbold, a German astronaut).

List of Contents

Foreword   15

PART I

Historical and Theoretical Aspects of World Population Growth

Chapter I
Introduction   19

Chapter II
Population Theory and Human Ecology   25

2.1 The Central Proposition of This Book   25
2.2 The Common Origins of Population Theory and Human Ecology   26
2.3 Epistemological Aspects and the Problem of Ethics   36

Chapter III
Intercultural Differentials in Human Reproduction and the Decline in World Fertility   45

3.1 Introductory Remarks   45
3.2 Differential Reproduction, Biography and Fertility   51
3.3 Causes of High Fertility and the Significance of Inter-Generational Transfers   67

Chapter IV
World Population Projections for the 21st Century   83

4.1 Introduction and Proposition   83
4.2 Methodological Aspects, Basic Terms and the Initial Data used for Population Projections   91

4.3	Impact of Alternative Fertility Scenarios on World Population Growth	94
4.4	Impact of Alternative Mortality Scenarios upon World Population Growth	117
4.5	Population Changes by Country and Region	121
4.6	Summary	123

Chapter V
World Population Growth, Development and the Environment: Dimensions of a Global Dilemma — 143

5.1	Preliminary Remarks	143
5.2	Demo-Ecnomic and Socio-Economic Feedback and Self-Regulatory Mechanisms	144
5.3	The Environment-Development Dilemma, as Illustrated by the Issue of the Greenhouse Gas, Carbon Dioxide	152

Chapter VI
Ethical Aspects of Population-Oriented Policies — 163

6.1	Ethical Antagonisms in Classical Population Theory	163
6.2	The Unity between Demography and Ethics	165
6.3	The Lethal Danger of Demographic Metaphors	174
6.4	Conclusions	182

Chapter VII
Technical Appendix — 185

Appendix 1:
1.	Population in the base year of 1990	185
2.	Fertility	185
3.	Mortality and life expectancy	188

Literature — 195

List of Figures and Tables (Part I)

Figures

Figure 1:	Phases of Demographic Transition	47
Figure 2:	Regional Differentials in the Net Reproduction Rates of the 328 Counties ("Kreise") in Western Germany before Reunification	58
Figure 3:	Distribution of the Net Reproduction Rates of the 328 Counties ("Kreise") in Western Germany before Reunification	59
Figure 4:	Dependence of the Intergenerational Transfer Quotient upon the Net Reproduction Rate	73
Figure 5:	World Population Growth since 1750 and Projections for the 21st Century	86
Figure 6:	Age Structure of World Population 1990, 2050 and 2100	87
Figure 7:	Decline in the Total Fertility Rate from 1960-65 to 1990-95 by Major Area	88
Figure 8:	Increase in Life Expectancy at Birth from 1960-65 to 1990-95 by Major Area	89
Figure 9:	Decline in the Total Fertility Rate of the World Population from 1962 - 1990 and Scenarios for the Decline to Replacement Fertility Level (TFR = 2.13) in the Future (Form of Decline: Hyperbolic)	95
Figure 10:	Decline in the Toral Fertility Rate of the World Population to Replacement Fertility Level (TFR = 2.13, Form of Decline: Hyperbolic)	96
Figure 11:	Decline in the Toral Fertility Rate of the World Population to Replacement Fertility Level (TFR = 2.13, Form of Decline: S-Shaped)	97

Figure 12:	Decline in the Toral Fertility Rate of the World Population to Replacement Fertility Level (TFR = 2.13, Form of Decline: Linear)	98
Figure 13:	Decline in the Toral Fertility Rate of the World Population to Replacement Fertility Level (TFR = 2.13, Form of Decline: Hyperbolic and S-Shaped)	99
Figure 14:	Comparison of Various Assumptions on Fertility Decline for the World Population	107
Figure 15:	8 Variants of World Population Growth - Hyperbolic Decline in Fertility, Medium Mortality Level -	108
Figure 16:	8 Variants of World Population Growth - Hyperbolic Decline in Fertility Below Replacement Level, Medium Mortality Level -	109
Figure 17:	8 Variants of World Population Growth - S-Shaped Decline in Fertility, Medium Mortality Level -	110
Figure 18:	8 Variants of World Population Growth - Linear Decline in Fertility, Medium Mortality Level -	111
Figure 19:	Forms of Decline in the Total Fertility Rate to Replacement Fertility Level and their Impact on World Population Growth (Various Target Years)	126
Figure 20:	Forms of Decline in the Total Fertility Rate to Replacement Fertility Level and their Impact on World Population Growth	127
Figure 21a:	Components of Population Change, World Population Projection No. 2060.R.M., Target Year for Replacement Fertility: 2060 (Form of Decline: *Hyperbolic,* Mortality Level: Medium)	128
Figure 21b:	Components of Population Change, World Population Projection No. 2060.R.M., Target Year for Replacement Fertility: 2060 (Form of Decline: *Linear*, Mortality Level: Medium)	129
Figure 22:	World Population Levels Resulting from Different Reductions in Mortality (Mortality Reductions Between 0 and 10 Percent, Fertility Assumption: *Hyperbolic* Reduction to Replacement Fertility Level by the Year *2060*)	130
Figure 23:	World Population Levels Resulting from Different Reductions in Mortality (Mortality Reductions Between 0 and 10 Percent, Fertility Assumption: *Linear* Reduction to Replacement Fertility Level by the Year *2070*)	131

Figure 24:	Scenarios of World Population Growth Based on Different Assumptions Concerning an Increase in Infant and Child Mortality (Malthus-Variants, *Hyperbolic* Fertility Decline)	132
Figure 25:	Scenarios of World Population Growth Based on Different Assumptions Concerning an Increase in Infant and Child Mortality (Malthus-Variants, *Linear* Fertility Decline)	133
Figure 26:	World Population Projections by Geographic Regions and Countries	134
Figure 27:	Average Annual Absolute Increments to Total Population of World Regions, 2000-2150	135
Figure 28:	The Surplus of Births over Deaths - Annual Population Change in Millions	136
Figure 29:	Number of Women of Fertile Age (15-49) for Different Fertility Paths	137
Figure 30:	Diagrammatic Representation of Demo-economic Interactive Effects	146
Figure 31:	System of Interaction between Demo-economic, Demo-Ecological and Socio-economic Effects	151
Figure 32:	Development of the Population of the Federal Republic of Germany, Ignoring Inward and Outward Migratory Flows	153
Figure 33:	Chains of Problems with Demographic Causes in Industrial and Developing Countries	155
Figure 34:	Correlation in Principle between Level of Development (Expressed in Terms of Per Capita Income and of Life Expectancy) and Energy Output, or Energy-Related CO_2 Emissions, in or about 1990	157
Figure 35:	Correlation between Population Trends and Energy-Related CO_2 Emissions in Industrial and Developing Countries	159
Figure 36:	Areas of the Cohort-Specific Mortality Rates in the Lexis Diagram	192
Figure 37:	Mortality Rates for Male World Birth Cohorts	193
Figure 38:	Mortality Rates for Female World Birth Cohorts	194

Tables

Table 1:	Factors of High Fertility and Corresponding Policy Concepts	69
Table 2a:	World Population Growth since the Birth of Christ	85
Table 2b:	The World Population Level in 2150, Based on Different Assumptions as to the Rapidity of the Decline in Fertility (TFR) to the Replacement Level of 2.13 Births per Woman	101
Table 3:	Comparison between the World Bank Population Projections of 1989/90, 1992/93 and 1994/95	112
Table 4:	World Population Growth Assuming a Hyperbolic Decline in Fertility up to 2060	113
Table 5:	The Impact of Delays in the *Hyperbolic* Decline in Fertility to the Replacement Level (TFR = 2.13), or to Just Under Replacement Level (TFR = 2.0 or 2.1)	114
Table 6:	The Impact of Delays in the *Linear* Decline in Fertility to the Replacement Level (TFR=2.13), or to Just Under Replacement Level (TFR = 2.0 or 2.1)	115
Table 7:	Dependence of the Number of Women in Reproductive Age (15-49) upon the Fertility Rate (Number of Women in Millions)	116
Table 8:	The Influence of Alternative Mortality Assumptions on the Outcome of World Population Projections (Target Year = *2060, Hyperbolic* Decline in Fertility)	138
Table 9:	The Influence of Alternative Mortality Assumptions on the Outcome of World Population Projections (Target Year = *2070, Linear* Decline in Fertility)	139
Table 10:	World Population Level Assuming a Sudden Increase in Infant and Child Mortality (Malthusian Variants, Target Year = 2060, *Hyperbolic* Decline in Fertility)	140
Table 11:	World Population Level Assuming a Sudden Increase in Infant and Child Mortality (Malthusian Variants, Target Year = 2060, *Linear* Decline in Fertility)	141
Table 12:	Population by Country, 1995 and 2100	142

PART II

Quantitative Projections and Simulations of World Population Growth for the 21st Century
(Graphs and Tables)

Appendix 2:		207
1.	Notation used to donate the population projection variants	207
2.	List of variables	208
3.	Synopsis of the Variants of Population Projections, Aggregate Figures for Males and Females in 1990, 2050, 2100, and 2150	209

Foreword

In 1958, the United Nations conducted a world population projection for the year 2000 which we can already say today will be accurate to within just 3% of the figure projected. This perhaps surprising degree of accuracy is not a matter of luck, for subsequent projections for 2000 made in the 1960s, '70s and '80s all yielded virtually identical results, all of them lying within the relatively narrow range of 6.1-6.3 billion. The world population projections set out in this book should not be regarded as forecasts which seek to predict population trends during the 21st century as accurately as possible: rather, these are *"if ..., then ... computations"* which show how the world population would develop if a certain pattern of fertility and mortality were followed in future. The actual future course of fertility and mortality will depend on economic, social and political developments in both industrial and developing countries, all of which are, or can be, shaped by domestic and international policy-making. Hence these computations can also be treated as information on the demographic consequences of particular policies, or as the basis for designing policies intended to prevent the demographic consequences which would inevitably arise if no policy efforts were made. Even if the number of children born per woman falls off extremely rapidly, the world population will grow to at least half as much again as today's figure simply because of its currently young age profile. One ought therefore to expect that, by the end of the 21st century, the world population will have risen from today's 5.7 billion to 11 billion or more. Whether the figure actually reached at the end of the 21st century might be 12 or 13 billion depends on the deeds or omissions of policy-makers during the coming decades.

    Financial support for printing this book and preparing the population projections set out in Chapter 4 and Part II was provided by the German World Population Foundation (*Deutsche Stiftung Weltbevölkerung*), and my kind thanks go to it for this assistance. I would like to thank Carsten Wessel, who at the time belonged to the staff of the *Institute for Population Research and Social Policy* at the *University of Bielefeld*, for so meticulously carrying out the empirical computations and for producing the tables. For another vital component of the book, its many graphs, I would particular like to thank Gabriele Lütkemeier. However, I take sole responsibility for the content of the book, and for any errors which may have occurred. I am also grateful to the foundations and academies listed in the introductory chapter, which invited me to deliver papers to a number of events in the run-up to the *International Conference on Population and Development* (ICPD) in Cairo in 1994, thus providing a vital stimulus to the task of compiling the book. Last but not least, my thanks go to Neil Johnson for his authoritative, cooperative approach in preparing the translation, and to Brigitte Ballhause, who carried out all of the lay-out and editing work needed to prepare the book for the printers.

Herwig Birg

University of Bielefeld, March 1995

PART I

Historical and Theoretical Aspects of World Population Growth

Chapter 1

Introduction

Just a brief look at the political realities of today's world is enough to show that humankind at the close of the 20th century does not consist of a unified entity, but breaks down into countless nation states, societies and population groups with different cultures and different interests; indeed, it is as if the term "humankind", which carries a pronounced, agreeable connotation of unity, refers to another world, and perhaps even stems from a completely different one or from a long-lost era in the past, having little in common with the demographic realities which this book will deal with. Things are not much different when we address the term of "world population". Like the idea of humankind, this term is based on a conception of homogeneity and unity which, taken of itself, is unfortunately little more than just an abstract construct. In fact, there is a general conviction that ideal constructs of this kind are more or less irrelevant to the world outside the covers of an academic book, and it is true that demonstrating their relevance is not a simple task. Nevertheless, deep down we are aware or we do sense that, if anything at all can tame or shape what we know as "reality", then it is the power of thought and that of language which gives it its force. An encouraging example from recent history is the revolution in eastern Germany and the former Soviet-bloc. The Leipzig demonstrators took to the streets in November 1989 chanting, "we are the people!". In the face of the government of what was then East Germany (i.e., the Democratic Republic) and also of a Soviet military presence still numbering 400,000 troops, these demonstrators set the ball rolling towards the official reunification of Germany which, as if by a miracle, was successfully concluded without a shot having been fired or a drop of blood being shed.

Events such as these quite abruptly display the power of ideas, language and concepts, and especially point up the distinction between the concepts of "people" and "population". Many are of the view that there is no longer any substantial difference between the two, and that they can be regarded as synonymous. That may indeed be so in everyday discourse. However, in the rare moments when the stream of history bursts its banks and changes course altogether, the future is utterly dependent on the power of thought and ideas upheld by language, and also on the subtle difference between terms such as "people" and "population". It would not have entered anyone's head at the Leipzig demonstrations to treat these two terms as synonyms, and nobody was heard chanting "we are the population!".

The "world population" is itself made up of numerous different "populations", which do not regard themselves as mere populations any more than the Leipzig demonstrators did. My reason for drawing attention to this distinction between a people and a population is the following. If a book devotes as much space to the quantitative aspects of population trends as this one does, its author needs to be all the clearer and all the more unequivocal about his own position with regard to the so-called "qualitative" aspects of population change. That, however, is easier said than done, as the first difficulties already arise in the fact that the usual parlance in this branch of science still lacks the degree of sensitivity which is so essential when dealing with such topics.

Problems are immediately raised by the fact that scientific literature persists in speaking of "quantitative'" and "qualitative" population developments which, however unwittingly, conjures associations with the biologistic era of demography when it was felt to be the done thing - in the scientific world too, unfortunately - to draw "qualitative" distinctions between human populations, speaking of "superior" and "inferior" races. We now know what dire consequences resulted from this intellectual and linguistic failure of which biologistic demography must stand accused. The Nazis' so-called "racial hygiene" led on in Germany to the governmentally organized slaughter of millions of people on an industrial scale. This era of history cannot be viewed independently of the history of demography, and it does form part of the background to this book.

Can the crimes of the Nazis be regarded as a form of "Big Bang" in the history of human cultural failure, just as the Big Bang in the theory of physics marks the absolute beginning of the development of the universe? From the moral point of view, the answer has to be Yes. However, that does not end the story as far as biologistic demography is concerned, for like all developments in the history of ideas, it has another, past history running up to it. That past history of biologistic demography is intimately bound up with the history of the biological theory of human genetics, which in turn is rooted in the materialist-rationalist philosophy of the modern era. J.-B. Lamarck's 18th-century theory of the inheritability of acquired characteristics in human beings could only have developed on the foundations of materialist-rationalist philosophy. When August Weismann discovered the true nature of genetic inheritance in 1885, refuting the theory of the inheritability of acquired characteristics when his own theory was published in 1892, it was already too late for the history of ideas to manage a radical change of course. Lamarckism lived on into the 20th century, in ideas such as the theory of inheritance put forward in the Stalin era by T.D. Lyssenko. By that time, political thought had developed onward on the basis of the inheritability of acquired characteristics for too long in a certain direction, triggering off political developments which were to prove irreversible. Examples of this nature can also be found in other fields of the history of science. One such idea is the view based upon philosophical dualism that the characteristics of humans as thinking, cultural beings depended upon their characteristics as physical beings. It was on this basis that the theory of eugenics developed, which was pushed onward during the 19th century, especially by Francis Galton in Britain. The aim of this school of thought was to "improve" humankind in biological terms by changing its genetic substance.

Now that molecular biologists have discovered the foundations of human genetics in the 20th century, the aims of the eugenicists in the 19th have regained currency, as their attainment appears almost within our reach. Experts believe it is possible that the genome project - which aims to completely decode the genetic material in humans - may be successfully completed by the year 2005. Could the dreams of the 19th-century eugenicists then come true? At the 1994 World Population Conference in Cairo in 1994, eugenics did not play any significant part in the official documents prepared by governmental delegations, nor in those of the UN itself. Yet anyone reading the media reports on the conference would find that a number of commentators could not resist giving free rein to their imaginations beyond the official agenda of the event. Their thoughts circled around the subjects of eugenics to such a degree that one wondered if they were not reporting on another conference altogether. The conference report in *TIME*, for example, concluded: "... though the world's numbers have leaped 1.7 billion between Budapest and Cairo, in those two decades the *qualitative* aspect of birth has also changed drastically. Science is shining its knowledge of human genes deep into the uterine cave, giving unimagined precision to the refrain that as the twig is bent, so shall the tree incline. In the developed world, this knowledge is opening the way for what Darwin would have called 'unnatural selection': choice on who should be brought to daylight. *Bioethics is knocking at the door of demographics"* (*TIME*, Sept. 19, 1994, p. 104 - this author's italics).

So will the demographers actually open that door? Does it even need opening now, or has it not stood wide-open for the last five hundred years in the history of ideas? Has there not always been a lively exchange of views on and about such matters?

Without doubt, the story of demography during the last two hundred years has been subject to the formative influence of the main strands of biological thought. Now, though, it is high time that biology finally gave up this lead role to the social sciences and humanities. Several important preliminary steps towards such a new beginning have been made this century, a good example in Germany being the work of Gerhard Mackenroth, to name the most important sociologist working in areas touching upon demography, and a number of other names could be added from the disciplines of anthropology and philosophy, from throughout Europe and the USA. Nevertheless, we are still a long way from achieving a new foundation for the science of demography. Indeed, if anything, that target is slipping still further away into the distance. The main reason for this is the renaissance of Malthusianism. If we replace the "food barrier" in Malthusian population theory by the "ecological barrier", and the "lower classes" by the population of the developing countries, all appearances would have it that Malthusian population theory can readily be applied to today's environmental problems and global population growth. This quirk of the theoreticians' minds is already having a fateful effect: population theory is being used as a justification for a proposal simply to let infants die in developing countries whose development cannot keep pace with the growth of their populations, ostensibly in order to prevent things getting still worse.

Another development giving grounds for pessimism is the revival of biological-materialist lines of thinking, e.g. in the form of theories purporting to identify racial differences in intelligence levels. Until such time as the groundwork laid for racism by the humanities and philosophy has been recognized, any attempt to refute it using the instruments of modern scientific research will be doomed to failure. What use is it if modern genetic science deprives racism of any kind of rational foundation, as the pioneering work of Luca and Francesco Cavalli-Sforza has done, if such research findings are then ignored for the sake of saving racism?

The close intellectual connections between biology and demography, especially between Charles Darwin's biological theory of evolution and Thomas R. Malthus' classic theory of population, are dealt with in Chapter 2 which follows, outlining the historical development of the science, while the political and ethical consequences of this theoretical interrelationship are the subject of the closing chapter. In between these two cornerstones are the three main chapters dealing, respectively, with this author's biographical theory of fertility, the quantitative projections of world population changes for the 21st century, and an analysis of the interrelationships between population growth, development and the environment, taking emissions of carbon dioxide (the "greenhouse gas") as an illustrative example.

These various chapters are based on what were originally separate contributions made on different occasions, either in German or in English. In fact, those occasions fitted very neatly into the thematic and chronological framework of my work over the past few years. Chapter 2, on Population Theory and Human Ecology, is the revised version of a paper presented to the European Population Conference in Paris in 1991 (which subsequently appeared in A. Blum & J.-L. Rallu [eds.]: *European Population. Vol. 2: Demographic Dynamics*, Paris 1993). Chapter 3, on Intercultural Differentials in Human Reproduction and the Decline in World Fertility, is based on an essay written for the interdisciplinary working group of the Werner Reimers Foundation, the participants in which come from a number of fields but primarily from those of biology, sociology and historiography. It was first published in German in the working group's report compilation (in: E. Voland [ed.]: *Fortpflanzung: Natur und Kultur im Wechselspiel*, Frankfurt 1991). Chapter 4, the World Population Projections for the 21st Century, stems from a research project sponsored by the *Deutsche Stiftung Weltbevölkerung* (= German World Population Foundation), which I reported upon at the World Congress of Sociology in Bielefeld in July 1994. A shortened account of these findings was published in German, as *"Die Eigendynamik des Weltbevölkerungswachstums"* (in: *Spektrum der Wissenschaft*, Sept. 1994). Chapter 5, on World Population Growth, Development and the Environment: Dimensions of a Global Dilemma, was originally written in German for the *Bundeszentrale für politische Bildung* (an adult education and public information institution) to accompany the federal government's publicity work in advance of the Cairo population conference (published in: Bundeszentrale für politische Bildung [ed.]: *Aus Politik und Zeitgeschichte*, supplement to the weekly Das

Parlament, Bonn, Sept. 2, 1994). Chapter 6, on Ethical Aspects of Population-Oriented Policies, came about at the invitation of Dr. Thomas, Director of the Lindenthal Institute in Cologne, who had asked me to present an antithetical paper to Julian Simon's population theory at a conference in the run-up to the Cairo event. The papers submitted by Julian Simon and myself will both be published in the forthcoming conference transcript. My talk was entitled "On the Demographic Aspects of Ethics and the Ethical Aspects of Demography" (*"Betrachtung über die demographischen Aspekte der Ethik und die ethischen Aspekte der Demographie"*). This closing chapter again takes up the issues introduced in Chapter 2 on the historical background. Its central thesis is that demography occupied a position at the centre of the social sciences in its beginnings in the 18th century, and that it is returning to that central position today as its central questions at that time - concerning the carrying capacity of the planet Earth - are more important now than ever before.

Chapter 2

Population Theory and Human Ecology

2.1 The Central Proposition of This Book

The postulate of this book is that the central topics of demography and human ecology are essentially the same and can be separated only artificially. The fact that population growth is one of the key determinants of the ecological crisis is the basis for this view. But there is another good reason: every important scientific problem has an ethical dimension. This is especially true of population theory and of human ecology. In the field of ecology, ethical debate has led to two diametrically opposed positions, those of "spaceship ethics" and "lifeboat ethics". Both concepts use arguments from population science, a fact which strengthens the close connection between population science and human ecology. "Spaceship ethics" draws a parallel between the situation on earth and that in a spacecraft, which depends upon solidarity among its crew for the success of its mission, and indeed the crew's survival. The viewpoint represented corresponds to those of one of the classic scholars of demography, J.P. Süssmilch. "Lifeboat ethics" propounds that the continued existence of mankind is best guaranteed if the rich nations of the world, already living on a seaworthy lifeboat, leave the rest to their fate swimming in the water. "Lifeboat ethics" is also echoed in classical population theory, namely in Thomas R. Matlhus' "Principle of Population". The objective of this chapter is to analyse the historical and epistemological connections between population science and ecology and so to stimulate interdisciplinary discussion and cooperation on the subject at hand.

2.2 The Common Origins of Population Theory and Human Ecology

(a)   Initial Methodological Remarks

Ecology has only recently become a matter for public discussion. This got under way in the 1970's as the effects of worldwide environmental pollution became known. The expression "ecology", however, has been in existence for 125 years. It was introduced in 1866 by the German zoologist Ernst Haeckel: " ... with 'ecology' is understood the whole science of the relationships between organisms and their surrounding environment, to which can be counted their 'conditions of existence' in a wide sense" (Haeckel, 1866: 286).

Much older than the definition of ecology as a science are real ecological problems. It is the general opinion that ecological problems first occurred in connection with the industrial revolution and the creation of modern industrialized societies, but in fact they are as old as humankind itself. Although some indigenous peoples lived in harmony with nature for hundreds or thousands of years, others changed natural conditions to a significant extent. The aboriginal inhabitants of Australia, for instance, converted the forested areas into prairie and even desert through systematic burning. Upon settling the Hawaiian islands in the 4th and 5th centuries the Polynesians wiped out more than half of the bird species then existing. Another example is that of the Mediterranean landscape. Plato describes ecological problems in pre-classical Greece in his dialogue "Kritias" with the words: "At the time we are speaking of these ravages had not begun. Our present mountains were high crests, what we now call the plains of Phelleus were covered with rich soil, and there was abundant timber on the Mountains, of which traces may still be seen. For some of our mountains at present will only support trees, but not so very long ago trees fit for the roofs of vast buildings were felled there and the rafters are still in existence. There were also many other lofty cultivated trees which provided unlimited fodder for beasts. Besides, the soil got the benefit of the yearly 'water from Zeus', which was not lost, as it is today, by running off a barren ground to the sea; a plentiful supply of it was received into the soil and stored up in the layers of nonporous potter's clay. Thus the moisture absorbed in the higher regions percolated to the hollows and so all quarters were lavishly provided with springs and rivers. Even to this day the sanctuaries at their former sources survive to prove the truth of our present account of the country. This, then, was the natural condition of the district at large, and it had received cultivation such as might be expected from true husbandmen, with no other vocation, who were also lovers of all that is nobel and men of admirable natural parts, possessed of an excellent soil, a generous water supply and an eminently temperate climate." (Plato, 1971: 1216-17).

Haeckel used the term "ecology" principally in connection with plant and animal ecology. The expression "human ecology", which places humankind at the centre of consideration, is first found in the 1920's, principally in the areas of human biology, the social sciences, geography and, of course, ecology. Two social science books with the title "Human Ecology" were published in 1950 in the United States which were principally concerned with aspects of settlement patterns (A.H. Hawley, J.A. Quinn, 1950). Shortly afterwards Eugene O. Odum defined "human ecology" as a boundary area lying between the social sciences and ecology in his mainly natural-science-oriented book "Fundamentals of Ecology" (Odum, 1953). He described the research field of human ecology as a task only possible through interdisciplinary cooperation. Paul R. and Anne H. Ehrlich took this course in their book "Population, Resources, Environment; Issues in Human Ecology" (Ehrlich and Ehrlich, 1970) and since then there has been a flood of publications in a similar vein.

The mass media report almost daily on themes of human ecology. News on the destruction of tropical rain forests and the virgin forests of North America, sea and lake pollution, the increasing temperature of the earth's atmosphere, the extinction of species, etc, etc, is spread in countless articles, books, radio and television programmes, seminars and congresses. Population science is being swept along by an ever- increasing volume of new literature. In the deluge of news of disasters, and of speculation, doomsday visions and fears about the future, demography - with its quantitative methods of population analysis and forecasting - has the role of offering a comparatively safe hold, like a solid raft in a raging torrent. The raft provides the basis for the scientific projection of population growth and thus for the expected anthropological pressure on the world's ecosystems. Thus population science is appearing increasingly as a public issue.

In Germany the complex of demography/ecology and demography/economics has been selected as one of the foci of adult education through the mass media.

For the winter semester 1991/92 Germany's radio stations broadcasted a series of 30 programmes compiled by an interdisciplinary team of scientists. Some universities and many of the 350 communal adult education centres offered courses parallel to the radio broadcastes. The German Institute for Research in Distance Education ("Deutsches Institut für Fernstudien) of the University of Tübingen published a didactic text accompanying each programme together with excercises for 18,000 students which were evalutated by computer.

The radio series was entitled "Human Ecology". The subtitle "World Population, Environment, Nutrition" demonstrates that population science occupies a central position in the range of topics presented from the natural and social sciences, economics, ecology and philosophy. Since I was responsible for the area of demography in this project I had to be very clear about the relationships that exist between human ecology and population science. I had determined three classes of relationship, each existing on its own level. The first level consists of the real phenomena of population and economic growth as part of the civilization process including the resulting socio- economic, demo-economic and demo-ecological problems, to mention only the most important classes within the network of problems resulting. On the second level are the connections in the historical development of the various sciences dealing with real problems, such as, biology, economics, sociology, ecology, statistics and - last but not least - demography. The third level comprises the relationships between the epistemological problems of these sciences. In Popper's ontology the epistemological level belongs to what he called "world 3", it is the world of thought, logical statements and timeless mathematical truths (Popper, 1979: 154-55). The scientific problems of ethics and the logical connections between the scientific problems of various disciplines also belong to "world 3". The logical relationships between scientific problems must not be confused with the relationships existing between real phenomena on the first level or with the historical connections between the sciences on the second.

In what follows, however, I shall not adhere strictly to the definitions of the three levels - in such a short chapter this is neither possible nor necessary. But there are points, such as the interpretation of Malthusian population theory, where I consider a clear analysis to be impossible unless differentiation is made between real, scientific-historical and epistemological relationships. The complexity of human ecological questions cannot be adequately discussed in any other way.

The history of real population problems (as part of level 1) and the history of population science (as part of level 2) have run so consistently parallel, and have influenced each other to such an extent, that their presentation can begin either with level 1 or with level 2. Since I am going to confine my considerations of real phenomena to those of the present and of the expected future, I shall put the historical aspects of level 2 first. My treatment of epistemological relationships will be separate and confined to ethical aspects. I shall return to the relationships between ethics and demography and examine them in more detail in Chapter 6.

(b) Human Ecological Approaches and the Demographic Carrying Capacity Analyses in Süssmilch's Population Theory

The usual present-day definition of "human ecology" is very wide: Human ecology is the science of the interrelationships between humankind (individuals, population groups) and other forms of life as well as between humankind and the environmental factors it influences. Though it appears clear and simple at first glance, upon further scrutiny this definition is not so much a watertight vessel as a wickerwork basket. What makes it "laeky" is the expression "humankind". According to the humanist Erasmus of Rotterdam man ist not born, but bred. Because human ecology is based on the concept of humankind it has to refer to anthropology which, however, is not a closed field, and consists of historical anthropology, biological anthropology, philosophical anthropology and other sub-anthropologies. The image of mankind presented by biological anthropology was and is more optimistic than that projected by social and philosophical anthropology. As a result of anthropological environmental destruction a sceptical, if not a negative, public image of humankind has been created. It is even possible that humanity's image will be so fundamentally changed by and through its continuing disregard of the environment that radically new values and a re-evaluation of humankind's cultural background will emerge.

How strongly the humanistic interpretation of man as the "pinnacle of creation" (Herder, 1784) has already changed can be seen from an historical review. We are now occupied more intensively than ever before with ecological questions because so many ecosystems are endangered. But Haeckel did not introduce the term "ecology" in 1866 in expectation of existent or future ecological crises. The difference between the ecology of the 18th and 19th centuries and that of today

29

is that of the motivation to work on ecological problems. For the demographer and theologist J.P. Süssmilch (1707-1767) the decisive motivation for his principal work was the wonderful harmony and order of nature and of the regularity of the laws governing demographic change. The formulation of his title "The Divine Order in Human Change Arising from Births, Deaths and Reproduction" (Berlin 1741) reflects his impression of an overall and wonderous "order of things". Süssmilch wrote that he received the impulse for his work from the English naturalist and theologist William Derham (1675-1735). Derham published a book in 1713 with the title "Physico-Theology" followed in 1714 by "Astro-Theology" and in 1729 by "Christo-Theology". Here again, the titles show that Derham wanted to demonstrate the hand of God in the harmonious structures, proportions and relations of animal and plant life just as Isaac Newton had done with his laws of gravity and mechanics of the planets. It was the following passage from Derham that inspired Süssmilch: "... and by a curious Harmony, and just Proportion between the increase of all Animals, and the length of their Lives, the World is through all ages well, but not over-stored. One Generation passeth away, and another Generation cometh, so equally in it's Room, to balance the Stock of the Terraqueous Globe in all Ages, and Places, and among all Creatures ..." (Derham, 1713: 171).

Süssmilch's contribution to population statistics and demography can be briefly summarized as follows: (1) He analysed the relationships of births and deaths to the population structure on the basis of church records for Prussian communities. From these relationships he derived methods for estimating the population of countries without population censuses. (2) He calculated the sex ratio at birth and defended the empirical value of 106 boys to 100 girls against the hypothesis of Nikolaus Bernoulli (1687-1759) and Abraham Moivre (1667-1754) that on the basis of probability theory the relation should be even at 100:100 and that any observed deviation would be random. (3) He calculated the differences in the proportions of the sexes according to age groups and analysed their regional disparities. (4) He performed mortality analyses according to the cause of death and, together with the mathematician Leonhard Euler, produced one of the first mortality tables. (5) He investigated regional differences in fertility and also regional and international differences in population growth. (6) Finally, he produced the first realistic forecast of the world's population (7 billion, see below).

Süssmilch's population analyses are a good example of early ecological and human ecological research. This is particularly apparent in his world population projection. It was based on an empirical carrying-capacity analysis and not, as per Malthus, on theoretical assumptions as to the patterns of growth in nutritional volumes and population. His demo-ecological analysis demonstrates a search for order and regularity - nowadays we would say for "system mechanisms" or for the laws of homoeostasis - and he only afterwards posed and answered the question of the world's maximum population. Süssmilch placed great value on his observation that humankind can change the natural carrying capacity of the world by means of knowledge and hard work. But he was not a dogmatic "populationist" who implicitly wished to increase the size of the population by all the argumentative means at his disposal. The "laws of order" were for him the most appropriate basis of population growth, not the artificial population measures of the mercantile state. Population growth would come to a halt automatically once the limits of the natural carrying capacity, including the efforts of man to improve it, were reached. This is in strong contrast to the "Principle of Population" propounded by Malthus who considered that violent "positive checks" such as wars or more or less violent "moral restraints" and "prudential checks" would be necessary to control the growth in population.

In the 17th and 18th centuries every piece of scientific work was seen as contributing towards proving or refuting the existence of God. Science and philosophy were circling around the questions of whether the God-sent miseries of this world such as wars, disease and natural disasters were really necessary and, if so, where the good might lie in them. Süssmilch didn't take on his life's work in demography out of scientific curiosity nor in order to create a scientific basis for his arguments for social policies and reforms to support the poor. The real motivation was to prove the existence of God by demographic means. Süssmilch's demography was a by-product of an attempt to provide an empirical proof of the existence of God. The central questions as to the sense and purpose of the calamities of this world were also answered by Süssmilch by empirical demographic means. In the third main chapter of this principal work of 1741, he reaches the conclusion that such calamities, also including the later Malthusian "positive checks", are not necessary and, in fact, are the sole responsibility of humankind itself.

I have made this point here for two reasons. Firstly, because it is highly relevant in our own time: modern thinkers are increasingly inclined to the hypothesis that the threatening ecological catastrophies are highly likely to lead to the destruction of human life on our planet. The second reason is the central role played by population theory as the basis for forecasting population levels and therefore for predicting inevitable future catastrophies. This is the decisive problem posed by Süssmilch in his third chapter which has the title "Are war and plague necessary, and how many people can live on the Earth?". In this chapter he counters Derham's theological arguments for the necessity of such disasters. He presents the detailed man-land carrying capacity analyses for various countries upon which he bases his world population forecasts. The result is that the world population can and will rise to seven billion, i.e. to approximately ten times the then existing world population of 750 million, before the limits of the carrying capacity are reached, and growth therefore comes slowly to a stop (Süssmilch, 1741: page 38 of the foreword and page 78 in the text). In the extended third edition published in Berlin in 1765 he computed a more or less hypothetical number of 13.932 billion (Süssmilch 1765, Vol. 2, p. 177). From this he reaches the conclusion "... (from my analyses it is) irrefutable that war and plague are not necessary, and indeed many hundreds of years can pass without these evils and the world will not be too full" (Süssmilch, 1741: 98). 57 years later Thomas Malthus published his "Principle of Population". In the preface we find: "It is an obvious truth, which has been taken notice of by many writers, that population must always be kept down to the level of means of subsistence; but no writer that the author recollects has inquired particularly into the means by which this level is effected: and it is a view of these means which forms, to my mind, the strongest obstacle in the way to any very great future improvement of society" (Malthus, 1798: 61). Had Malthus read Süssmilch's work? He uses tables from Süssmilch's book without even mentioning the conclusions that Süssmilch derived from them. We don't know whether Malthus ignored Süssmilch's arguments because he couldn't speak German, or whether he had the tables translated but not the text. It is, however, certain that the history of population science would have been different had Malthus fully considered Süssmilch's ideas and not simply used his book as a data bank.

(c) The Effects of Malthusian Population Theory on Biology and Economics

Süssmilch's population theory directly relates to ecological questions, so much so that one can postulate an identity between population theory and population ecology in his work. In Malthus' population theory there is also a direct connection between the size of the population and agricultural/ecological carrying-capacity; but more important are the indirect connections made with the development of economic theory and - separately - with evolution theory. The indirect effects described are long-term and they are, in fact, increasing in our times in unexpected ways. In the meanwhile one doesn't have to be a prophet to suppose that we will be confronted with a renaissance of Malthusianism. This new trend is already apparent in some recent book titles, e.g. P. Neeurath's recent (1994) work: From Malthus to the Club of Rome *and Back*.

This is particularly astonishing since neither of the two basic postulates of Malthusian theory has proven to be valid; neither the assumption that food supply increases only arithmetically nor the other that the lower classes react to improved living and income conditions by increasing their fertility and population growth. The Malthusian postulates were rejected as early as the beginning of the 19th century (Charles Hall 1805, William Hazlitt 1807, James Grahame 1816, John Weyland 1816, Georg Ensor 1818, Pierce Ravenstone 1821, Michael Thomas Sadler 1830 and others), and in fact the Malthusian "principle of population" was refuted by Süssmilch's work in 1741 even before the theory was propounded. Nevertheless, although the theory - scientifically seen - no longer exists, Malthusianism is still very much alive, especially in connection with human ecological problems. Why is this?

The first reason has to do with its impact on the theory of biology. In his autobiography and in his diaries Charles Darwin wrote that the "principle of population" had given him the inspiration for his theory of selection, which is the basis for the theory of evolution (Darwin, 1958). There is, in fact, an obvious similarity between the Malthusian "positive checks" and the mechanism of selection. This is even demonstrated in the way in which the "principle of population" is formulated: "... nature has scattered the seeds of life abroad with the most profuse and liberal hand. She has been comparatively sparing in the room and the nourishment necessary to rear them. The germs of existence contained in this spot of earth, with ample food, and ample room to expand in, would fill millions of worlds in the course of a few thousand years. Necessity ... restrains them within the prescribed bounds. The race of plants and the race of animals shrink under this great restrictive law. And the race of man cannot, by any efforts of reason, escape from it. Among plants and animals its effects are waste of seed, sickness, and premature death. Among mankind, misery and vice" (Malthus, 1798: 71-72).

This biological view had significant effects on the theory of fertility which plays a central role in human ecology. Biologists define two types of reproduction strategies of which one, the so-called "r-strategy", has direct reference to Malthus. Primitive forms of life which employ the r-strategy bank on the sheer quantity of their offspring whereas forms with a better-developed nervous system rely on the "c-strategy" in which preference is given to the quality of offspring rather than its quantity. The "c" here stands for carrying capacity, i.e. these life forms adjust the number of their offspring to the carrying capacity of the relevant ecological systems. In doing this they exercise "reproductive self-constraint". Specialists in quality are the large mammals and birds. Into which class does mankind fall? This question, of course, is rhetorical but nevertheless justifiable because Malthus created his population theory to describe the reproductive behaviour of man, and not that of animals. But the "Malthusian parameter r"-signifying the maximum possible rate of reproduction - is used in biology for the reproductive behaviour of the lower forms of life, not for higher forms employing the "c-strategy". Of course, no biologist would maintain that mankind reproduces according to the "r-strategy". Nevertheless, biologists do judge the effects of man's reproductive behaviour on ecological systems to be catastrophic, even though we reproduce ourselves - biologically seen - on the basis of the "c-strategy"; to quote one of the contemporary German biological anthropologists: "Man has obviously used his intelligence primarily to rapidly continue the old Darwinian contest of "survival of the fittest" with increasingly sophisticated cultural and technological means. He has eliminated the factors limiting population size by means of his inventions with ever increasing success and speed, and thereby pushed the 'carrying capacity' supporting his own population growth always in an upward direction. Thus ecological and economic crises and catastrophies were inevitable in the long term. 'That the grandiose ecological success of our species is presenting us, and our natural surroundings, with increasing problems is not a result of abandonment of our natural virtues but because we have followed them almost blindly and consistently' (Markl, 1984). It has to be noted here that the 'natural virtues' named with undisguised sarcasm are in fact the result of billions of years of natural selection and 'survival-of the-fittest' optimization" (Vogel, 1986: 27/28).

This biological interpretation is not generally convincing and I think it contains a contradiction: if, in fact, the characteristic of the c-strategy is that animals adapt more successfully to the ecological carrying capacity the more highly developed they are, then why should man in particular, without doubt the most highly developed animal, be in the position of not being able to apply the c-strategy to such good effect as lower animals? If artificial interference in the human ecological balance is causing the crises then mankind can correct the mistakes, or at least those that have not already led to irreversible ecological damage.

The second reason for Malthus becoming more relevant to human ecology lies in the effects of his population theory on the development of the economic sciences. Malthus himself was one of the founders of classical economics. His supposition that wage increases above the minimum subsistence level are impossible in the long term because the birth rate and therefore also the supply of labour thereby increases, was adopted by David Ricardo as a basis for his classical wage theory. The scientific standing of Malthus' main economic publication, the "Principles of Political Economy" is far higher than his extremely polemic "Principle of Population", which he conceived as a political challenge and published anonymously. Nevertheless, the effects of his "Principle of Population" on economic theory were highly significant in that they contributed to a widening in the division between the liberal British and socialist German, or continental, schools of economic theory. Karl Marx and Friedrich Engels were well aware of the analogy between the selective mechanism of "positive checks" in population growth and the selective mechanism of economic competition which pushes the weakest out of the market (Engels, 1974: 501). The close intellectual ties between economic liberalism and Malthusian population theory compelled Marx and Engels not only to damn the population theory but also to propose a social utopia opposed in the extreme to the liberal position.

In the 20th century the division of economic theory into liberal and social currents induced a polarization in the economic theory of international development and ideologization of aid policies. This has caused difficulties in the realization of international aid programmes for the developing countries and in many cases has blocked it completely. As to economic theory itself, after the changes in eastern Europe it remains to be seen whether socialist ideals actually belong to the past or not. It is also possible, even probable, that critical ecological conditions will lead to a revision of liberal economic theory. The first signs of this have already been provided by reforms in methods of calculating the social product. For instance, in Germany the national accounting system is planned to be extended to incorporate an "ecological accounting system". A fitting phrase is provided by U. von Weizsäcker (1989: 143): "Prices have to reflect the ecological truth". This "ecological truth" might well lead us to a new "economic truth".

2.3 Epistemological Aspects and the Problem of Ethics

(a) Epistemological aspects

Not many demographers know that the further development of Malthusian population theory took place within the framework of the economic sciences and not that of demography. This occurred because classical economics gave way to its neoclassical successor in which the model of static equilibrium developed into one of dynamic equilibrium growth (R.M. Solow, R.F. Harrod, E.D. Domar, E.S. Phelps and others). In the static model, population was a stationary variable, but in the neoclassical model of "equilibrium growth" and the models of the "golden rule of accumulation" the population grew geometrically along with the national product and other principal variables of the national accounting.

The change of paradigm is revolutionary from the viewpoint of population theory. The model of "equilibrium growth" is in direct contrast to the "Principle of Population". The sense and purpose of Malthus' "Principle" was to prove that a geometrically growing population must lead to a society's economic and moral breakdown. The neoclassical growth model, however, demonstrated that technological advance allowed a continuous increase in per capita income, even when the population grew geometrically. The neoclassical economists therefore maintained nothing more or less than that steady growth in prosperity was possible for decades, if not for centuries. The idea of perfected material and social living conditions had already been propagated in the course of the French Revolution by the social revolutionaries such as Godwin and Condorcet. In the subtitle of the first edition of the "Principle of Population" Malthus named Godwin and Condorcet as the principle addressees of his theory. His objective was to destroy the postulate of everlasting ideal conditions using demographic arguments. All he in fact achieved was the opposite: the economists refuted Malthus by theoretically demonstrating the possibility of the existence of permanent improvement in economic living conditions, and the economic growth of their own time supported them; the biologists also defied Malthus by recognizing the "positive checks" of population as a mechanism effecting improvements in the biological conditions for existence via the selection principle.

Malthus therefore instigated developments in the economic sciences and biology which were the opposite of what he had intended. Something similar happened in the political economy through the reactions of Marx and Engels. So to my knowledge, population theory is the only field which has not seen any consequences comparable to those that took place in the theories of evolution and economics. But this could still occur, even if very late, if population theory is revised. It is now becoming vital to re-examine population theory in connection with global ecological problems; it would be dangerous indeed to advocate solutions to the environmental crisis that were based on a population theory whose validity were dubious.

The main cause for concern is what is known as the "theory of demographic transition". The micro economic theory of fertility can also be doubted. But I do not wish to comment on this theory here since no macro-demographic statements and projections of population growth exist which are based on micro economic arguments. There is more criticism of the transition theory from outside demography than from within; whether it constitutes a theory at all is being questioned because it is too descriptive and because the decisive characteristic of a theory, namely the existence of a core of theoretically relevant, non-trivial statements and hypotheses, is lacking. Gerhard Mackenroth further developed the theory of demographic transition in a sound way in his book "Population Science" (*"Bevölkerungslehre"*), and one can say much the same of Adolphe Landry (1934), but, as Mackenroth admits, his theory of demographic transition lacks a decisive theoretical core (Mackenroth, 1953: 328-9).

Whatever one thinks personally about such theoretical questions it remains a fact that the departments of the United Nations, the World Bank and other organisations responsible for producing world population projections receive little help from population theory in making assumptions on future changes in fertility. I myself as a forecaster have tried to improve this unsatisfactory situation by developing a theory of fertility (the "Biographical Theory of Fertility") which provides a justification for forecasting assumptions that is lacking in the theory of demographic transition (Birg, 1987 and 1991a; Birg, Flöthmann, Reiter 1991b). The essence of the thinking behind this can be summarized briefly as follows (for a detailed description see chapter 3.2): Firstly, the low level of fertility in developed countries is not a temporary phenomenon but a permanent, unavoidable, though unwanted, consequence of the economic, social and cultural processes of development which, in the industrialized countries, has led to a continuous increase in the freedom of biographical choice and, as a result, to a correspondingly steady decline in the willingness to enter into the long-term biographical commitments of marriage and/or having children. Secondly, in those countries which are not yet fully developed but which are following a route leading to the western form of development, in which individuals have legal, cultural and material freedoms of biographical choice, a similar decrease will occur. Lastly, in those countries remaining below a critical level of development in which the individual implicitly has no freedom of biographical choice, there can also be no satisfactory freedom of choice with respect to fertility. In such countries the effective logic of biographical decisions in the western democracies - a minimization of the risk elements in long-term commitments - cannot apply and result in voluntary relative childlessness, and hence in a decrease in the net reproduction rate to a value of one or less. The intensity of world population growth depends critically upon the share of the total taken up by the Third World population at any one time. At the moment nobody can say how large this is. The longer a large part of the world's population belongs to this critical category the more probable it is that the total population will exceed - even considerably exceed - the stationary endpoint of eleven or twelve billion currently being suggested.

(b)   "Spaceship Ethics" versus "Lifeboat Ethics"

A fundamental experience derived from the history of philosophy is that everyone who deliberates upon a problem of a certain level of complexity has to decide between two viewpoints, or "noting systems" as Henri Bergson called them, namely between the viewpoints of realism and idealism. The history of population theory is a good example of this experience: on the primary level are the real problems; the historical changes and the transformation of the basic ethics of human reactions are their consequences. In spite of the fundamental implications that practical ethics has had for human behaviour, there has been little progress in the theory of ethics as philosophy has developed over the years. The British philosopher Bernard Williams probably correctly maintains that there are only about five books which contain something new to the theory of ethics, whereas the number of publications in which this small basis has been merely repeated and slightly varied is countless. A large part of the literature of demography falls into that countless category, but I would go so far as to maintain that its classics, Süssmilch's "Divine Order" and Malthus' "Principle of Population", are essentially theories of ethics in which the science of demography plays a secondary role (Birg, 1990). How important the ethical influence of demography in fact is, can be seen from the paradigm conflict of human ecology or ecology, whose opposing positions are represented by "spaceship ethics" on the one hand and "lifeboat ethics" on the other, exactly as represented by the two classical theories.

The expression "spaceship ethics" comes from a short, but extremely important, article by Kenneth E. Boulding. Boulding explains the meaning of his metaphor thus: "The closed earth of the future requires economic principles which are somewhat different from those of the open earth of the past. For the sake of picturesqueness, I am tempted to call the open economy the 'cowboy economy', the cowboy being symbolic of the illimitable plains and also associated with reckless, exploitative, romantic and violent behaviour, which is characteristic of open societies. The closed economy of the future might similarly be called the "spaceman" economy, in which the earth has become a single spaceship, without unlimited reservoirs of anything, either for extraction or for pollution, and in which, therefore, man must find his place in a cyclical ecological system which is capable of continuous reproduction of material forms even though it cannot escape having inputs of energy. The difference between the two types of economy becomes most apparent in the attitude towards consumption (Boulding, 1966: 9).

After this was published in the 1960's came the Club of Rome discussion of the Earth's limited resources. A certain relaxation then followed and the official opinion of the United Nations at present is that: "It no longer seems likely that we will run out of minerals or sources of energy. Known reserves of most minerals have increased, not declined, with time and use. Exploration and new technology have opened up new sources" (Nafis Sadik, 1990: 10).

In place of the global resource problem then came the environmental problems, destruction of the rain forests, pollution of the seas and lakes, rivers and groundwater, the extinction, and hence removal from the evolution process, of certain biological species, the climate problem, and many more. In answer to the question "what has posterity ever done for me ..., why should we not maximize the welfare of this generation at the cost of posterity?" Boulding gave an answer which simultaneously provides a definition of the expression "ethics": "The only answer to this, as far as I can see, is to point out that the welfare of the individual depends on the extent to which he can identify himself with others, and that the most satisfactory individual identity is that which identifies not only with a community in space but also with a community extending over time from the past into the future" (Boulding, 1966: 11).

Boulding's position is described nowadays by the term "spaceship ethics". One could speak of an "unavoidable common interest" between all populations of the earth. The expression "unavoidable common interest" makes it clear that "spaceship ethics" is the result of the existence of real problems and thus corresponds to a position of philosophical realism. Boulding actually used the metaphor "spaceship Earth" and not "spaceship ethics". This is understandable in that Boulding's ethical position is valid not only for closed systems like the Earth but also for open systems. If we should one day learn how to tap the energy of the sun the earth would no longer be - at least in this respect - a closed system, but that would not alter Boulding's ethical position in the slightest.

The term "spaceship ethics" was introduced by the biologist Garret Hardin to characterize Boulding's position and in particular to differentiate the "spaceship ethics" from his own which he described as "lifeboat ethics": "Metaphorically each rich nation amounts to a lifeboat full of comparatively rich people. The poor of the world are in other, much more crowded lifeboats. Continuously, so to speak, the poor fall out of their lifeboats and swim for a while in the water outside, hoping to be admitted to a rich lifeboat, or in some other way to benefit from the goodies on board. What should the passengers of a rich lifeboat do? This is the central problem of 'the ethics of a lifeboat'" (Hardin, 1974; 561). Hardin proposed three alternative courses of action: 1. The boat with the rich rescues everybody and then goes down itself: "complete justice, complete catastrophe". 2. The boat with the rich fills up all the free places regardless of the fact that safety regulations demand that some of them should remain unoccupied. There are then two consequences: (a) Sooner or later one has to pay for not

observing the safety regulations. (b) Since there is not enough room for everyone still in the water a choice has to be made: should the "best" be chosen, or those most in need, or simply those that come first? What does one say to the others?
3. No one is given refuge and the safety factor thus remains. The consequence is that the "survival of the people in the lifeboat is then possible (although we shall have to be on our guard against boarding parties)".

Hardin recommended the third course of action: "... so long as there is no true world goverment to control reproduction everywhere it is impossible to survive in dignity if we are to be guided by spaceship ethics ... without a world government that is sovereign in reproductive matters mankind lives, in fact, on a number of sovereign lifeboats. For the foreseeable future survival demands that we govern our actions by the ethics of a lifeboat. Posterity will be ill served if we do not" (Hardin, 1974; 568). Hardin is a biologist, he quotes Nietzsche who regards having a conscience as a form of "disease". Does Hardin regard eugenics and genetic engeneering as a form of therapy? If so, with this point of view he would find himself in accordance with the well-known Nazi racial population ideology.

The logic of his argument is: firstly, we have to act in such a way as to consider the requirements of future generations; secondly, because the poor are more numerous and multiply faster than the rich, they impair the rights of future generations much more than the rich; thirdly, as a consequence ethical principles are best fulfilled if only the rich survive.

The arguments are formally/logically correct, but they have to be rejected because they are based on the false premise that the poor influence the interests of future generations more than the rich. In fact, quite the opposite is true: Although the rich nations (the industrialized countries) comprise only approximately a quarter of the world's population, they produce and consume, for instance, 80% of the commercially produced energy. Because of their high energy consumption they emit three times as much carbon dioxide as the developing countries, and this is responsible for the greenhouse effect (see chapter 5, section 3). Similar remarks apply to sulphur dioxide, one of the causes of *"Waldsterben"* (our dying forests).

Other authors have already commented on this point: "Hardin's statement about saving lives in poor countries is even more applicable to the rich. Every life preserved in the United States threatens the resources and environment of the planet many more times than a life preserved in, say Bangladesh" (Ehrlich and

Ehrlich, 1977: 922). I don't want to take this discussion further here, but want to move on to another point, namely that of the epistemological relationship between lifeboat ethics and Malthus' population theory. A detailed analysis of the arguments of lifeboat ethics is presented in chapter 6.

The metaphor used by Malthus of "nature's mighty feast" where "there is no vacant cover" for the poor man corresponds exactly to Hardin's lifeboat metaphor: nature has not reserved a place for everybody at this table (Malthus) nor in the lifeboat (Hardin). The poor are morally of less worth than the rich because they do not control their sexual urges (Malthus) and therefore overstretch the carrying capacity of the earth (Malthus and Hardin). Thus the rich have a morally better right to survive than the poor (Malthus and Hardin). Conclusion: *helping the poor is immoral.*

The metapohor of the laden table is indicated in encyclopaedias as being the typical core of Malthusian theory. The decisive piece of text in chapter six of his fourth book, however, has been eliminated in all Malthus editions with the exception of the first edition of the "Second Essay" of 1803. The important quotation is: "A man who is born into a world already possessed, if he cannot get subsistence from his parents ... and if the society do not want his labour, has no claim of right to the smallest portion of food, and, in fact, has no business to be where he is. At nature's mighty feast there is no vacant cover for him. She tells him to be gone, and will quickly execute her own orders, if he does not work upon the compassion of some of her guests" (Malthus, 1803: 531).

Indeed, the similarity, or even identity, with the lifeboat argumentation goes one step further: if the rich were to share the lifeboat with the poor for reasons of equity, the boat would fill up with people who do not have such moral scruples, an ethically undesirable consequence. Malthus: "... if these guests get up and make room ... other intruders immediately appear demanding the same favour ... the order and harmony of the feast is disturbed ... the happiness of the guests is destroyed ..." Hardin: "The net result of conscience-stricken people relinquishing their unjustly held positions is the elimination of their kind of conscience from the lifeboat" (Hardin, 1974: 562).

(c) Conclusion

In the contest between the metaphors "spaceship", "lifeboat" and "nature's feast" we are not concerned with poetic honours but with a matter of life or death. When Hardin postulates that the "freedom to breed is intolerable" (Hardin, 1968: 1243) this means that he denies the majority of humankind the right to live, since in most developing countries survival without support from children is impossible when sick or old. Satisfactory social support systems are not available. How currently relevant this Malthusian doctrine is in the ecology debate can be seen from remarks such as: "It is a mistake to think that we can control the breeding of mankind in the long run by an appeal to conscience ... 'A bad conscience', said Nietzsche, 'is a kind of illness' ... Freedom to breed will bring ruin to us all ... an appeal to independently acting consciences selects for the disappearance of all conscience ..." (Hardin, 1968: 1246 & 1248).

Derham used a metaphor in 1713 in his "Physico-Theology" which corresponds to the spaceship, not the lifeboat, metaphor; he wrote of the "ball of earth and water" upon which all lifeforms can exist. Süssmilch used the mother metaphor: "The earth can be called the mother of all things, not because she has given all things birth but because that which she does bring forth she upholds and nourishes" (Süssmilch, 1741). At the present time there is neither a material reason nor a moral justification for replacing this viewpoint in the ecology debate with the Malthus/Hardin metaphor and its derived "lifeboat ethics". This should be broadcast principally by demographers because the ecologists derive their ethical arguments from population science. The human race is still small enough in number that its members could congregate (albeit not exist) on the island of Mallorca. The population of West Berlin lived for 30 years without any hinterland in an area with 4,200 inhabitants per km^2, and the majority preferred this life to the available alternatives in West Germany.

The agricultural production potential of the land and water area of the planet is sufficient to support a population of at least double that of today. The ecological consequences of production and consumption have already led to some irreversible environmental changes but much of the destruction is reversible and is being reversed. Technological advance is making it possible to employ increasingly compatible methods of production. The world could become a fertile garden. In my opinion this is a realistic, not an idealistic, view. We should reject an idealism of the type propounded by the "Principle of Population".

Chapter 3

Intercultural Differentials in Human Reproduction and the Decline in World Fertility

3.1 Introductory Remarks

There is no area of demographic research more complex than fertility theory. It hardly comes as a surprise, therefore, that the most widely established approach to date has been the comprehensive, historically-oriented theory of demographic transition, with its wealth of source material from social and economic history (for an overview see C. Chesnais, 1992). Since the emergence of the theory of transition in the first half of the 20th century, particular variants have been developed in each of a number of countries with their own demographic researchers (F. Oppenheimer, 1901; L. Brentano, 1911; J. Wolf, 1912 and 1913; W.S. Thomson 1929 and 1946; K. Davis, 1945 and 1950; F.W. Notestein, 1945 and 1953). Significant examples of this are the work done in France by Adolphe Landry (1909 and 1934), and the theory developed in Germany by August Lösch (1936), Werner Sombart (1938) and Gerhard Mackenroth (1953). The advantage of transition theory, namely its capability of integrating continually new source material relevant to the countries involved, has been obtained at the cost of the disadvantage that it lacks a firm theoretical basis. Because every country has undergone its own peculiar demographic development in the past, there is a considerable temptation to apply transition theory schematically to any country at all, including the developing countries of today. Yet we ought to be aware that most developing countries now have substantially different demographic, economic and cultural starting conditions from those the industrial countries had 100 or 200 years ago. The birth rate in present-day developing countries is much higher and the death rate much lower, so the population growth rate which results from the differential between the two is in many cases twice as high as it was in the industrial countries during their pre-transition phases *(Figure 1)*. Another important point to consider is that the demographic transition from the pre-industrial to the industrial phase occurred in the western industrial countries over the space of one to two centuries, whereas the developing countries today only have a matter of a few decades available tothem. Any delay would jeopardize the development process due to the high rate of population growth, thus disrupting if not even preventing the process of industrial transformation which is regarded as the real prerequisite for demographic transformation. This situation is so patently obvious that transition theory, in spite of its rich source material, ought not to play the significant role in demography which it does. Its success can probably best be explained by the fact that it is very schematic and straightforward; indeed it is similarly simple and schematic, and apparently similarly successful, to Thomas Malthus' theory.

Because dozens of populations exist side-by-side today in societies with the most varied levels of development, the world of demography is extremely multifaceted for the researcher. Fertility theory, already highly complex in its own right, is made still more so by having what are, in effect, asynchronous developments existing simultaneously: several historical dimensions are present in parallel, and their reciprocal impact upon one another also needs to be analysed. While there are still some populations on Earth which can be said to be in a prehistoric stage of development, some others have by now reached a "post-post-industrial" stage. In between the two poles, there are so many intermediate stages and cultural peculiarities to consider that it is beyond the cognitive capacity of any researcher to take in this wide variety in its entirety, let alone to explain these populations' demographically relevant aspects of behaviour in one single, cogent approach. So it is simply inconceivable that we shall ever have a fertility theory available to us which can fully do justice to its object.

One could of course sonsider the possibilities of expanding transition theory in such a way that it at least embraces the most relevant aspects of fertility. Particularly significant among such aspects are the religious and cultural foundations of reproductive behaviour. Even in the 1970s, authors such as J.C. Caldwell stood by the objective of expanding or restating the theory of transition, as exemplified by Caldwell's essay "Toward a restatement of demographic transition theory" (1976). Yet we have not come any closer to achieving that goal in the interceding years. Indeed, John and Pat Caldwell's own enquiries during the 1980s found that the religious and cultural roots of behaviour pertinent to demo-

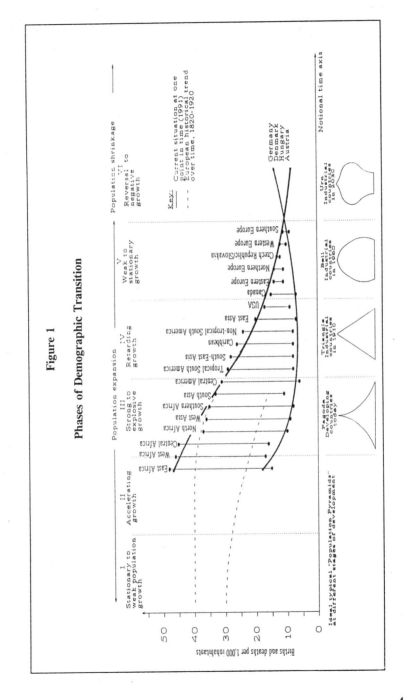

Figure 1

Phases of Demographic Transition

graphy, which have not played the part in transition theory they would have deserved, are still highly significant today in the developing countries, that is in the majority of the world's populations, especially in Africa and Asia. The high birth rate typical of many African cultures, relative to European and Asian countries, would appear particularly significant as far as fertility theory is concerned. To explain the major difference between the birth rates in Africa and Eurasia, Caldwell draws upon J.R. Goody's anthropological theory. Although Goody's theory in fact deals with the proto-historic period of human development, it is nevertheless highly relevant in explaining current fertility differentials between African and Eurasian countries, since people's reproductive behaviour today is partly shaped by religions and cultures, even though the origins of those religions and cultures lie in the earliest historical times. According to Caldwell, or Goody, the difference in fertility rates is ultimately attributable to differing interests in land ownership between these two groups of cultures. The Caldwells summarize Goody's hypothesis as follows:

"After the Neolithic revolution, ancient people livng on alluvial plains and valley bottoms from the Mediteranean to northern India found that these regions could be made to produce surplus grain, and thus wealth, for anyone who could maintain control over enough land. A few people could produce enough food to support many more. The resulting battle for wealth and privilege based on control of land area led to a society stratified by social class and to a determination on the part of each class not to be reduced to the circumstances of the classes below it. This aim was achieved by strict control over land and other property, by the marriage of children to families from the same class and by managing dowry and heritance. (Some societies even adopted primogeniture to reduce the fragmentation of inherited property, by passing most of it to the first-born son.) Fertility took second place to ensuring the right match by the outlawing of women's sexual activities outside marriage and to maintaining indisputable inheritance by identifying and anathematizing illegitimacy. Africa escaped the gains and losses of the Eurasian system, according to Goody's theory, not by conscious rejection but because it had no great alluvial valleys suited to irrigation or good temperate soils that were moist the year round. Its agriculture was carried out on upland soils unsuited to the plow, which yielded only small surpluses beyond the food needed by the families cultivating them. Just as the African system of belief in ancestors reinforced its social structure, so the popular religions of Eurasia - Buddhism, Hinduism, Judaism, Christianity and Islam -

grew up across Eurasia's agricultural heartland, from the Mediterranean to the Ganges. These religions did not preach sustained inequality; religions must convince not only those who are advantaged but also those who are not. Instead they preached the virtuous life. This virtuous life, however, tended to include strong female sexual restraint, guidance in marriage by one's parents and marriage within one's social class - all factors that acted to sustain inequality. Bolstered by the wealth generated in their home regions, Eurasian belief systems were exported to many places where the economic conditions that had fostered their growth did not prevail. By diffusion these religions conquered the rest of Europe and by migration, the Americas and Australasia. The diffusion was not complete, of course, and so the lines of power in northern European and North American families were never as absolute as in those of the Mediterranean, Middle East or India."(Caldwell and Cladwell 1990: 86)

The logical chain of thought in Goody's hypothesis is this: The circumstances of the natural environment determine what the optimum strategy for survival and for living should be, and the optimum means of organizing agricultural labour. So the religious and cultural superstructure, particularly the kinship system, adapts to suit the living conditions dictated by Nature. Soil fertility in Africa is generally low. Consequently, increasing the number of hands to do the work is a more worthwhile investment than more equipment for intensive cultivation. The fertility of women is crucial to the yield obtained from cultivating the soil, as more children means more labour. Hence possession of fertile women is more important than possessing land. In Europe and Asia, on the other hand, the yield obtained from the land is not primarily dependent on the number of people available to work it but upon the acreage available. The composition of the family is adapted to the desire to bequeath this valuable land to one's own descendants: hence, the nuclear family in Eurasian societies consists of parents and their common, natural descendants. In Africa, mothers and their children form the basic social unit. Whereas a bride-price has to be paid to obtain a woman in African cultures, in their Eurasian counterparts a dowry is given to anyone prepared to marry a daughter.

Up to this point, the line of argument can be appreciated. But how does one comprehend the fact that, in Africa, the predominating form of socio-religious basis for society is found in ancestral cults while in Eurasia the typical form is that of monotheistic religion? Explaining that is considerably more difficult. Could it be that individuals living in competitive isolation in their nuclear families in the Eurasian cultures had to rely upon one common god to bridge the gap with their fellows in the rest of society, whereas the ancestral cults - probably the oldest form of worship - have simply been retained by Africa's clan and tribal societies as this form of socio-religious coexistence had always fulfilled the need for proximity with other people? This is not the place to speculate on how religions emerged. Indeed, in the present context this question in itself is not even so very important. For as far as today's reproductive behaviour is concerned, the question of *why* monotheistic religiousness predominates in Eurasia and ancestral cults in Africa is not as significant as the actual fact that all cultures, including "atheistic" ones (if there is, or has ever been, any such thing) are built on some form of religious basis - the term, incidentally, should not be confused with attachment to churches, which is on the wane in most societies.

These considerations are moving us into philosophical territory. It cannot, of course, be up to fertility theory to advance the frontiers of philosophy, or the philosophy of religion, but on the other hand it is impossible to conceive of how a proper basis for fertility theory can be found without taking philosophical considerations into account. And if not philosophy, or a philosophically reflective demography, what other discipline could do justice to the extraordinary complexity of fertility as an object of research? Plato spoke of people participating in "eternal life" by way of their individual reproduction, so for him this was evidently a philosophical matter *par excellence*. Süssmilch too held that people performed "a form of creation" in the process of reproduction. Certainly, it is not enough simply to subsume reproduction under, for example, the category of utility-maximizing behaviour - all the more so as a great deal still needs to be done to explain the significance of economic factors in the context of culturally-informed behaviour. According to Max Weber's theory of capitalism, for example, the accumulation of capital and the resulting dynamism of competitive societies is derived from a religiously-motivated factor, i.e. non-economic influences, namely the will to perform in modern man which has been encouraged by the Protestant ethic. To explain reproductive behaviour today and how this should be built into world population projections, we have need of a theory which will also incorporate among its determining factors the fundamental cultural mood and the metaphysical aspects driving human behaviour in the 20th century.

Such a theory will not only have to explain the secular downward *trend* in fertility, but also the low *absolute level* it has reached in those societies where the trend is now drawing to a close. The theory of demographic transition has not treated this problem of the absolute level, since it is a central postulate of the theory that it ought not to be possible for the net reproduction rate to fall below 1.0 for any sustained length of time (G. Mackenroth, 1953: 410). We now know that the low fertility seen in many advanced societies and also in the advanced regions of Asian developing countries is not a merely temporary deviation from some "equilibrium" at which net reproduction is exactly 1.0 or above 1.0, but has become a quite normal state of affairs. This new situation, which some demographers describe as the "second demographic transition", needs to be a central focus of modern fertility theory (van de Kaa, 1987; Cliquet 1991).

3.2 Differences in Reproduction, Biographies and Fertility

Just some of the reasons cited in the literature for the low fertility in industrial countries are the introduction of collective old-age pensions, the increased activity rate of women, the expansion of education, the instability of relationships, changes in society's system of values, the rationalization of the sphere determined by our personalities (Max Weber's "disenchantment of the world"), changes in psychological motivation, and socio-economic processes like urbanization. Conversely, an absence of these factors is seen as the main cause of high fertility in the developing countries, together with the continued existence there of factors which now belong to the past in industrial countries, such as high infant and child mortality, the lack of social insurance systems, marriage at a young age, and so on. While all these factors really do exist, they are still not suitable to serve as a basis for a theory of reproductive behaviour, as they tend to be phenomena which have accompanied the secular downward trend in fertility, as a product of the times, but which have not generally had a causal impact upon it.

In their historical development, theoretical biology and the theory of population have been very closely interrelated in the past. Collaboration between the disciplines of demography, biology and other natural and social sciences could also prove fruitful in the present day in developing a more complex theory of human reproduction. One of the bases of evolution in the world of nature, via natural and gender selection, is individual variability. In the case of humanity, the variability predetermined by Nature as a biological given is supplemented by a category of the *possible* opened up by our individual cognitive capabilities, and analysing the latter is primarily the task of the social sciences and humanities. That is to say the human individual, endowed with consciousness and the ability to make choices, develops his/her own ideas of life alternatives, reaching beyond natural givens into the realm of the possible. For that reason, it will never be possible to develop an appropriate theory of human reproduction based *solely* on biological considerations.

Developing a theory entails finding a common explanatory denominator for a variety of facts and arguments which may appear to be irreconcilable. A theory of human reproduction needs to take biological, psychological, cultural, societal, economic and historical facts all into consideration; however, if this is not to occur merely by adding together an accumulation of interdiscipinary or multidisciplinary knowledge, the process of distilling out a common theoretical basis must lead to the creation of a set of conceptual instruments which are appropriate to the phenomenon one is seeking to explain. There is hardly a better way of showing a theory's specific qualities, such as its explanatory power and practicability, than by applying it to a specific question: in the case of the biographical theory of fertility under discussion here, the question of *differential reproduction* would appear particularly well suited to act as that object of application.

All theories of fertility are made up of statements of multi-causal, but non-deterministic, links between certain dependent and independent variables, at the level of individuals, groups, or regional or national populations. In cases where these functions are reduced to the bare essentials for didactic reasons or to aid understanding - expressing them in mathematical formulae has proved a particularly effective instrument in this regard - they are known as "models", so in our case we have a variety of models of reproductive behaviour. In such models reproduction (the dependent variable) is expressed as a number of live-born children per woman (or sometimes, per man).

On the basis of three elements consisting of (1) dependent variables, (2) independent variables and (3) functional relationships between the two, the term "differential reproduction" may be defined in three ways. *Firstly*, the adjective "differential" may be taken to apply exclusively to the *dependent* variable, i.e. differential reproduction will be said to exist if the number of children per woman differs between two individuals or groups, regardless of what the cause of that difference might be. In this rudimentary definition which predominates in public coverage of the topic, the *independent* variables (i.e. the varied collection of explanatory factors) have just as small a part to play as any differences there might be in the nature of the links between the two sets of variables. In the *second case*, the term "differential" may apply to the *independent* variables to which changes in the dependent variables are attributed. This tends to be the definition of the term chosen in scientific studies, particularly when multivariate statistical analysis is used. The *third* definition, to be used in the argument which follows, takes the term "differential" to apply to the *nature of the functional link* between the dependent and independent variables. Using this definition, "differential reproduction" is said to occur when the combination of factors influencing the reproductive behaviour of individual A is different (i.e., made up of a different set of variables) from that affecting individual $B's$ behaviour; alternatively, though the actual bundles of variables may be identical, the specific factors involved may operate in different directions or with differing intensities, which will result in differing empirical parameters for the variables. In the case of the third definition of the term "differential", multivariate statistical analysis can only be used for descriptive purposes, since one of the preconditions on which it is based - the same functional relationship for all samples - is not fulfilled.

Quite involuntarily, every human being is different as a biological entity, for each individual is so genetically unique that the laws of probability rule out any duplication. As a cultural entity, each person then truly does become an individual (in its literal sense of an indivisible being incapable of being reduced to anything else), as (s)he develops an ego on the basis of his/her self-perception which maintains a separate existence from the non-ego, taking shape in a process of self-development; the latter process might, with reference to Charles Darwin's theory of biological selection and evolution, be termed cultural self-selection, because it entails continually assessing and selecting alternative development paths. Human behaviour, particularly reproductive behaviour, is predicated upon the existence of individuality and variability. However, biological selection and cultural, personality-forming self-selection not only have variability as a precondition, but they also give rise to it, whether in biological evolution, in the evolution of human culture, in perception, thought, language, or in the individual behaviour attached to particular personalities.

In the process of personality development, individuality is chiefly developed via interaction between the ego and questions of meaning. Although the "meaning" of behaviour, lending direction and coherence to the indvidual's actions, is

53

invariably predefined by society which means that it is not entirely individual, that "meaning" nevertheless is not established unless the individual experiences it for him/herself, which in effect is what actually creates it. A commonly-used phrase in German speaks of someone *giving* meaning (or sense) to something. Of course, it is possible to adopt the values put forward by others or by society at large, including values which influence reproduction, but those values have to be imbued with meaning by *individuals*, or else they will remain abstract and ineffective. So the values of reproductive behaviour need like any others to be given substance by the individual; if they were not, reproductive behaviour would be no more than passive conformity to prescribed patterns, or would follow blind biological instincts.

The observation made above, that both biological and cultural evolution are not only predicated upon variation but also generate it, will be assumed to be valid as the theoretical propositions are developed below. The objection that, in the cultural sphere in particular, individuality is frequently swamped and substantial uniformity generated - as in the cases of political or religious mass phenomena such as the idolization of dictators like Hitler, Stalin or Mao - cannot be accepted as a counter-argument for, as already stated, a worldview, a value or a belief can only be adopted by people *giving* meaning to them. And they can only do so in an *individual* act, even if the final outcome is more rather than less uniformity.

Reproductive behaviour, then, as a specifically human form of behaviour, is individual behaviour, which means that any theoretical explanation of it has to start out from the level of the individual, known as the micro level. On the other hand, many of the environmental conditions within which individuals behave, e.g. the legal framework, social role-models, economic prospects and the regional pattern of life, which thus determine the scope for individual action, simultaneously apply to larger groups of people in the same way - say, to a particular age cohort - which means that the micro and macro levels interact with one another in giving rise to any particular pattern of individual behaviour. Despite this, the fact remains that reproductive behaviour, like any other human behaviour, is conducted by individuals.

Today we live in an era in which personality-oriented values dominate group-oriented ones. This circumstance, combined with the realization that individuality and variability constitute the natural (albeit frequently concealed) disposition of human behaviour in general and reproductive behaviour in particular, means that it is absolutely essential to use the third of the definitions of "differential" set out above when discussing differential reproduction - i.e. to assume that differences occur in the manner in which the independent variables influence the dependent one. It is true that economic variables such as a woman's personal income or the household income earned by a couple will, in the same way as other variables like the availability of nursery-school places, generally tend to exert their influence in the same *direction* upon the probability of children being born; however, the intensity of influence exerted by those factors, and indeed also by "values", will vary due to the effects of personality-forming self-selection by individuals upon their own behaviour.

One would expect this fundamental truth of the individuality of personal behaviour to have been substantially reflected in scientific enquiries into reproductive behaviour. Yet that is not the case: in all empirical studies built around models working with analytical methods such as regression or event-history analysis, or using other multivariate methods, the assumption is made along the lines of the *second* of the above definitions that the nature of the functional relationship will be *the same* in all of the individuals or population groups sampled. Because, as has been made clear, this assumption is not and cannot be fulfilled in reality, the findings of such studies using multivariate methods can only be interpreted as a sophisticated description of functional relationships, but not as explanations in the strict theoretical sense.

Starting out from the idea of utility and from the principle of rational choice, researchers in microeconomics have developed sophisticated models of consumer behaviour, and these have been projected by Gary Becker and numerous other economists on to reproductive behaviour. Similarly, the theory of games has been used to explain people's choice of partner, again closely associated with reproductive behaviour. However, this approach to theory-building has not yet brought much promise of success when applied *empirically* to explain fertility. Rather, the microeconomic paradigm's chances of success need to be viewed somewhat sceptically, for the following reasons. Based on the principle of rational choice, microeconomic models concentrate on demonstrating how an optimum choice can be made with regard to a specific target function from among a set of alternative decisions (options) and also constraints on those decisions (e.g. budgetary restrictions). Meanwhile, the problem as to how the elements in this set of choices themselves come about is left aside. So if a particular option is not actually named as one of the alternatives, it cannot form part of the theory. This is a serious shortcoming, for the question of whether or why a particular option does or does not form part of the range of alternatives available for a particular subject is often more interesting and far more important than determining the optimum choice on the basis of a fixed set of alternatives, preferences and behavioural constraints.

The biographical theory of fertility described below, which has been empirically tested using population data for Germany, is also based on the principle of rational choice. However, it differs from the microeconomic behavioural models in that it does not place prime emphasis on how an optimum choice can be obtained from a prescribed set of alternatives (in this case, biographical options), but focuses on the issue of why certain elements in a set of biographical options may apply to one individual but not to another. The biographical theory is in agreement with microeconomic theory in as far as it takes the view that all human beings are constantly choosing between or among alternatives, but it differs strictly from microeconomic theory by taking into account the fact that a person normally *does not choose* the actual set of options from which those continual decisions have to be made. The biographical theory of fertility treats biographical alternatives as the cumulative outcomes of numerous actions which, in and of themselves, an individual would not normally directly relate to reproductive behaviour yet which, when regarded ex post as part of his/her life-course, will prove to have been *preliminary* decisions which would later influence reproductive behaviour because, intentionally or otherwise, they determine the range of reproductive options available to that person.

Thus, whether or not a particular decision-making situation even arises at a particular point in a person's life, i.e. whether "reproduction" is among the options available, is strongly dependent on other decisions the person has made in *earlier* phases of his/her life. The choice of which trade to learn or what subjects to study, the choice of job, frequently also linked to a choice of what area to live in, the choice of spouse or partner: all of these add up to a sequence of decisions which are linked in the sense that the choice made at any one of these stages, which may be a more or less optimum choice according to the criteria applying to *that* situation, will simultaneously determine what options will become, or indeed *can possibly* become, available for *future* decision-making situations. It often does not become clear to people until some time later that by choosing, say, a certain course of education or training, they have already gone quite a way down the road towards a later occupational choice. People have varying degrees of awareness of this inter-temporal interdependence between biographically important decisions during the course of their lives. The more clearly they do perceive this reality, the greater consideration they will give to it when deciding whether or not to have children.

A reproductive decision is more than a straightforward decision as to whether or not to have a child: it is also a decision for or against a certain biographical path taken as a whole. Such a decision entails what in German would be termed *langfristige Festlegung*, i.e. firmly setting down certain factors for the long term, the closest available English translation being *long-term commitment*. The term is intended to reflect the *irreversible consequences* which exist de facto for the remainder of a person's life, regardless of whether the person recognizes this as a commitment voluntarily entered into, or merely accepts the consequences because there is no other alternative. Whenever a woman in a developed society decides to have a child, she is also making a preliminary decision on how many and what kind of options she can retain in the occupational field; conversely, the outcome of a career decision will determine what options can or cannot be available for future family and reproductive decisions. The situation described here generally does not apply in the *developing countries*, or only to a lesser extent, but that does not mean to say that the biographical theory of fertility is inapplicable to developing countries. The chief difference between industrial and developing countries is that the set of biographical decision-making options available to individuals in developing countries tends to be severely restricted. However, there are also populations in the less-developed regions of *industrial* countries whose members have to shape their biographies within substantially restrained living conditions. This reduced biographical freedom of choice in less-developed regions of industrial countries is a very significant factor in the current context, as it provides an explanation for pronounced regional differences in fertility within a country. In Germany, for example, the difference in fertility between *regions* is greater than that between different *generations* from the same region. The evidence is that the less developed a region is, the higher its fertility tends to be (*Figures 2 and 3*). Just as the biographical theory of fertility explains *interregional* fertility differences within industrial countries, so too it is able to explain a considerable portion of the *international* fertility differentials - say, between developed and less-developed countries - provided that the religious and cultural circumstances are taken into consideration which work alongside socio-economic living conditions in influencing the amount of scope for biographical

Figure 2

Regional Differentials in the Net Reproduction Rates of the 328 Counties ("Kreise") in Western Germany before Reunification

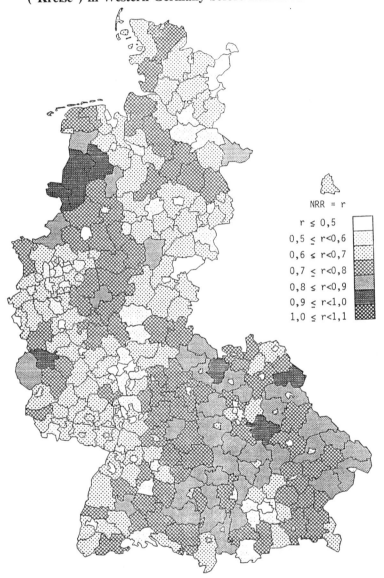

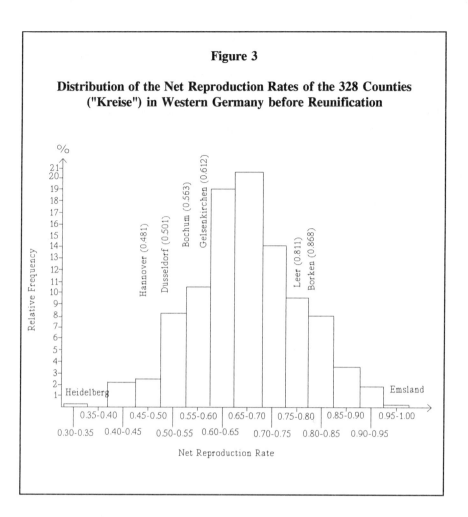

Figure 3

Distribution of the Net Reproduction Rates of the 328 Counties ("Kreise") in Western Germany before Reunification

choices and the concrete biographical options available. These considerations are particularly important when setting assumptions as to future fertility trends for the world as a whole in order to make world population projections: the biographical theory of fertility allows conclusions to be drawn from the pace of change in social and economic living conditions (which crucially influence individuals' freedom of biographical choice) for the likely future rate of decline in the world total fertility rate.

Returning now from this short digression on the theory's application to the essential elements of the theory itself, it is necessary to elaborate on a number of further distinctions between it and microeconomic fertility theory. The fact that education-related or training-related, occupational and reproductive decisions are all intermeshed in a superordinate, dynamic, intertemporal linkage can, in principle, also be taken into account by dynamizing microeconomic models; however, there is still one more aspect which underlines the need to develop a theory especially for the purpose of explaining reproductive behaviour, i.e. a theory which is autonomous in a certain sense and which differs fundamentally from a micro*economic* theory. The aspect in question is the special character of the biographical commitments entailed in partnerships (marital or quasi-marital) and in having children. Certainly, long-term commitments are also entered into in the economic sphere in the form of purchase and investment decisions (e.g., for consumer durables), but while the irreversibility of the consequences of such decisions consists solely in the fact that changing one's mind generates considerable costs, in the case of choosing a life-partner or of taking on the obligations associated with parenthood the irreversibility becomes a *matter of principle*, as the underlying ethical criteria involved cannot be weighed against each other or substituted for in the way that economic costs can.

Though it is possible to view an individual's biography from an economic viewpoint, as a dynamic, utility-maximizing decision-making process in which future decisions are cumulatively predetermined by those of an earlier time-period, parallel to this economic logic for the decision-making linkage there are also additional logics in operation, that of developmental psychology and also a social logic, neither of which can be reduced to economic terms. The need to take psychological and social factors into account means that economic variables, which are fairly readily measurable, need to be analysed for their interaction with other factors which are barely quantifiable, if at all. These implications are frequently rejected by sociologists concentrating on qualitative aspects, as they maintain that a person's identity and the internal coherence of his/her biography are inaccessible to any form of quantitative analysis. A different point of view is advocated by this author, for although it is true that the internal coherence of anyone's biography belongs to a monadically closed internal world accessible only to the individual in person, to the extent that such coherence is also manifested in the economic, psychological and social logic of his/her biography it is nevertheless also reflected in phenomena belonging to the external world, and as such it is amenable to scientific analysis. If this were not the case, we would not be able, for instance, to communicate linguistically, on the basis of signs which only belong to the external world in the form of sounds. When the basic building-blocks of a biography are added together to form a sequence of events or states, this is comparable to the development of a sequence of letters, syllables and words to make up a sentence, to the creation of a tune by adding together a set of single notes or chords, or to the way in which long DNA sequences are formed to store or convey our genetic codes. A feature all of these examples have in common is the inexhaustible variation which is possible in the final result together with the insurpassable precision of the information conveyed - all of which provides an ideal basis for the forces of cultural and personal selection to operate.

In order to present the main hypotheses of the biographical theory of fertility, I shall first introduce a number of basic concepts. Biographical *elements* consist of "chapters", phases and states into which a biography can be divided up from the economic, development-psychological, social or demographic point of view. The term *biographical sequence* will be used to describe an ordered set of consecutive biographical elements. Several different sub-sequences can be identified in every biography, among which the following are especially significant as far as reproductive behaviour is concerned: (a) *economic life-course*, consisting of an ordered set of different stages of bread-winning; (b) *psychobiography* (as used by Ch. Bühler, F. Massarik and E.H. Erikson), the ordered set of psychological development phases; (c) *social life-course*, the ordered set of stages of socialization and social attachment, and (d) *family* or *demographic biography*, the ordered set of family events such as finding a new partner, separating, or having children. In analyses of reproductive behaviour, it has also proved fruitful to include a further category of (e) *migrational biography* to cover changes in place of residence or place of work during a person's life.

The total number, in abstract terms, of *sequences* which can possibly be constructed from a given set of biographical elements using mathematical operations (permutation, variation, combination or any of these together) are together referred to as the *biographical universe*. This is a realm of biographical possibilities, and for the time being it is of theoretical interest only. To illustrate, the four elements of "occupational training", "job", "partner commitment" and "birth of first child" can, in theory, be combined in a total of 24 possible biographical sequences, all of which are different permutations of the four elements. In this oversimplified case, then, the biographical universe contains 24 sequences of elements. If there are five elements, the number of potential sequences rises to 120, while for seven elements the figure is 5,040 and for ten elements it is 3,628,800; the general mathematical expression is that a biographical universe containing n elements will include $n!$ potential sequences. Biographical models with a high level of differentiation can also be formed on the basis of variations and combinations (with or without the facility for elements to be repeated). These mathematical constructs are also relevant when empirical surveys are carried out, as the models can have any possible degree of precision in approaching real-life biographies.

Only a very small portion of the sequences contained in the mathematically-constructed biographical universe actually bear any resemblance to the biographical decisions taken in practice. This subset of sequences of relevance to human action, which also exist as relevant alternatives in the individual's conceptual world - regardless of whether those conceptions are "false" or illusionary - are termed a *virtual biography*. This encompasses a considerably smaller number of sequences than the biographical universe, yet the number is still generally large enough to give rise to the following central questions: (1) On what do the amount and the nature of the biographical elements relevant for any particular individual depend? (2) By what mechanisms is the virtual biography selected from the biographical universe, and an individual's actual biography - i.e. one specific sequence - selected from that virtual biography? (3) What are the consequences of the continual expansion of the biographical universe in the course of economic and social development, as new elements emerge such as new occupations or career opportunities? (4) What are the consequences of the diminution of biographical restraints in the course of civilization, e.g. reduced social control, the roll-back of religious influence, and a weakening of the significance for an individual's biographical options of his/her class origins or family's social standing? The field of research outlined by these questions is an extensive one, but since the purpose of developing a theory should not be to find ultimate answers to questions but to formulate questions in such a way that the search for answers will yield new discoveries, a number of hypotheses (or basic propositions) need to be set up at the outset, however daunting the amount of work needed to test them may appear to be at the time. The biographical theory of fertility includes two basic propositions, or rather groups of propositions (Birg 1987 and 1991).

First basic proposition: (1.1) The size of the biographical universe and also of virtual biographies is continuously increasing, both because of the removal of social, normative and economic constraints and because of the emergence of new ways of establishing a livelihood. (1.2) The larger the biographical universe or a virtual biography, the greater the number of options will be that are *eliminated* as a result of a biographical commitment, especially a demographically relevant commitment such as a close (e.g. marital) partnership or the birth of a child. (1.3) Hence as the range of biographical possibilities broadens, so too does the risk inherent in any biographical commitment. (1.4) In societies with market economies, in which individual behaviour is chiefly derived from the *principle of competition*, the risk associated with commitments made in one's family biography is greater than any made in one's educational or economic life-course, as the long-term consequences of family commitments are irreversible not only from the practical, economic point of view but also on the basis of ethical principles. (1.5) The risks associated with family commitments can be postponed or avoided altogether by deliberately not having children, whereas the commitments made during an educational, training or occupational career cannot be so readily postponed or avoided because of the societal or institutional dictates which stem from the standardization of economic life-courses. (1.6) As a result, familial decisions like having children, which can be more readily postponed than other commitments, are indeed pushed on into later biographical phases, thus reducing the probability of such demographically relevant biographical commitments actually being made. (1.7) If biographical decision-making is too heavily burdened by a surfeit of biographical freedom, the following anomaly may occur: the family commitment of childbirth is used instrumentally to deliberately reduce biographical freedom and to lend stability to a person's virtual biography, if such stability appears unattainable by any other means. This form of behaviour is increasingly apparent among teenagers growing up in socially unstable circumstances in the USA.

Second basic proposition: (2.1) There are two different types of biographical mobility: the first is a change from one biographical element or state to another *within the same* biographical sequence, whereas the second is a change from one biographical sequence to another. (2.2) Different population groups view biographical mobility either as a positive instrument which can be used actively to shape one's life-course (the idea of mobility as a resource), or else as a negative compulsion to adjust to exogenous changes in circumstances (mobility as forced adaptation). (2.3) People can be divided into two groups: for individuals in group A, high biographical mobility has a positive effect on the probability of long-term commitments being entered into such as having children, while for those in group B it has a negative impact.

These hypotheses can be tested both by historical comparisons and by means of inter-individual analyses. Models for this purpose can be built up on the individual, micro, group and macro levels. In all such cases, *longitudinal* data and analysis are essential, since biographical relationships are a classic example of intertemporal relationships. To be able to put these hypotheses to the test in the strict sense of the expression, very detailed empirical material is required, and this was indeed obtained in the *biographical survey* used for the purpose. The findings of the survey have already been reported elsewhere (Birg 1987 and 1991a; Birg, Flöthmann, Reiter 1991b, 1991c). Let us instead endeavour here to interpret historical development processes in the light of biographical theory. The proposition is as follows: The process of industrialization and modernization has created a mushrooming growth in individuals' scope for biographical development, the consequence of which has been a decrease in fertility from generation to generation in the industrial countries, to below replacement level. Since the factors giving rise to that decrease continue to operate, an autonomous increase in fertility back above replacement level cannot be expected. This provides an explanation for the phase of a net reproduction rate below replacement fertility which transition theory claimed could only ever occur for short periods and would not be possible as a persisting phenomenon. The following factors have historically acted in combination in the course of population and economic development:

(1) Beginning in the 18th century in Europe, scientific progress coupled with the principle of competition led to a more pronounced *division of labour*, and to increased *occupational specialization*, which in turn produced rapid growth in

industrial production and in the number of ways of earning a living (the number of "positions").

(2) As a result of the increasing production of goods, different branches of the economy became more intensively intermeshed, and there was a similar intensification in the interchange of goods and services between producers, in interregional trade, and in the social interaction among individuals participating in the economy. More intensive interaction over time allowed individuals to compare their ways of life with those of other people and to reflect upon their personal convictions and values, thus reducing the influence of religious and other values and norms and thus giving rise to the *pluralism of values*.

(3) Competitive pressure to raise the productivity of labour forced firms or other employers to steadily increase their relative capital intensity (i.e. the amount of physical and intellectual capital per employee or per unit of output), generating a trend towards larger businesses, and hence also towards larger settlements. The result was the urbanization of industrial societies and the emergence of an *urban settlement system*.

(4) Urbanization on the one hand and increased real incomes on the other led to a change in production and consumption patterns which included an increased share in the national product and in employment taken up by the *tertiary (i.e. service) sector*. New jobs were created in this sector, especially in the towns and cities, and these were increasingly occupied by women. This meant that female biographies changed much more dramatically over time than those of the male population. As women became better trained and educated and increasingly began to work more outside their homes, they attained an increasing level of biographical autonomy, and as a result gave more conscious consideration to the *biographical opportunity cost* of the long-term commitment of having children.

Both for men and for women, these processes mainly led to a proliferation of the possibilities available for building up an occupational, social and cultural living; hence they increased biographical decision-making freedom but at the same time increased the corresponding biographical risk.

People in the industrial countries, and also in the rapidly-developing regions or in particular social strata in the developing countries, now have to decide at an increasingly young age, on the basis of an ever-increasing number of options, what courses of education or training they wish to pursue or how they would like to specialize for particular occupations. Furthermore, the chances for people to abandon a particular career in favour of some other biographical option are growing ever slighter once they have made a particular commitment. In an effort to reduce the resulting risks attached to long-term biographical commitments and to keep a certain number of options open, people now tend to postpone some commitments or even to avoid making them altogether. One result of this pattern of behaviour is that those commitments in a personal or family life-course which can be delayed or avoided (commitment to a partner, marriage, having children) are increasingly having to take a back seat relative to other commitments in people's economic life-courses which cannot be put off in the same way (choosing educational and training courses, a career, a specific job). To put these findings in general terms, as part of the civilizing process the range of life-course alternatives broadens (i.e., the biographical universe expands), but this is associated with increased pressure to make decisions, and growing specialization in the world of work make it increasingly difficult to reverse biographical commitments in that area at some later date in favour of a new, different career. Consequently, there is a general tendency to avoid long-term biographical commitments relating to the family, and this has pushed the net reproduction rate in developed societies below the replacement level of fertility, which in countries such as Germany would result in a dramatic drop in the population were it not for large-scale immigration. To make the point clear, Germany's population net of all migration flows could be expected to fall from 80 million in 1990 to just 48 million in 2050 (Birg and Flöthmann 1993d).

Although the demo-economic functional relationships described above are primarily observable in the highly developed industrial countries, as economic and social progress also takes place in the developing countries the points discussed above will apply to an ever-increasing portion of their populations too. Long-term population projections reaching into the 21st century normally assume that living conditions will also increasingly improve in the developing countries. Indeed, it is important that ample consideration should be given to the impact of these factors linked to the civilizing process upon the speed of decline in the world's birth rate when long-term projections are made. Conversely, any ommissions and delays occurring in the development process, which will be accompanied by delays in the decline of the world birth rate, will have to be paid for in later years in the form of famine, human suffering and environmental destruction.

3.3 Causes of High Fertility and the Significance of Inter-Generational Transfers

If industrial and developing countries are compared with one another with reference to the logic of deciding in favour of or against having a child, an essential distinction can be observed. In the industrial countries, the biographical freedom of choice available is greater than it has ever been in their entire history, while the extent of such freedom for the majority of the population in developing countries - i.e., excluding the middle and upper classes - is next to nothing. Of course, in reality there are various shades of grey between these two extremes. Nevertheless, the general point can be made that if countries are ranked in order of their level of development this tends to be reflected in a corresponding ranking for the level of biographical freedom of choice, and also that the theory described in the previous section is all the more applicable the higher a particular country is placed in the development rankings. If a "pyramid" were to be drawn showing the number of people in each of the parts of the world with different development levels (as a counterpart to the age-cohort pyramid used to show population structures), one would indeed find by far the largest number of people in the low development levels at the base of the pyramid. The top priority for policy-makers has to be one of raising the poorest countries' development levels into the area where the biographical decision-making logic portrayed above begins to operate. Obviously, different policy concepts are needed in the range below that critical stage of development from those which operate in countries which are already above it. Another point which is clear is that the decline in the total fertility rate for the world population from 5.0 children per woman in 1960-65 to 3.3 in 1990-95, and the corresponding decline in developing countries from 6.1 to 3.6 children per woman, must have different causes from the biographically determined decline which can be expected to operate in future once the critical development threshold has been crossed. Three possible factors determining high fertility can be distinguished, and there are different policy concepts for dealing with each type (see *Table 1*).

The relative importance of the factors set out in the table varies between different cultures or countries. Rather than examining such differences in too much detail, let us focus on an aspect which is significant for all cultures and all countries, namely the material and immaterial transfers made between the younger, middle-aged and older generations.

The following considerations will be based on the idea that each generation passes through three phases as it grows older. During childhood and youth, each generation starts out as a recipient of material support from its parents' generation. During its mid-phase, each generation provides material support to two other generations, i.e. to its children and to its parents who have now grown old. Finally, it enters the third phase during which it in turn is a net recipient of assistance from its children who have now entered the mid-phase.

The validity of the conclusions drawn below is not impaired by the fact that generations are linked with one another not only by material support but also by immaterial assistance and mutual affection. The difference between material or immaterial assistance on the one hand and the emotional qualities on the other is that the latter can be both given and received at any time during an individual's life, i.e. during any phase of his/her generation. But the point of particular interest here is that the provision of material and/or economic forms of assistance depends closely on the particular phase of the life-cycle - or simply, the age - reached by the providers, whereas such assistance is most intensely needed and received in those parts of the life-cycle in which the recipients are too young or too old to be able to provide much or any assistance of their own. Because of this, the relative sizes of the generations in demographic terms are all the more significant for the balance between material and immaterial support received and given during an entire life-course.

So every generation in the sequence of generations is linked both to the preceding and to the succeeding one by way of inter-generational transfers, which raises the question of how significant the size of a particular generation, as determined by the birth rate, will be for the ratio of assistance received to assistance given. Let the following be the notation used to analyse this relationship:

Table 1

Factors of High Fertility and Corresponding Policy Concepts

Factor 1:	*Policy 1:*
The number of *unwanted* births is high.	Classic family-planning measures, e.g. improved health and sex education, making effective means of birth control available.
Factor 2:	*Policy 2:*
The number of births needed to *compensate* for high infant and child mortality is high.	Health-oriented development policy, e.g. courses in motherhood, nursing for small children, hygiene, nutrition, immunization against childhood diseases.
Factor 3:	*Policy 3:*
(a) The number of children *wanted* for social and economic reasons is high.	(a) Classic development-policy measures, e.g. changing motivation patterns via education, eliminating the need to have children as a living form of social insurance, improving the position of women in society.
(b) The number of children *wanted* for religious, cultural and traditional reasons is high.	(b) Promotion of cultural development and information programmes which aim to develop an appreciation of the real purposes behind demographically relevant commandments and prohibitions contained in cultural and religious traditions (e.g., the preference for sons). (See the final chapter of this book).

G_x = the size of generation x
G_{x-1} = the size of generation x's parental generation
G_{x+1} = the size of generation x's children's generation
α_x = the services rendered and assistance given by generation x per head of its children's generation
β_x = the services rendered and assistance given by generation x per head of its parents' generation

The value of the services rendered and assistance given by generation x to its children's generation can be obtained by multiplying the size of its children's generation by the services per head of that generation, i.e. by the expression $\alpha_x G_{x+1}$. Likewise, the services and assistance rendered to the parental generation is $\beta_x G_{x-1}$. That means that generation x provides a *total amount of service and assistance* to other generations of

$$\alpha_x G_{x+1} + \beta_x G_{x-1} \qquad (1)$$

Correspondingly, generation x in turn will *receive* a total of

$$\alpha_{x-1} G_x + \beta_{x+1} G_x \qquad (2)$$

from its predecessor and successor generations.

The services/assistance given or received (α or β) have the index x appended to them because each generation can potentially have its own approach to these activities.

The ratio of the services/assistance received and given to or by generation x is referred to as the *"inter-generational transfer quotient for generation x"*:

$$T_x = \frac{\alpha_x G_{x+1} + \beta_x G_{x-1}}{\alpha_{x-1} G_x + \beta_{x+1} G_x} \qquad (3)$$

This quotient will inevitably depend on the relative sizes of the three generations of G_{x-1}, G_x and G_{x+1}. For example, one important aspect of a favourable quotient for generation x is that the number of its children, i.e. G_{x+1} should not be too large. However, because the same argument applies to all generations, including the preceding one G_{x-1}, generation x's size when in the denominator of the transfer quotient would be all the smaller, making its transfer coefficient *less favourable*, the more the parental generation G_{x-1} kept down the number of children it had for the sake of improving *its own* transfer quotient. In other words, this is a trans-generational, dynamic optimization problem. The problem can best be expressed by asking what ratio between the generations G_{x-1}, G_x and G_{x+1} will yield the optimum, i.e. the lowest, transfer quotient. The numerical ratio between two consecutive generations is termed the *net reproduction rate* (NRR). Since any particular NRR always relates *two* generations to one another, the *three* generations involved in our transfer quotients can be represented by *two* net reproduction rates, as follows:

$$\frac{G_x}{G_{x-1}} = NRR_{x-1} \tag{4a}$$

$$\frac{G_{x+1}}{G_x} = NRR_x \tag{4b}$$

By substituting these expressions into the definitional equation for the transfer quotient, we obtain:

$$T_x = \frac{\alpha_x NRR_x + \beta_x \frac{1}{NRR_{x-1}}}{\alpha_{x-1} + \beta_{x+1}} \tag{5}$$

To begin with, let us seek to establish the optimum value of the transfer quotient when net reproduction rates and the "assistance output" rates α and β specific to the generations are equal, i.e. when

$$NRR_x = NRR_{x-1} = NRR \tag{6a}$$

$$\alpha_x = \alpha_{x-1} = \alpha \tag{6b}$$

$$\beta_x = \beta_{x+1} = \beta \tag{6c}$$

In this case, instead of equation (5) we have the simplified expression

$$T = \frac{\alpha NRR + \beta \dfrac{1}{NRR}}{\alpha + \beta} \tag{7}$$

The net reproduction rate yielding the optimum, i.e. lowest, value for the transfer coefficient is found by setting the derivative of T with respect to NRR to zero. The result is:

$$NRR^{opt} = \sqrt{\frac{\beta}{\alpha}} \tag{8}$$

The dependence of the transfer quotient upon the net reproduction rate as expressed in equation (7) is portrayed graphically in *Figure 4*. As the net reproduction rate increases, the transfer quotient initially falls, as the support provided to the older generation is spread among more people in the middle generation. However, because the effort they need to make for the young generation also increases as a result, the optimum value of the transfer quotient is reached with a net reproduction rate of exactly one. For all NRR figures above that, the transfer quotient increases in proportion.

The conclusions which can be drawn from this outcome are directly apparent from equation (8) above (showing the optimum NRR):

(a) A country's optimum net reproduction rate does *not* depend on the actual level of per capita assistance provided to the succeeding generation (α) or to the older generation (β), but on the *ratio* of the latter to the former (β/α). So if *both* forms of support are larger in country B than in country A by the same margin, that will not affect the optimum net reproduction rate.

(b) The larger the amount of assistance provided per capita to the *younger generation* (α) relative to that provided per capita to the *older generation* (β), the lower the optimum net reproduction rate will be, and vice versa.

(c) If the value of the assistance given to the younger and older generations is equal on a per capita basis ($\alpha = \beta$), the *optimum net reproduction rate = 1*, re-

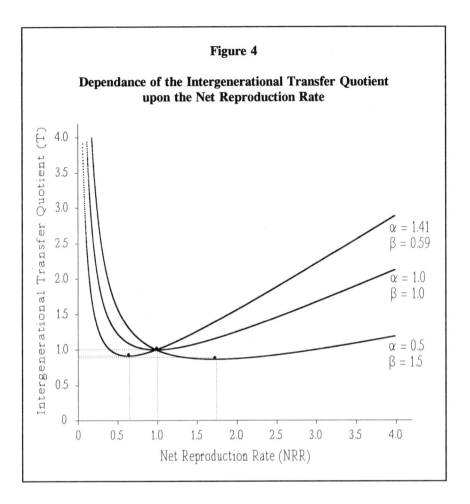

gardless of the actual amount of support transferred from generation to generation: thus the population will remain constant without any need for immigration or emigration.

(d) If the assistance given to the young generation is *greater* than that given to the older one ($\alpha > \beta$), the *optimum net reproduction rate* < *1*, which means *the population will decline if there is no net immigration.*

(e) If the assistance given to the young generation is *less* than that given to the older one ($\alpha < \beta$), the *optimum net reproduction rate* > *1*, which means *the population will grow if there is no net emigration.*

(f) The social and economic power to determine the relative amounts of per capita assistance given to the young and the old normally lies with the generation in the middle which is active in the working world. It is to the advantage of this active generation if it keeps a damper on the amount of assistance given to the young per head while favouring assistance to the old, particularly since this generation has already left its own phases of childhood and youth, in which it was a recipient, whereas its phase of old-age when it will again require support still lies ahead. Consequently, in any society which, like numerous developing countries does not protect children from being exploited by the middle generation (e.g. by prohibiting child labour or passing laws for the benefit of children and young people, say on school provision) one would expect the balance of assistance provided to shift in favour of the older generation, making $\beta > \alpha$, and the *optimum net reproduction rate* > *1*, resulting in persisting population growth. *Figure 4* outlines these links by examining three examples:

Example 1:
α = 0.50
β = 1.50
NRR_{opt} = 1.732

Numerous developing countries with net reproduction rates of approximately 1.7 (e.g. in South-East Asia, Central and South America) correspond to example 1.

Example 2:
$\alpha = 1.00$
$\beta = 1.00$
$NRR_{opt} = 1.00$

In example 2, more assistance per capita is provided to the younger generation relative to the older than was the case in example 1, and that has reduced the net reproduction rate. This example represents an ideal case in which a population remains constant when viewed net of migratory flows. Its net reproduction rate is 1.00 (approx. 2 children eventually reaching adult age and reproducing themselves per woman).

Example 3:
$\alpha = 1.41$
$\beta = 0.59$
$NRR_{opt} = 0.65$

The effort made on behalf of the younger generation relative to that made for the older is higher still in this case. The figures in example 3 were chosen so as to reflect roughly the circumstances in *Germany* today. In this case, the net reproduction rate is 0.65. Please note that the optimum net reproduction rate depends solely on the *ratio* of α to β, and not on the absolute value of either parameter. That being the case, the figures shown in the example for α and β do not actually have to agree with the *absolute* parameters existing in the real world. One may conclude from this example that the objective of maintaining a constant population, with a net reproduction rate of 1.0, without the need for net immigration will be unattainable as long as the assistance provided to the younger generation (per head of that generation) is greater than that given, per head, to the older generation. The per capita inter-generational transfer in favour of the younger generation cannot be found simply by examining statistics on family or household income and expenditure, for these figures are, firstly, themselves influenced by government policy on families, and secondly, they fail to take into account any of the government services and infrastructure provided to the younger or to the older generation. What is needed is an assessment which takes in all real payments or transfers of assistance, so that would have to include such items as expenditure on the educational system etc. The same naturally applies to the support given to the older generation. Many of the real provisions made by the state are economic quantities which cannot be directly captured in statistical information, but they can certainly be empirically estimated using statistics as a basis, though the necessary research input is high.

Another issue to be addressed in this theoretical treatment is that of what effects can be expected to be generated if an ever-greater proportion of the transfers per head of the younger or older generation are no longer made by individuals or families but by society as a whole or by government bodies. Suppose the sum of individual services (α^i) and societal services (α^s) per head of the younger generation is constant, and likewise for the services to the older generation:

$$\overline{\alpha} = \alpha^i + \alpha^s \qquad \alpha^i = \overline{\alpha} - \alpha^s \qquad (9)$$

$$\overline{\beta} = \beta^i + \beta^s \qquad \beta^i = \overline{\beta} - \beta^s \qquad (10)$$

Let us further assume that the members of the middle generation only bear their individual share of the services given, although they have been, or will later be, recipients both of the individual and of the societal assistance given to younger and older people. Based on these assumptions, the numerator of the transfer quotient, showing the services or assistance given out, will only contain the individual items whereas the denominator will show both the individual and societal transfers received by the same generation during its lifetime:

$$T_x = \frac{\alpha^i NRR_x + \beta^i \dfrac{1}{NRR_{x-1}}}{(\alpha^i + \alpha^s) + (\beta^i + \beta^s)} \qquad (11)$$

Here too, let us begin by assuming a net reproduction rate which remains constant from generation to generation ($NRR_{x-1} = NRR_x = NRR$), this yields the following *optimum net reproduction rate* where the transfer quotient is at a minimum:

$$NRR^{opt} = \sqrt{\frac{\overline{\beta} - \beta^s}{\overline{\alpha} - \alpha^s}} \qquad (12)$$

The derivation of the optimum net reproduction rate is based on legally and culturally defined standards for the assistance provided, per capita, to the younger or older generation. If these findings are applied to the situation, say, in Germany, the following statements can be made:

Summary (with reference to Germany):

I. The greater the proportion of the assistance provided (per capita) to people in *the late, old-age*, phase of the life-cycle which is *borne by society* at large or by the state, the *lower* the optimum net reproduction rate will be, all other factors being equal. In Germany, for example, the birth rate began to decline at the time a collective insurance programme for old-age pensions was introduced (in the Bismarckian social reforms of the 1890s), thus backing up this finding. Of course, one should not take that to mean that the introduction of a state social insurance scheme was the *only* factor behind the fall in the birth rate.

II. The greater the proportion of the assistance provided (per capita) to *children and young people* which is *borne by society* at large or by the state, the *higher* the optimum net reproduction rate will be. It is this functional relationship which nurtures the hope in industrial countries that it will be possible to raise the net reproduction rate substantially with the help of government policy towards families.

III. Whether the net reproduction rate is greater than, equal to or less then unity, or in other words whether the population net of migration will grow, remain constant or shrink in the long term, depends on the *ratio* between the portion of per capita assistance provided by society at large to the older generation and the portion of per capita assistance it provides to the younger generation.

IV. For example, the introduction of *nursing-care insurance* in Germany in 1995 has raised the proportion of per capita services to the older sections of the population which is borne by society or at least collectively, the effect of which is to *lower the optimum net reproduction rate*. So in a population like Germany's which is already shrinking without net immigration, the introduction of nursing-care insurance for senior citizens will mean that net immigration needs to be even higher than it already was in order to maintain a constant population. (In the early 1990tees the number of refugees asylum seekers and other immigrants was above one million per annum so that Germany's population grew despite of the birth deficit.)

Nursing-care insurance thus intensifies the cause of Germany's negative population trend, which is the actual reason for introducing the insurance scheme in the first place. From the purely demographic point of view, then, the measure is counter-productive, apart from which it breaches the principles laid down in the Federal Constitutional Court's much-publicized judgment of July 7, 1992 (on pension rights for the women who had worked to clear the rubble in Germany's cities after the World-War-II bombings), because it increases still more the transfer payments made by families with several children to pensioners with few or no children, instead of reducing this "inverse solidarity".

So far, we have set out to establish the optimum net reproduction rate on the basis of the functional relationship between the NRR and the inter-generational transfer quotient, while assuming that the net reproduction rate sought or obtained will be equal in all generations. In other words, we imagined that what might be termed a *"community of generations"* existed as the focus of people's actions, linking the different sections of the population together in a chain of consecutive generations giving assistance and reciprocating it.

Let us now drop this rather idealistic conception in favour of a more realistic view, enquiring what the optimum number of children per woman will be if the focus of action is not the community of generations but a single one, generation x. So the new question posed is: What are the optimum patterns of reproductive behaviour and family structure in terms of the transfer quotient for the *generation under examination* if it seeks solely to optimize the benefits to *itself*?

To answer this question, we must first return to the definition of the transfer quotient for generation x supplied in equation (3), but instead of the net reproduction rate we must now focus upon the *completed fertility rate* (CFR, i.e. the number of live-born children per 1,000 women during the full course of their lives). The latter is often a more appropriate measure, as the CFR values for different generations are easier to establish empirically.

The size of generation x can be expressed as the product of the number of women in its parents' generation (W_{x-1}) and the number of children per woman. If the number of women is also measured in thousands like the CFR, we obtain the following sizes for the three successive generations in (3):

$$G_x = W_{x-1} CFR_{x-1} \tag{13a}$$

$$G_{x+1} = W_x CFR_x \tag{13b}$$

$$G_{x-1} = W_{x-2} CFR_{x-2} \tag{13c}$$

Substituting for the generations in (3) using the definitions expressed in (13a to 13c) gives:

$$T_x = \frac{\alpha_x W_x CFR_x + \beta_x W_{x-2} CFR_{x-2}}{W_{x-1} CFR_{x-1} (\alpha_{x-1} + \beta_{x+1})} \tag{14}$$

Now dividing (14) by $W_{x-1} CFR_{x-1}$, we have:

$$T_x = \frac{\alpha_x \dfrac{W_x CFR_x}{W_{x-1} CFR_{x-1}} + \beta_x \dfrac{W_{x-2} CFR_{x-2}}{W_{x-1} CFR_{x-1}}}{\alpha_{x-1} + \beta_{x+1}} \tag{15}$$

W_x and W_{x-1} can be substituted for in equation (15) by the following expressions:

$$W_x = w W_{x-1} CFR_{x-1} \tag{16a}$$

$$W_{x-1} = w W_{x-2} CFR_{x-2} \tag{16b}$$

where w represents the proportion of live-born females in the generation concerned. If we assume $w = \frac{1}{2}$, we obtain the following equation to match equation (5):

$$T_x = \frac{\alpha_x \frac{1}{2}CFR_x + \beta_x \frac{1}{\frac{1}{2}CFR_{x-1}}}{\alpha_{x-1} + \beta_{x+1}} \qquad (17)$$

If generation x wishes to minimize its transfer quotient, the following three quantities in equation (17) are unalterable from its point of view:

CFR_{x-1}

α_{x-1}

β_{x+1}

Obviously, generation x has no influence over the average number of children born to its parents' generation (CFR_{x-1}) which determines its own size. Similarly, α_{x-1} represents the per capita assistance generation x received from its parents during its childhood and youth, while β_{x+1} is the assistance, per capita, which it will receive from its own children when it enters old-age. The only quantitites which generation x *can* influence in a bid to minimize its transfer quotient are the number of children it has (CFR_x), the amount of assistance it provides per child (α_x) and the amount of assistance it provides per head to its parents' generation (β_x). The outcome of this is directly apparent from equation (17):

Taking generation x's point of view in isolation, its transfer quotient will be at an optimum when the values for the number of generation x's children per woman, the amount of assistance α_x provided per child and the amount of assistance per head provided to the parental generation (β_x) are all at their lowest.
In contrast to the outcome of the trans-generational optimization problem considered prior to this one, the transfer quotient is now at its lowest when the number of children pr woman is *zero*. So if generation x were to optimize its own benefits without any regard for what would happen if other generations acted in the same way - i.e., if it chose to violate the universal ethical principle laid down in Immanuel Kant's *categoric imperative* - there would be a persistent decrease in the number of children per woman, with all the consequences that entailed (see *chapter 6*).

Such a trend is indeed in evidence in the demographic data for western industrial countries over the past 100 years. Nevertheless, we should not conclude from this, as other people often do, that an increasing number of people now gear their reproductive behaviour to a model of their own hedonistic self-interest without paying any heed to the overall consequences of such behaviour if it becomes a general pattern. One of the prime counter-arguments against a willy-nilly condemnation of productive behaviour and against likening this to ethically offensive hedonism is the mere fact that the most vital prerequisite of any ethical behaviour is the freedom to act as one chooses. This is a precondition which, given the growing economic restraints upon the actions of individuals and families which have resulted from the dominance of the working world over biographical and demographic options in competitive societies, has to be regarded as being breached in many cases today.

Conclusions:

The deductions made above allow the following conclusions to be drawn for any future decline in the total fertility rate in the developing countries and in the world as a whole. There are two routes towards attaining a net reproduction rate of 1.0 which will maintain a constant population in the long run. The first of these is the path of successful, civilizing development based on positive emotional relations between the generations, with balanced inter-generational transfers of material and immaterial assistance. The second path is one of reckless competitive struggle not only between different social groups but also between generations. Both of these paths lead to a reduction in the birth rate for the world population, but two entirely different worlds stand at the end of them: one world of humanity and peace, the other of destruction and chaos. Which of the two paths is taken by the countries of this world will be decided by the individuals and the populations who inhabit them. Nothing on Earth can therefore be more important than educating and fully enlightening those people.

Chapter 4

World Population Projections for the 21st Century

4.1 Introduction and Proposition

Up to the mid-18th century, it was still an open question as to whether the world population had grown or diminished since the olden days. It was not until demography developed along with regular censuses being carried out in a number of different European countries during the 18th century that a clearer picture emerged. It is now thought probable that the population of the world around the time of the birth of Christ lay between 200 and 400 million. Today (1995), there are estimated to be 5.7 billion people, i.e. about twenty times as many, living on the planet Earth.

In the first one-and-a-half milennia A.D., world population growth was extraordinarily slow. The average annual rate during that period was well below 0.1%. As industrialization got under way around 1750, the growth in the world's population took a considerable leap, yet still remained well below 1% until the end of the 19th century. The 20th century, though, will go down in population history as the century which brought a unique acceleration in growth. In other words, not only the world population has grown markedly but also the growth rate as such, so the pace of that growth has hotted up (see *Figure 5*, lower graph). This phenomenon of increasing growth rates is referred to as *hypergeometric population growth*. The rate grew from 0.5% in 1900 to 0.8% in 1950 and then to 2.1% in the early 1970s. If the world population figure for 1975 - when the Earth had 4.07 billion inhabitants - were to have continued growing steadily at that same rate for 100 years, that would have meant a world population of 32 billion in 2075. The rate of world population growth has in fact fallen off from its early-1970s peak of 2.1% to reach approximately 1.5-1.6% at pre-

83

sent (1995). However, in spite of that decline the *absolute* population figure is still increasing - the in-built momentum is rather like that of a supertanker which, even as it is slowing down, can still travel some miles before it is brought to a stand. The present rate of increase in absolute terms is approx. 90-100 million each year, or approx. 1 billion per decade (see *Figures 27* and *28*). The time needed by the world population to increase by another billion has shortened from 121 years in 1805 to just 11 years in present times (see *Table 2a*).

Public interest in the issue of world population growth is largely concentrated upon the double question of how long the population will continue to grow (i.e., up to which year) and what level it will have reached by that time, likely to be in the late 21st or early 22nd century. As long as the number of live births per woman, defined as the *total fertility rate* (TFR), remains above 2.13 (the *replacement fertility level* which corresponds to a *net reproduction rate* (NRR) of 1.0) on a world average, the population will go on increasing. Because of the relatively young profile of the world population, even after the replacement fertility level has been attained and subsequently maintained, it will in fact still go on growing for between 50 and 100 years more. The crucial question is therefore how many decades will be needed before the total fertility rate comes down to the replacement fertility level of 2.13 live births per woman.

The present-day (period 1990-95) total fertility rate is 1.91 in the industrial countries, 3.64 in the developing countries, and 3.26 for the world as a whole (United Nations World Population Prospects, The 1992 Revision). If the two separate rates for the industrial and developing countries were each to continue unchanged, the effect on the world average total fertility rate would be for it to rise rather than fall as projections assume: for example, by the year 2050 it would have risen to 3.39 from the current 3.26. In view of the indisputable rise in the developing countries' share of total world population, it is fair to ask how probable it is that the world's total fertility rate really will have come down to replacement level by the year 2060 or even by the year 2055 as assumed, for example, by the *World Bank* in its latest estimates (World Population Projection, 1992-93 and 1994-95 Editions). That question will be addressed in this chapter.

Over the past few decades, the average total fertility rate for the world population as a whole has fallen considerably, from 4.98 live births per woman in the 1960-65 period to 3.26 in 1990-95 (UN, 1993: 216; see *Figure 7*). This pronounced absolute drop has diverted attention from the fact that the actual pace of the decline has slowed steadily during those three decades. Indeed, if the high

Table 2a

World Population Growth since the Birth of Christ

	Year	Number of years needed to reach next billion
200 - 400 Millions	0	1800 years
⋮	⋮	
First Billion	1805	
Second Billion	1926	121 years
Third Billion	1960	34 years
Fourth Billion	1974	14 years
Fifth Billion	1987	13 years
Sixth Billion	1998	11 years
Seventh Billion	2010	12 years
Eighth Billion	2023	13 years
Ninth Billion	2040	17 years
Tenth Billion	2070	30 years
Eleventh Billion	c. 2100	30 years

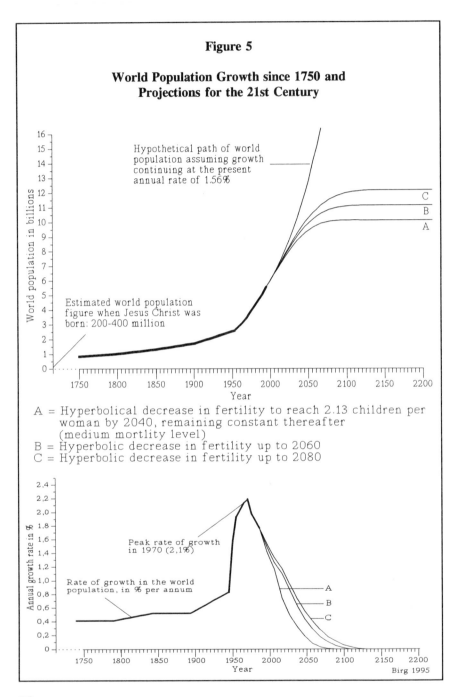

Figure 6

Age Structure of World Population 1990, 2050 and 2100

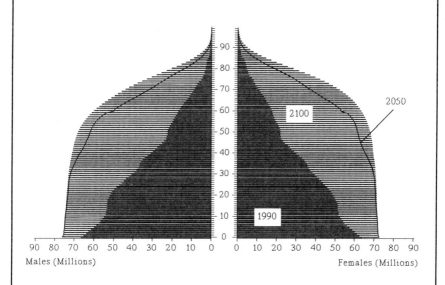

Population Projection No. 2060.R.M.

Target year for replacement fertility
level (TFR = 2.13): 2060
Form of fertility decline: Hyperbolic
Mortality level: Medium

Total population: 1990 5 275 Million
2050 9 824 Million
2100 10 674 Million

Figure 7

Decline in the Total Fertility Rate from 1960-65 to 1990-95 by Major Area

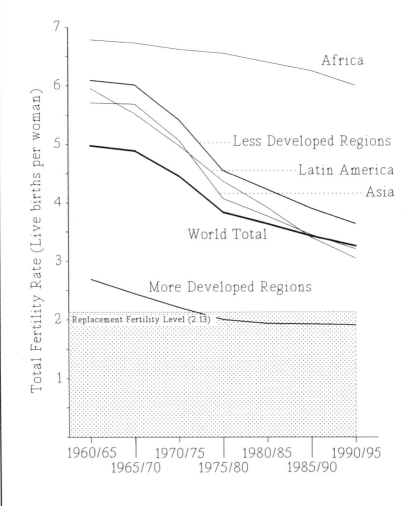

Source of Data: UN (Ed.), World Population Prospects - The 1992 Edition, New York 1993

Figure 8

Increase in Life Expectancy at Birth from 1960-65 to 1990-95 by Major Area

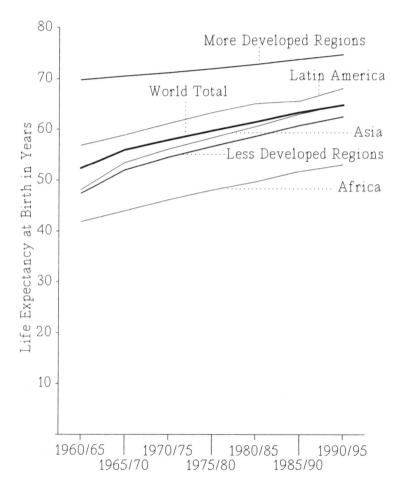

Source of Data: UN (Ed.), World Population Prospects - The 1992 Edition, New York 1993

rate of decline between 1965-70 and 1975-80 (-2.4 per cent p.a.) had been maintained, the total fertility rate ought to reach replacement level at the end of this decade: A number of statistics help to illustrate how much the pace of decline has slowed: between the second half of the 1960s and the second half of the 1970s, the TFR fell by 1.05 live births per woman; between the second half of the 1970s and the second of the 1980s, the corresponding fall was less than half of that, at only 0.41 live births per woman (1975-80: 3.84; 1985-90: 3.43). The *proposition* which will be put forward here is that the pace of decline in the total fertility rate is likely to continue slackening in the decades ahead. The proposition is not based simply on a projection of earlier trends, but on the following three substantive arguments:

1. People in the developing countries are likely to realize that, given the inadequacy of state unemployment and sickness benefits and old-age pensions, two children who attain adult age will not be sufficient to safeguard their parents' economic livelihood, to maintain family networks of mutual assistance or to comply with religious precepts and cultural norms.

2. Because of this, it will be all the more difficult to achieve further reductions in the level of fertility the lower that level has already sunk. In order to reduce the number of children per woman by the same amount each decade, ever greater efforts will be called for on the part of development, population and family-planning policies. That in turn will mean that so many funds will be required that donor countries will have to substantially increase the assistance they provide.

3. As their relative demographic weighting increases, the developing countries' contribution towards the world total fertility rate will also steadily increase, so that a growing proportion of development and population policy efforts will need to be devoted even just to counterbalancing the increase in world total fertility rate caused by that change in weighting alone.

These propositions do not contradict the findings of the Demographic and Health Surveys (DHS) or the Family Planning Surveys (FPS) conducted by *Johns Hopkins University* in 40 developing countries during the 1980s (Robey 1992 and 1994). When the results of these were published in December 1992, the figures were misunderstood all around the world as implying that the situation was now easing (Stevens, 1994). Yet demographic researchers see no reason at present to revise any earlier population projections downwards - quite the reverse. The UN's *Population Division* did not make any adjustments at all to its 1990 assumptions when making its 1992 estimates of the future trend in the total fertility rate in developing countries, while the latest publications on the subject by the *World Bank* (1992-93 and 1994-95 revisions) actually revised the forecast TFR slightly upwards for the second half of the 21st century. According to the revision of 1992-93 the TFR in 2075 ist estimated at 2.08, and according to the revision of 1994-95 at 2.09.

4.2 Methodological Aspects, Basic Terms and the Initial Data used for Population Projections

(a) Initial Population, Fertility, Mortality and Projection Method

The population projections presented in this book have been prepared using the same method as those published by the World Bank and the UN Population Division, namely what is known as the *cohort survival method*. So as to be able to delineate as clearly as possible between the influence of the age profile and that of fertility and mortality rates on the final results obtained, the base population in 1990 was differentiated by 100 different years of age and by gender (the source of the initial data for *5-year* age groups is K.C. Zachariah and My T. Vu, 1988)). Taking 1990 as the *base year*, the next step is to calculate the number of males and females in each age cohort who are expected to survive into the following year, according to the statistical survival probability for the gender and age- group. When that operation is complete, one year is added to the age of each of the 200 cohorts, and the same procedure is then repeated for the surviving 1991 population thus obtained, and for each subsequent year until the end of the projection period is reached. Hence a projection running until the year 2100 which has 1990 as its base year will call for 110 computational steps, and the number of people surviving into, say, 2050 will be calculated on the basis of the projected population in 2049. The survival probabilities for the world population needed to apply this method were computed separately for each age cohort and each gender. The parameters used also took account of the fact that the survival probabilities of younger people are rising considerably faster than those of older age-groups in the population (for details see *technical appendix 1*).

The *number of live-born* children in any given year of the projection period less the figure deducted for infants dying before they reach one year of age gives the world population in the 0-1 age-group for the start of the following year. The method used to calculate the number of live-born children each year is as follows: First the number of women in each of the 31 age cohorts (from 15 to 45 years old) who have survived until that year in the projection is identified from the calculations already made. Then the number of women in each of those cohorts is multiplied by the corresponding age-specific fertility rate (of which there are again 31 different rates), and the aggregate number of live births for the year is established by adding all of the age-specific results together. The *age-specific fertility rate* is nothing more than the probability that a woman in a particular age-group will give birth to a child during the following year. Starting out at a very low value at age 15, the age-specific fertility rates are distributed along a bell-shaped curve which returns to zero around the age of 45 years. The age-specific fertility rates all add together to give the *total fertility rate* (see technical appendix).

(b)   Basic Terms: Replacement Fertility Level, Momentum of Population Growth and "if-then"-Statements on the Future

The *replacement fertility level* is the particular total fertility rate which, at a predetermined mortality level (derived from the measure of survival probabilities), allows just enough children to be born to replace their parents' generation. On the basis of the present and future life expectancies which have been used and assumed for these projections, that replacement fertility rate is 2.13 live births per woman. In other words, every 100 women need to give birth to 213 children for the population to sustain itself in the long run.

However, even assuming that the world's total fertility rate, at some point in the future, were to reach the replacement fertility level, the population itself would continue to *grow* for a further 50 to 100 years because of the *demographic momentum* inherent in the relatively young age profile, before it attained a stationary state in which both the total population figure and the age profile remained stable. In such a stationary state, the *net reproduction rate* (NRR) equals 1. The net reproduction rate is the ratio of the size of a new generation to that of its parents' generation. As a general rule, if the NRR is greater than one (>1), the population will grow, if $NRR<1$ it will fall, and if it equals 1, it will remain constant in the long run. To illustrate, the net reproduction rate in the world is currently 1.314 implying an increase of 36% from one generation to another (in approx. 25 years).

The methods of demographic projection allow a precise answer to be given to the following *hypothetical question*: Assuming the total fertility rate were to come down to the replacement fertility level of 2.13 live births per woman in just one year, by how many people, or by what percentage, would the world population continue to grow? And that answer is that the world population would grow from 5.3 billion in 1990 to 7.3 billion in 2040, or in other words by approx. 40%! The significance of this hypothetical calculation is that it clearly demonstrates the importance of attaining replacement fertility as early as possible. If it were not attained in one year as in the hypothetical case just cited, but in an equally hypothetical period of 10 years, the world population would then go on growing until the year 2050, and would stabilize at the higher level of 7.9 billion. Such computations will be illustrated in more detail and on a systematic basis below.

The computations, projections and simulations shown here should *not* be regarded as *population forecasts or prophecies*; rather they consist of *"if ... then ..." statements* with regard to the future. That is to say, these statements as to future developments will prove true if the assumptions on which they are based are fulfilled. The consequences for fertility and mortality derived from these if-then conditions can be ascertained with a high degree of accuracy.

4.3 Impact of Alternative Fertility Scenarios on World Population Growth

(a) Alternative Patterns of Decline and Target Years for Fertility Reduction (= Fertility Paths)

The target year is the description given to the future year at which the world total fertility rate is expected to have fallen from the 3.4 live births per woman registered in the base year (1990) to the replacement fertility level of 2.13 live births per woman. The alternative target-year scenarios reflect varying degrees of optimism in the assumed rapidity with which fertility will decline in future. As has been pointed out, these are *not* forecast values, but alternative sets of if-then assumptions, and the current purpose is to investigate the consequences flowing from particular assumptions of this kind. As there is no special need here to examine particular target years, an interval of 10 years has been chosen, giving the sequence of 2000, 2010, 2020, ..., 2060 (i.e. the target year assumed in the World Bank's projections of 1992-93), 2070, ..., 2100. It would be equally possible to make the calculations for any other target year in between e.g. for the year 2055 (World Bank Projections 1994-95). Of course, each specific target year gives rise to its own variant projection of world population growth.

In addition to the target year for the reduction in fertility, it is also necessary to establish what *form* that reduction should take, i.e. what the pattern of decline might be. The proposition made in section 1 above, that as fertility goes on falling it will become increasingly difficult to achieve any further decline, is best reflected in the assumption that the fertility curve will take the shape of a concave *hyperbola*. As alternatives to the hyperbolic curve, calculations have also been carried out on the assumption that the fall in fertility describes an *S-curve* (with the fastest rate of decline in the middle of the period and slower initial and final rates of decline) and finally also assuming a *linear reduction* (*see Figures 9-13*). Hence the following variants of population projections have been computed for each of the target years selected, as follows:

Figure 9
Decline in the Total Fertility Rate of the World Population from 1962-1990 and Scenarios for the Decline to Replacement Fertility Level (TFR = 2.13) in the Future (Form of Decline: Hyperbolic)

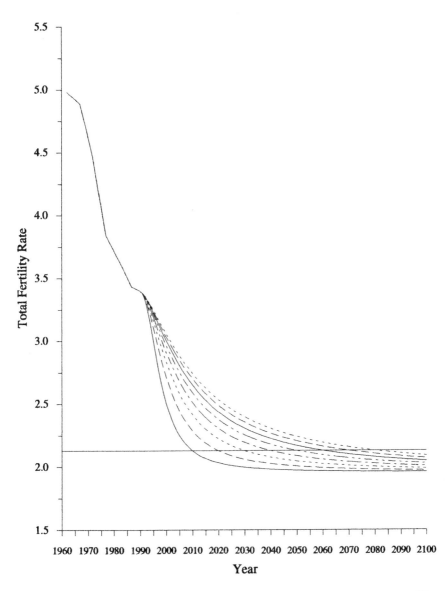

Figure 10
Decline in the Total Fertility Rate of the World Population to Replacement Fertility Level (TFR = 2.13)
(Form of Decline: Hyperbolic)

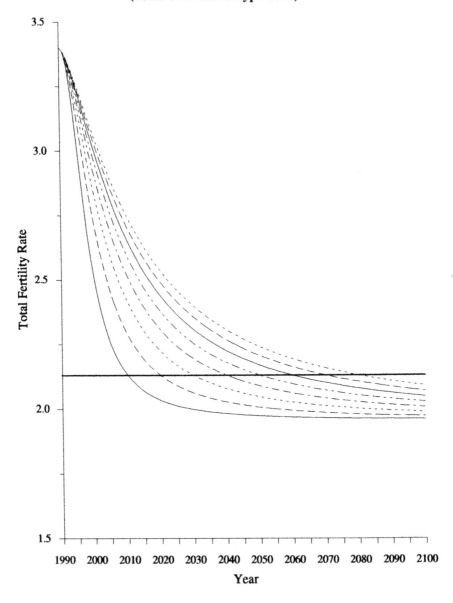

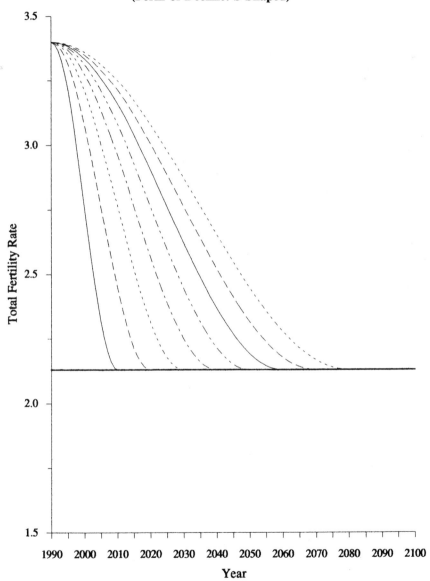

**Figure 11
Decline in the Total Fertility Rate of the World Population
to Replacement Fertility Level (TFR = 2.13)
(Form of Decline: S-Shaped)**

Figure 12
Decline in the Total Fertility Rate of the World Population to Replacement Fertility Level (TFR = 2.13)
(Form of Decline: Linear)

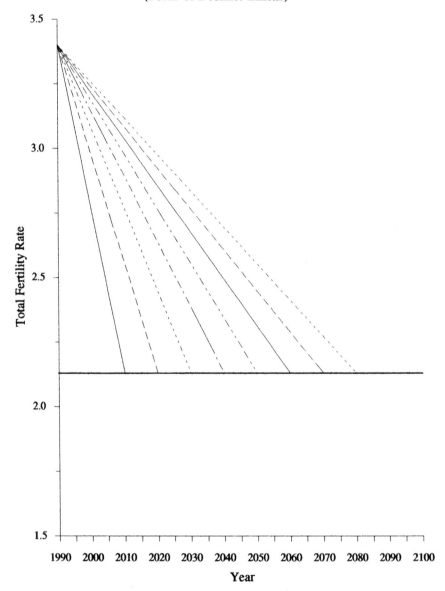

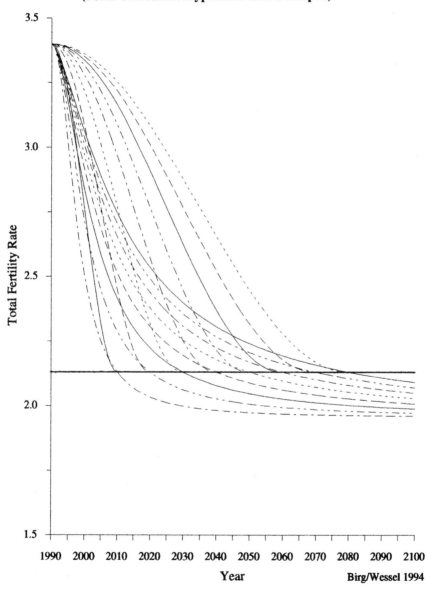

**Figure 13
Decline in the Total Fertility Rate of the World Population
to Replacement Fertility Level (TFR = 2.13)
(Form of Decline: Hyperbolic and S-Shaped)**

Birg/Wessel 1994

Pattern of decline   Target year for attaining
in fertility   replacement fertility
                     level or intersection

- Hyperbolic
- S-curve   2000, 2010, ..., 2060, ..., 2100, ...
- Linear

Each combination of a particular target year and a particular pattern of decline gives rise to its own *path of fertility decline over time* (or *"fertility path"* for short) and to a corresponding population projection. In the case of the S-curve and linear fertility paths, fertility was assumed to remain constant at replacement level once the target year had been reached. The same approach was also adopted for the hyperbolic path, but an additional variant was also computed in which fertility continued to decline beyond the target year.

(b)   Population Projections for Alternative Fertility Paths and the Differences between Global and Country-Specific Population Projections (Aggregation Effects)

For the *"medium variant"* of the World Bank's population projections, 2060 or 2055 were chosen as the target years with constant fertility thereafter. When one of those target years, e.g. 2060, is chosen here, along with other alternative target years, the fertility paths arising from the different types of decline produce the projections set out in *Table 2b*. The population figure for the year 2150 emerging from the World Bank's projection is 11.4 billion(*Table 3*), whereas the figure produced by the projections discussed here, on the lower variant, is just 10.7 billion. How does this discrepancy arise? To examine one possibility, the hyperbolic time path chosen here is compared with the World Bank's assumption on the decline of fertility in *Figure 14*. Readers will notice that the hyperbolic curve runs above the World Bank's assumed fertility curve from 2035 onwards. If anything, then, one would expect a *higher* projection than the World Bank's to result, and not a lower one.

The reason for this discrepancy is what is known as the *aggregation effect*, the essence of which will be illustrated below. The population projections made by

Table 2b

The World Population Level in 2150, Based on Different Assumptions as to the Rapidity of the Decline in Fertility (TFR) to the Replacement Level of 2.13 Live Births per Woman

The number of years needed, starting in 1990, for fertility to reach replacement level, by the target year of...	Target year	World population in 2150, in billions, assuming different forms of decline in fertility (TFR) to the same final value of 2.13 live births per woman by the target year stated		
		Form 1	Form 2	Form 3
20 years	2010	8.3	8.6	8.7
30 years	2020	8.8	9.5	9.5
40 years	2030	9.3	10.4	10.5
50 years	2040	9.7	11.4	11.5
60 years	2050	10.2	12.5	12.7
70 years	2060	10.7	13.7	13.9
80 years	2070	11.2	15.1	15.3
90 years	2080	11.7	16.5	16.8
100 years	2090	12.2	18.2	18.5
110 years	2100	12.7	19.9	20.3

Form 1: Very rapid decline in fertility in the early years, slackening off over time (hyperbolic function intercepting x-axes in the target year, after intersection constant)

Form 2: S-shaped decline in three fertility phases:
phase 1 - weak initial decline, but increasingly accelerating;
phase 2 - very pronounced decline;
phase 3 - decline easing off again (sine-function)

Form 3: Equal decline in fertility each year until the target date (linear function)

the World Bank and by the UN Population Division are based on separate computations for more than 150 countries around the world, which are subsequently added together to obtain the world total. This approach is known as a *disaggregated projection*. By way of contrast, the projections under discussion have been prepared on an *aggregated* world basis from the outset. One might at first think that the aggregated and disaggregated projections would be identical in their outcomes provided that they used the same base data and that all the underlying fertility and mortality assumptions were the same. However, that is not the case, as will be demonstrated by the following example.

Suppose we prepare one population projection for the world as a whole on an aggregate basis, and that we then make a second projection in which the world population is subdivided into two large parts, one for the industrial and one for the developing countries (a disaggregated projection). In the latter case, the projection for the world as a whole is obtained by adding together the two sub-populations for the industrial countries and the developing countries. Suppose also that we apply the same assumptions on future fertility trends to both the aggregated and disaggregated projections. For the sake of simplicity, we maytake a constant total fertility rate both in the industrial and in the developing countries, but with the latter higher than the former. Now, if we similarly assume a constant total fertility rate for the aggregated projection, this is where the discrepancy arises, for in the case of the disaggregated computation method the assumption of constant fertility in each sub-group would actually imply an increase in the world total fertility rate over time, since it is calculated as the weighted average of the specific fertility rates in the industrial countries on the one hand and the developing countries on the other. Provided that the TFR in each of the two sub-groups remains constant, that weighted average will inevitably increase because the developing countries with their higher specific fertility rate will take up an increasing relative share of the world population while the relative share of the industrial countries, with their lower fertility rate, declines. Thus precisely *because* we have supposed that the TFRs are constant in both the developing countries and the industrial countries, it is *impossible* for the world TFR to remain constant in the disaggregated projection method - it *must inevitably* increase. Conversely, one can conclude that if the world fertility path of a disaggregated population projection derived from specific country figures is the same as the fertility path underlying an aggregated world population projection, then the fertility assumptions made must have been *different*. As will be seen from *Figure 14*, the fertility paths for the target year of 2060 in the projection presented here and for the World Bank's projection are broadly the same, which means that the underlying fertility assumptions must be *different*, with a lower assumed fertility in this study than in the World Bank projection with the same target year. Consequently, the projected eventual population figure is also lower, since both projections work with the same base population and with largely identical mortality assumptions (for further examples of aggregation effects see Lutz and Prinz 1991 and Birg 1980, with computations of regionally differentiated population projections for the more than 300 counties in former West Germany). From these considerations, we can conclude that it will be necessary to select a higher fertility path if we wish to compare the population projections presented here with those of the World Bank and the UN Population Division. The comparison can readily be made if a higher fertility path is chosen instead of the path with 2060 as the target year. The figures in *Table 2b* show that the hyperbolic fertility path with a target year in the 2080-85 range would fit such a comparison: by shifting the target 20-25 years further forward in time to 2080-85, we obtain a fertility path equivalent to that of the World Bank's projection, and the resulting projected population figures are in the same order of magnitude.

Another possible way of attaining comparability between aggregated and disaggregated population projections is to choose an S-curve or linear decline in fertility instead of the hyperbolic curve, as the resulting fertility level is invariably higher in either of these alternative cases for any given target year. However, the fertility with a target year of 2060 then turns out higher than in the World Bank's projection: the linear fertility path produces a projected population in 2150 of 13.9 billion, and the S-curve path a projection of 13.7 billion (*Table 2b*). The population level projected by the World Bank is now arrived at by bringing the target closer in time, to the years 2045-50 for the linear option or 2040-45 for the S-curve option.

Table 2b and *Figures 15-18* show the resulting aggregated population projections for various alternative target years and patterns of fertility decline. Further computations are presented in **Part II** of this book. The following important findings should be particularly pointed out:

The outcome of population projections is curcially dependent on the pattern of decline in fertility:

1. Given a medium mortality trend and a replacement fertility level of 2.13, *choosing which pattern* of fertility reduction to assume results in a discrepancy, taking the target year of 2060 as an example, of approximately 3 billion in the final population figure projected (difference between 10.7 billion for a hyperbolic and 13.7 billion for a linear reduction in fertility). If the target year chosen is 2070, that discrepancy widens to 4 billion, and if it is 2080, to 5 billion. Even if the relatively close target year of 2030 is chosen, there is still a discrepancy in the final total of 1.2 billion.

2. The results obtained using S-curve and linear fertility paths are quite similar, and the final population projections they give when the target year for replacement fertility is 2060 lie approximately 30% above the final level obtained when a hyperbolic fertility path is assumed.

To sum up, not only the target year for replacement fertility and the replacement level itself are significant, but the actual pattern of fertility decline is an important factor in population growth in its own right, and the latter has received too little attention to date.

(c) Path Effects

In *Figure 19*, a linear fertility path with 2060 as the target year (curve "C") is superimposed on a hyperbolic curve with 2080 as the target year (curve "B"). Although one would normally expect a higher final population to result from selecting the more distant target year, in fact the population curve for the linear/2060 case tracks substantially above that based on the hyperbolic fertility path to 2080. The reason for this is that the aggregate of the TFR values for each successive calendar year is considerably greater for the linear path than for the hyperbolic, even though the target year for the latter comes so much later.

One could now go on to examine what happens if both the target year and the sum of the TFR values are the same for two fertility curves. This case is illustrated in *Figure 20*. The linear and S-curved paths shown here share the same target year of 2060, and the sums of their TFR values are also virtually identical. Nevertheless, the population curve derived from the S-curved path exceeds the curve derived from the linear fertility path not just until the intersection of the paths in the year 2024, but right on until 2076 before it begins to grow more slowly than the other. This phenomenon will be termed the *"path effect"*. Its explanation lies in the momentum of population growth due to the cumulative impact of the age profile on the total population figure. The existence of such path effects further underlines the importance of the pattern of fertility decline for future trends in total population. This conclusion has important connotations for policy-makers, namely that any time lost in reducing fertility levels will lead to an increased overall population figure for many decades, even if that lost time is subsequently made up by a more urgent policy approach.

(d)   The Impact upon World Population Growth of Delays in Reducing Fertility

There are a number of ways in which the decline in fertility rates may be delayed:

Case 1:   For a given pattern of fertility decline, replacement fertility may not be attained until a much later date than the original target.

Case 2:   Even if replacement fertility is indeed attained by the target year, a delay may occur along the way if the path of decline follows the slower S-curve or is linear instead of following the rapid, hyperbolic curve. As shown in the previous section, the result may be an eventual total population which is higher by 3—5 billion.

Case 3:   The lowest level of fertility eventually attained may still exceed the replacement level, meaning that the world population will not reach an upper limit, but will go on growing indefinitely.

These three cases may occur together in a variety of different combinations. Due to space constraints, it will have to suffice here to conclude with a short examination of the case in which replacement fertility is not actually reached. To demonstrate this, a computation has been made (see *Table 4*) based on a final fertility level of 2.17 live births per woman instead of 2.13, with the following result:

Final fertility rate in the year 2060 (hyperbolic decline)	Population level in the year 2100, in billions
2.13	10.7
2.17	11.4

The difference between the fertility rates is 1.9%, whereas the difference between the corresponding population levels in 2100 is 6.5%. The absolute difference is one of 700 million people. Nevertheless, more important than the absolute difference is the high degree of sensitivity with which population growth responds to small increases in fertility (*Table 5*).

If the final fertility rate attained is *below* the replacement fertility level, the world population will still continue growing for a number of decades because of the in-built momentum, then reaching a maximum in the 21st or 22nd century before declining thereafter (see *Figure 16*). *Tables 5 and 6* show the results emerging from three different final fertility rates (2.0, 2.1 and 2.13), assuming a hyperbolic or a linear decline in fertility. *Table 7* and *Figure 29* show the dependence of the growth in the number of women in reproductive age upon the fertility path.

(e) Note on the Precision of World Population Projections to Date

The Population Division of the United Nations' Department of Economic and Social Affairs has been regularly drawing up world population projections since the 1950s. Those projections have in fact proved very reliable. If the projections for the year 2000 which were made in 1958, 1962, 1982 and 1992 are compared, the degree of accuracy achieved is astonishingly good. It is possible to say this today as the world population figure for 2000 is already almost settled at this stage.

Because the projection period is now only 10 years long, the authors' projections for the year 2000 presented here all lie within a relatively narrow range, between 6.1 billion (with 2010 as the target year) and 6.2 billion (with 2080 as the target year). The UN's projections since 1958, with the exception of the deviating projection made in 1962, equally fit into a range which is hardly any broader. The following table shows the medium variants in each case:

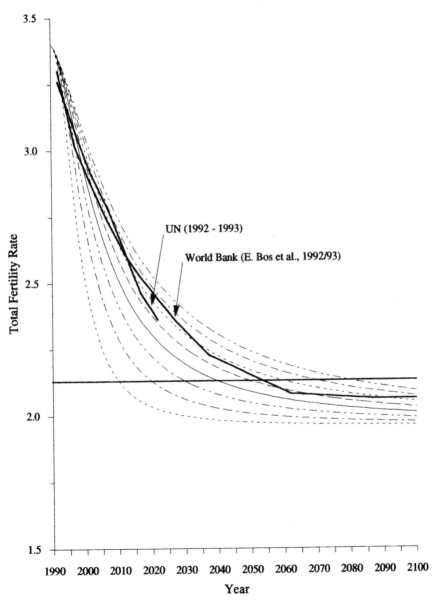

**Figure 14
Comparison of Various Assumptions on Fertility
Decline for the World Population**

Figure 15
8 Variants of World Population Growth
- Hyperbolic Decline in Fertility, Medium Mortality Level -

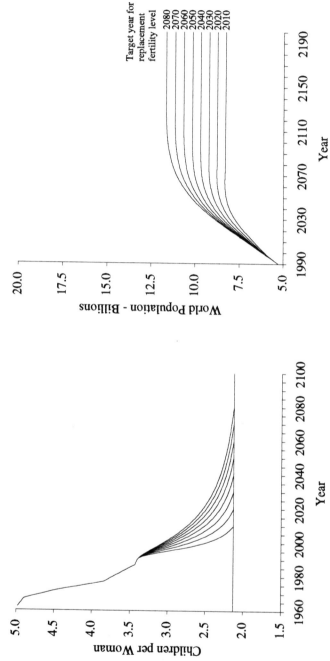

108

Figure 16
8 Variants of World Population Growth
- Hyperbolic Decline in Fertility Below Replacement Level, Medium Mortality Level -

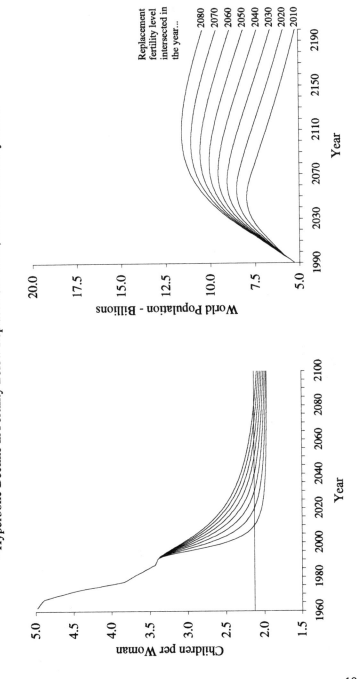

109

Figure 17
8 Variants of World Population Growth
- S-Shaped Decline in Fertility, Medium Mortality Level -

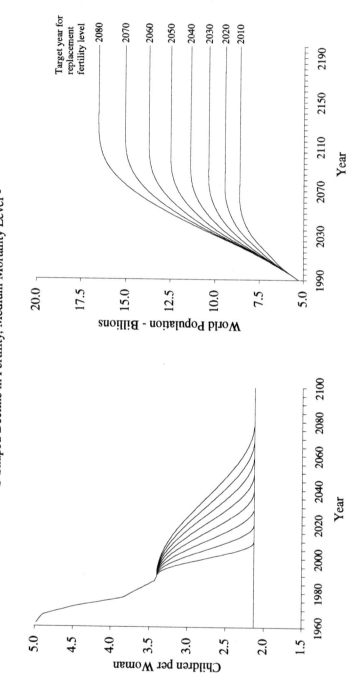

110

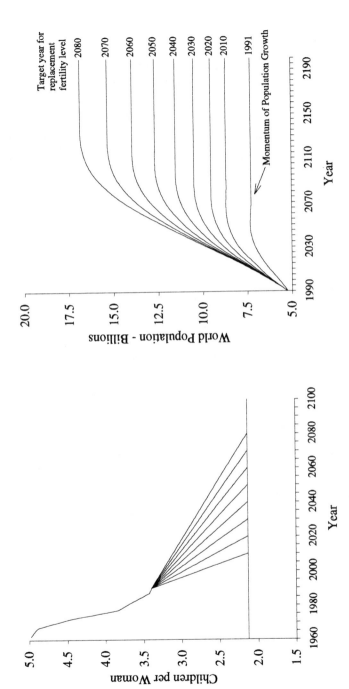

Figure 18
8 Variants of World Population Growth
- Linear Decline in Fertility, Medium Mortality Level -

Table 3

Comparison between the World Bank Population Projections of 1989/90, 1992/93 and 1994/95

(figures in millions)

	1989/90 Projection			1992/93 Projection			1994/95 Projection		
	1990	2050	2150	1990	2050	2150	1990	2050	2150
World	5285	10035	11499	5268	10055	12078	5266	9578	11401
Developing Countries	4074	8716	10186	4053	8623	10610	4051	8219	10013
Industrial Countries	1211	1319	1314	1214	1433	1469	1215	1367	1399
Africa	651	2275	3042	627	2079	2954	627	1999	2827
Americas of which	721	1146	1200	721	1201	1308	715	1178	1294
Latin America	441	814	871	441	839	935	435	804	906
North America	280	332	329	280	362	373	281	374	388
Asia	3100	5728	6367	3103	5811	6817	3174	5638	6509
Europe and former USSR	787	843	846	790	922	954	723	721	726
Oceania	27	42	45	27	43	46	27	42	46

Compiled from: (a) R. A. Bulatao et al.: World Population Projections 1989-90 Edition, Baltimore and London, 1990; (b) E. Bos et al.: World Population Projections 1992-93 Edition, Baltimore and London, 1992; (c) E. Bos et al.: World Population Projections 1994-95 Edition, Baltimore and London, 1994.

Table 4

World Population Growth Assuming a Hyperbolic
Decline in Fertility up to 2060 (in Billions)

| | final fertility value in the year 2060 [1] ||
	TFR = 2.13	TFR = 2.17
1990	5.3	5.3
2050	9.8	10.1
2100	10.7	11.4
2150	10.7	11.8
2200	10.7	12.2

[1] assuming constant fertility thereafter, and the medium mortality variant

Table 5

The Impact of Delays in the Decline in Fertility of the Replacement Level (TFR = 2.13), or to Just Under Replacement Level (TFR = 2.0 or 2.1)

Length of time needed for fertility decline	World population in 2150, in billions assuming final fertility values of...		
	TFR = 2.0	TFR = 2.1	TFR = 2.13
20 years (= 2010)	5.9	7.7	8.3
30 years (= 2020)	6.2	8.2	8.8
40 years (= 2030)	6.4	8.6	9.3
50 years (= 2040)	6.7	9.0	9.7
60 years (= 2050)	6.9	9.4	10.2
70 years (= 2060)	7.2	9.9	10.7
80 years (= 2070)	7.4	10.3	11.2
90 years (= 2080)	7.6	10.8	11.7
100 years (= 2090)	7.9	11.2	12.2
110 years (= 2100)	8.1	11.7	12.8
120 years (= 2110)	8.4	12.2	13.3
130 years (= 2120)	8.6	12.7	13.8
140 years (= 2130)	8.8	13.2	14.4
150 years (= 2140)	9.1	13.7	14.9

Assumption: Hyperbolic fertility decline, medium mortality level

Table 6

The Impact of Delays in the Decline in Fertility to the Replacement Level (TFR = 2.13) or Just Under Replacement Level (TFR = 2.0 or 2.1)

Length of time needed for fertility decline	World population in 2150, in billions assuming final fertility values of...		
	TFR = 2.0	TFR = 2.1	TFR = 2.13
50 years (= 2040)	8.9	10.9	11.5
60 years (= 2050)	10.0	12.0	12.7
70 years (= 2060)	11.1	13.2	13.9
80 years (= 2070)	12.4	14.6	15.3
90 years (= 2080)	13.8	16.1	16.8
100 years (= 2090)	15.4	17.7	18.5
110 years (= 2100)	17.1	19.6	20.3
120 years (= 2110)	19.0	21.5	22.3
130 years (= 2120)	21.0	23.5	24.3
140 years (= 2130)	23.1	25.7	26.5
150 years (= 2140)	25.2	27.8	28.6

Assumption: Linear fertility decline, medium mortality level

Table 7

Dependence of the Number of Women in Reproductive Age (15 - 49) upon the Fertility Path (Number of women in millions)

Year	Fertility path: Target year for replacement fertility							
	2010	2020	2030	2040	2050	2060	2070	2080
1990	1314	1314	1314	1314	1314	1314	1314	1314
2000	1560	1560	1560	1560	1560	1560	1560	1560
2010	1797	1802	1804	1805	1806	1806	1807	1807
2020	1891	1938	1965	1983	1996	2005	2012	2018
2030	1932	2014	2074	2117	2150	2175	2195	2212
2040	1937	2042	2135	2209	2267	2314	2353	2385
2050	1897	2013	2122	2223	2307	2378	2438	2489
2060	1922	2025	2135	2241	2344	2434	2512	2580
2070	1916	2024	2131	2241	2350	2456	2552	2637
2080	1912	2021	2128	2236	2348	2459	2568	2669
2090	1917	2023	2130	2239	2348	2462	2575	2688
2100	1915	2023	2129	2239	2348	2460	2575	2692
2110	1915	2022	2130	2238	2348	2460	2574	2692
2120	1915	2022	2130	2238	2348	2460	2574	2691
2130	1915	2022	2130	2238	2348	2460	2574	2691
2140	1915	2022	2130	2238	2348	2460	2574	2691
2150	1915	2022	2130	2238	2348	2460	2574	2691
2160	1915	2022	2130	2238	2348	2460	2574	2691
2170	1915	2022	2129	2238	2348	2460	2574	2691
2180	1915	2022	2129	2238	2348	2459	2574	2691
2190	1914	2022	2129	2238	2347	2459	2574	2691
2200	1914	2022	2129	2238	2347	2459	2574	2691

Medium mortality level. See projection variants 2010 R.M.,..., 2080 R.M. in **part II** of this book.

	Projected population in the year 2000
1958 UN projection	6.3 billion
1962 UN projection	6.6 billion
1982 UN projection	6.1 billion
1992 UN projection	6.2 billion
The author's projection	6.1-6.2 billion

The precision of projections made in the past does not necessarily mean that they will achieve a correspondingly high degree of precision in the future. Thus it is all the more important to demonstrate the potential scope for variation by portraying alternative scenarios, in the form of "if ..., then ..." projections.

4.4 The Impact of Alternative Mortality Scenarios upon World Population Growth

(a) Assumptions on Changes in Life Expectancy

The trend in life expectancy has been computed separately for each individual age cohort within the world population. It is assumed that improvements in health conditions and the overall standard of living will lead to an increase in the average life expectancy of men and women together from 68.5 years for those who are now almost 20 years of age (the 1975 age cohort) to 73.8 years for those born in 2030. No further improvement in life expectancy has been assumed for those born later than the year 2030. Nevertheless, because at least some of the people born in 2030 can be expected to live on beyond the end of the 21st century, the calendar-year life expectancy (according to the period concept conventionally used, rather than the cohort concept used here) will in fact continue to rise, though only slightly, until the end of that century (for detials see technical appendix).

The life expectancies assumed by the World Bank and the UN Population Division are more optimistic than those underlying the projections presented here. The World Bank supposes that the average period-concept life expectancy of the two sexes will have increased to 82.3 years by the end of the 21st century (1992-93 estimates). This entails an optimistic assumption that the differential in life expectancies between the industrial and developing countries will by that time have narrowed to just three years (85 years for the industrial countries, 82 years for the developing countries). In 1990, that differential was still 12.4 years (74.3 years in the industrial, 61.9 years in the developing countries).

The author does not share the above optimism. In reality, a more likely presumption is that rapid population growth will create nutrition problems and trigger a number of demographically and politically determined development crises, all of which will prevent health conditions and overall living standards from reaching the levels which would be necessary to attain the long life expectancy of 82 years. For the sake of comparison, it is worth noting that the average current male life expectancy in an industrialized country like Germany is 72.2 years, and the female life expectancy 78.7 years.

(b) The Impact upon World Population Growth of Alternative Assumptions on General Mortality Trends and the Influence of AIDS

Overall life expectancy is a complex measure computed from 200 separately ascertained cohort life expectancies i.e. 100 each for males and females. The probability of mortality (x) is the complementary quantity to the probability of survival (y), i.e. $x = 1-y$. If a change is made to the assumed life expectancy in a population projection, this entails altering 100 male and 100 female age-specific mortality rates, similar to the 31 age-specific fertility rates encountered earlier.

How pronounced, then, are the changes in population projections which result from changed assumptions on mortality? *Table 8* and *Figure 22* show the results of population projections based on a hyperbolic fertility decline with a target year of 2060, with alternative scenarios for a reduction in mortality rates of 1%, 2%, ..., and 10%. A similar variant is presented in *Table 9* and *Figure 23* for the target year of 2070 and a linear decline in fertlity. Readers will notice that the impact of changes in mortality is comparatively slight relative to changes in fertility: for example, a 5% reduction in mortality in the case illustrated in *Table*

8 would give rise to a total population of 10.9 billion in the year 2100, as against 10.7 billion with mortality unchanged. A 10% reduction in mortality would lead to a total population of 11.1 billion in the same year.

These findings also illustrate why the influence of AIDS upon world population growth has been estimated to be relatively limited in all demographic surveys to date. For example, the main distinction between the first two World Bank projections for Africa contained in *Table 3* is that AIDS was considered as a factor in the later projection (1992/93) whilst it did not play any major part in the earlier projection of 1989/90. The overall difference in Africa's projected population in 2050 is 196 million people. The second projection assumes slightly higher fertility rates than the first, so that under normal circumstances with unchanged mortality a higher rather than a lower population figure would have been expected to result. Consequently, the overall impact of AIDS as projected can be assumed to amount to less than 10% of the population of the continent in the year 2050.

(c) The Impact upon World Population Growth of an Increase in Child and Infant Mortality

The computations presented in this section were carried out under the dark shadow cast by an issue which was the focus of discussion at the *Deutsches Institut für Ärztliche Mission* (Medical Mission Institute) in Tübingen in November 1993. *Maurice King*, in a controversial article in *The Lancet*, had put forward the idea that the movement towards "demographic entrapment" faced by the developing countries as their populations grew too large could only be retarded -- and therefore had to be retarded - by deliberately settling for an increase in child and infant mortality, for the consequence of not doing so would be the destruction of the Earth's ecosystem by overpopulation (King 1990 and 1993; Kind and Elliot 1993). The proposition harks back to Thomas Malthus' classic population theory proposed in 1798. This mode of thinking also provides the basis for *lifeboat ethics* and, taken to its logical conclusion, creates the maxim that to provide aid is immoral. *Maurice King* propounded his ideas in person at the Tübingen conference, and it was the author's task to respond in a separate paper. That response included a whole series of counter-arguments, some of them ethical but others demographic in their essence. I shall return to the ethical objections in chapter 6, and at this point I shall concentrate on the demographic core argument. Let us therefore scrutinize the proposition that an increase in mortality by consciously allowing children in developing countries to die offers the only means of solving the problem of overpopulation on the planet Earth.

Six population projections have been prepared based on the assumption of a hyperbolic decline in fertility with the target year for the replacement fertility level set at 2060, in which child and infant mortality is increased by 50%, 100%, ..., 300% (*Table 10* and *Figure 23)*. Another six variants are based on the assumptions of a linear reduction in fertility for the same target year (*Table 11* and *Figure 25*). This extreme form of hypothetical experiment produced the following results:

1. An increase in child and infant mortality even of up to 300% would, assuming a hyperbolic decline in fertility with 2060 as the target year for 2.13 live births per woman, still be unable to prevent the continuation of population growth at least until the year 2030 (hyperbolic case or 2050 (linear case), albeit in a less pronounced form. The initial population figure in the base year of 1990 (5.3 billion) would not be reached again until 2080 (hyperbolic case) or 2135 (linear case) even if child and infant mortality rose by 300%.

2. In the scenario in which child and infant mortality increases by 50%, population growth continues until the year 2080 (hyperbolic case) or 2100 (linear case), when it reaches a peak of 9.5 or 12.2 billion. Without any increase in child and infant mortality, the world population in 2100 is projected at 10.7 billion (hyperbolic case) or 13.8 bilion (linear case), or 1.2 (1.6) billion more. Thus, in percentage terms, a 50% increase in child and infant mortality leads in both the hyperbolic and the linear cases to a 12% reduction in the population in 2100.

The *conclusion* from these calculations is as follows: The grim recommendations made by Maurice King and his Malthusian school are not suited to the objective decisively reducing in population growth, nor to resolving other, population-related problems. Thus the pursuit of such an aim as a matter of deliberate policy would not yield success. While demographically ineffective on the one hand, it would also be quite ghastly in its dehumanizing impact. By resorting to such means, we would cast aside all the objectives we live for. Its inner contradictions push Malthusian policy to the point of absurdity. The fact that such thinking nevertheless has so many supporters is largely a manifestation of a lack of seriousness in analysing demographic problems rather than of ethical incapacity. Consequently, it is a worthwhile exercise to contribute to a clearer insight into the nature of the problems involved by means of rational argument.

4.5 Population Changes by Country and Region

The method of population projection used here for the world as a whole can equally be applied separately to individual countries, but additional account then needs to be taken of inward and outward migratory flows. There are many countries in which annual net immigration has almost equalled - or in Germany's case, even exceeded - the number of live-born children from the domestic population. As far as these countries are concerned, the quality of any population projection depends extraordinarily heavily on how well migratory flows can be projected. A migration projection in turn requires painstaking research into economic trends - this is beyond the scope of demographic computations alone, and can only be dealt with by expanding the demographic projection procedures to become a demo-economic model.

The World Bank subdivides its world population projections by country, so it would be desirable for it to base them on a demo-economic rather than a purely demographic projection model. The fact that it has not so far done so restricts the realism of the projections. Taking Germany as an example, one has to criticize the fact that the World Bank assumes zero net immigration for the country during the next century, even though it has had a net intake of immigrants for several decades, and has considerably more immigrants per 1,000 population even than a classic immigration country such as the United States or Canada.

In spite of these deficiencies in the country results, there are certain central findings made by the World Bank projections which come out approximately the same in all projection models and do not depend so heavily on migration assumptions. These central findings are naturally particularly reliable if the country results are aggregated to give projections for groups of countries or world regions.

The following key features can be identified.

(1) Absolute population growth is by far the greatest in the Asian countries, while relative growth is highest in Africa (*Figures 26* and *27* and *Table 3*). In the first quarter of the 21st century, Asia's population is set to grow by approx. 45 million per annum, and Africa's by 25-30 million per annum.

(2) Africa and Latin America have the greatest population momentum of all the continental groupings:

Africa	1.5
Latin America	1.5
North America	1.1
Asia	1.4
Europe	1.0
Oceania	1.2
World	*1.4*

In some countries within Africa, the population momentum has values well in excess of 1.5, examples being Nigeria (1.6), Kenya (1.7), Algeria (1.7), Libya (1.7) and Botswana (1.8). High country values are also found in Latin America, such as Venezuela (1.6), Costa Rica (1.6), Guatemala (1.7), Honduras (1.7) and Nicaragua (1.8). On a comparative basis, the population momentum in large Asian countries is relatively low: China (1.3), India (1.4) and Indonesia (1.4). It is chiefly the Moslem countries in Asia which have high values: Pakistan (1.6), Iran (1.7), Uzbekistan (1.7), Tajikistan (1.8) and Syria (1.8).

The most significant changes likely to occur in the rankings of the world's most populous countries by the end of the 21st century are that India will then have the largest number of inhabitants (1,813 million), ahead of China with 1,630 million. Pakistan and Nigeria will by that time have pushed the USA down from third to fifth place:

Population (million)

		1995	2100
1.	India	934	1,813
2.	China	1,199	1,630
3.	Pakistan	129	379
4.	Nigeria	111	355
5.	United States	263	344
6.	Indonesia	193	338

Other changes in the ranking of the top 20 countries are shown in *Table 12*. Germany, which currently occupies 12th position with its 81 million inhabitants, will no longer be among the 20 largest countries due to its shrinking population, and Japan will similarly fall back from 8th to 20th position (its population decreasing from 125 to 107 million).

As regards these purely quantitative computations, it should be stressed that population-induced problems do not primarily depend on the actual number of inhabitants, but on changes in the age profile or the ethnic or social composition of the population, and on its culturally determined capacity to solve political and social problems. Whether or not policy-makers can successfully deal with population-induced problems in any particular country chiefly depends upon whether its economy and society can adapt quickly enough to changing demographic conditions. When it comes to coping with ecological problems, a population's consuming and producing habits are far more important than its sheer numbers. This point will be looked at in more detail in *Chapter 5*.

4.6 Summary

International discussion of population issues is chiefly centred around the demographic world population projections published by two United Nations institutions, namely by the *World Bank* and by the Population Division of the *UN Department for Economic and Social Information and Policy Analysis* (previously named the Department of International Economic and Social Affairs). These population projections are not a reflection of current prospects, nor are they forecasts or prophecies, but computations which predict exactly what would happen to future population patterns if a particular set of assumptions were met (*"if ..., then ..." statements*). The "if..." conditions consist of assumptions on the future trends in fertility (as expressed by the total fertility rate, or number of live births per woman) and in mortality (the decrease in mortality or increase in life expectancy). If those assumptions on fertility and mortality should be borne out in reality, then the statements derived from them regarding the future population size will also be correct.

The fertility assumptions underlying the UN population projections are made in the following way. Target years are cited by which time the number of live births per woman (TFR) is assumed to have fallen from 3.3 in the early 1990s to the replacement fertility level. Replacement fertility level refers to the number of live-born children per woman at which the world population will cease to grow in the long term (i.e., some time after the end of the 21st century). At the mortality levels currently assumed and used in this book, that replacement level of fertility is 2.13 live births per woman. In its medium variant, the World Bank takes 2060 (1992-93 estimates) or 2055 (1994-95 estimates) as its target year for replacement fertility. On this optimistic assumption, the world population is projected to grow from 5.3 billion in 1990 to 11.7 (or 11.0) billion in 2100. Population growth, on this projection, will come to a stop by 2150, when the world total will be 12.1 (11.4) billion.

The author's own population projections are computed for the world as a whole (=aggregate projections). They add a number of additional variants to those contained in the UN projections, by including further target years which are both more optimistic than 2060 (i.e., earlier targets such as 2030 or 2040) or more pessimistic (later years) and computing the consequential changes in the world population. Further variations have been included by calculating the impact of different patterns of decline in fertility. For any particular target year, the reduction in the number of live births per woman may, for example, be swift in the initial period but becoming slower over time (i.e., following a hyperbolic curve), or it may be equal each year (i.e., linear). The projections shown here also vary the mortality assumptions, both to take account of the impact of AIDS and to estimate the consequences for world population growth of deliberately allowing child and infant mortality to rise (i.e., by allowing children in developing countries to die), as advocated by a currently influential Malthusian school of thought.

The most important findings of the alternative population projections presented here are:

1. The final population figures computed for the planet Earth of 10.7 billion in the year 2150 (for the assumptions see *Table 2b*, first column) will be exceeded if it does not prove possible by means of development and family policies to achieve a fall in the number of children born per woman in the developing countries from the current level of 3.6 to just *2.5 by 2020-25 and 2.3 by 2025-30*. The author is sceptical as to whether this objective can be achieved, for people in the developing countries will find that just two children are insufficient to insure against economic and social risks in countries which lack adequate state provision for unemployment, sickness and old age, especially now that traditional help networks in extended families and local communities are breaking down as economies and societies undergo modernization processes. This could result in a slackening pace of fertility decline in years to come, and the consequence of that in turn would be heavier population growth than has so far been allowed for in the UN's population projections.

2. The simulations show that the impact of mortality changes is substantially less than that of fertility changes. For example, AIDS is not expected to have any decisive effect in reducing population growth. The reduction in the eventual population of Africa in the year 2050 resulting from AIDS is estimated at less than 10%.

3. Special significance attaches to the future trend in child and infant mortality. Yet even here, variations in mortality still have a relatively low impact on population growth overall. Even if infant and child mortality were to increase by 50%, for example, the world population would still continue to grow up to the period 2080-2100. At that peak level, the total would be only 12% lower than with the initially assumed mortality rates. These alternative mortality scenarios were calculated in order to demonstrate that any policy following the inhumane recommendations of Malthusian population theorists who advocate deliberately allowing children born in developing countries to die would still not succeed in preventing population growth, quite apart from the ethical unacceptability of such policies.

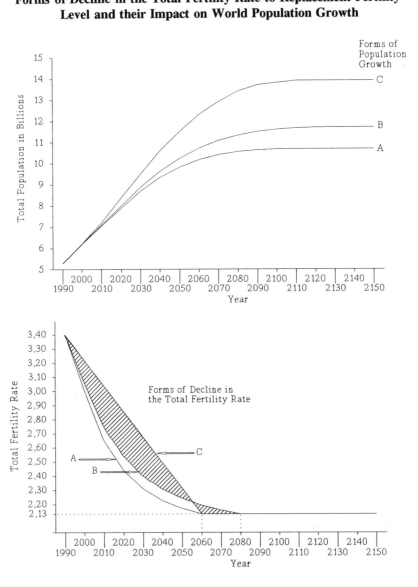

Figure 19

Forms of Decline in the Total Fertility Rate to Replacement Fertility Level and their Impact on World Population Growth

Figure 20

Forms of Decline in the Total Fertility Rate to Replacement Fertility Level and their Impact on World Population Growth

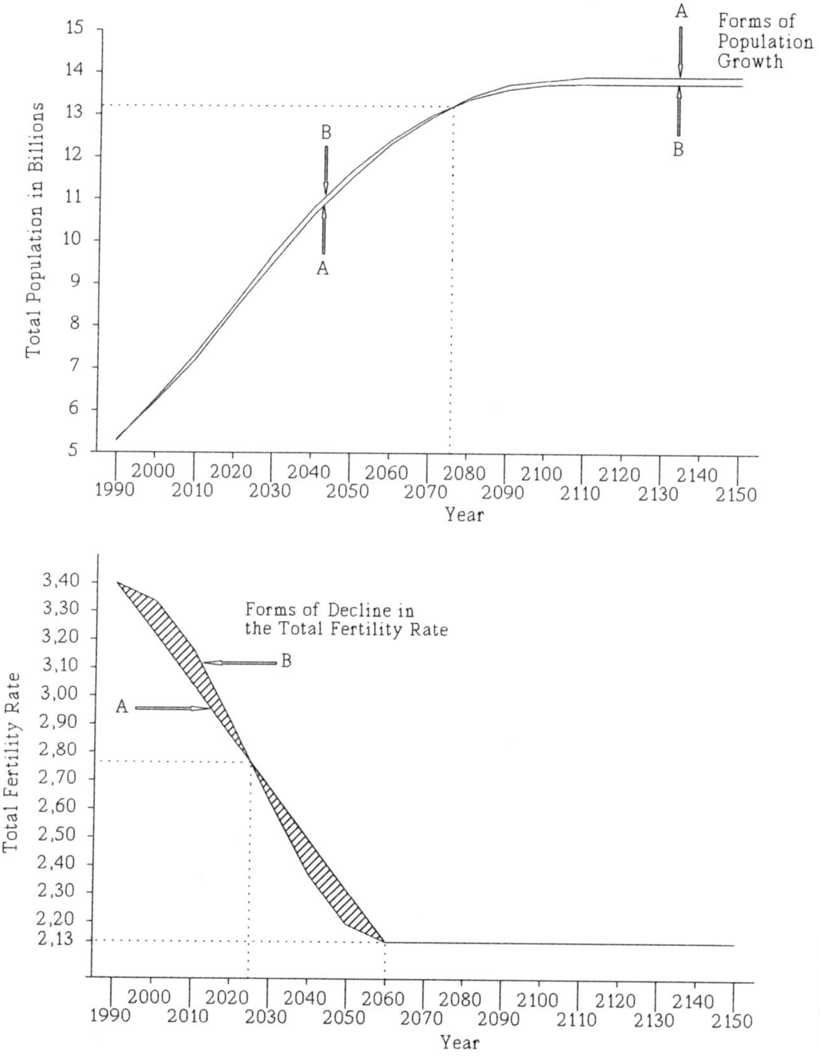

127

Figure 21 a
Components of Population Change
World Population Projection No. 2060.R.M
Decline to Replacement Fertility Level (2.13)
Mortality Level: Medium

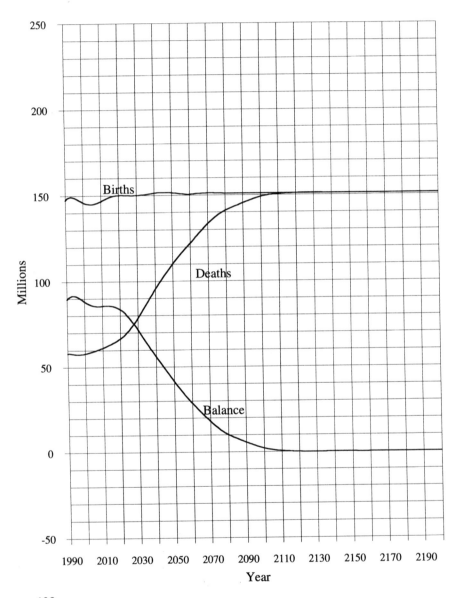

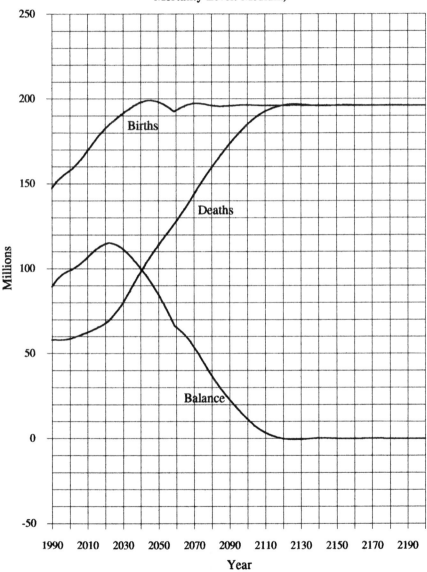

**Figure 21b
Components of Population Change
World Population Projection No. 2060.R.M.
Target Year for Replacement Fertility:2060
(Form of Fertility Decline: Linear,
Mortality Level: Medium)**

Figure 22
World Population Levels Resulting from
Different Reductions in Mortality
(Mortality Reductions Between 0 and 10 Percent,
Fertility Assumption: Hyperbolic Reduction to Replacement
Fertility Level by the Year 2060)

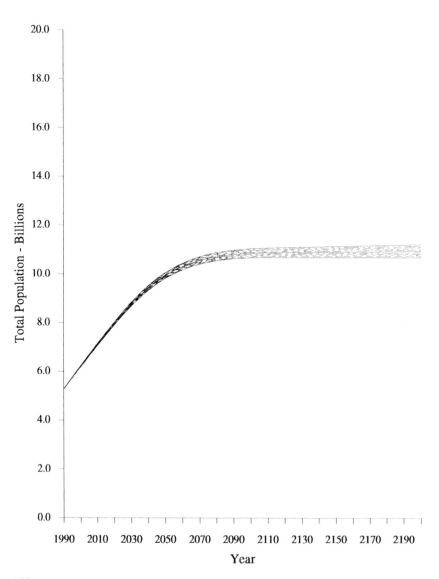

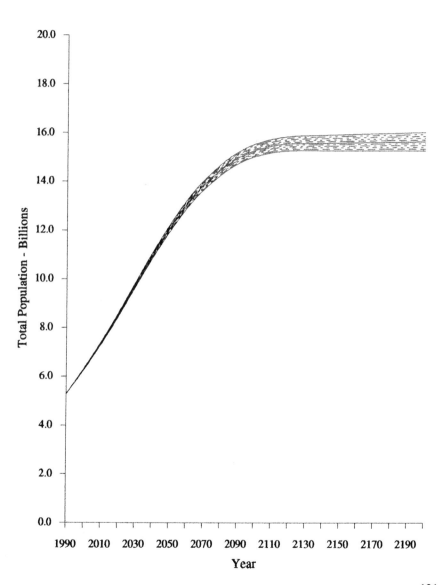

**Figure 23
World Population Levels Resulting from
Different Reductions in Mortality
(Mortality Reductions Between 0 and 10 Percent,
Fertility Assumption: Linear Reduction to Replacement
Fertility Level by the Year 2070)**

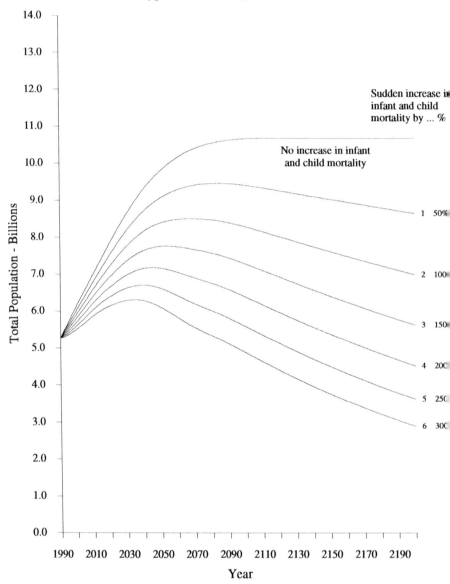

**Figure 24
Scenarios of World Population Growth Based on
Different Assumptions Concerning an Increase in
Infant and Child Mortality (Malthus-Variants,
Hyperbolic Fertility Decline)**

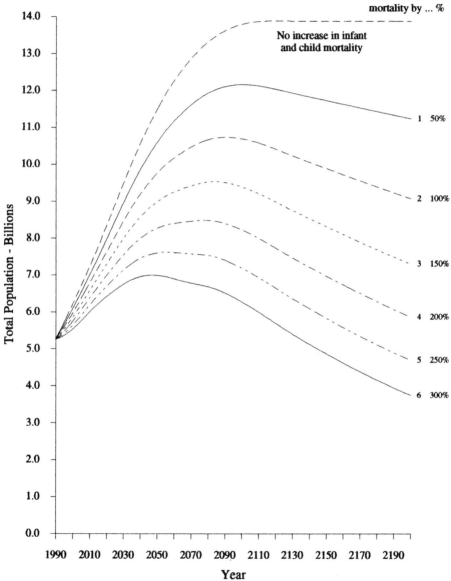

Figure 26

World Population Projections by Geographic Regions and Countries

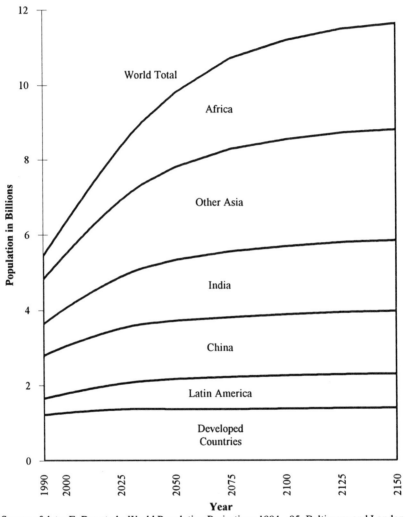

Source of data: E. Bos et al.: World Population Projections 1994 - 95, Baltimore and London, 1994.

Figure 27

Average Annual Absolute Increments to Total Population of World Regions, 2000 - 2150

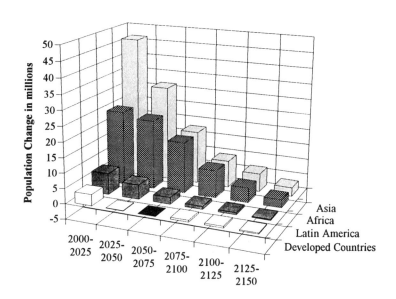

Source of data: E. Bos et al.: World Population Projections 1994 - 95, Baltimore and London, 1994.

Figure 28

The Surplus of Births over Deaths - Annual Population Change in Millions

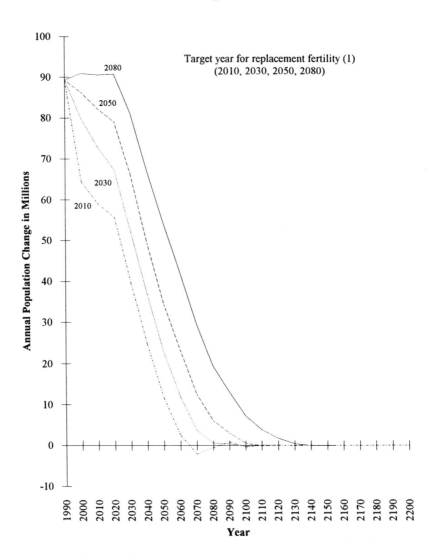

(1) Medium mortality level

Figure 29

Number of Women of Fertile Age (15 - 49) for Different Fertility Paths

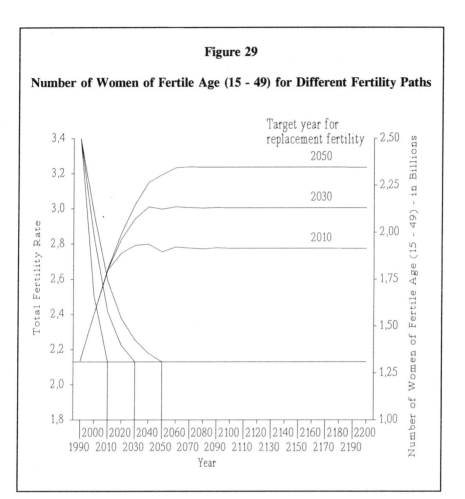

Table 8
The Influence of Alternative Assumptions on the Outcome of World Population Projections
Reduction in Mortality Rates

Year	0%	1%	2%	3%	4%	5%	6%	7%	8%	9%	10%
					population figures in 1000						
1990	5274612	5274612	5274612	5274612	5274612	5274612	5274612	5274612	5274612	5274612	5274612
2000	6179936	6184726	6189531	6194350	6199183	6204032	6208894	6213772	6218665	6223573	6228496
2010	7042654	7051118	7059617	7068150	7076718	7085322	7093962	7102638	7111351	7120102	7128891
2020	7896185	7908271	7920409	7932602	7944848	7957150	7969508	7981923	7994396	8006928	8019520
2030	8686097	8701914	8717802	8733764	8749798	8765908	8782094	8798357	8814699	8831121	8847623
2040	9330948	9350623	9370394	9390262	9410230	9430298	9450469	9470744	9491125	9511613	9532210
2050	9823846	9847269	9870816	9894488	9918287	9942216	9966277	9990472	10014802	10039271	10063881
2060	10177586	10204435	10231434	10258586	10285892	10313356	10340979	10368765	10396716	10424836	10453126
2070	10415512	10445494	10475654	10505995	10536520	10567232	10598133	10629227	10660517	10692006	10723697
2080	10555673	10588180	10620894	10653818	10686954	10720308	10753881	10787679	10821705	10855962	10890455
2090	10634933	10669501	10704292	10739310	10774558	10810042	10845765	10881730	10917943	10954407	10991128
2100	10673851	10710348	10747084	10784064	10821292	10858771	10896507	10934503	10972764	11011295	11050100
2110	10685944	10724124	10762560	10801254	10840212	10879437	10918935	10958710	10998766	11039109	11079744
2120	10688213	10727949	10767951	10808225	10848775	10889605	10930719	10972124	11013823	11055822	11098126
2130	10687175	10728420	10769945	10811752	10853848	10896236	10938922	10981910	11025206	11068814	11112741
2140	10686548	10729274	10772290	10815602	10859213	10903128	10947353	10991893	11036752	11081937	11127453
2150	10686579	10730803	10775330	10820164	10865309	10910771	10956556	11002667	11049110	11095892	11143017
2160	10686039	10731761	10777798	10824156	10870838	10917850	10965197	11012884	11060918	11109303	11158046
2170	10685684	10732898	10780441	10828316	10876529	10925086	10973990	11023249	11072868	11122852	11173208
2180	10685379	10734091	10783143	10832542	10882293	10932400	10982870	11033708	11084920	11136512	11188490
2190	10684982	10735188	10785750	10836673	10887961	10939620	10991656	11044074	11096882	11150084	11203687
2200	10684634	10736336	10788408	10840854	10893680	10946892	11000495	11054497	11108902	11163717	11218949

Fertility assumptions: Target year of 2060 for replacement fertility, hyperbolic decline

Table 9
The Influence of Alternative Assumptions on the Outcome of World Population Projections
Reduction in Mortality Rates

Year	0%	1%	2%	3%	4%	5%	6%	7%	8%	9%	10%
					population figures in 1000						
1990	5274612	5274612	5274612	5274612	5274612	5274612	5274612	5274612	5274612	5274612	5274612
2000	6226719	6231554	6236404	6241268	6246147	6251040	6255948	6260871	6265809	6270763	6275731
2010	7263292	7271982	7280707	7289465	7298259	7307089	7315955	7324858	7333798	7342775	7351791
2020	8406721	8419432	8432197	8445016	8457890	8470820	8483807	8496852	8509955	8523118	8536341
2030	9614606	9631684	9648135	9666060	9683361	9700738	9718193	9735726	9753340	9771035	9788813
2040	10785893	10807722	10829651	10851679	10873810	10896045	10918385	10940832	10963388	10986053	11008831
2050	11876315	11903078	11929969	11956991	11984145	12011434	12038859	12066424	12094129	12121978	12149973
2060	12845864	12877524	12909342	12941320	12973462	13005769	13038245	13070891	13103711	13136707	13169883
2070	13634925	13671478	13708224	13745164	13782302	13819640	13857182	13894930	13932889	13971060	14009448
2080	14250967	14292201	14333666	14375366	14417304	14459484	14501911	14544586	14587515	14630702	14674151
2090	14714132	14759771	14805676	14851853	14898304	14945035	14992049	15039352	15086948	15134842	15183038
2100	15011333	15061070	15111111	15161460	15212123	15263103	15314407	15366039	15418005	15470310	15522959
2110	15179841	15233165	15286829	15340837	15395196	15449910	15504985	15560428	15616243	15672439	15729020
2120	15253364	15309742	15366489	15423613	15481118	15539011	15597299	15655986	15715081	15774590	15834519
2130	15267843	15326782	15386116	15445853	15505999	15566560	15627543	15688955	15750803	15813094	15875837
2140	15262824	15323942	15385477	15447435	15509822	15572646	15635914	15699633	15763810	15828453	15893570
2150	15261433	15324618	15388235	15452292	15516794	15581750	15647167	15713051	15779411	15846255	15913591
2160	15262833	15328173	15393962	15460208	15526918	15594098	15661757	15729901	15798539	15867680	15937330
2170	15261332	15328820	15396776	15465209	15534126	15603533	15673439	15743851	15814777	15886227	15958208
2180	15260903	15330511	15400606	15471197	15542289	15613893	15686014	15758661	15831843	15905567	15979844
2190	15260656	15332407	15404666	15477440	15550736	15624563	15698928	15773840	15849308	15925340	16001945
2200	15259941	15333827	15408242	15483192	15558686	15634731	15711336	15788510	15866261	15944598	16023531

Fertility assumptions: Target year of 2070 for replacement fertility, linear decline

139

Table 10
World Population Level (in 1000) Assuming a Sudden Increase in Infant and Child Mortality (Malthusian Variant)

Variant	I (+50 %)			II (+ 100 %)			III (+ 150 %)		
Age	Males	Females	Total	Males	Females	Total	Males	Females	Total
1990	2657196	2617416	5274612	2657196	2617416	5274612	2657196	2617416	5274612
2000	3055615	3003112	6058727	2994345	2947906	5942250	2935588	2894846	5830433
2010	3435064	3394083	6829147	3325713	3298554	6624267	3221039	3206796	6427835
2020	3790143	3775391	7565534	3622379	3629530	7251909	3463752	3490902	6954654
2030	4102685	4122941	8225626	3870978	3920454	7791432	3653352	3729008	7382360
2040	4338736	4396280	8735016	4041597	4134899	8176496	3764297	3889160	7653458
2050	4497695	4587708	9085404	4133733	4264114	8397847	3796402	3961778	7758181
2060	4592795	4708429	9301225	4166877	4323665	8490542	3774855	3966371	7741226
2070	4642632	4776864	9419497	4166010	4339043	8505053	3730847	3935365	7666212
2080	4659716	4805786	9465501	4145304	4328155	8473458	3680016	3891568	7571584
2090	4652728	4805670	9458397	4104734	4292720	8397454	3613722	3828109	7441830
2100	4628493	4784511	9413004	4048754	4237137	8285892	3533932	3745656	7279588
2110	4594056	4750710	9344766	3984699	4171637	8156336	3448410	3656276	7104686
2120	4555767	4711796	9267563	3917658	4102100	8019758	3361077	3564308	6925385
2130	4516690	4671389	9188079	3850780	4032045	7882824	3275087	3473058	6748145
2140	4478255	4631510	9109764	3785366	3963450	7748816	3191649	3384493	6576142
2150	4440291	4592315	9032606	3721151	3896277	7617428	3110373	3298367	6408740
2160	4402451	4553177	8955628	3657863	3830003	7487866	3031033	3214219	6245252
2170	4365025	4514449	8879474	3595735	3764936	7360671	2953795	3132302	6086097
2180	4327915	4476084	8803999	3534655	3700995	7235650	2878513	3052482	5930994
2190	4291094	4437998	8729092	3474592	3638101	7112693	2805134	2974664	5779798
2200	4254605	4400259	8654864	3415566	3576296	6991862	2733640	2898849	5632489

Variant	IV (+ 200 %)			V (+ 250 %)			VI (+ 300 %)		
Age	Males	Females	Total	Males	Females	Total	Males	Females	Total
1990	2657196	2617416	5274612	2657196	2617416	5274612	2657196	2617416	5274612
2000	2879304	2843900	5723204	2825454	2795035	5620489	2773999	2748219	5522218
2010	3120943	3118734	6239677	3025328	3034295	6059623	2934098	2953405	5887503
2020	3313892	3359244	6673136	3172443	3234300	6406743	3039062	3115824	6154886
2030	3449151	3548150	6997301	3257743	3377441	6635184	3078521	3216460	6294982
2040	3505757	3658305	7164063	3264947	3441609	6706556	3040888	3238379	6279266
2050	3484046	3679519	7163565	3195102	3416212	6611314	2928094	3170792	6098886
2060	3414382	3634840	7049222	3083257	3327461	6410719	2779418	3042715	5822132
2070	3333947	3563454	6897401	2972334	3221088	6193423	2643246	2906186	5549431
2080	3259662	3492844	6752506	2880374	3129027	6009401	2538583	2797372	5335955
2090	3174374	3407713	6582087	2781825	3027733	5809558	2431622	2684668	5116290
2100	3077451	3304868	6382319	2673341	2910021	5583362	2316194	2556772	4872966
2110	2977197	3198193	6175390	2563869	2791560	5355429	2201967	2431094	4633061
2120	2876457	3090599	5967056	2455269	2673941	5129209	2089916	2308018	4397935
2130	2778318	2985062	5763380	2350489	2559711	4910200	1982790	2189572	4172362
2140	2683914	2883564	5567478	2250607	2450877	4701485	1881621	2077797	3959418
2150	2592711	2785637	5378348	2154927	2346746	4501673	1785544	1971769	3757313
2160	2504493	2690839	5195332	2063214	2246849	4310063	1694280	1870963	3565243
2170	2419536	2599357	5018711	1975482	2151302	4126784	1607760	1775416	3383177
2180	2337092	2510985	4848077	1891459	2059811	3951270	1525634	1684736	3210371
2190	2257616	2425591	4683206	1811001	1972183	3783189	1447697	1598666	3046362
2200	2180855	2343118	4523973	1733978	1888309	3622286	1373752	1517010	2890762

Target year = 2060, hyperbolic decline in fertility

Table 11
World Population Level (in 1000) Assuming a Sudden Increase in Infant and Child Mortality (Malthusian Variant)

Variant	I (+50 %)			II (+ 100 %)			III (+ 150 %)		
Age	Males	Females	Total	Males	Females	Total	Males	Females	Total
1990	2657196	2617416	5274612	2657196	2617416	5274612	2657196	2617416	5274612
2000	3075113	3021870	6096983	3012240	2965240	5977480	2951934	2910802	5862736
2010	3528683	3484844	7013528	3412245	3383319	6795563	3300774	3285786	6586560
2020	4001097	3980626	7981722	3815305	3819341	7634646	3639780	3666163	7305943
2030	4475424	4486102	8961526	4209673	4254091	8463764	3960356	4034935	7995291
2040	4903341	4947370	9850711	4552074	4638625	9190700	4224776	4348752	8573528
2050	5260817	5334729	10595546	4819840	4943123	9762963	4411881	4577851	8989732
2060	5533801	5634634	11168435	5008761	5161504	10170266	4526382	4722899	9249281
2070	5741467	5868389	11609856	5144101	5321640	10465741	4599561	4818326	9417887
2080	5888649	6040883	11929532	5232826	5433899	10666724	4640317	4879754	9520071
2090	5964393	6138663	12103056	5257833	5478568	10736401	4625211	4881153	9506365
2100	5983890	6174261	12158151	5231579	5464640	10696219	4563859	4827836	9391695
2110	5961549	6161573	12123122	5168615	5408145	10576760	4471056	4737903	9208959
2120	5915623	6118563	12034186	5085006	5324706	10409712	4360798	4624743	8985542
2130	5863355	6064490	11927845	4996854	5232349	10229203	4248050	4505087	8753137
2140	5813340	6012042	11825382	4911857	5142722	10054579	4139716	4389653	8529369
2150	5764614	5962027	11726641	4829022	5056325	9885347	4034726	4278620	8313346
2160	5715150	5910869	11626018	4746601	4970022	9716623	3931557	4169210	8100767
2170	5666624	5860553	11527177	4666027	4885547	9551574	3831409	4062914	7894322
2180	5618511	5810886	11429398	4586823	4802695	9389518	3733809	3959484	7693294
2190	5570648	5761358	11332007	4508828	4721008	9229836	3638583	3858484	7497067
2200	5523303	5712383	11235686	4432252	4640819	9073071	3545862	3760152	7306015

Variant	IV (+ 200 %)			V (+ 250 %)			VI (+ 300 %)		
Age	Males	Females	Total	Males	Females	Total	Males	Females	Total
1990	2657196	2617416	5274612	2657196	2617416	5274612	2657196	2617416	5274612
2000	2894155	2858522	5752677	2838862	2808367	5647229	2786016	2760304	5546320
2010	3194164	3192165	6386329	3092310	3102378	6194688	2995109	3016346	6011456
2020	3474095	3520787	6994882	3317837	3382921	6700757	3170610	3252279	6422889
2030	3726688	3828093	7554781	3507914	3633043	7140958	3303311	3449282	6752593
2040	3920102	4076808	7996910	3636776	3821893	7458669	3373584	3583149	6956733
2050	4034835	4237408	8272244	3686717	3920366	7607083	3365652	3625370	6991022
2060	4083645	4316624	8400269	3677727	3940608	7618335	3305981	3592902	6898884
2070	4103713	4355373	8459085	3652710	3929903	7582613	3242983	3539228	6782211
2080	4105668	4374305	8479973	3623847	3913707	7537554	3190216	3494389	6684605
2090	4059584	4341053	8400620	3554600	3853253	7407853	3104453	3413239	6517691
2100	3972123	4257041	8229164	3448562	3746033	7194594	2986101	3289131	6275232
2110	3858405	4142417	8000822	3321248	3614050	6935297	2851131	3145884	5997015
2120	3730475	4008429	7738905	3182877	3466557	6649434	2708066	2990860	5698926
2130	3602166	3870441	7472608	3046147	3317491	6363638	2568475	2836514	5404990
2140	3479667	3738345	7218013	2916610	3176001	6092610	2437338	2691327	5128665
2150	3361798	3611978	6973776	2792940	3041573	5834513	2313165	2554435	4867600
2160	3247199	3488842	6736041	2673894	2911915	5585809	2194781	2423687	4618468
2170	3136840	3370191	6507031	2560215	2788049	5348265	2082719	2299878	4382597
2180	3030226	3255704	6285931	2451361	2669558	5120919	1976365	2182480	4158845
2190	2927142	3144933	6072074	2347055	2555954	4903009	1875375	2070945	3946320
2200	2827628	3038009	5865637	2247242	2447252	4694494	1779593	1965170	3744763

Target year = 2060, linear decline in fertility

141

Table 12

Population by Country, 1995 and 2100

Population in millions			
Country	1995	Country (rang order 1995)	2100
(1) China	1199	India (2)	1813
(2) India	934	China (1)	1630
(3) United States of America	263	Pakistan (7)	379
(4) Indonesia	193	Nigeria (10)	355
(5) Brazil	161	United States of America (3)	344
(6) Russian Federation	149	Indonesia (4)	338
(7) Pakistan	129	Ethiopia (22)	334
(8) Japan	125	Brazil (5)	275
(9) Bangladesh	121	Bangladesh (9)	247
(10) Nigeria	111	Iran (15)	198
(11) Mexico	90	Zaire (27)	191
(12) Germany	81	Mexico (11)	177
(13) Viet Nam	74	Philippines (14)	166
(14) Philippines	69	Viet Nam (13)	160
(15) Iran	65	Russian Federation (6)	155
(16) Turkey	61	Egypt (21)	116
(17) Thailand	60	Afghanistan (37)	113
(18) United Kingdom	58	Turkey (16)	109
(19) France	58	Tanzania (35)	108
(20) Italy	58	Japan (8)	107
Source: E. Bos et al.: World Population Projections 1992-93 Edition, Baltimore and London, 1994.			

Chapter 5

World Population Growth, Development and the Environment: Dimensions of a Global Dilemma

5.1 Preliminary Remarks

People's anxieties over the dangers inherent in population trends have always been more acutely inflamed by the expected consequences of population *changes* (i.e., by the processes in train) than by any negative *present state* which has resulted from the population changes of the past. A typical example of process characteristics being paid more attention than current-state characteristics is provided by the problem of the environment: even though the environmental damage already caused both by demographic and by economic developments is very substantial, the attention of the general public is directed quite markedly towards the possible negative consequences of demographic changes in the mid- to-long-term future. There is a good reason why we perceive processes more intensely than present or past states: after all, any state is ultimately a state in transition to some other state. In a realistic perspective, it can even be said that the peculiar feature of states, namely their duration, is really a rather rare phenomenon, not only in the history of nations and cultures but also in the lives of individuals, and that flux (often inappropriately referred to as a "state" of flux) is the crucial feature both of nature and of social reality. So it is more than just understandable, it is also highly logical that even in the classic phase of population theory in the 18th century, when the *world* population was still well away from a state of overpopulation, the theoreticians' main concern was with the question of whether the underlying tendency in global demographic processes lead to self-destructive world population growth or whether there might be certain hidden self-regulatory mechanisms at play which would at least make a comparatively harmonious development possible, even if it were not guaranteed from the outset.

In answer to this question, the optimists and pessimists are, as usual, irreconcilable, though the contrariety of their positions is actually less than it would seem. Whereas the pessimists, following in the tradition of Malthus, believe there is little likelihood of humanity recognizing the dangers flowing from its own proliferation and coping with them by making rational use of its capabilities, the optimists are convinced that there is no such thing as an absolute limit imposed by Nature on the growth and development of humankind, because it has the capacity to adapt its natural habitat to cope with the new needs arising out of that growth and development. One point these differing positions do have in common is that they take Nature's role of the most powerful adversary as a given factor, generally failing to give due consideration to the fact that we too all form part of that adversary, "Nature". Even though the two positions are diametrically opposed in terms of how they believe the game will end, the distinctions between them with regard to interpreting the rules of the game or its purpose are much less marked than the conclusions they choose to draw from viewing human existence and development as a form of game.

This is not intended to put the case for one side or the other. Rather, the intention is to describe and analyse some of the processes which give rise to the problem. The example of "global warming" has been chosen for this purpose, as most climatologists have now agreed that the undeniable increase in the mean temperature of the Earth's atmosphere does indeed have a man-made component to it, whereas expert opinion is much more divided on the significance of demographic development as a factor in the problems of food and resources scarcity.

5.2 Demo-Economic and Socio-Economic Feedback and Self-Regulatory Mechanisms

Do mechanisms of self-regulation operate between demo-economic and socio-economic variables, ensuring that world population growth will become steadily weaker, effectively coming to a stand "on its own"? To investigate this issue, the arguments discussed in demography and economics will be brought together by summarizing the essential demo-economic variables and the reciprocal effects they exert on each other in one overall scheme (see *Figure 30*). The place to start when discussing the interactive effects shown in *Figure 30* is with the growing world population. This is directly linked to the size of the workforce, and for the sake of simplicity I have left the additional influences of age and gender structure as well as social patterns of earning behaviour out of account (*arrow 1*). For its part, the size of the workforce influences the gross national product (*arrow 2*), which in turn affects the volume of savings and investment in the economy (*arrow 3*); dependent on the latter are the volume and value of the real capital (e.g. manufacturing facilities, infrastructure) deployed in the economy. The larger the amount of productive capital per employee (the capital intensity), the larger will be the amount of goods and services each employee can produce (the productivity of labour), and the higher per capita incomes will be (*arrow 4*).

Another chain of impacts also starts out from the population, and works through as far as per capita income. It is a plausible assumption that, in a population with plenty of young, well-educated or trained, mobile people with the latest in scientific and technical knowledge available to them, more new inventions will be made and innovations introduced than in another population which is demographically older, in which people are more inclined to follow a reflective, backward-looking lifestyle, stressing the virtues of a relaxed approach, of maturity and of appreciating the essentials in things. Certainly the alternatives, namely the reverse assumption that technological progress is more intensive the older the population, or the idea that there is no connection at all between a population's age structure and technological change, are both rather implausible (*arrow 5*).

Apart from numerous other influential factors, technological progress also depends on the overall level of output in the economy (the tendency is for technical innovation to be made where mass-production techniques are used, with large product runs, automation, etc.). So another arrow (*arrow 6*) points from GNP, as a measure of the amount of goods and services produced, to technological progress. In this particular schematic view, we shall concentrate on this quantitative aspect as manifested in GNP as the source of such progress (other aspects include the quality of education, and cultural factors such as the will to succeed), and now return to per capita income, which is directly dependent on the intensity of technological progress.

Figure 30

Diagrammatic Representation of Demo-economic Interactive Effects

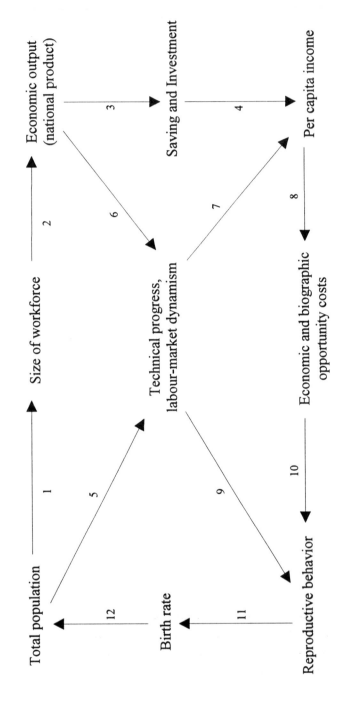

I turn now from the economic to the demo-economic interactive relationships, i.e. those in which economic and demographic factors influence one another. The higher a country's per capita income level the higher, if other circumstances remain the same (this *ceteris paribus* condition is always implicitly assumed), will be the income forgone if a parent (usually a woman) devotes her/his time to raising children and not to earning an outside income. This is described as the *economic opportunity cost* (*arrow 8*): it is not a "cost" in terms of money actually spent, but in terms of income that could otherwise have been earned.

At this point, the biographical theory of fertility can also be brought into the picture, enhancing the concept of opportunity cost previously used only in an economic sense, to speak of *biographical opportunity costs*. These are possible biographical alternatives and life-course elements primarily existing in the minds of individuals which would be lost from the spectrum of possibilities, having become unrealizable alternatives, once long-term commitments had been made such as marriage (or similar firm partner-ties) and having children. The entire set of conceivable life-course alternatives available to an individual is, to recall Chapter 3, referred to as the *biographical universe*. An individual's biographical universe will shrink if particular potential life-courses are eliminated as a result of long-term, irreversible biographical commitments, and these eliminated alternatives are what we refer to as biographical opportunity costs.

The number and form of the alternative life-courses in any individual's biographical universe vary according to that person's character, origins, education and social environment, but they also depend on a number of other quantities from the macro level, particularly the level of technological progress a society has attained. In the course of economic development, new technologies give rise to new occupations and fields of activity, while other occupations die out over time. Looked at historically, the spectrum of biographical and economic livelihoods has expanded steadily since industrialization first set in, that is to say, individuals' biographical universes have grown. The consequence of this for the birth rate in industrial countries has been that, since the early 20th century, "one" has no longer simply "had" children, as Thomas Mann once commented on the topic, but has reflected on the pros and cons of having a family as it pertains to shaping or preserving one's own identity, making this a calculated biograpical decision.

The biographical theory of fertility presented in Chapter 3 states that the long-term trend in the variety of biographical development potential is upward, so the biographical opportunity costs and risks of entering into commitments are also rising. As shown earlier, the result is that long-term commitments therefore tend to be avoided, meaning that more and more potential births no longer occur and childlessness increases (*arrow 9*). Furthermore, biographical opportunity costs are especially high in just the age-range which is most important as regards starting a family (20-35 years) compared with the situation for people later on in life, and within that range they also tend to increase from one birth cohort to another, with the result that the decision to have children is postponed, sometimes for so long that a couple prefers not to have any at all (*arrow 10*). In sociological literature, this is referred to as the *transition in values*, as a parallel process to the *demographic transition*. The biographical theory does not run counter to these sociological and economic theories of fertility, but integrates them in an interdisciplinary approach.

Hence the change in reproductive behaviour and the shift in social values, however unplanned or even undesired they may be, should be seen as an inevitable result of the socio-economic development process. The further a country has progressed along the road of development, the stronger is the impact of the introduction and expansion of collectively-funded welfare-state institutions such as retirement pension and health insurance schemes (now also supplemented in Germany by nursing-care insurance for people's old-age) as a further factor supplementing those relating to individual biographies. The upshot of this is that the birth rate tends to fall all the more short of the level needed to maintain a constant population the greater individual prosperity and collective welfare provision have become (*arrow 11*). Having returned to the birth rate, that brings us back to the start of the interactive loop portrayed in *Figure 30* but now, at the close, the reduced birth rate produces a slowdown, or possibly even a reversal, in the growth of the population (*arrow 12*), as is the case in Germany today. This model can also be applied to developing countries in which the industrialization process is encouraging a demographic transition. The regions in this group to which it applies most are a number of countries and urban areas in Asia where the *"revolution in reproductive behaviour"* has already brought with it a sharp fall in birth rates (Leete and Alam, 1993).

This section began by asking what happens if the population is growing. The effects generated by growth lead, after they have worked through the demo-economic system, to feedback effects which dampen down the population growth seen at the outset. So does this mean we are looking at a self-regulating system ensuring that population growth "... must ultimately come to a halt on its own, without the need for forceful, extraordinary means ...", as Süssmilch presumed as long ago as 1741, while Malthus rejected the idea of a self-regulating mechanism?

As far as we know or can presume today, the change in population levels does at least partly regulate itself via demo-economic feedback effects. However, that does not mean that we merely need to sit back and hope that self-regulation will put a stop both to the drastic population growth in developing countries and to the threat of severe shrinkage in the industrial countries, to establish a state of equilibrium. The likelihood is that these forces, though they operate in the right direction, are not adequate to bring relief by themselves:

- In the especially poor developing countries, the demo-economic mechanisms are severely impaired by the sheer scale of human distress, to the extent that they virtually cease to operate. In these countries, the general rule is that the population *grows* all the faster, the greater the initial destitution, and in this situation no self-regulation can be said to occur (this is the *"spiral of poverty"*).

- In the especially rich industrial countries, the self-regulatory mechanism is similarly questionable, but for the converse reasons. There is nothing to suggest that *population shrinkage* in these countries can be arrested by any other means than by persisting mass immigration (the *"spiral of prosperity"*).

How does this bear upon the world population as a whole? The population growth in the poor countries and shrinkage in the rich ones do not cancel each other out in an unproblematic overall average. Policy-makers therefore have to endeavour to exert some control over demo-economic processes. The crucial question is whether it will be possible, by means of integrated development, population, health and family policies, to reduce the birth rate in developing countries quickly enough to allow the development of civilization at least to keep pace with population growth, and quickly enough for us not to lose the race against time.

The difficulty of this policy task of breaking the spirals of poverty or prosperity by means of rational economic, societal, social and environmental policies becomes obvious once the demo-economic interactive relationships from *Figure*

30 are further supplemented by demo-ecological and socio-economic interrelationships. This gives us the system portrayed in *Figure 31* and consisting of four groups of variables, under the headings of population, economy, society and environment. The interrelationships within the subsystem of the economy are especially significant, since public expectations and hopes of increased prosperity are founded on the economic system's capacity to produce output. The crucial quantity in this regard is per capita income: if this is too low, virtually all of a country's national income has to be used simply to satisfy basic needs. The portion of national income not used for consumption but set aside for productive investment is not enough to ensure the formation of an adequate amount of *material productive capital* (consisting of industrial plant, infrastructure, transport and telecommunications systems, etc.) and of *immaterial, human capital* (knowledge and occupational skills generated by education and training). Human capital in its broadest sense also includes certain forms of behaviour rooted in cultural background and religious beliefs, such as the will to perform, contractual fidelity, or a general sense of responsibility for society as a whole. A small stock of capital results in too low a level of *capital intensity* (i.e. the amount of productive material and immaterial capital deployed per employee), which in turn depresses the economy's *productivity* (the amount of goods and services produced per employee), meaning that sufficient capital resources are not available to raise the population's per capita income. So that closes the circle, since incomes above subsistence level are a precondition for more savings and investment, for a larger stock of capital, for increased productivity and hence for higher incomes. The feedback effects from the economic system to produce a reduction in the birth rate, illustrated in *Figure 31*, are too weak to act as a self-regulatory mechanism if the per-capita income level is too low to start with. This is the origin of the *"spiral of poverty"*, also known variously as the *"poverty trap"*, the *"population trap"* or the *"Malthusian trap"*.

For the industrial countries, meanwhile, analagous but converse terms can be coined such as the *"prosperity trap"* or the *"immigration trap"*. In the most advanced countries where per capita income is especially high, the wealth of the population leads to a reduction of the birth rate in two ways. Firstly, a high per capita income also means that the economic and biographical opportunity costs of having children are high; secondly, there are enough resources available to finance a particularly close-meshed network of social security systems (unemployment, accident, pension and health insurance schemes). In Germany, another

Figure 31

System of Interaction between Demo-economic, Demo-ecological and Socio-economic Effects

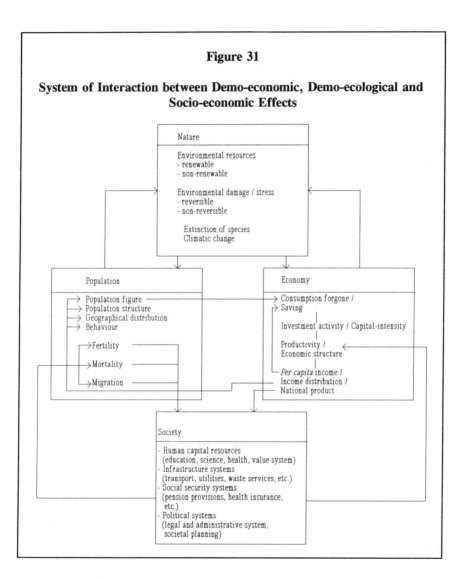

element was added to that network in 1994, namely nursing-care insurance for the old and infirm. As a result, Germany's birth rate is some way below that of comparable countries such as the USA. Indeed, its net reproduction rate is 30% below the level needed to maintain a constant population. The current number of children per woman is approximately 1.4, which also takes the immigrant population into account; although the latter's birth rate is higher than that of the native German population, it too is below the level of two children per woman. Were it not for a steady flow of immigration, Germany's population would, as pointed out earlier, fall from 80 million in 1990 to just 48 million in 2050 (see *Figure 32*). If the shortfall in births were to be fully compensated for by more immigration, the proportion of the total population accounted for by immigrants would pass the 50% mark in a matter of decades (Birg and Flöthmann, 1993d). If the constitution were to continue in force in its present form, that would leave the majority of the population without the right to vote or to be elected. The term *"immigration trap"* is a manifestation of the element of inevitability about this trend, because the inner dynamism of population shrinkage is such that countries like Germany reach a certain point at which they cannot choose whether they want to open their doors to immigration or not, and because they will need to adapt their political and constitutional systems (particularly the law on citizenship) to suit the demographic realities, whether they wish to or not.

5.3 The Environment-Development Dilemma, as Illustrated by the Issue of the Greenhouse Gas, Carbon Dioxide

In theory the world community - assuming that such a thing actually existed - would have the power, the scientific and technical capability and the economic potential to create paradise on Earth while still conserving Nature to the greatest possible degree. As we all know, the reason this is not happening is that a world community, or humanity as a whole, simply do not exist as subjects of action. The main human actors are either the individual, family, social group, tribe or, at the most, the nation state. The powerful supranational or international acting subjects that humanity needs to solve its global problems have yet to be developed. And what are the prospects of this succeeding? A glance at the situation in

Figure 32

Development of the Population of the Federal Republic of Germany, Ignoring Inward and Outward Migratory Flows

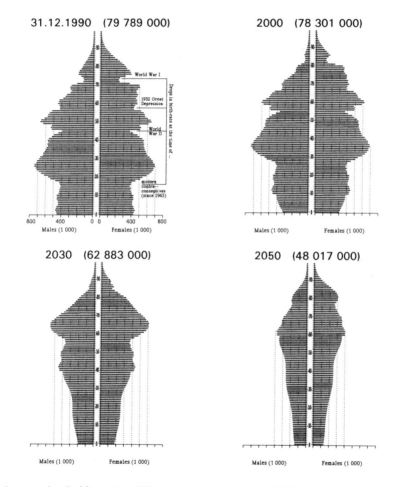

Assumes that fertility and mortality rates remain constant at 1990 levels.

Note: The constriction at age 10 in 2000, age 40 in 2030, and age 60 in 2050 is the result of the pronounced drop in the birth rate in former East Germany after reunification between 1989 and 1991.

Bosnia, Somalia or Rwanda gives grounds for scepticism.

The fact that, so far at least, there is no such thing as a world community except in the heads and hearts of visionaries and idealists, is in itself evidence that the environmental problem, whatever its scientific and technical dimesnions might be, is in essence a social problem we have on our hands, which we need to resolve in the social, societal and political fields, or ultimately in the field of our culture in its broadest sense, before the problem can be dealt with in economic and technical terms. Only from this cultural perspective can we begin to understand why global environmental problems - climatic change, extinction of species, depletion of the protective ozone-layer and the utter destruction of sensitive terrestrial and marine ecospheres - give rise to such a general sense of despondency: our awareness that these problems could, in principle, be avoided or technically solved brings it home to us that our failure is culturally rooted.

So the prime task now is to attain problem-solving *capability* on the cultural level so that we can go on to solve the problems in the real world. This touches upon a question which has remained in the background to date in public debate: What feedback effects upon the ethical principles underlying individual action are generated by the change in individuals' demographically relevant patterns of behaviour, via the avenue of the consequences they have for society and the economic system? In other words, do the demo-economic interactive relationships described in a technical, abstract way in the preceding section also have cultural and ethical side-effects which are destabilizing the demographic foundations of society?

It goes without saying that both the countries with shrinking populations and those with growing ones are demographically endangering their societies, each in their own way. There is a logical consistency to the associated problems which makes it virtually unnecessary to comment upon them in any detail here, and they are simply listed in summary form (in *Figure 33*). Although cross-border environvironmental problems are last in this list, in truth they have the most far-reaching consequences of any future problems. This can be usefully illustrated by looking at the example of the dangers of man-made climatic change due to emissions of carbon dioxide, the main "greenhouse gas".

Figure 33
**Chains of Problems with Demographic Causes
in Industrial and Developing Countries**

Industrial countries (low birth rate)	Developing countries (high birth rate)	World (high birth rate)
1. Threat of a shrinking population	1. Population growth	Worldwide poplation growth from 5.5 to over 10 billion inhabitants
2. Demographic ageing	2. Mass youth unemployment	
3. Institutions of the welfare state (care for the old and the sick) placed in jeopardy	3. General lack of state support systems for today's younger generations once they grow old	Increasing international disparities between rich and poor countries
4. Polarization of society into reproductive and non-reproductive sections	4. Extreme differences in the living conditions of different social strata	Growing supranational urgency for action to be taken. Population trends further amplify environmental problems
5. Shortage of labour and large-scale immigration	5. Refugees from poverty, from environmental degradation, and from civil war; asylum-seekers	
6. Ethnic and inter-cultural tensions and conflict		
7. Increased need for government intervention	7. Conflicts projected outwards, with the risk of war	
8.	<- Cross-border environmental problems ->	

According to the findings of the German *Bundestag's* Commission of Enquiry on the Protection of the Earth's Atmosphere, the amount of CO_2 greenhouse gas emitted due to energy use in the industrial countries in the mid-1990s is estimated at 18.4 billion metric tons, while the quantity emitted by the developing countries is put at only 5.6 billion metric tons. Expressed per head of population, the gap between the industrial and developing countries is wider still (Deutscher Bundestag, Enquete-Kommission "Schutz der Erdatmosphäre, Vol. 2, 1990: 869):

Industrial countries: 14.7 metric tons per capita per annum
Developing countries: 1.3 metric tons per capita per annum
World: 4.2 metric tons per capita per annum

The dangers resulting from the man-made greenhouse effect are portrayed frequently enough in the media, so it is sufficient here to name a few headline aspects of the problem: the rise in sea levels, changes in precipitation patterns, wind speeds and the frequency of storms, shifts in vegetation zones, melting of perma-frost, changes in the prevalence of pests, the dissemination of illnesses, etc. The climate changes have a great many different impacts on the economy, especially on agriculture, food supplies, transport and settlement systems, etc. From the wealth of instances cited by the Commission of Enquiry, here is just one telling example: "Regions in which the proportion of land available for agricultural use is relatively low and which, according to climatic simulations, can expect a reduction in soil humidity, are the following: the Maghreb, West Africa, the Horn of Africa, Southern Africa, Western Arabia, parts of South-East Asia, Mexico, Central America, parts of Eastern Brazil, ...". Special attention also needs to be paid to grain-exporting regions; for example, the greater part of inland North America is, say the climatic models, also likely to suffer a reduction in soil humidity (op.cit., Vol. 1, 1990: 297).

There are two main problems for international efforts to cut energy-related emissions of CO_2: the first is the increasing demand for energy stemming from economic growth in the developing countries, and the second is the huge discrepancy between per capita emissions in industrial and developing countries. Making the *"right to development"* proclaimed by the UN a reality thus clashes head-on with the *right to a healthy environment* which is also proclaimed, while both of these are impaired by the *right of demographic self-determination* if that entails the rate of population growth failing to decline, or to decline fast enough.

Figure 34

Correlation in Principle between Level of Development (Expressed in Terms of Per Capita Income and of Life Expectancy) and Energy Output, or Energy-Related CO_2 Emissions, in or about 1990

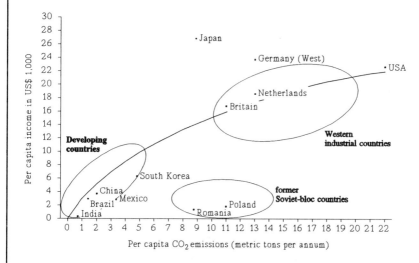

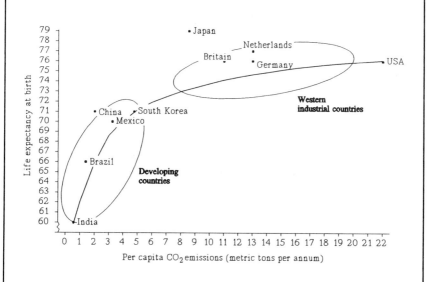

The dilemma is illustrated by two correlations in *Figure 34*. The two most important indicators of a country's level of development can be taken to be its *per capita income* and the *life expectancy* of its population. There is a positive correlation between both of these and *per capita CO_2 emissions*. That implies that scaling back CO_2 emissions in the developing countries or preventing their increase would have to be paid for by concessions on their development objectives.

The principle of justice demands that developing countries should be granted the right to produce the same level of per capita CO_2 emissions as the industrial countries. If a demand is simultaneously made that worldwide emissions of this gas at least must not be allowed to grow any further, the two demands in combination can only be fulfilled if, for example, per capita emissions in the developing countries double while those of the industrial countries are reduced by 85%. This scenario is illustrated in *Figure 35* (labelled *"World I"*). On these assumptions, per capita emissions in 2050 would be uniform around the world at 2.27 metric tons per head and per annum. Although it would not achieve any reduction, this scenario would at least allow a stabilization of absolute CO_2 emissions which otherwise would be growing throughout the world. This *"World I"* scenario is probably unrealistic, for two different reasons: firstly, an 85% reduction in per capita emissions in the industrial countries would appear to be unenforceable and, secondly, a mere doubling of per capita emissions in the developing countries is probably insufficient to allow enough leeway for the economic growth necessary to generate the increased per capita incomes to which they aspire, since the ageing production facilities often found in these countries have a low energy-efficiency. If the *World I* scenario were nevertheless sucessfully achieved, because of the large and growing populations in the developing countries their share of total energy-related CO_2 emissions would be 20 billion metric tons in 2050, while that of the industrial countries would be just 3.3 billion metric tons, and the two together would be just over 23 billion compared with today's total of 24 billion metric tons (see the lower portion of *Figure 35*). That would mean that today's ratio of emissions would be *reversed*: the industrial countries currently generate more than three times the amount of CO_2 emitted by the developing countries, but by the year 2050 they would be responsible for *six times as much as the industrial countries.*

Figure 35

Correlation between Population Trends and Energy-Related CO_2 Emissions in Industrial and Developing Countries

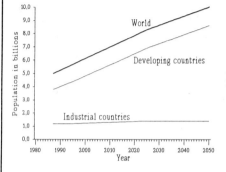

Population projections issued by the UN Population Division

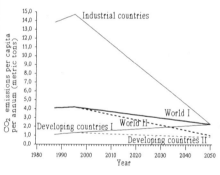

Key

World I:
This author's assumptions

World II:
The *Bundestag* Commission's[1] reduction targets for the world as a whole

Developing countries I:
A path allowing developing countries gradually to catch up
(Alternative to the Commission's[1] target)

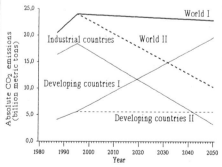

Developing countries II:
The *Bundestag* Commission's[1] target for developing countries

Industrial countries:
Reduction path for the industrial countries in accordance with the *Bundestag* Commission's[1] requirements and the author's assumptions

[1] Commission of the German *Bundestag* "Schutz der Erdatmosphäre"

The German *Bundestag's* Commission of Enquiry proposes a much more drastic reduction scenario, in which total world emissions fall from today's (1995) level of 24 billion metric tons to 10 billion metric tons in 2050. Here too, the industrial countries are expected to reduce their per capita emissions by 85%, but the developing countries are also called upon to scale back their per capita emissions, from 1.3 metric tons in 1995 to 0.81 metric tons in 2050 (this is the *World II* scenario in *Figure 35*). Although this proposal by the *Bundestag* Commission would better serve the environmental objective, it would also be a denial of the right to development, or would violate the principle of justice (the claim to equal per capita emissions). The dilemma is insoluble.

The impact of population growth on the environment can be divided into a quantitative and a qualitative component, the former being the number of people, and the latter their patterns of behaviour. The question of which of these components is the more significant is of great importance to the search for appropriate problem-solving strategies. As far as industrially manufactured goods and the consumption of commercially produced energy are concerned, the per capita consumption of resources and emission of environmentally damaging substances in industrial countries is more than ten times the corresponding level in developing countries. So it is patently obvious that immediate measures to safeguard the environment have to be taken in the industrial countries. The chief demands currently being expressed in this regard are geared to raising energy-efficiency in particular and efficient resource utilization in general in the industrial economies. A general eco-technological revolution in modes of production and consumption is intended to put an end to the current profligacy of the industrial countries, transforming their position to a new form of prosperity which the developing countries will also be able to imitate. If these objectives are to be made a reality, it is fundamentally important to give adequate consideration to the wide variety of reciprocal interactions occurring between the population, the environment and economic and scientific progress.

These proposals are primarily aimed at the qualitative, behaviourally-determined component of the population's impact on the environment. They promise immediate results, and should be implemented with top priority. However, when one turns to the environmental improvements which are necessary in the long term, taking the needs of future generations into account, the quantitative component to the environmental impact of population growth becomes crucially important. For example, thanks to its large population and vigorous economic growth

China may already have become the world's second largest emitter of carbon dioxide after the USA within just 10 years. In terms of sulphur dioxide emissions, China is already about to overtake the USA even today.

The worst scenario would be one in which the negative environmental effects flowing from the quantitative and qualitative demographic factors occurred in combination and amplified one another. And that is precisely what is now happenning. People in the developing countries have quite understandably set their sights on attaining the same form of consumer prosperity, as quickly as possible, which more and more people in the industrial countries are now recognizing as a blind alley. So they want to do exactly those things which we most criticize about ourselves, i.e. they want to consume as much as possible. There is no evidence to suggest that people in the developing countries are in some way "better" human beings than those in the industrial countries, or that Hindu, Confucian or Moslem cultures are superior to Occidental cultures with regard to global environmental problems. In fact, this author is convinced that the contrary is more likely to apply, for the ideas of human rights and of the individual's responsibility towards nations or towards humanity in its entirety are ideas which developed in the culture of the Occident, even if the actual practices of these countries - especially their colonial policies - have little in common with their cultural achievements. As we endeavour to stem global environmental problems, these ideas of human rights and of individual responsibility for the world as a whole will yet prove vital to our survival. But of course, the crux of the matter is that we must put those ideas into practice. To do so, we must help achieve a breakthrough for societal progress of a kind which Malthus' population theory maintains is impossible on demographic grounds.

In spite of the growing long-term significance of the demographic factor for the environment as well as other spheres, humanity will not perish due to its population problems; the much greater perils stem from our way of dealing with them, both in intellectual and in practical, political terms. One-sidedly emphasizing the demographic factor is therefore just as deleterious a thing as playing it down or ignoring it.

Chapter 6

Ethical Aspects of Population-Oriented Policies

6.1 Ethical Antagonisms in Classical Population Theory

Demography deals with the lives of individuals and peoples, and its core subject areas include the problems of survival for individuals, and the transmission of human life from one generation to the next. Ethics, too, addresses human life, particularly the good life or questions associated with right living, and it does so especially intensely in instances where matters normally assumed to be self-evident have been called into question and ethics itself has thus become controversial. Given that ethics and demography share the same object, it is only natural that the two spheres should have been treated in combination by the classic population theorists, and indeed appeared virtually inseparable right into the first third of the 19th century. For Johann Peter Süssmilch, population statistics and demographic methodology were not an end in themselves, but served the higher purpose of providing empirical proof of the existence of God. The second idea which lay at the centre of Süssmilch's line of argument was the proposition that the evils of this world - ranging from the horrors of war via the wretched living conditions of the poor through to the illnesses and plagues attributable to inadequate hygiene and poor public health - were not God's will, i.e. had *not* been sent by God as a trial or punishment and hence were *not* *"necessary"*, but had been caused by humanity itself, and that both governments and the governed could be held responsible for them. By putting forward this proposition, Süssmilch not only risked disassociation from the Church and theological doctrine, but also the prospect of conflict with political rulers, in particular with FriedrichII of Prussia, who allowed him to continue more out of tolerance than out of any affinity with his ideas, and accepted him as a member of the Berlin Academy of Sciences. To put paid to these evils which could no longer be passed off as acts of God, Süssmilch demanded political reforms, some of which he was also able to put into practice. In short, as far as Süssmilch was concerned, demography was the most effective instrument available to conceive a new ethics which would serve the reform of the social system and of society as a whole.

The grand classic population theorist, Thomas Robert Malthus, did not conduct his demographic studies merely for their own sake either. His underlying purpose is evident from the full title of his principal work, namely: "An Essay on the Principle of Population as it Affects the Future Improvement of Society with Remarks on the Speculations of Mr. Godwin, M. Condorcet, and other Writers". Here too, demography plays a subservient role, this time to provide evidence as part of a fundamental hypothesis of moral philosophy and politics. The substance of this proposition was diametrically opposed to that of Süssmilch. For the latter, the rules and order of demographic processes provided the proof that the Earth was able to support or "carry" considerably more people than were living on it during his time, and the term "living" itself did not, as in Malthus' propositions, merely mean physical survival, but living better, in better health and with greater dignity. The thrust of Malthus' arguments was the opposite in as far as his theory sought to demonstrate that political and societal progress was impossible precisely because the Earth was overpopulated even at that time with its approximately one billion human inhabitants, and because any improvement in the living conditions of the "lower classes" would - according to this central proposition - increase the birth rate and hence the rate of population growth, with the inevitable consequence that the excess population would be annihilated by war, disease and destitution - i.e. by an increased death rate - to bring the overall population level back within the bounds of its means of subsistence. In this view, the evils of the world could not be overcome by human action, but were necessary according to the *"laws of Nature"* and hence constituted the will of God until such time as humanity realized the moral imperative of holding its sexual instincts in check and changing its reproductive behaviour. At no point in his comprehensive world does Malthus address the fact that sexual intercourse need not necessarily lead to conception, since all cultures at all times have been aware of and made use of some form or other of contraception. So we have to assume that it was despite his better knowledge that he chose to equate the biological sexual urge with a supposed reproductive instinct.

One of the main foundation-stones of Malthusian theory is the claim that food supplies tend to grow at a slower rate than the population which consumes them. The whole theoretical edifice thus stands or falls on the reliability of this hypothesis. Yet although this proposition is demonstrably wrong, that has not prevented Malthusianism living on to this day, and indeed it still appears to have a vigorous future ahead of it. One reason for this is that the theory can be readily reformulated by substituting the "ecological barrier" for the "food barrier" as the main constraint on population size, and by exchanging the theory's original division of society into "upper" and "lower classes" for a new division of the whole world into "industrial and developing countries". Giving this ecological bent to Malthus' theory would appear to allow its basic tenet to be upheld, that the global progress in the political and societal spheres needed to raise the living standards of four-fifths of the world's population living in the developing countries is actually impossible for demographic reasons. *Eco-Malthusianism* is also used to lend weight to a new, particularly menacing variety of demographic moralism which is known according to the metaphor of *lifeboat ethics* and is touting the argument that it is immoral to lend help to the developing countries because this will only amplify the root-cause of the problem, i.e. worldwide population growth.

6.2   The Unity between Demography and Ethics

Following this retrospective on the *historical* unity between demography and ethics in the classical theory of population, I shall turn now to an outline of the *systematic* associations between the two. Since we are dealing in this context with ethics in its most universal sense and not with any particular set of ethical codes such as those of the Occidental/Christian or Oriental/Buddhist cultural spheres, I shall endeavour to approach the problem from as neutral a cultural standpoint as possible, and begin by posing one essential question. A point all ethical systems have in common is the demand for maxims of action which can be universally applied, as manifested in Immanuel Kant's categorical imperative: "So act that the maxim of your will could always hold at the same time as a principle establishing universal law" (I. Kant, 1956: 30). My own question in this regard is: What is the source of this commonality among ethical systems, especially bearing in mind the tremendous, often contradictory variety of ideas, convictions and rules of human action which otherwise predominate on matters of ethics and morality?

My response is as follows: The demand for universal applicability in ethics is actually a secondary principle which derives its sense from another fundamental principle which all ethical systems have *in common*. Hans Jonas describes this fundamental principle as the principle of the perpetuity of human life and of human development on Earth. The sense, meaning and validity of the principle of universal applicability cannot be properly grounded without resorting to the principle of perpetuity; certainly, this author has no knowledge of any attempts to substantiate it in any other way. In his book *The Imperative of Responsibility* Jonas derives from the principle of perpetuity, by also referring back to Kant's categorical imperative, the following ethical maxim: So act that the perpetuity of human life on this Earth remains possible. This maxim for action applies chiefly to behaviour which is ecologically relevant and also to reproductive behaviour. In other words, Hans Jonas' ethics of responsibility, like those of Süssmilch and Malthus before it, incorporates some fundamental demographic maxims. However, Jonas' principle of responsibility may be said to be more radically demographic than Süssmilchian or Malthusian ethics, for as he succintly notes: "... the categorical commands only *that* there be *human beings*, with the accent equally on the *that* and the *what* of obligatory existence. For me, I admit, this imperative is the only one which really fits the Kantian sense of the categorical, that is, the unconditional" (H. Jonas, 1984: 43).

I do not intend in the context of this book to enter into a detailed account of Hans Jonas' ethics of responsibility. What should be said, however, is that he sees the risks and hazards of modern technology as a problem which threatens humanity and hence as a metaphysical question which ethics has not hitherto had to face, namely "... should humanity exist, and if so, why?" (H. Jonas, 1987: 48). The answer Jonas provides is at once metaphysical and ontological: the population-related imperative derived from the principle of perpetuity makes us "... not responsible to the future human individuals but to the *idea* of Man, which is such that it demands the presence of its embodiment in the world. It is, in other words, an ontological idea, which does not, however, as the 'ontological proof' alleges-concerning the concept of God, guarantee the existence of its subject already with the essence - far from it! - but says that such a presence *ought* to be and to be watched over, thus making it a duty to us who can endanger it. It is this ontological imperative, emanating from the idea of Man, that stands behind the prohibition of a *va-banque* gamble with mankind. Only the idea of Man, by telling us *why* there should be men, tells us also *how* they should be" (H. Jonas, 1984: 43).

I believe Hans Jonas' ethics of responsibility is well grounded, and well capable of obtaining a consensus, yet being so amenable to approval also poses a problem. The increasing urgency of demographic problems both in the industrial countries (in the form of population shrinkage and immigration) and in the developing countries (population growth, environmental destruction, mass unemployment and political and societal destabilization) amply demonstrates that ethical problems, quite apart from their theoretical or metaphysical relevance, are in fact primarily *practical* problems. Although inspired contributions to theory such as Hans Jonas' ethics of responsibility are helpful and most welcome as supportive providers of greater certainty, that alone is not enough to deal with the tasks at hand: what are really needed are unequivocal recommendations for human action capable of being put into practice, which will both be able to be and have to be improved upon if and when, at some distant future time, the theoretical problems of ethics should finally be resolved.

Jonas, too, stresses that one of the essential features of ethics in its role as a science of practical action is that it is inevitably fraught with conflict. He writes, for example: "... it is ethically inconceivable that the field of biomedical technology could refrain from lowering the rate of child mortality in 'underdeveloped' countries which have high birth rates, even if that could result in still more ghastly destitution due to overpopulation. One could list any number of bold enterprises in the field of large-scale technology which began as a blessing to humanity but which serve to illustrate the dialectic, or the double-edged quality, of most such enterprises." (H. Jonas, 1987: 50). He continues "The same means with which [progress] promises to eliminate poverty in the Third World and to multiply the material prosperity of the whole of humanity which, thanks to that progress, continues to grow ... threaten by their very success in the short term to create what may be incurable environmental devastation in the long term ..." (H. Jonas, 1987: 60-61). "It was virtuous to do what one could, to surpass the good with the even-better, to multiply our capabilities in all fields, to achieve more and more, and greater and greater things. But ought we in future to move on to still greater achievements in all fields? Should we, for example, aim to vastly improve our own longevity?" (H. Jonas, 1987: 70).

The last of the above quotations takes up one of the main themes of classic population theory, namely a proposition put forward by the Marquis de Condorcet - Malthus' adversary whom he addresses in *The Principle of Population* - that there was nothing, in principle, which should act as an obstacle to the enhancement of human life-expectancy. It may indeed turn out that Condorcet was right: according to some scientists working in gerontological genetics, the prospect of being able to artificially prolong people's lives by means of genetic engineering is becoming more and more technically feasible. Scientists are already making this idea a reality for lower life forms. In the view of leading experts in the field, the human lifespan could be increased to the biblical figure of 600 years.

The purpose of addressing Hans Jonas' ethics of responsibility was to demonstrate that, even in spite of a certain amount of progress in ethical theory, we are still a long way from solving the practical problems of demographic ethics. Let us now resume these considerations by returning to the principles of perpetuity and of universal applicability. My proposition was that the idea of the permanence of human life on Earth is the fundamental principle shared by all major systems of ethics, and that the principle of universal applicability is derived from that, which means that it too is common to all major ethical systems, playing the part of a practical rule of implementation in realizing the fundamental, perpetuity principle. If this postulate is valid, it follows that the principle of universal applicability and all specific ethical actions required to comply with it must acquire their ethical qualities solely from their capability, which must be empirically verified, of realizing the perpetuity principle's inherent aim, i.e. of guaranteeing the conditions which will allow human life on Earth to persist and to develop. When subjected to this empirical suitability test, the ethical directives given both by the great world religions and by non-religious, philosophical ethical systems actually prove quite problematic. I should like to address two aspects of these problems.

1. All religious systems of ethics, Christian or non-Christian, which lead to more than two children being born per woman, or which generate a net reproduction rate of more than 1.0 after mortality has been taken into account, imply on-going population growth and are therefore *irreconcilable* with the principle of perpetuity. The demographically relevant doctrines of the great world religions have yet to be thoroughly examined in terms of what average number of children or what

net reproduction rate the actions they recommend would ultimately lead to. A survey of these implications, which is an important project for the future, should not only appraise religious statements in and of themselves, but also how they are interpreted by religious authorities and how they are translated into practical reproductive behaviour by families and individuals.

Pending such a thorough examination of the major religions, I would venture to suggest that all religions have a tendency to be *pronatalistic*. Some religions, such as certain forms of Hinduism, include a clear, overt *imperative to reproduce*. In other religions, though they may not express such an imperative directly, a close reading of the scriptures indicates that it also exists. However, directly or indirectly, i.e. by way of cultural traditions, all great religions ultimately have a pronatalistic impact. To put it slightly differently, a basic pronatalistic preference and an underlying pronatalistic tendency are inherent in all systems of values which are based on *religious* ethics. As for *philosophically*based systems of ethics, it should be noted that Hans Jonas' ethics of responsibility also contains a clearly manifest *"duty to reproduce"*: "It is this sort of duty that is involved in a responsibility for future mankind. It charges us, in the first place, with ensuring that there *be* a future mankind - even if no descendents of ours are among them - and sedond, with a duty toward their *condition*, the quality of their life. The first duty contains within itself the duty of procreation (even if not necessarily that of everybody) and like the latter is not simply derivable, by extension, from the duty of the begetter toward the life already begotten. If there is such a duty, as we would like to suppose, our discourse has yet to show a sanctioning ground for it" (H. Jonas, 1984: 40).

A more important point than the fact that religious and ethical systems contain pronatalistic recommendations for action is the fact that they do *not* contain action recommendations for the eventuality of population growth developing a negative impact due to an excessively high birth rate (not to a low death rate or migratory flows), the indirect consequences of which could jeopardize the very foundations of ethics itself. It is true that even in Ancient Greece or Rome the abandonment of live-born children was broadly practised and ethically accepted as a means of adjusting the size of a family to the capacity of the land to provide it with a living. However, in the works of philosophy and literature handed down to subsequent generations this behaviour was not systematically justified in the shape of a well-reflected, ethical and religious theory of reproductive behaviour. The fact that religions have still not really confronted the problem of global population growth even today may well represent the most serious of the demographically generated threats to the future development of humankind.

I do not wish to refute that the Catholic and Protestant churches, for example, have given their attention to this problem in many information events, congresses and memoranda. The point I wish to focus on is not whether the churches have taken up and addressed this problem, but what (or, one ought to say, what little) they have actually done to solve the problem. My complaint is not that there has been a lack of practical activity, e.g. in the field of development aid, but primarily that they have been found wanting in getting to grips with the basic scientific and ethical problems of population trends. The two *propositions* I wish to make on this point are as follows.

(I) The majority of the world's inhabitants belong to world religions or cultures which are pronatalistic in their impact, and they are hardly encouraged by their religious and cultural authorities, if at all, to reflect upon their reproductive behaviour in the light of the global, macrodemographic consequences this has. This situation is inevitable as long as the religious authorities have *themselves* failed to recognize the necessity to scrutinize the basic tenets of religions to appraise their consistency with the principle of the perpetuity of human life on Earth, and then to make changes to them - which I can find no better term to describe than a *"cultural revolution"* - to adapt them to the demographic/ethical demands derived from the perpetuity principle.

(II) A cultural revolution of this nature is predicated upon a worldwide, intercultural consensus on the objective of the perpetuity of human life and human development on Earth. A fundamental precondition for that in turn is genuine, deep-seated intercultural communication. Yet how can we expect, for example, a North American or European coffee-drinker to have anything more than an abstract, cool relationship with an African coffee-producer based solely on their respective roles in the coffee market if - as is the case in Germany, say - even normal interhuman relations based on a special feeling of mutual belonging within the same country or nation state are frowned upon as a nationalistic vestige of history, and if the real emotion of this feeling of mutual belonging is disdained as a manifestation of political backwardness, or simply denied altogether? Common ethical values across national and cultural boundaries only develop - if everything goes well - in the course of a process of intercultural communication, from the combined effects of mutual affection, a belongingness also recognized in the mind, and solidarity supported by reason. The people of Europe are only in the early stages of that process, which they will have to undergo and complete; we should also realize that the dynamism of population growth is such that we are in a race against time.

2. Demographically, humankind is divided into two worlds, one of which is growing and the other either static or in decline. The comments made in the previous section may have given the false impression that the demographic plight of the countries with *growing* populations constitutes the main problem in every respect. However, I take a different view, namely that although the world is under threat because of its rapid overall population growth, if it should one day perish it will not do so *because of* the population-related problems in themselves, but because of its inadequacies in dealing with them on an intellectual or cultural plane.

The main factor giving grounds for concern is a lack of sincerity in approaching these problems. Although the demographically-determined problems of a shrinking population and mass immigration in a country such as Germany are now gradually being recognized and discussed, two decades too late in Germany's case, even now the discussion still concentrates almost exclusively on the *effects* of the demographic trend. The *causes* of this shrinkage, which I refer to as a *"spiral of prosperity"* as a corollary to the *"spiral of poverty"* in which many developing countries find themselves (see Chapter 5), are hardly ever dwelt upon. If those causes of population shrinkage are actually analysed, then here too one encounters a unity between ethics and demography, and it is probably that very unity which inhibits us from discussing the causes, as that would call for a rather embarrassing discussion of the fundamental values of society.

This author's view, the theoretical foundations of which are sketched out in Chapter 3, can be summarized as follows. First of all, the motor of economic and social change, which we have accepted as the guarantor of a high and growing level of prosperity even though it also generates social hardship and injustice for some, is technological progress in the economy. This process of change also has the effect of creating a high, continual dynamism in the labour market: for one thing, that drastically shortens the personal planning horizons of members of the workforce (there is a threat of unemployment as a consequence of innovation), and for another, it raises the economic and biographical opportunity costs of entering into family commitments. As a result, the greater the success of a society's economy the lower its level of fertility tends to be. I have proposed that this relationship should be termed the *"demo-economic paradox"* (Birg, 1993a). The decline in fertility caused by the spiral of prosperity is then followed by a decline in the size of the population itself. A further effect of economic success is thus a reduction in the number of young recruits to the workforce, and mass immigration due to demographic factors. The cultural and societal consequences of immigration are now being rationalized ex post as a positive phenomenon, in the vision of a "multicultural society"; however, this ignores the fact that the immigration was neither desired nor planned *ex ante*, i.e. it was not consciously brought about and politically set in motion as a positive development, but bore down upon society rather like an unstoppable force of nature and, in Germany's case for example, was accepted in silence by the majority of intellectuals. We still have time and still have the chance to overcome that silence, to integrate the positive aspects of what has so far tended to be a merely declamatory multicultural vision into a genuine blueprint for the future which we also inwardly accept, and to institute the political programmes and legislation which will make that a genuine gain for society.

Like the changes in society resulting from immigration, the changes in reproductive behaviour and the structure of families were neither desired nor planned *ex ante*. Nevertheless, the changes have been rationalized ex post as a positive phenomenon by the use of such terms as the "transformation of values" (*Wertewandel*), and simultaneously accepted as inevitable. Thus the *"Wertewandel"* ideology turns the western industrial countries' loss of demographic substance from an undesired development *ex ante* into a change which is seen after the event as positive in principle. In reality though, this supposed transformation of values has not changed the values themselves at all. It is not "values" which have "been transformed" but our own ideology with regard to those values. As shown in Chapter 2, it is absolutely essential to draw a proper distinction between the ideology of values and the underlying values themselves for the purposes of analysing population theory and the real history of population change.

How should this all be understood and fitted into place from the perspective of social philosophy and social psychology? It hardly appears possible at present to provide a discerning answer, as any discussion of the causes of these phenomena, certainly in the discipline of demography in Germany or in the general public, has barely even begun. However, what one could do at this stage is to put forward the following provisional proposal. There has always been a tacit conviction in the past that the portion of society which manages to assert itself economically and socially - in the face of whatever opposition - over the weaker portion will multiply and thus not only reproduce itself (i.e., in biologists' terms, its "own genes") but also society as a whole. In a number of industrial countries with extremely low birth rates, there is no longer any basis for that conviction. In the countries concerned, the economic and social competitive struggle has meant that, when all individual reproductive decisions are aggregated, the birth rate can no longer ensure that the population is maintained without net immigration. It is possible to speak of the *demographic self-exploitation* of society; A. Schumpeter must have had something of this kind in mind when, addressing the subject of the rationality of reproductive behaviour, he spoke of capitalism destroying its own foundations (A. Schumpeter, 1942). The causative principle at work here, namely the rational behavioural principle of market competition, which is the core element of interhuman behaviour in competitive societies, also applied to the countries of the former socialist bloc, whose populations' daily lives in practice differed drastically from the ideological positions proclaimed. In other words, the essential factor is not the formal political constitution but the concrete living conditions of ordinary people, and hence the *ethical* constitution of interhuman relations within a society. If personal success in such a competitive society can only be had on the basis of others' lack of success - i.e., if this is inherent in the system - it is bound to be the case that many of the things which could stand in the way of success are sacrificed to it, including the wish to live as part of a family and to have children. In terms of practical policy, there are a number of implications of this for the industrial countries, three of which I would like to touch upon here:

(I) Can a society continue to exist in the long run if it borrows its demographic substance from other societies, compensating for its shortfall in births by immigration, as Germany, for example, has now been doing for several decades?

(II) Given a situation in which the birth rate has been persistently falling short of the level necessary for maintaining the population level, is it not essential to adapt the political constitution to take full account of demographic realities, making that constitution an honest one by including an article on immigration, which would guarantee a facility for incomers to take up permanent residence and serve as the basis for legislation on immigration and integration that would be institutionally protected from the cycle of shifting governmental majorities?

(III) What changes are necessary in elementary interhuman relations in the industrial countries to encourage families to demographically reproduce not only themselves but also the society they together make up? An answer to this last question is offered by one of the most prominent thinkers of Europe's Enlightnment, David Hume, who propounded the idea in his ethical theory, which can deservedly be termed a "demographic" theory, that all ethical values, especially the fundamental idea of justice, share common roots in the interhuman relations among family members, the relationship between parents and their children, and between the two parents. These elementary relationships give rise, according to Hume, to the virtue of gratitude - mutual gratitude between husband and wife and children's gratitude to their parents - which in turn serves as the basis for all societal virtues, especially the idea of *justice* (D. Hume, 1777). Hans Jonas, who makes no reference to Hume's theory in his ethics of responsibility, speaks of these elementary virtues as the only class of altruistic behaviour handed to us by *Nature*: "... and indeed, it is in this one-way relationship to dependent *progeny*, given with the biological facts of procreation, and *not* in the mutual relationship between independent adults (from which, rather, springs the idea of reciprocal rights and duties) that one should look for the origin of the idea of (basically one-sided) responsibility in general ..." (H. Jonas, 1984: 39). That brings us to a point at which the unity between demography and ethics will be glaringly evident, and at which any separation of the two could only appear artificial. I should like to conclude by looking at two examples which illustrate the practical significance of that unity.

6.3 The Lethal Danger of Demographic Metaphors

Can the principles of an ethical code be upheld if the pursuit of those principles tends on a long-term historical view to be of no real use in achieving a more dignified existence for all humankind, that is to say if it tends to hinder rather than to encourage such a development? Or to put the question in more general terms, must not ethics itself satisfy some criterion if it is to deserve to be termed "ethical", and if so, what should that criterion be? Anyone answering "yes" to the first question, that is who does not accord an absolute status to ethics but assigns a task to it, regarding the fulfilment of that task as a subservient rather than a dominant role, will have no objection to the response given by David Hume to the second question: "It appears, that there never was any quality recommended by any one, as a virtue or moral excellence, but on account of its being *useful*, or *agreeable* to a man *himself*, or to *others*. For what other reason can ever be assigned for praise or approbation? Or where would be the sense of extolling a *good* character or action, which, at the same time, is allowed to be *good for nothing*? All the differences, therefore, in morals, may be reduced to this one general foundation, and may be accounted for by the different views, which people take of these circumstances" (D. Hume, 1777: 336).

There are three reasons why the Humeian theory of ethics and morality is pertinent to the subject of this chapter. Firstly, the theory is the most general philosophical theory of ethics known to this author, which in itself makes it relevant to the issues of population ethics we are dealing with. Secondly, Hume himself applied it to the questions set out herein and elaborated the relationship between his ethics and demography: according to Hume the origin of all the utility generated by virtue, ethics and morality lies in the family, i.e. at the heart of the object of demographic research too. Thirdly, its reference to the concept of *"utility"* means that Hume's theory offers the possibility of providing norms with a foundation which is free of metaphysics: this aspect is crucial with a view to the ethics we need for the future, with universal and hence intercultural validity. The philosopher Norbert Hoerster speaks of a "truly exciting relevance [to our present and future needs]" when addressing this *"metaphysics-free" grounding for norms* (N. Hoerster, 1981: 148). He refers in this context to the work of J.L. Mackie, who is said to have first discovered this possibility (L. Mackie, 1980).

Most certainly, the demographically-determined problems of this world are such that there is hardly any more pressing task for philosophy at present than to establish the grounding for an ethics which will do justice to those problems, by elaborating orientational aids and setting standards for the necessary policy measures, as has recently been undertaken by Vittorio Hösle (1994). Hans Jonas' ethics of responsibility is a particularly well-elaborated endeavour to set such standards. Jonas postulates an important obligation to properly take in information on fundamental scientific knowledge, which also includes the findings of population projections (H. Jonas, 1987: 66). The ethical obligation to keep informed of the condition of this world must also apply equally to philosophers themselves (and indeed to all of humanity), and not merely to "the politicians", whom we are often so happy to leave to "carry the can". I believe the traditional attitude of philosophers, shunning the humble concerns of the everyday world, is (to put it mildly!) not especially beneficial to fulfilling the aim of ensuring that the scientific knowledge which is generally available be allowed to have a genuine impact.

The contribution philosophy has to make towards solving future problems does not consist exclusively of elaborating convincing foundations for the principles which guide human action, as David Hume, Hans Jonas and Vittorio Hösle have done. In addition to this substantiating role, philosophy also plays an "ordering" role which is of immense importance; I understand this to include such things as performing the elementary tasks of testing theories and arguments, to ensure that they are free of logical contradictions, and generally weeding out errors and falsehoods. In the field of population theory and population philosophy, few yet pay much attention to these tasks. That is the only possible explanation for the fact that questionable theories and doctrines on population development such as Malthusian population theory not only continue to exist but can also be revivified, or that truly ghastly ethical recommendations such as *"lifeboat ethics"* have generated so little protest. I should like to illustrate what I mean when I invite philosophy to ensure the maintenance of intellectual order by citing two examples below. A more systematic characterization of the potential for cooperation between demography and philosophy has already been published (Birg, 1990).

Example 1: The population theory of Julian Simon

Julian Simon's theory occupies a special position in as far as it takes up some of the stances adopted by the optimistic population theories of mercantilism, which in effect takes it a step back before the classic theories of Süssmilch and Malthus (J. Simon, 1981). However, it is not the fact that Simon's theory seeks its basis in the pre-classical period and builds upon an essentially normative, consciously metaphysical enhancement of the value of human life which makes it questionable in my eyes - quite the reverse. My reservations are of a different, much more straightforward nature. In the view of mercantilistic population theory, a large population is the best indicator of the well-being of any political "commonwealth" and of the contentment of the individuals within it. Simon comes to a similar judgment as he develops the idea that people in historic times have only ever achieved progress to attain a better life when they have been *up against* the need to solve problems. In Simon's view, the fact that humankind is growing ever larger causes an increase in the demographically-determined pressure to find problem solutions, which in turn will lead to an ever greater capability of doing so. Hence population growth has a double causative role, firstly by exacerbating the problems themselves and secondly by generating their solutions. Simon's conclusion is that the Earth cannot have too many human inhabitants:

"What does it mean to like the idea of more people? To me it means that I do not mind having more people in the cities I live in, seeing more children going to school and playing in the park. I would be even more pleased if there were more cities, more people in unsettled areas -even another planet like this one. I believe that this particular value is in the best spirit of Judeo-Christian culture, which is the foundation for much of our modern Western morality: In Biblical terms, be fruitful and multiply. It also accords with the spirit and logic of the *utilitarian* philosophers, starting with *Jeremy Bentham*, whose thinking underlies much of our legal and social philosophy, as well as modern economic thinking." (J. Simon, 1981: 337).

First of all, I should like to declare a quite unscientific affinity: the idea that the greatest possible number of people can live happily together on Earth in dignified circumstances has a great appeal to me, too. Indeed, I am convinced that humanity's scientific knowledge and economic potential would be sufficient to achieve paradise on Earth for twice the number of people who currently inhabit it. However, these possibilities go to waste because humankind does not act as one body, but in the form of individuals, families, tribes or, at best, nations and alliances among nations. The United Nations is still far from constituting "humankind" as an actor, as we all would wish.

I would like to summarize my criticism of Simon's theory in four main points. (a) It does *not* necessarily follow, from the underlying statement that human progress has always been attained in the teeth of pressing problems, that *all* problems *invariably* give rise to progress. Population-related problems refute any such conclusion more tellingly than any others. The carrying-capacity of the

Earth is restricted, as is that of a bridge: if a bridge has held up for a long, long time this still does not prove that it is capable of bearing *any* load at all, and the collapse, when it comes, usually comes suddenly. (b) The era to which Simon's theory might most appropriately have been applied is now behind us. At best, the theory is applicable to the era of human history in which there appeared to be an inexhaustible supply of unsettled land and resources, that is, to the age of discovery, the "modern era", and the era of mercantilism itself, in which Simon's ideas have their origin. (c) The theory has nothing to say about the *costs* of progress. Only the positive effects of population growth are cited, yet what it ought to do is to establish a net effect by comparing benefits *and* costs. It is true, on the one hand, that many of the quantities associated with population growth have been showing continual progress. However, it is equally undeniable that other indicators are deteriorating as population growth continues apace: indicators such as "the number of dead per war" or "the number of extinct animal and plant species". We even now face the possibility that humanity in its entirety could be wiped out by nuclear warfare. (d) When resources grow scarcer - and Simon does not deny that they are doing so - their prices increase, and this too he admits. Before the stage is reached at which those scarcer resources can be substituted for by alternative materials, their prices will attain such a level that they are no longer affordable for poor countries. In other words, the resources issue is inseparably linked to the issue of distributive justice. World population growth means there is a tendency towards greater scarcity and hence also towards greater injustice. That in turn raises the probability of discontent and conflict. The theory has nothing to say on these matters.

To sum up: Simon bases his theory on a fundamental metaphysical and utilitarian principle that human life is a high value in its own right, and that a great deal of human life must therefore have a higher value than a smaller amount. The reverse side of this sublime metaphysical argument is the banality of the concrete statements derived from it, which tend to be pre-scientific in character. Neverthless, the author does find the theory appealing - scientific or not. Yet what help can an *appealing* metaphysical theory be to us? In truth, metaphysics' lack of "utility" ought to be a source of major concern to Julian Simon the utilitarian: "Metaphysical experience is devoid of any capacity to be verified which might lend it validity to the common man" (Karl Jaspers). Yet that "common man" is the very person utilitarianism seeks to address.

Example 2: Lifeboat ethics

"Lifeboat ethics" was introduced into the debate on the ethics of population by the American biologist Garett Hardin in his article *"Living on a Lifeboat"* (1974). His argument can be summarized as follows. Some countries are rich, but others are poor. The poor countries cannot all develop into rich ones, since economic progress is all used up by the growing population, and since the Earth's resources are finite. As those resources are increasingly exhausted, the poor countries are encountering bottlenecks which threaten their survival, and that in turn is a threat to the whole world. The situation of humanity is analagous to that of the passengers on a sinking ship: the number of inhabitants on Earth exceeds the planet's carrying capacity, so the ship sinks. People in the rich countries have seaworthy lifeboats available, which would allow them to survive. However, the people in the poor countries have no means of survival, and are doomed to go under. Is it ethically right or wrong to allow the people still thrashing about in the water to clamber aboard the lifeboats? The response provided by lifeboat ethics is unequivocal and alarming: it is, says the theory, *immoral* to provide help! The basis for this "ethical" maxim is that if *all* of the people already in the lifeboats were magnanimous (as the principle of universal applicability demands) and sacrificed their own lives in order to allow in someone else currently still in the water, the lifeboats would eventually be full of people who had *no* scruples about surviving at others' expense. As a result, the overall moral state of the world would deteriorate. Ergo, providing help is immoral.

The line of argument appears logically consistent, i.e. if one accepts the premises one must also accept the conclusions. It is one of philosophy's vital tasks to solve this riddle. My own proposal as to how to go about this contains four main points: (a) The theory depends on a number of further premises not explicitly named, the verity of which is open to doubt: a particularly dubious premise is the idea that anyone begging for help is necessarily morally inferior. In reality the wish to be helped may not be a matter of moral inferiority but could flow, for example, from a lack of information on the others' capacity to provide that help. In a typical case of that kind, those seeking help may quite simply overestimate their potential helpers' economic means. However, it is also possible that those seeking help have good reason to be convinced that the chances of survival are unjustly distributed between the rich and the poor. (b) A criticism flowing from a point of principle is that lifeboat ethics uses a metaphor indicating a marginal situation of human existence - i.e., a sinking ship - in which too little time is available to eliminate the cause of the problem. One particular feature of this situation, for example, is that there is no opportunity to build any more lifeboats. But the real situation of humankind in the present day *cannot* be equated with the conditions for survival in this marginal situation. For the moment at least, we do still have time today to develop the poorer countries and to adjust the birth rate of the world population to the limits of the Earth's carrying-capacity. (c) The fact is that the problem which lifeboat ethics sets out to solve would not have developed in the first place if humankind had spent the two centuries which have elapsed since the publication of Malthus' population theory endeavouring to find solutions to population-linked problems instead of colonizing and exploiting the resources of those countries which are now placed in the dock by lifeboat ethics, which only goes to show that the root causes of the problem do not lie in the system-inherent difficulties of a marginal existential situation but in an insufficient or false awareness of the true nature of population problems and, as a consequence of that false awareness, a lack of will-power to solve them. (d) Even if one is prepared to accept the logic of the marginal situation, the theory ought still to be rejected because any call for an *ethical* decision must, as a matter of general principle, be predicated upon people being able to act upon their own free will, and this cannot be so lightly assumed in the situation of existential anxiety symbolized by a sinking ship.

To sum up: The analogy with a lifeboat is a false one, for demographically-relevant behaviour is *not* a form of action which flows from the inevitabilities of a marginal situation but is an *everyday* form of action, and the problems to which it gives rise develop only slowly, which also leaves time to set about solving them. Hence to liken population-generated problems to the survival problems of the shipwrecked is a **crucial error** - or else it is a **trick** played with the tools of logic to present us with the illusion of a necessary ethical conclusion. Once this error has been resolved, the ethical inconsistencies and contradictions derived from it also vanish.

I have deliberately made reference to Malthus' principle of population in this context because a similar metaphor can be found in Malthus' work to that used by Hardin, and Malthus used it to construe an analogy just as false as that of the lifeboat used in today's debate. Malthus' metaphor is that of *"Nature's mighty feast"*, at which a *"vacant cover"* is not provided for everyone, as humankind is supposedly too numerous. This too was a false metaphor, since humanity sets out its own "cover" with Nature's help: the size of the feast is not finite, and in fact any number of "covers" have been added since the publication of Malthus' "principle of population", and five times the number of people are now seated at table than at that time, with scope for the number to go on growing, which of course it will. Malthus exposes his underlying thinking in this passage from the second (1803) edition of *The Principle of Population*, which was deleted from later editions:

*"A man who is born into a world already possessed, if he cannot gut subsistence from his parents on whom he has a just demand, and if the society do not want his labour, has no claim of **right** to the smallest portion of food, and, in fact, has no business to be where he is. At nature's mighty feast there is no vacant cover for him. She tells him to be gone, and will quickly execute her own orders, if he do not work upon the compassion of some of her guests. If these guests get up and make room for him, other intruders immediately appear demanding the same favour. The report of a provision for all that come, fills the hall with numerous claimants. The order and harmony of the feast is disturbed, the plenty that before reigned is changed into scarcity; and the happiness of the guests is destroyed by the spectacle of misery and dependence in every part of the hall, and by the clamorous importunity of those, who are justly enraged at not finding the provision which they had been taught to expect. The guests learn too late their error, in counteracting those strict orders to all intruders, issued by the great mistress of the feast, who, whishing that all her guests should have plenty, and knowing that she could not provide for unlimited numbers, humanely refused to admit fresh comers when her table was already full"* (Malthus, 1803: 532).

Hardin harks back to Malthus' principle of population in his lifeboat ethics. Modern *Malthusianism with an ecological bent*, or the ethics based upon it, chiefly associated with the name of Maurice King, also draws upon those principles and calls for children in developing countries to be deliberately allowed to die as a means of restricting population growth (King, 1990 and 1993). King's theory also regards itself as an ethical theory: it is in the interests of future generations, that is an *ethical* choice, to allow children to die in developing countries. As a critical response to this position, I ask readers to refer to the projection findings set out in Chapter 4 (section 4.4) which will speak for themselves.

The main point to note is that the ethical theories propounded by Hardin and King are both varieties of Malthusian theory, and Malthus' theory itself turns out on closer inspection to be a *theory of class built on moral-philosophical foundations*, for in Malthus' view the members of the "lower classes" chiefly have that station in life because of a *moral* inferiority and not, as Marx later proposed, because of their lack of property. While something can be done about dispossession by reforming the distribution of property, how can one do anything to overcome the stigma of *moral* inferiority? When compared with Malthus' moral-philosophical theory of class, Karl Marx's economic theory of class is veritably harmless. Perhaps that explains why nobody hated Malthus' ideas more than Marx did. The fact that Marx's ideas have been outlived by those of Malthus raises the fear that we are still not sufficiently aware of the intrinsic dangers of Malthusianism.

6.4 Conclusions

1. Nowhere else does the need to distinguish clearly between theory and practice lead to such painful experience as the separation between the theory of ethics and ethical practice with regard to demographically determined problems. The theory/practice differential is insoluble as a problem in itself. Unfortunately, Plato was only right *in theory* when he said that good could only be born out of good. Because, in practice, good can arise from bad and vice versa, a well-meaning scientific theory such as that of Julian Simon can nevertheless tragically contribute to a worsening of conditions in the real world.

2. Plato and his Renaissance successors, Thomas Morus, Tommaso Campanella and Francis Bacon, apart from their utopias for the ideal state, invariably also offered the blueprint of a population utopia. The last governmental and population utopias experienced by humanity vanished in the ashes of Nazism and Stalinism. What may come in future, we do not know. It is said that the time for utopias is now past. But it must never be said that the time for a utopia of justice has passed. Therefore, population problems are not only of practical importance, but they are also fundamentally significant.

3. Even without any governmental utopia or any universally valid theory of ethics, humankind is not left entirely helpless. It has a great wealth of cultural experience to fall back on, which is as relevant as ever to the present day. In politics, for example, Max Weber's observation is still very apt, that politics is like slowly hand-drilling through a hard wooden board: it has to be done with passionate determination, but with a keen eye. What this principle means when applied to population-determined ethical problems is that the task of ethics should be one of perfecting the art (and not just the science) of developing guidelines for action which are not only free of contradiction but also practicable, to the effect that ethical conflicts, even if they cannot actually be avoided, are at least minimized. Ethics, in other words, is a *preventive* science of action. Once conflicts and dilemmas have appeared, even the best system of ethics no longer has simple solutions to offer.

Chapter 7

Technical Appendix

Appendix 1

1. Population in the base year of 1990

The population projections are all calculated with 1990 as the base year. The 1990 population figures were obtained from the World Bank's publication (K.C. Zachariah and My T. Vu, *"World Popultion Projections, 1987-88 edition"*). The figures in that volume are classified into five-year age groups. The author subsequently broke these down into single-year age groups, in such a way that the sum of the single-year age groups still matches the population in the corresponding five-year age group. The reclassified data avoid any implausible jumps between neighbouring age groups.

2. Fertility

The total fertility rate (TFR) of the world population in the base year of 1990 was 3.40. On the mortality assumptions set out in the next section (taking the medium variant), the replacement fertility level (TFR*) is 2.13. The projections assume that the total fertility rate falls steadily to replacement fertility level, reaching that level in a given target year (t*). Alternative projections are provided for different patterns of decline, namely linear, hyperbolic, and S-curve. For all three alternative decline patterns, projections have been prepared on the assumption that the total fertility rate remains constant at 2.13 from the target year

185

onwards. In the case of the fertility path with a hyperbolic decline pattern, a further alternative of the path intersecting replacement fertility level was also considered, and the final fertility levels reached in these cases are as follows:

Target year (TFR=2.13 intersected)	Final level reached by TFR
2010	1.957
2020	1.960
2030	1.966
2040	1.974
2050	1.982
2060	1.992
2070	2.002
2080	2.010

The mathematical formula for the linear fertility path is

$$TFR_t = TFR_0 - \frac{TFR_0 - TFR^*}{t^* - t_0} (t - t_0) \qquad (1)$$

where

$$\begin{aligned} t &= 1990, 1991, \ldots, t^* \\ t^* &= \text{target year} \\ TFR^* &= 2.13 \\ TFR_0 &= 3.40 \\ TFR^t &= TFR^* \text{ when } t > t^* \end{aligned}$$

The formula for the S-curve fertility path is

$$TFR_t = TFR^* + \frac{TFR_0 - TFR^*}{2} \left(1 + \cos\left(\frac{180}{t^* - t_0}(t - t_0)\right)\right), \qquad (2)$$

where $TFR_t = TFR^*$ when $t > t^*$.

The formula used for the hyperbolic fertility path is

$$TFR_t = \frac{\gamma}{b+(t-t_0)^x} + c \qquad (3)$$

where $TFR_t = TFR^*$ when $t > t^*$, where a = 130, b = 90 and c = 1.956, and where the parameter x varies with the target year as follows:

$$x = \frac{\log\left(\frac{\gamma}{TFR^*-c} - b\right)}{\log(t^*-t_0)} \qquad (4)$$

As mentioned above, in the case of the hyperbolic fertility path the additional alternative of the target year being intersected was calculated.

After the TFR had been calculated using one of the above formulae, it was then broken down into age-specific fertility rates, (f_x):

$$TFR = \sum_{x=15}^{45} f_x \qquad (5)$$

A typical, single-peaked distribution curve was assumed when breaking down the TFR according to the age x of the women giving birth to the next generation. The shape of curve chosen was the mean of the distributions typically observed in Brazil and Indonesia. The share (γ_x) of the total fertility rate in the base year (TFR_0) taken up by each of the age-specific birth rates

$$\gamma_x = f_{x,0}/TFR_0, \quad x = 15, \ldots, 45 \qquad (6)$$

was used as the basis for calculating age-specific birth rates in any particular future year:

$$f_{x,t} = \gamma_x \, TFR_t \qquad (7)$$

3. Mortality and life expectancy

The main purpose of computing these projections was to elaborate the significance for future population growth of different patterns of fertility decline and to compare the findings with those of the World Bank and the Population Division of the United Nations. The differences made apparent by that comparison were chiefly intended to reflect the discrepancies between fertility models. For that reason, we endeavoured as far as possible to apply the same mortality assumptions as those of the World Bank. Attaining such a parity in mortality assumptions was made more complex by the fact that the World Bank uses a cross-sectional concept in its mortality assumptions whereas we chose to apply the longitudinal concept. In the former case, mortality and life-expectancy computations are derived from particular calendar years, whereas in the longitudinal approach they are based on particular birth cohorts. As it is possible to transform data between the two concepts, we were able to ensure that the mortality assumptions made herein substantially conform to those made by the World Bank. The inevitable slight differences which occur are negligible, particularly since the influence of mortality on the outcome of a world population projection is in any case much smaller than that of fertility, which was the prime focus of attention.

In the various estimates it has made since 1985, the World Bank began by revising upwards the assumed increase in life expectancy within the world population. However, in its most recent estimate for 1994-95, it has made a slight downward correction:

Life expectancy (both sexes)

Edition	1990	2020/25	2025/30	2025/50	2075/100
1985	64.44	72.05			
1987-88	64.44	71.45	72.32		
1992-93	64.44	72.95	74.04	75.96	82.36
1994-95	64.44	71.47	72.30	74.33	81.68

The assumed life expectancies shown above vary from one year of birth to another, the assumption being that they will increase gradually until the year

2029. The life expectancy for the birth cohort born in 2029, computed from the age-specific mortality probabilities, is 73.8 years, so the underlying mortality assumptions are broadly in line with the 1987-88 World Bank projections written forward to the year 2100, which the World Bank itself approached once again in its own 1994-95 projection.

Though the last birth cohort assumed to have increased its life expectancy is, as stated above, that born in 2029, some of the people involved will actually live as long as the year 2129. For that reason, the life expectancy based on *calendar years* (cross-sectional concept) will continue to increase until 2129, even though the *a priori* life expectancy of the *birth cohorts* was assumed only to increase until cohort 2029.

To make the population projections, one needs not only to know the life expectancies but also the age-specific and gender-specific mortality probabilities, right up to the last calendar year for which the projection is made. The method used to calculate these mortality probabilities is set out below.

Step 1

First of all, the mortality assumptions underlying the World Bank's population projection (1987-88 edition) were established. In its estimates published in 1985 and in 1987-88, the World Bank gave population figures for the years 1980, 1985, 1990, ..., 2030, subdivided into 5-year age groups and also by gender. The survival probabilities for each of the 5-year age groups can be obtained from those figures. For example, those born in the period 1975-79 are referred to as the 1975-79 birth cohort. In the year 1980, they constituted the 0-4 age group. The probability of their survival into the 5-9 age group is found by dividing the size of the 5-9 age group in 1985 by that of the 0-4 age group in 1980. Likewise, the probability that that same age cohort will go on to reach the ages of 10-14 is found by dividing the size of the 10-14 age group in 1990 by that of the 5-9 age group in 1985. The survival probabilities of the world birth cohorts for 1975-79, 1980-84, 1985-89, ..., 2025-29 were computed for each gender in turn by this method. After that, the survival probabilities of single-year age cohorts were distinguished by means of linear interpolation. The survival probabilities (p_x) for individual age cohorts were then converted into mortality probabilities (q_x): $q_x = 1-p_x$. When dealing with the 0-4 age group and calculating infant mortality rates, a more sophisticated, non-linear interpolation procedure was used to reflect the fact that mortality rates fall off much more quickly during the first year of infants' lives than in their second, third and fourth years.

Step 2

Step 1 yields age- and gender-specific death rates for the 1975-79, ..., and 2025-29 birth cohorts, located in the area ABC of the lexis diagram (*Figure 36*). The next task, in Step 2, is to extrapolate the mortality probabilities for the 1975-79, ..., 2025-29 cohorts up to the year 2129 (area BCDE in the lexis diagram - *Figure 36*). The outcome of this operation is shown in *Figures 37 and 38*. As can be seen, the curves showing the mortality probability of the various birth cohorts reduce by stages, i.e. the younger a cohort it is, the lower its mortality curve is placed on the graph. The curves derived from the World Bank's figures which only reached ahead until 2030 would normally end at the age of 50-55 for the 1975-79 birth cohort, 45-49 for the 1980-84 cohort, and so on, i.e. the curves would grow shorter and shorter, the younger the age cohort. This is not apparent in the figure, where the curves shown have all been extrapolated to age 100. However, what is strongly apparent is the important point that the gaps between the curves are especially wide while people are still *young*, i.e. in the part of the curves still covered by the World Bank's figures. With increasing age, the downward staggering of the curves gradually decreases, i.e. the reduction in mortality from cohort to cohort gradually falls off. With increasing age, then, the curves grow closer and closer, which means that the individual cohort branches come together into a corridor which narrows with increasing age (however, please note the logarithmic scale). The upper boundary of this corridor represents high mortality probabilities. The figures found here are comparable to those relating to the life table of the early years of the Federal Republic of Germany (the 1949-51 life table), when living conditions were particularly unfavourable with hunger and destitution. The lower boundary of the corridor represents low mortality probabilties, comparable to the Federal Republic in 1986-88, when living conditions had considerably improved and the life expectancy in Germany had returned to that of other industrial nations.

Step 3

Step 2 yields the mortality probabilities shown in the area ABDE of the lexis diagram (*Figure 36*). The next task, in Step 3, is to derive the mortality probabilities in areas DHI and BEL. The mortality probabilities in area DHI were interpolated from the mortality probabilities of the 1975 birth cohort (area ICD) and the mortality probabilities in the calendar year 1990. The latter are broken down into three parts, namely the mortality probability for the 0-14 age group (area GI), for the 15-74 age group (area IK), and for the 75-100 age group (area HK). We are familiar with the mortality probabilities in area GI from Step 2. Those in area IK were derived from the 1990 and 1995 population figures, and those in area HK were taken from the deaths table for the Federal Republic of Germany in 1949-51. We are also familiar with the mortality probabilities in area BEL from Step 2, which are equal to the mortality probabilities for the 2029 birth cohort, and remain constant for succeeding birth cohorts.

Variants for mortality trends

The mortality probabilities for the 1990-2029 period set out in the lexis diagram (*Figure 36*, rectangle GHEL) represent the **medium mortality assumption**. These are the foundation on which the other two mortality scenarios are based. The **"low mortality"** and **"high mortality"** variants are obtained by decreasing (increasing) the medium variant by 15%.

Figure 36

Areas of the Cohort-Specific Mortality Rates in the Lexis Diagram

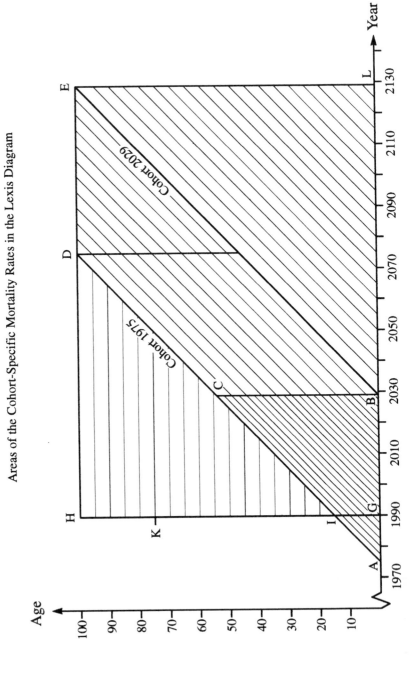

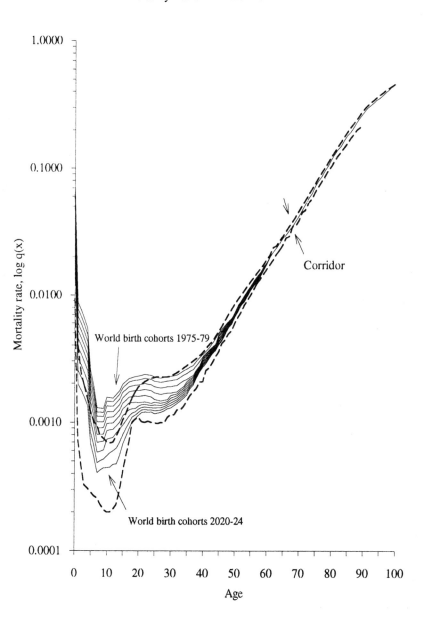

Figure 37

Mortality Rates for Male World Birth Cohorts

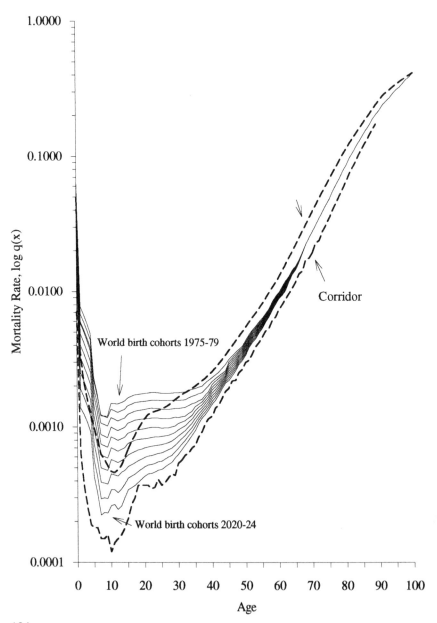

Figure 38
Mortality Rates for Female World Birth Cohorts

Literature

Alam, I.; Leete, R., Variations in Fertility in India and Indonesia. In: R. Leete; I. Alam (Eds.): *The Revolution in Asian Fertility*; Oxford, 1993.

Beaver, S. E., *Demographic Transition Theory Reinterpreted*; Lexington, Mass., 1975.

Becker, G. S., *A Treatise on the Family*; Cambridge: Harvard University Press, 1981.

Becker, G. S.; Barro, R. J., Altruism and the Economic Theory of Fertility. In: K. Davis; M. S. Bernstam; R. Ricardo-Campbell (Eds.): *Below-Replacement Fertility in Industrial Societies*; Cambridge: Cambridge University Press, 1987.

Bernstam; R. Ricardo-Campbell (Eds.): *Below-Replacement Fertility in Industrial Societies*; Cambridge: Cambridge University Press, 1987.

Becker, H. A. (Ed.), *Life Histories and Generations*; Utrecht, 1991.

Bernstam, M. S., Competitive Human Markets, Interfamily Transfers, and Below-Replacement Fertility. In: K. Davis; M. S. Bernstam; R. Ricardo-Campbell (Eds.): *Below-Replacement Fertility in Industrial Societies*; Cambridge: Cambridge University Press, 1987.

Birg, H., *Long-Term Population Projections for the 343 Counties of the Federal Republic of Germany* [Berechnungen zur langfristigen Bevölkerungsentwicklung in den 343 kreisfreien Städten und Landkreisen der Bundesrepublik Deutschland] In: Vierteljahrshefte zur Wirtschaftsforschung, No. 2, 1980; pp. 191-216.

Birg, H., *A Biography Approach to Theoretical Demography*, Materials of the Institute for Population Research and Social Policy, University of Bielefeld, Vol. 23; Bielefeld, 1987.

Birg, H., *Towards a Philosophical Population Theory* [Unterwegs zu einer philosophischen Demographie]. In: Zeitschrift für Bevölkerungswissenschaft, No. 3/4; Bopppard, 1990.

Birg, H., A Biographic/Demographic Analysis of the Relationships Between Fertility and Occupational Activity for Women and Married Couples. In: H. J. Siegers; J. De Jong-Gierveld; E. van Imhoff (Eds.): *Female Labour Market Behaviour and Fertility*; Berlin/Heidelberg, 1991a.

Birg, H.; Flöthmann, E.-J.; Reiter, I., *A Biographic Theory of Demographic Reproduction* [Biographische Theorie der demographischen Reproduktion]; Frankfurt/M./ New York, 1991b.

Birg, H.; Flöthmann, E.-J.; Reiter, I., Biographic Analysis of the Demographic Characteristics of the Life Histories of Men and Women in Regional Labour Market Cohorts as Clusters of Birth Cohorts. In: H. A. Becker (Ed.): *Life Histories and Generations*; Utrecht, 1991c, pp. 145-182.

Birg, H., *Der Konflikt zwischen Spaceship Ethics und Lifeboat Ethics und die Verantwortung der Bevölkerungstheorie für die Humanökologie*. In: Deutsche Gesellschaft für die Vereinten Nationen (Ed.): Dokumentationen, Informationen, Meinungen, Nr. 40; Bonn, 1991d.

Birg, H., *Interpretation of the Differentials in Human Reproduction on the Basis of the Biographic Theory of Fertility* [Differentielle Reproduktion aus der Sicht der biographischen Theorie der Fertilität]. In: E. Voland (Ed.): Fortpflanzung: Natur und Kultur im Wechselspiel; Frankfurt/M., 1992, pp. 189-215.

Birg, H., *Demographic Impact of Political Action* [Demographische Wirkungen politischen Handelns]. In: H.-U. Klose (Ed.): Altern hat Zukunft - Bevölkerungsentwicklung und dynamische Wirtschaft; Opladen, 1993a, pp. 52-79.

Birg, H., Population Theory and Human Ecology. In: A. Blum; J.-L. Rallu: *European Population, II. Demographic Dynamics*, Paris: Editions John Libbey, 1993b, pp. 509-523.

Birg, H.; Flöthmann, E.-J., *Population Projections for the Unified Germany* [Bevölkerungsprojektionen für das vereinigte Deutschland bis zum Jahr 2100]. In: German Bundestags Commission on Climate Change ["Schutz der Erdatmosphäre"] (Ed.): Studienprogramm, Band 3, Teilband 2: "Energie", Bonn: Economica, 1995. A Summary of this Report is included in: Deutscher Bundestag, Enquete-Kommission "Demographischer Wandel", Zwischenbericht, Drucksache No. 12/7876, Bonn, June 14, 1994.

Birg, H., *Dynamics of World Population Growth* [Die Eigendynamik des Weltbevölkerungswachstums]. In: Spektrum der Wissenschaft; 9/1994.

Bongaarts, J., *A Framework for Analyzing the Proximate Determinants of Fertility*, Population and Development Review, 4, 1978, pp. 105-132.

Bongaarts, J., Projection of the Mortality Impact of AIDS in Africa. In: W. Lutz (Ed.): *The Future Population of the World - What Can we Assume Today?*; London, 1994.

Bos, E. et al., *World Population Projections 1992-93 Edition. Estimates and Projections with Related Demographic Statistics*; Baltimore/London, 1992.

Bos, E. et al., *World Population Projections, 1994-95 Edition. Estimates and Projections with Related Demographic Statistics*; Baltimore/London, 1994.

Boulding, K. E., The Economics of the Coming Spaceship Earth. In: H. Jarrett (Ed.): *Environmental Quality in a Growing Economy*; Baltimore, 1966.

Brentano, L., *Die Malthussche Lehre und die Bevölkerungsbewegung der letzten Dezennien*, Königlich Bayerische Akademie der Wissenschaften, Bd. 24, 3. Abteilung; München, 1909.

Bucht, B., Mortality Trends in Developing Countries: A Survey. In: W. Lutz (Ed.): *The Future Population of the World - What Can we Assume Today?*; London, 1994.

Bulatao, R. A. et al., *World Population Projections, 1989-90 Edition. Short and Long-Term Estimates*; Baltimore/London, 1990.

Caldwell, J. C., *Toward a Restatement of Demographic Transition Theory*. In: Population and Development Review, Vol. 20, No. 4, Sept./Dec., 1976.

Caldwell, J. C.; Oruboloye, I. O.; Caldwell, P., *Fertility Decline in Africa: A New Type of Transition?*; In: Population and Development Review, No. 2, 18; 1992.

Caldwell, J. C., The Asian Fertility Revolution: Its Implications for Transition Theories. In: R. Leete; I. Alam (Eds.): *The Revolution in Asian Fertility*; Oxford, 1993.

Carr-Saunders, A. M., *World Population: Past Growth and Present Trends*; Oxford: Clarendon Press, 1936.
Chesnais, J.-C., *The Demographic Transition - Stages, Patterns and Economic Implications*; Oxford, 1992.
Cleland, J., A Regional Review of Fertility Trends in Developing Countries: 1960-1990. In: W. Lutz (Ed.): *The Future Population of the World - What Can we Assume Today?*; London, 1994.
Cliquet, R. L., *The Second Demographic Transition: Fact or Fiction*, Council of Europe, Population Studies No. 23; Strasbourg, 1991.
Coale, A. J., *Population Density and Growth*. In: Science (133), 1961, pp. 1931-1932.
Coale, A. J., *The Demographic Transition Reconsidered*. In: IUSSP Conference, Liege, 1973, pp. 53-72.
Coale, A. J., *A Reassessment of World Population Trends*, Population Bulletin of the United Nations, No. 14; New York, 1982.
Coale, A. J., *Population Trends in China and India (a Review)*, Proceedings of the National Academy of Sciences of the United States of America, Vol. 80; Washington, 1983.
Coale, A. J., Demographic Effects of Below-Replacement Fertility and Their Social Implications. In: K. Davis; M. S. Bernstam; R. Ricardo-Campbell (Eds.): *Below-Replacement Fertility in Industrial Societies*; Cambridge: Cambridge University Press, 1987.
Coale, A. J.; Freedman, R., Similarities in the Fertility Transition in China and Three Other East Asian Populations. In: R. Leete; I. Alam (Eds.): *The Revolution in Asian Fertility*; Oxford, 1993.
Cofala, J., *Modeling Acid Rain in Southeast Asia*. In: International Institute for Applied System Analysis/ IIASA (Ed.): Options, Winter 1993; Laxenburg, 1993.
Condorcet, A. Marquis de, *Entwurf einer historischen Darstellung der Fortschritte des menschlichen Geistes*; Köln, 1977.
Council on Environmental Quality (Ed.), *The Global 2000 Report to the President*; Washington, D. C., 1980.

Darwin, Ch., *The Autobiography of Charles Darwin*. In: Nora Barlow (Ed.); London, 1958.
Davis, K., *The World's Demographic Transition*. In: Annals of the American Academy of Political and Social Science, No. 273 (Jan.), 1945, pp. 1-11.
Davis, K.; Blake, J., *Social Structure and Fertility: An Analytic Framework*. In: Economic Development and Cultural Change, 4, 1956, pp. 211-235.
Davis, K.; Bernstam, M. S.; Ricardo-Campbell, R., (Eds.), *Below-Replacement Fertility in Industrial Societies*; Cambridge: Cambridge University Press, 1987.
Davis, K., Low Fertility in Evolutionary Perspective. In: K. Davis; M. S. Bernstam; R. Ricardo-Campbell (Eds.): *Below-Replacement Fertility in Industrial Societies*; Cambridge: Cambridge University Press, 1987.
Davis, K.; Bernstam, M. S. (Eds.), *Resources, Environment, and Population: Present Knowledge, Future Options*; New York/Oxford, 1991.
Demeny, P., *On the End of the Population Explosion*, Population and Development Review, Vol. 5, No. 1; New York, 1979.

Demeny, P., *A Perspective on Longterm Population Growth*, Population and Development Review, Vol. 10, No. 1; New York, 1984.
Demeny, P., Pronatalist Policies in Low-Fertility Countries: Patterns, Performance, and Prospects. In: K. Davis; M. S. Bernstam; R. Ricardo-Campbell (Eds.): *Below-Replacement Fertility in Industrial Societies*; Cambridge: Cambridge University Press, 1987.
Demeny, P., *Population and Development*, IUSSP Distinguished Lecture Series, International Union for the Scientific Study of Population; Liege, 1994.
Derham, W., *Physico-Theology or, a Demonstration of the Being and Atributes of God, from his Works of Creation*; London, 1713. Reprint: Hildesheim, New York, 1976.
Deutscher Bundestag, Enquete-Kommission "Schutz der Erdatmosphäre" (Ed.), *Schutz der Erde*, Vol. 1 und 2; Bonn, 1990.
Dublin, L. I.; Lotka, A.; Spiegelman, M., *Length of Life*; New York, 1949.
Dupâquier, J.; Fauve-Chamoux, A.; Grebenik, E. (Eds.), *Malthus Past and Present*; London/New York: Academic Press, 1983.
Durand, J. D., *Historical Estimates of World Population: An Evaluation*; Population and Development Review; New York, 1976.

Ehrlich, P. R.; Ehrlich, A. E.; Holdren, J. P., *Ecoscience: Population, Resources, Environment*; San Francisco, 1977.
Engels, F., Umrisse zu einer Kritik der Nationalökonomie. In: K. Marx u. F. Engels: Schriften; Berlin, 1974.
Ensor, G., *An Inquiry Concerning the Population of Nations, Containing a Reflection of Mr. Malthus' Essay on Population*; London, 1818. In: Ch. Sugiyama; A. Pyle (Eds.); Reprint: London, 1994.
Espenshade, T. J., Population Dynamics with Immigration and Low Fertility. In: K. Davis; M. S. Bernstam; R. Ricardo-Campbell (Eds.): *Below-Replacement Fertility in Industrial Societies*; Cambridge: Cambridge University Press, 1987.

Faaland, J., *Population and the World Economy in the 21st Century*; Oxford, 1982.
Feeney, G., Fertility in China: Past, Present, Prospects. In: W. Lutz (Ed.): *The Future Population of the World - What Can we Assume Today?*; London, 1994.
Festy, P., *La Fécondité des pays occidentaux de 1870 a 1970*. Travaux et Documents, Cahier No. 5; Paris: INED, 1979.
Frejka, T., *The Prospects for a Stationary World Population*, Scientific American 228; 1973.
Frejka, T., *Long-Term Prospects for World Population Growth*, Population and Development Review; 1981.
Frejka, T., Long-Range Global Population Projections: Lessons Learned. In: W. Lutz (Ed): *The FuturePopulation of the World - What Can we Assume Today?*; London, 1994.
Fritsch, B., *Mensch, Umwelt, Wissen*; Zürich, 1994.

Glantz, M. H., On the Interactions Between Climate and Society. In: K. Davis; M. S. Bernstam (Eds.): *Resources, Environment, and Population: Present Knowledge, Future Options*; New York/Oxford, 1991.

Grahame, J., *An Inquiry into the Principle of Population, Including an Exposition of the Causes and theAdvantages of a Tendency to Exuberance of Numbers in Society, a Defence of Poor-Laws* ...; London, 1816. In: Ch. Sugiyama; A. Pyle (Eds.); Reprint: London, 1994.

Haeckel, E., *Allgemeine Entwicklungsgeschichte der Organismen*; Berlin, 1866.

Hall, C., *Effects of Civilization on the People in European States, with Observations on the Principal Conclusions in Mr. Malthus' Essay on Population*; London, 1805. In: Ch. Sugiyama; A. Pyle (Eds.); Reprint: London, 1994.

Hardin, G., *The Tragedy of the Commons*. In: Science, Vol. 162, 1968, pp. 1243-1248.

Hardin, G., *Living on a Lifeboat*. In: BioScience, No. 24, 1974, pp. 561-568.

Haub, C., *World and United States Population Prospects*, Population and Environment, Vol. 12, No. 3; New York, 1991.

Hawley, A. H., *Human Ecology: A Theory of Community Structure*; New York, 1950.

Hayflick, L., Biological Aspects of Aging. In: S. Preston (Ed.): *Biological and Social Aspects of Mortality and Length of Life*; Liege, 1982.

Hazlitt, W., *A Reply to the 'Essay on Population'*; London, 1807. In: Ch. Sugiyama; A. Pyle (Eds.); Reprint: London, 1994.

Hecht, J., *The Future Was their Business: Some Examples of Demographic Projections in the Eighteenth Century* [L'avenir etait leur affaire: de quelques essais de prevision demographique au XVIIIeme siecle], European Journal of Population, Vol. 6, No. 3; Amsterdam 1990.

Heilig, G. K., How Many People Can Be Fed on Earth? In: W. Lutz (Ed.): *The Future Population of the World - What Can we Assume Today?*; London, 1994.

Herder, J. G., *Ideen zur Philosophie der Geschichte der Menschheit*; Hildburghausen, 1873.

Hoerster, N., Epilogue. In: D. Hume, *Dialoge über natürliche Religion*; Stuttgart, 1981.

Hoesle, V., *Moral Ends and Means of World Population Policy*, Paper Presented at the 13th World Congress of Sociology, University of Bielefeld, 1994 (to be published).

Hofstadter, R., *Social Darwinism in American Thought*; Boston, 1944.

Hume, D., *Enquiries Concerning Human Understanding and Concerning the Principles of Morals*. Reprinted from the Posthumous Edition of 1777 and Edited with Introduction, Comparative Tables of Contents, and Analytical Index by L. A. Selby-Bigge; Oxford, 1975.

Hume, D., *Eine Untersuchung über die Prinzipien der Moral*; Stuttgart, 1984.

Inoue, S.; Wils, A. B., United Nations Population Projections; In: W. Lutz (Ed.): Future Demographic Trends in Europe and North America: What Can we Assume Today?; San Diego/London, 1991.

Johnson, S. P., *World Population - Turning the Tide. Three Decades of Progress*; London/Dordrecht/Boston, 1994.

Jonas, H., *The Imperative of Responsibility. In Search of an Ethics for the Technological Age* [Das Prinzip Verantwortung]; Chicago/London, 1984.

Jonas, H., *Technik, Medizin und Ethik*; Frankfurt/M., 1987.

Kant, I., *Critique of Practical Reason*. Translated with an Introduction by L. W. Beck; New York, 1956.

Keyfitz, N., *Demography in the Twenty-First Century: The Uses of Forecasting*, International Population Conference/Congres International de la Population, Vol. 1; Florence, 1985.

Keyfitz, N., Toward a Theory of Population - Development Interaction. In: K. Davis; M. S. Bernstam (Eds.): *Resources, Environment, and Population: Present Knowledge, Future Options*; New York/Oxford, 1991.

Keyfitz, N., The Effect of Changing Climate on Population; In: I. M. Mintzer (Ed.): *Confronting Climate Change: Risks, Implications and Responses;* Cambridge, 1992.

Keyfitz, N., Beyond Stable Theory: Comparison of Intercohort Changes in the USSR, USA and Europe. In: W. Lutz; S. Scherbov; A. Volkov (Eds.): *Demographic-Trends and Patterns in the Soviet Union before 1991*; London, 1992.

Keyfitz, N., Seven Ways of Causing the Less Developed Countries' Population Problem Disappear - in Theory. In: European Journal of Population, Vol. 8, No. 2; 1992.

Keyfitz, N., Culture and the Birth Rate. In: IUSSP (Ed.): International Population Conference, Montreal, 1993, pp. 299-323.

Keyfitz, N., The World Population Debate: Urgency of the Problem. In: The Royal Society (Ed.): *Population - The Complex Reality*. A Report of the Population Summit of the World's Scientific Academies; London, 1994.

King, M., *Health is a Sustainable State*. In: The Lancet, Sept. 15, 1990, pp. 664-667.

King, M., *Population Growth, Entrapment and the Sustainability of Health*. In: German Institute for Medical Mission (Ed.): The Consequences of Population Growth for Health Care Programmes; Presentations and Discussions of the Conference held at the Institute on 11th and 12th November 1993, pp. 7-12.

King, M.; Elliot, Ch., *Legitimate Double Think*. Typescript Distributed on the Conference in Tübingen, Nov. 1993.

Kingsley, D. (Ed.), *Below Replacement Fertility in Industrial Societies*, Population Council, New York, 1987.

Knodel, J.; Van De Walle, E., *Demographic Transition and Fertility Decline: The European Case*. In: IUSSP Conference, Sydney, 1967, pp. 47-55.

Knodel, J., *The Decline of Fertility in Germany, 1871-1939*. Princeton: Princeton University Press, 1974.

Kuczynski, R. R., The International Decline of Fertility. In: L. Hogben (Ed.): *Political Arithmetic*; London, 1938, pp. 47-72.

Kuznets, S., Population Trends and Modern Economic Growth: Notes Towards an Historical Perspective. In: *The Population Debate, Dimensions and Perspectives*, Papers of the World Population Conference in Bucharest; New York, 1975, pp. 425-433.

Landry, A., *Les trois théories principales de la population*. In: Scientia, 6 (3), 1909, pp. 3-29.
Landry, A., *La révolution démographique*; Paris, 1934.
Landry, A., *Traité de demographie*; Paris, 1945.
Lee, R. D. et al. (Eds.), *Population, Food and Rural Development*; Oxford, 1988.
Lee, R. D., Long-Run Global Population Forecasts: A Critical Appraisal; In: K. S. Davis, M. S. Bernstam (Eds.); *Resources, Environment and Population: Present Knowledge, Future Options*; New York/Oxford, 1991.
Leete, R.; Alam, I. (Eds.), *The Revolution in Asian Fertility*; Oxford, 1993.
Leete, R.; Alam, I., Fertility Transition of Similar Cultural Groups in Different Countries. In: R. Leete; I. Alam (Eds.): *The Revolution in Asian Fertility*; Oxford, 1993.
Leisinger, K. M.; Schmidt, K., *All Our People - Population Policy with a Human Face*; Washington, D. C., 1994.
Lösch, A., *Was ist vom Geburtenrückgang zu halten?*; Heidenheim, 1932.
Lösch, A., *Bevölkerungswellen und Wechsellagen*; Jena, 1936.
Lutz, W.; Scherbov, S., *Sensitivity of Aggregate Period Life Expectancy to Different Averaging Procedures*, Population Bulletin of the United Nations, No. 33; 1992.
Lutz, W. (Ed.), *The Future Population of the World - What Can we Assume Today?*; London, 1994.
Lutz, W.; Goldstein, J. R.; Prinz, C., Alternative Approaches to Population Projection. In: W. Lutz (Ed.): *The Future Population of the World - What Can we Assume Today?*; London, 1994.
Lutz, W.; Prinz, C.; Langgassner, J., The IIASA World Population Scenarios to 2030. In: W. Lutz (Ed.): *The Future Population of the World - What Can we Assume Today?*; London, 1994.
Lutz, W.; Prinz, C.; Langgassner, J., Special World Population Scenarios to 2100. In: W. Lutz (Ed.): *The Future Population of the World - What Can we Assume Today?*; London, 1994.

Mackenroth, G., *Bevölkerungslehre - Theorie, Soziologie und Statistik der Bevölkerung*; Berlin, 1953.
Mackie, J. L., *Hume's Moral Theory*; London, 1980.
Malthus, Th. R., *An Essay on the Principle of Population, as it Affects the Future Improvement of Society with Remarks on the Speculations of Mr. Godwin, M. Condorcet and Other Writers*; London, 1798. Reprint: Harmondsworth, 1970.
Malthus, Th. R., *An Essay on the Principle of Population*; London, 1803.
Malthus, Th. R., *Versuch über die Bedingungen und Folgen der Volksvermehrung* [The Principle of Population], London, 1803. Translated by F. H. Hegewisch; Altona, 1807.
Malthus, Th. R., *Principles of Political* Economy; London, 1820.
McIniscon, J., *An Examination of Opinions Maintained in the Essay on the Principles of Population*; London, 1827. In: Ch. Sugiyama; A. Pyle (Eds.); Reprint: London, 1994.

McNicoll, G., Economic Growth with Below-Replacement Fertility. In: K. Davis; M. S. Bernstam; R. Ricardo-Campbell (Eds.): *Below-Replacement Fertility in Industrial Societies*; Cambridge: Cambridge University Press, 1987.
Meadows, D. L.; Zahn, E.; Milling, P., *Die Grenzen des Wachstums. Bericht des Club of Rome zur Lage der Menschheit*; Hamburg, 1973.
Meadows, D. H.; Meadows, D. L.; Randers, J., *Beyond the Limits*; Post Mills, 1992.
Merrick, T. W., *World Population in Transition*, Population Bulletin, Vol. 41, No. 2; Washington, D.C., 1986.
Mombert, P., *Bevölkreungslehre*; Jena, 1929.

Neurath, P., *From Malthus to the Club of Rome and Back*; London, 1994.
Notestein, F. W., Population: The Long View. In: E. Schultz (Ed.): *Food for the World*; Chicago: University of Chicago Press, 1945, pp. 36-57.
Notestein, F. W., *The Economics of Population and Food Supplies: Economic Problems of Population Change*. In: Proceedings of the 8th International Conference on Agricultural Economists; New York: Oxford University Press, 1953, pp. 13-31.

Odum, E. P., *Fundamentals of Ecology*; London, 1953.
Oppenheimer, F., *Das Bevölkerungsgesetz des Th. R. Malthus und der neueren National-ökonomie*; Berlin/Berne, 1901.

Peng, X., Regional Differentials in China's Fertility Transition. In: R. Leete; I. Alam (Eds.): *The Revolution in Asian Fertility*; Oxford, 1993.
Plato, *Kritias*, The Collected Dialogues of Plato Including the Letters. E. Hamilton, H. Cairns (Eds.); Princeton: Princeton University Press, 6th Printing, 1971.
Polanyi, K., *The Great Transformation*, 1944. Deutsche Übersetzung von H. Jelinek; Frankfurt, 1978.
Popper, K. R., *Objektive Erkenntnis*; Hamburg, 1973.
Popper, K. R., *Objective Knowledge. An Evolutionary Approach*; Oxford, 1979.
Preston, S. H. (Ed.), *Biological and Social Aspects of Mortality and Length of Life*; Liege, 1982.
Preston, S. H., The Decline of Fertility in Non-European Industrialized Countries. In: K. Davis; M. S. Bernstam; R. Ricardo-Campbell (Eds.): *Below-Replacement Fertility in Industrial Societies*; Cambridge: Cambridge University Press, 1987.
Preston, S. H., Changing Values and Falling Birth Rates. In: K. Davis; M. S. Bernstam; R. Ricardo-Campbell (Eds.): *Below-Replacement Fertility in Industrial Societies*; Cambridge: Cambridge University Press, 1987.
Preston, S. H., Population and the Environment. In: The Royal Society (Ed.): *Population - the Complex Reality*. A Report of the Population Summit of the World's Scientific Academies; London, 1994.

Quinn, J. A., *Human Ecology*; New York, 1950.

Ravenstone, P., *A Few Doubts as to the Correctness of Some Opinions Generally Entertained on the Subjects of Population and Political Economy*; London, 1821. In: Ch. Sugiyama; A. Pyle (Eds.); Reprint: London, 1994.

Robey, B. et al., *The Reproductive Revolution: New Survey Findings*, Johns Hopkins University Population Program, Population Reports, Series M, No. 11; Baltimore, Oct. 1992.

Robey, B. et al., *Familienplanung in Entwicklungsländern*. In: Spektrum der Wissenschaft, Feb.1994.

Sadler, M. T., *The Law of Population: A Treatise in Six Books, in Disproof of the Superfecundity of Human Beings, and Developing the Real Principle of Their Increase*; London, 1830. In: Ch. Sugiyama; A. Pyle (Eds.); Reprint: London, 1994.

Sadik, N., *The State of World Population 1990*, United Nations Population Fund; New York, 1990.

Sadik, N., *Healthy People - in Numbers the World Can Support*, World Health Forum, Vol. 12, No. 3; Geneva, 1991.

Schultz, T. P., The Value and Allocation of Time in High-Income Countries: Implications for Fertility. In: K. Davis; M. S. Bernstam; R. Ricardo-Campbell (Eds.): *Below-Replacement Fertility in Industrial Societies*; Cambridge: Cambridge University Press, 1987.

Schumpeter, J. A., *Capitalism, Socialism and Democracy*; New York, 1942.

Simon, J., *The Ultimate Resource*; Oxford, 1981.

Simon, J.; Steinmann, G., The Economic Implications of Learning-By-Doing for Population Size and Growth. In: European Economic Review, No. 26, 1984, pp. 167-185.

Sombart, W., *Vom Menschen - Versuch einer geisteswissenschaftlichen Anthropologie*; Berlin, 1938.

Süssmilch, J. P., *Die Göttliche Ordnung in den Veränderungen des menschlichen Geschlechts, aus der Geburt, Tod und Fortpflanzung desselben erwiesen*. First Edition: Berlin, 1741. Third Edition: Berlin, 1765.

Thompson, W. S., *Population*. In: American Journal of Sociology, 34 (6), 1929, pp. 959-975. Thompson, W. S., *Population and Peace in the Pacific*; Chicago, 1946, pp. 22-35.

Umpleby, S. A., *The Scientific Revolution in Demography*. In: Population and Environment: A Journal of Interdisciplinary Studies, Vol. 11, No. 3; Spring, 1990, pp. 159-174.

United Nations (Ed.), *The Future Growth of World Population*; New York, 1958.

United Nations (Ed.), *The Determinants and Consequences of Population Trends. New Summary Findings on Interaction of Demographic, Economic and Social Factors*, Vol. I and II; New York, 1973.

United Nations (Ed.), *Global Estimates and Projections of Population by Sex and Age: The 1984 Assessment*; New York, 1987.

United Nations (Ed.), *World Demographic Estimates and Projections 1950-2025*; New York, 1988.

United Nations (Ed.), *World Population Prospects 1990*, Population Studies No. 120; New York, 1991.

United Nations (Ed.), *Concise Report on the World Population Situation in 1989*. With a Special Report on Population Trends and Policies in the Least Developed Countries; New York, 1991.

United Nations (Ed.), *Long-Range World Population Projections. Two Centuries of Population Growth: 1950-2150.*; New York, 1992.

United Nations (Ed.), *World Population Prospects - the 1992 Revision*; New York, 1993.

U.S. Bureau of the Census, *World Population Profile: 1991*, Report WP/91 Government Printing Office; Washington, D.C., 1991.

Van de Kaa, D., *Europe's Second Demographic Transition*. In: Population Bulletin, 42, No. 1; 1987.

Vogel, Chr., Populationsdichte-Regulation und individuelle Reproduktionsstrategien in evolutionsbiologischer Sicht; In: O. Kraus (Ed.): *Regulation, Manipulation und Explosion der Bevölkerungsdichte*; Göttingen, 1986.

Weaver, L. C., Social Security in Asian Society. In: K. Davis, M. S. Bernstam, R. Ricardo-Campbell (Eds.): *Below-Replacement Fertility in Industrial Societies: Causes, Consequences, Policies*; Population and Development Review, Supplement to 12; 1986.

Weizsäcker, U. v., *Erdpolitik*; Darmstadt, 1989.

Westoff, C. F., Reproductive Preferences and Future Fertility in Developing Countries. In: W. Lutz (Ed.): *The Future Population of the World - What Can we Assume Today?*; London, 1994.

Weyland, J., *The Principles of Population and Production as they are Affected by the Progress of Society; With a View to Moral and Principal Consequences*; London, 1816. In: Ch. Sugiyama; A. Pyle (Eds.); Reprint: London, 1994.

Willekens, F., Life Table Analysis of Staging Processes. In: H. A. Becker (Ed.): *Life Histories and Generations*, Vol. II; Utrecht, 1991, pp. 477-518.

Williams, B., *Morality. An Introduction to Ethics*; London, 1976.

Wolf, J., *Der Geburtenrückgang. Die Rationalisierung des Sexuallebens in unserer Zeit,* [The Fertility Decline]; Jena, 1912.

Wolf, J., *Das Zweikindersystem im Anmarsch und der Feldzug dagegen*; Berlin, 1913.

World Commission on Environment and Development (Ed.), *Our Common Future*, Oxford University Press, London, 1987.

Zachariah, K. C.; Vu, M. T., *World Population Projections, 1987-88 Edition. Short- and Long-Term Estimates*; Baltimore/London, 1988.

PART II

Quantitative Projections and Simulations of World Population Growth for the 21st Century
(Graphs and Tables)

Appendix 2

1. Notation used to donate the population projection variants

The projection variants are all donated using a uniform code. Here is an example:

2050.R.H.

In this instance,

2050	=	target year for the attainment of replacement fertility level
R	=	total fertility rate remains constant at replacement level (TFR = 2.13) after the target year
H	=	high mortality variant
M	=	medium mortality variant (as an alternative to **H**)
L	=	low mortality variant (as an alternative to **H**)

If the target year is followed by the letter **B** (below) instead of **R** (replacement), this means that replacement fertility level is intersected in the target year, falling below it in subsequent years. For more details on final fertility levels, see *Appendix 1* (section 1).

In contrast to the variants with linear and S-curve fertility paths discussed in Chapter 4, all of the variants in **Part II** are based on a **hyperbolic** decline in fertility.

For each target year, the variants are arranged in ascending order. First come the three **R** variants (for high, medium and low mortality scenarios), and then the **B** variants (again for high, medium and low mortality scenarios).

2. List of variables

Birth rate (‰)	Number of births per 1,000 inhabitants
Death rate (‰)	Number of deaths per 1,000 inhabitants
Growth rate (%)	Births minus deaths, as percentage of population
Total fertility rate (TFR)	Number of children born per 1,000 women (TFR = $\Sigma\, f_x$, where f_x signifies the age-specific number of live births per 1,000 women aged x years)
GRR	Gross reproduction rate
NRR	Net reproduction rate
IMR	Infant mortality rate
E(0)	Life expectancy at birth (i.e., at age 0)

3. Synopsis of the Variants of Population Projections Aggregate Figures for Males and Females in 1990, 2050, 2100, and 2150

Population in the base year 1990 in millions: Males 2 657, Females 2 617, Total 5 275

	2050			2100			2200		
Variant	Males	Females	Total	Males	Females	Total	Males	Females	Total
				(in thousands)					
2010RH	3 987 427	4 072 119	8 059 546	3 950 044	4 061 086	8 011 130	3 866 596	3 974 718	7 841 314
2010RM	4 099 157	4 164 895	8 264 052	4 115 457	4 206 352	8 321 809	4 113 581	4 203 789	8 317 370
2010RL	4 222 425	4 267 119	8 489 544	4 299 225	4 366 878	8 666 103	4 388 003	4 456 358	8 844 361
2010BH	3 833 365	3 923 148	7 756 513	3 341 970	3 456 633	6 798 603	2 398 234	2 481 231	4 879 465
2010BM	3 943 081	4 014 308	7 957 389	3 488 844	3 586 421	7 075 265	2 556 832	2 629 045	5 185 877
2010BL	4 064 311	4 114 899	8 179 210	3 653 153	3 730 856	7 384 009	2 734 233	2 793 092	5 527 325
2020RH	4 172 905	4 253 717	8 426 622	4 171 462	4 288 362	8 459 824	4 083 404	4 197 589	8 280 993
2020RM	4 287 311	4 348 495	8 635 806	4 346 041	4 441 657	8 787 698	4 344 325	4 439 594	8 783 919
2020RL	4 413 291	4 452 741	8 866 032	4 539 990	4 611 102	9 151 092	4 634 234	4 706 426	9 340 660
2020BH	4 098 328	4 181 765	8 280 093	3 718 401	3 842 229	7 560 630	2 716 301	2 809 738	5 526 039
2020BM	4 211 738	4 275 727	8 487 465	3 880 491	3 985 187	7 865 678	2 895 796	2 977 003	5 872 799
2020BL	4 336 710	4 379 148	8 715 858	4 061 545	4 144 038	8 205 583	3 096 528	3 162 594	6 259 122
2030RH	4 343 965	4 420 708	8 764 673	4 393 043	4 516 224	8 909 267	4 300 494	4 420 750	8 721 244
2030RM	4 460 730	4 517 271	8 978 001	4 577 015	4 677 832	9 254 847	4 575 332	4 675 666	9 250 998
2030RL	4 589 100	4 623 319	9 212 419	4 781 434	4 856 496	9 637 930	4 880 703	4 956 734	9 837 437
2030BH	4 313 544	4 391 410	8 704 954	4 073 768	4 204 468	8 278 236	3 051 461	3 155 445	6 206 906
2030BM	4 429 897	4 487 628	8 917 525	4 249 615	4 359 257	8 608 872	3 252 810	3 343 023	6 595 833
2030BL	4 557 848	4 593 327	9 151 175	4 445 703	4 530 959	8 976 662	3 477 901	3 551 082	7 028 983
2040RH	4 498 847	4 571 610	9 070 457	4 616 900	4 764 480	9 363 380	4 519 154	4 645 523	9 164 677
2040RM	4 617 710	4 669 773	9 287 483	4 810 267	4 916 252	9 726 519	4 808 005	4 913 441	9 721 446
2040RL	4 748 203	4 777 439	9 525 642	5 025 057	5 103 858	10 128 915	5 128 948	5 208 845	10 337 793
2040BH	4 491 206	4 564 263	9 055 469	4 404 073	4 539 801	8 943 874	3 396 453	3 510 837	6 907 290
2040BM	4 609 964	4 662 337	9 272 301	4 592 248	4 705 133	9 297 381	3 620 132	3 719 150	7 339 282
2040BL	4 740 352	4 769 912	9 510 264	4 801 725	4 888 209	9 689 934	3 870 081	3 950 108	7 820 189
2050RH	4 640 383	4 709 280	9 349 663	4 842 977	4 978 070	9 821 047	4 710 891	4 873 463	9 614 354
2050RM	4 761 150	4 808 914	9 570 064	5 045 419	5 155 601	10 201 020	5 043 952	5 154 565	10 198 517
2050RL	4 893 573	4 918 064	9 811 637	5 270 430	5 351 621	10 621 751	5 380 685	5 464 505	10 845 190
2050BH	4 640 383	4 709 280	9 349 663	4 709 709	4 849 054	9 558 763	3 746 965	3 871 479	7 618 444
2050BM	4 761 150	4 808 914	9 570 064	4 908 948	5 023 808	9 932 756	3 993 180	4 100 694	8 093 874
2050BL	4 893 573	4 918 064	9 811 637	5 130 382	5 216 993	10 347 375	4 268 180	4 354 705	8 622 885

Variant	2050			2100			2200		
	Males	Females	Total	Males	Females	Total	Males	Females	Total
				(in thousands)					
2060RH	4 767 565	4 832 840	9 600 405	5 069 330	5 208 622	10 277 952	4 966 840	5 105 729	10 072 569
2060RM	4 890 041	4 933 806	9 823 847	5 280 391	5 393 461	10 673 852	5 284 376	5 400 258	10 684 634
2060RL	5 024 192	5 044 300	10 068 492	5 514 450	5 597 344	11 111 794	5 637 191	5 725 004	11 362 195
2060BH	4 767 565	4 832 840	9 600 405	4 992 458	5 134 355	10 126 813	4 100 201	4 234 511	8 334 712
2060BM	4 890 041	4 933 806	9 823 847	5 201 673	5 317 576	10 519 249	4 368 948	4 484 636	8 853 620
2060BL	5 024 192	5 044 300	10 068 492	5 433 845	5 519 808	10 953 653	4 669 038	4 761 682	9 430 720
2070RH	4 877 438	4 939 536	9 816 974	5 293 774	5 436 021	10 729 795	5 197 720	5 343 064	10 540 784
2070RM	5 001 387	5 041 652	10 043 039	5 512 985	5 627 742	11 140 727	5 530 049	5 651 320	11 181 369
2070RL	5 137 030	5 153 310	10 290 340	5 755 831	5 838 986	11 594 817	5 899 302	5 991 202	11 890 504
2070BH	4 877 438	4 939 536	9 816 974	5 254 442	5 398 086	10 652 528	4 454 230	4 597 969	9 052 199
2070BM	5 001 387	5 041 652	10 043 039	5 472 705	5 588 968	11 061 673	4 745 499	4 868 910	9 614 409
2070BL	5 137 030	5 153 310	10 290 340	5 714 580	5 799 357	11 513 937	5 070 486	5 168 857	10 239 343
2080RH	4 973 447	5 032 733	10 006 180	5 514 490	5 658 651	11 173 141	5 434 190	5 586 153	11 020 343
2080RM	5 098 681	5 135 857	10 234 538	5 741 410	5 856 870	11 598 280	5 781 672	5 908 465	11 690 137
2080RL	5 235 626	5 248 532	10 484 158	5 992 524	6 075 032	12 067 556	6 167 761	6 263 844	12 431 605
2080BH	4 973 447	5 032 733	10 006 180	5 497 751	5 642 532	11 140 283	4 807 666	4 960 454	9 768 120
2080BM	5 098 681	5 135 857	10 234 538	5 724 263	5 840 388	11 564 651	5 121 257	5 252 043	10 373 300
2080BL	5 235 626	5 248 532	10 484 158	5 974 962	6 058 179	12 033 141	5 470 970	5 574 682	11 045 652

Table 1
Projected Total Population
World Population Projection No. 2010.R.H
Decline to Replacement Fertility Level (2.13); Mortality Level: High
- Millions -

Age Year	0-4	5-9	10-14	15-19	20-24	25-29	30-34	35-39	40-44	45-49	50-54	55-59	60-64	65-69	70-74	75+	Total
1990	625	563	528	519	490	436	380	342	282	230	214	186	160	123	87	108	5275
2000	590	645	609	555	518	508	479	424	367	327	264	209	184	149	113	121	6062
2010	548	540	578	637	599	545	508	496	464	406	345	298	229	168	131	149	6639
2020	585	567	539	535	570	628	589	533	494	477	438	372	300	240	163	169	7198
2030	564	574	579	563	534	529	562	617	575	515	468	438	382	301	214	225	7638
2040	564	556	559	570	573	556	527	520	549	595	544	473	409	355	273	289	7913
2050	568	564	559	553	554	563	566	547	515	502	520	547	477	384	292	351	8060
2060	563	561	563	560	554	546	546	554	553	528	487	461	455	443	341	383	8098
2070	562	558	558	558	557	554	546	537	534	535	523	485	427	374	324	439	8073
2080	562	559	557	555	553	551	550	545	533	519	506	491	458	394	305	401	8038
2090	560	557	557	555	552	549	545	542	537	526	505	477	443	398	327	398	8028
2100	559	556	555	554	552	549	545	539	532	523	509	483	442	386	316	410	8011
2110	558	555	554	552	550	547	544	540	532	521	504	481	445	392	316	400	7992
2120	557	553	553	551	549	546	542	538	532	521	504	479	442	390	318	402	7976
2130	555	552	552	550	548	545	542	537	530	519	504	479	441	388	315	402	7959
2140	554	551	550	549	547	544	540	536	529	518	502	477	441	388	315	400	7942
2150	553	550	549	548	545	543	539	535	528	517	501	476	439	387	315	400	7925
2160	552	549	548	547	544	541	538	534	527	516	500	475	439	386	314	399	7908
2170	551	548	547	545	543	540	537	532	526	515	499	474	438	385	313	398	7891
2180	550	546	546	544	542	539	536	531	525	514	498	473	437	384	313	397	7875
2190	548	545	545	543	541	538	535	530	523	513	497	472	436	384	312	396	7858
2200	547	544	543	542	540	537	534	529	522	512	496	471	435	383	311	395	7841

Table 2
Components of Population Change
World Population Projection No. 2010.R.H
Decline to Replacement Fertility Level (2.13); Mortality Level: High

Year	Males Births	Males Deaths - Thousands -	Males Balance	Females Births	Females Deaths - Thousands -	Females Balance	Total Births	Total Deaths - Thousands -	Total Balance
1990	75539	29422	46117	71783	28562	43221	147322	57985	89338
2000	61579	30308	31272	58517	27162	31354	120096	57470	62626
2010	60666	33576	27091	57649	28586	29064	118316	62161	56154
2020	61730	37496	24234	58660	31283	27377	120390	68779	51611
2030	59208	44236	14972	56263	37210	19053	115471	81446	34025
2040	59926	51507	8419	56946	45100	11846	116872	96607	20265
2050	59883	57124	2759	56905	51577	5328	116788	108701	8087
2060	59451	60333	-882	56494	56029	465	115945	116362	-416
2070	59508	61562	-2054	56549	58612	-2064	116057	120174	-4118
2080	59348	60158	-810	56396	57418	-1022	115744	117576	-1832
2090	59189	59812	-623	56246	56663	-417	115435	116475	-1040
2100	59096	60128	-1031	56157	57277	-1120	115253	117405	-2151
2110	58958	59729	-771	56026	56850	-824	114984	116579	-1595
2120	58832	59656	-824	55906	56713	-807	114737	116368	-1631
2130	58711	59575	-864	55791	56698	-907	114503	116273	-1771
2140	58584	59400	-816	55670	56509	-838	114254	115908	-1655
2150	58460	59293	-834	55552	56404	-852	114012	115698	-1686
2160	58336	59168	-833	55435	56294	-860	113771	115463	-1692
2170	58211	59036	-825	55317	56163	-847	113528	115199	-1671
2180	58088	58915	-827	55199	56049	-850	113287	114964	-1677
2190	57965	58789	-824	55082	55930	-848	113047	114719	-1672
2200	57841	58663	-822	54965	55809	-845	112806	114473	-1666

Table 3
Demographic Indicators
World Population Projection No. 2010.R.H
Decline to Replacement Fertility Level (2.13); Mortality Level: High

Year	1990	2000	2010	2020	2030	2040	2050	2060	2070	2080	2090
Birth Rate ‰	27.9	19.8	17.8	16.7	15.1	14.8	14.5	14.3	14.4	14.4	14.4
Death Rate ‰	11.0	9.5	9.4	9.6	10.7	12.2	13.5	14.4	14.9	14.6	14.5
Growth Rate %	1.69	1.03	0.85	0.72	0.45	0.26	0.10	-0.01	-0.05	-0.02	-0.01
Total Fertility Rate	3.400	2.506	2.130	2.130	2.130	2.130	2.130	2.130	2.130	2.130	2.130
GRR	1.684	1.203	1.051	1.035	1.038	1.041	1.038	1.039	1.039	1.039	1.039
NRR	1.5	1.1	1.0	1.0	1.0	1.0	1.0	1.0	1.0	1.0	1.0
IMR - Males	67.2	53.4	39.5	26.3	24.6	24.6	24.6	24.6	24.6	24.6	24.6
IMR - Females	62.8	47.9	31.8	18.8	17.0	17.0	17.0	17.0	17.0	17.0	17.0
IMR - Both Sexes	65.0	50.6	35.7	22.5	20.8	20.8	20.8	20.8	20.8	20.8	20.8
E(0) - Males	65.36	66.12	67.01	67.99	68.39	68.39	68.39	68.39	68.39	68.39	68.39
E(0) - Females	68.43	69.71	71.16	72.53	73.25	73.25	73.25	73.25	73.25	73.25	73.25
E(0) - Both Sexes	66.90	67.91	69.08	70.26	70.82	70.82	70.82	70.82	70.82	70.82	70.82

Year	2100	2110	2120	2130	2140	2150	2160	2170	2180	2190	2200
Birth Rate ‰	14.4	14.4	14.4	14.4	14.4	14.4	14.4	14.4	14.4	14.4	14.4
Death Rate ‰	14.7	14.6	14.6	14.6	14.6	14.6	14.6	14.6	14.6	14.6	14.6
Growth Rate %	-0.03	-0.02	-0.02	-0.02	-0.02	-0.02	-0.02	-0.02	-0.02	-0.02	-0.02
Total Fertility Rate	2.130	2.130	2.130	2.130	2.130	2.130	2.130	2.130	2.130	2.130	2.130
GRR	1.039	1.039	1.039	1.039	1.039	1.039	1.039	1.039	1.039	1.039	1.039
NRR	1.0	1.0	1.0	1.0	1.0	1.0	1.0	1.0	1.0	1.0	1.0
IMR - Males	24.6	24.6	24.6	24.6	24.6	24.6	24.6	24.6	24.6	24.6	24.6
IMR - Females	17.0	17.0	17.0	17.0	17.0	17.0	17.0	17.0	17.0	17.0	17.0
IMR - Both Sexes	20.8	20.8	20.8	20.8	20.8	20.8	20.8	20.8	20.8	20.8	20.8
E(0) - Males	68.39	68.39	68.39	68.39	68.39	68.39	68.39	68.39	68.39	68.39	68.39
E(0) - Females	73.25	73.25	73.25	73.25	73.25	73.25	73.25	73.25	73.25	73.25	73.25
E(0) - Both Sexes	70.82	70.82	70.82	70.82	70.82	70.82	70.82	70.82	70.82	70.82	70.82

Graph 1

Projected Total Population
World Population Projection No. 2010.R.H
Decline to Replacement Fertility Level (2.13)
Mortality Level: High

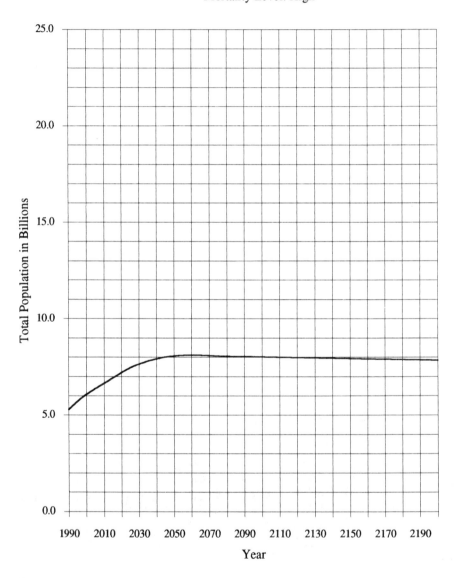

Graph 2

Components of Population Change
World Population Projection No. 2010.R.H
Decline to Replacement Fertility Level (2.13)
Mortality Level: High

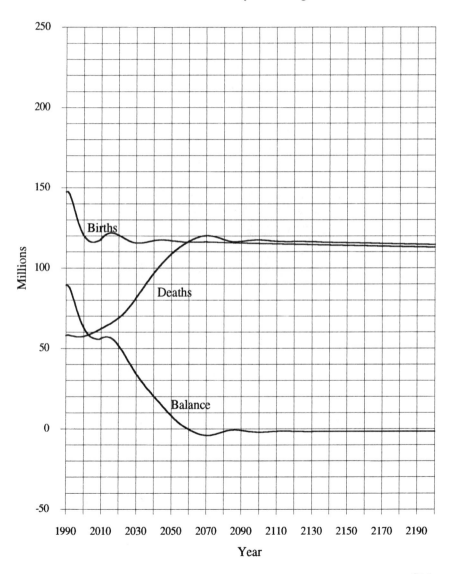

Graph 3

Age Structure of World Population 1990, 2050 and 2100

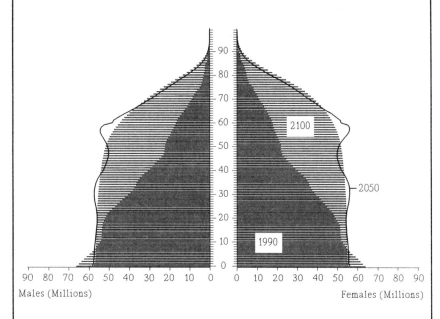

Population Projection No. 2010.R.H.

Target year for replacement fertility level (TFR = 2.13):	2010
Form of Fertility Decline:	Hyperbolic
Mortality Level:	High

Total population:	1990	5 275 Million
	2050	8 060 Million
	2100	8 011 Million

Table 1
Projected Total Population
World Population Projection No. 2010.R.M
Decline to Replacement Fertility Level (2.13); Mortality Level: Medium

- Millions -

Age Year	0-4	5-9	10-14	15-19	20-24	25-29	30-34	35-39	40-44	45-49	50-54	55-59	60-64	65-69	70-74	75+	Total
1990	625	563	528	519	490	436	380	342	282	230	214	186	160	123	87	108	5275
2000	591	646	609	555	519	508	479	424	367	327	264	209	185	149	114	124	6071
2010	550	543	580	638	600	545	508	496	465	408	346	299	231	170	133	157	6671
2020	588	570	543	538	573	629	590	535	496	479	441	375	305	246	169	186	7264
2030	569	578	583	567	538	532	566	620	578	518	472	444	391	312	226	257	7751
2040	570	562	565	575	578	561	531	524	554	601	551	482	421	370	292	339	8077
2050	575	571	565	559	560	569	572	553	521	509	528	558	491	401	314	417	8264
2060	571	570	571	568	561	554	554	561	560	536	497	472	470	465	366	459	8334
2070	572	568	567	567	566	562	554	546	542	544	534	498	442	393	350	527	8334
2080	573	569	568	565	562	561	559	554	543	529	517	505	476	415	330	488	8315
2090	572	569	568	567	563	559	556	553	548	537	518	492	461	421	355	481	8320
2100	572	569	568	566	564	561	557	551	544	536	523	499	462	410	344	498	8322
2110	572	569	568	566	563	560	557	553	545	535	519	498	466	416	344	488	8319
2120	572	569	568	566	563	560	556	552	546	536	520	497	463	415	347	490	8320
2130	572	569	568	566	563	560	557	552	545	535	521	498	463	414	345	491	8319
2140	572	569	568	566	563	560	557	552	545	535	520	497	464	415	346	490	8319
2150	572	569	568	566	563	560	557	552	545	535	520	497	463	414	346	490	8319
2160	572	569	568	566	563	560	557	552	545	535	520	498	463	414	345	490	8318
2170	572	569	568	566	563	560	557	552	545	535	520	497	463	414	346	490	8318
2180	572	569	568	566	563	560	557	552	545	535	520	497	463	414	346	490	8318
2190	572	569	568	566	563	560	557	552	545	535	520	497	463	414	346	490	8318
2200	572	569	568	566	563	560	557	552	545	535	520	497	463	414	346	490	8317

Table 2
Components of Population Change
World Population Projection No. 2010.R.M
Decline to Replacement Fertility Level (2.13); Mortality Level: Medium

Year	Males			Females			Total		
	Births	Deaths	Balance	Births	Deaths	Balance	Births	Deaths	Balance
		- Thousands -			- Thousands -			- Thousands -	
1990	75539	29422	46117	71783	28562	43221	147322	57985	89338
2000	61599	29409	32190	58535	26390	32145	120134	55799	64335
2010	60740	32015	28725	57719	27333	30386	118459	59348	59111
2020	61937	35408	26529	58857	29657	29200	120794	65065	55729
2030	59545	41524	18020	56583	35044	21539	116128	76568	39560
2040	60372	49531	10842	57370	43453	13917	117742	92984	24759
2050	60453	55838	4615	57446	50428	7018	117899	106266	11633
2060	60150	59609	541	57158	55305	1854	117308	114913	2395
2070	60329	61434	-1105	57329	58356	-1027	117658	119790	-2132
2080	60294	60421	-128	57295	57712	-417	117589	118133	-544
2090	60259	59940	319	57263	56785	477	117522	116725	797
2100	60290	60477	-187	57292	57512	-220	117581	117988	-407
2110	60275	60249	27	57278	57304	-27	117553	117553	0
2120	60272	60253	19	57275	57216	59	117547	117469	78
2130	60275	60323	-49	57277	57339	-62	117552	117662	-110
2140	60270	60269	0	57272	57276	-3	117542	117545	-3
2150	60268	60281	-13	57271	57278	-7	117539	117560	-20
2160	60267	60285	-19	57270	57292	-22	117536	117577	-41
2170	60264	60275	-11	57267	57278	-11	117531	117553	-21
2180	60262	60277	-14	57265	57279	-14	117528	117556	-29
2190	60260	60275	-14	57264	57279	-15	117520	117553	-29
2200	60258	60272	-13	57262	57275	-13	117520	117546	-27

Table 3
Demographic Indicators
World Population Projection No. 2010.R.M
Decline to Replacement Fertility Level (2.13); Mortality Level: Medium

Year	1990	2000	2010	2020	2030	2040	2050	2060	2070	2080	2090
Birth Rate ‰	27.9	19.8	17.8	16.6	15.0	14.6	14.3	14.1	14.1	14.1	14.1
Death Rate ‰	11.0	9.2	8.9	9.0	9.9	11.5	12.9	13.8	14.4	14.2	14.0
Growth Rate %	1.69	1.06	0.89	0.77	0.51	0.31	0.14	0.03	-0.03	-0.01	0.01
Total Fertility Rate	3.400	2.506	2.130	2.130	2.130	2.130	2.130	2.130	2.130	2.130	2.130
GRR	1.684	1.203	1.051	1.035	1.038	1.041	1.038	1.039	1.039	1.039	1.039
NRR	1.5	1.1	1.0	1.0	1.0	1.0	1.0	1.0	1.0	1.0	1.0
IMR - Males	67.2	51.4	36.8	23.7	21.4	21.4	21.4	21.4	21.4	21.4	21.4
IMR - Females	62.8	46.2	29.6	16.9	14.8	14.8	14.8	14.8	14.8	14.8	14.8
IMR - Both Sexes	65.0	48.8	33.2	20.3	18.1	18.1	18.1	18.1	18.1	18.1	18.1
E(0) - Males	65.36	66.65	67.98	69.34	70.09	70.09	70.09	70.09	70.09	70.09	70.09
E(0) - Females	68.43	70.20	72.05	73.74	74.76	74.76	74.76	74.76	74.76	74.76	74.76
E(0) - Both Sexes	66.90	68.43	70.02	71.54	72.43	72.43	72.43	72.43	72.43	72.43	72.43

Year	2100	2110	2120	2130	2140	2150	2160	2170	2180	2190	2200
Birth Rate ‰	14.1	14.1	14.1	14.1	14.1	14.1	14.1	14.1	14.1	14.1	14.1
Death Rate ‰	14.2	14.1	14.1	14.1	14.1	14.1	14.1	14.1	14.1	14.1	14.1
Growth Rate %	0.00	0.00	0.00	0.00	0.00	0.00	0.00	0.00	0.00	0.00	0.00
Total Fertility Rate	2.130	2.130	2.130	2.130	2.130	2.130	2.130	2.130	2.130	2.130	2.130
GRR	1.039	1.039	1.039	1.039	1.039	1.039	1.039	1.039	1.039	1.039	1.039
NRR	1.0	1.0	1.0	1.0	1.0	1.0	1.0	1.0	1.0	1.0	1.0
IMR - Males	21.4	21.4	21.4	21.4	21.4	21.4	21.4	21.4	21.4	21.4	21.4
IMR - Females	14.8	14.8	14.8	14.8	14.8	14.8	14.8	14.8	14.8	14.8	14.8
IMR - Both Sexes	18.1	18.1	18.1	18.1	18.1	18.1	18.1	18.1	18.1	18.1	18.1
E(0) - Males	70.09	70.09	70.09	70.09	70.09	70.09	70.09	70.09	70.09	70.09	70.09
E(0) - Females	74.76	74.76	74.76	74.76	74.76	74.76	74.76	74.76	74.76	74.76	74.76
E(0) - Both Sexes	72.43	72.43	72.43	72.43	72.43	72.43	72.43	72.43	72.43	72.43	72.43

Graph 1

Projected Total Population
World Population Projection No. 2010.R.M
Decline to Replacement Fertility Level (2.13)
Mortality Level: Medium

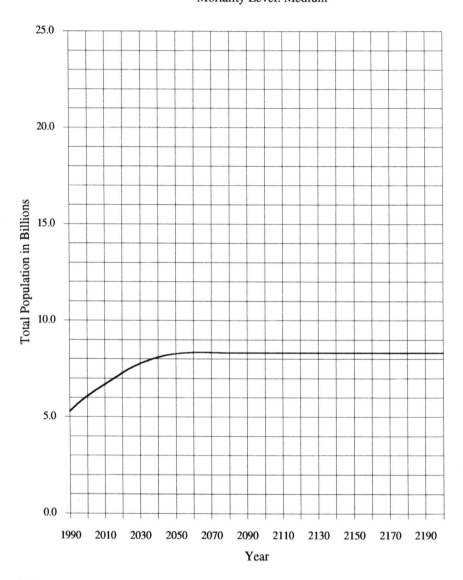

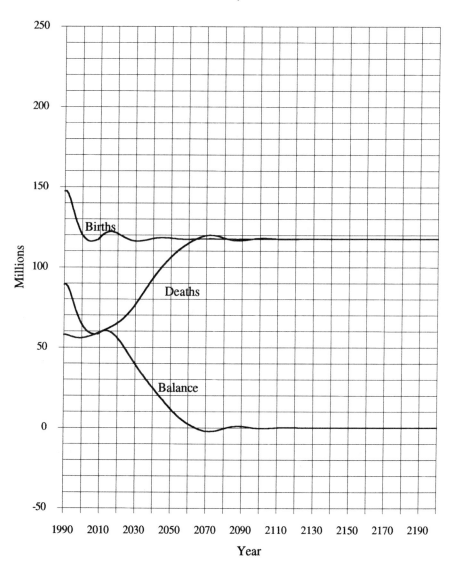

Graph 3

Age Structure of World Population 1990, 2050 and 2100

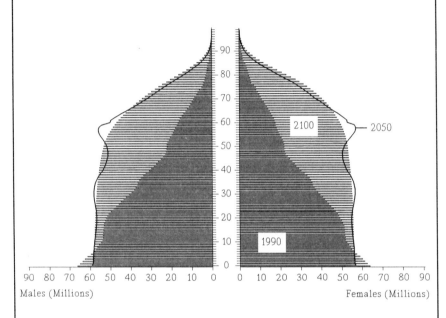

Population Projection No. 2010.R.M.

Target year for replacement fertility
level (TFR = 2.13): 2010
Form of fertility decline: Hyperbolic
Mortality level: Medium

Total population: 1990 5 275 Million
2050 8 264 Million
2100 8 322 Million

Table 1
Projected Total Population
World Population Projection No. 2010.R.L
Decline to Replacement Fertility Level (2.13); Mortality Level: Low
- Millions -

Age Year	0-4	5-9	10-14	15-19	20-24	25-29	30-34	35-39	40-44	45-49	50-54	55-59	60-64	65-69	70-74	75+	Total
1990	625	563	528	519	490	436	380	342	282	230	214	186	160	123	87	108	5275
2000	593	647	609	555	519	508	479	425	367	328	265	210	185	150	115	126	6079
2010	553	545	582	640	600	546	509	497	466	409	347	301	233	172	136	166	6703
2020	592	574	546	541	575	631	592	537	498	481	444	379	310	252	176	205	7333
2030	574	583	587	571	541	536	569	623	581	522	477	451	400	323	239	295	7872
2040	576	568	570	580	583	566	536	529	559	607	558	491	432	386	312	401	8255
2050	582	578	572	566	566	575	578	559	527	515	537	570	506	420	337	500	8490
2060	580	578	579	576	568	561	561	568	568	544	506	484	487	488	394	555	8597
2070	582	578	576	576	575	571	563	554	551	553	545	512	459	414	379	638	8625
2080	584	580	578	575	572	571	569	564	553	540	529	520	494	438	357	599	8624
2090	584	581	580	578	574	570	566	564	559	549	531	507	480	445	385	590	8644
2100	586	582	580	578	576	573	569	563	557	549	537	516	482	434	374	610	8666
2110	587	584	582	580	577	573	570	566	559	549	535	516	487	442	375	601	8681
2120	588	585	583	581	578	575	571	566	560	551	537	515	485	441	379	604	8700
2130	589	586	584	582	579	576	572	568	561	552	538	518	486	441	378	608	8718
2140	591	587	585	583	580	577	573	569	562	553	539	518	488	443	379	607	8736
2150	592	588	587	585	582	578	575	570	564	554	540	519	488	444	380	609	8754
2160	593	590	588	586	583	579	576	571	565	555	541	521	490	444	380	610	8772
2170	594	591	589	587	584	581	577	572	566	556	542	522	491	446	381	611	8790
2180	595	592	590	588	585	582	578	574	567	558	544	523	492	446	382	613	8808
2190	597	593	592	589	586	583	579	575	568	559	545	524	493	447	383	614	8826
2200	598	594	593	591	588	584	581	576	569	560	546	525	494	448	384	615	8844

Table 2
Components of Population Change
World Population Projection No. 2010.R.L
Decline to Replacement Fertility Level (2.13); Mortality Level: Low

Year	Males Births	Males Deaths - Thousands -	Males Balance	Females Births	Females Deaths - Thousands -	Females Balance	Total Births	Total Deaths - Thousands -	Total Balance
1990	75539	29422	46117	71783	28562	43221	147322	57985	89338
2000	61618	28498	33120	58554	25607	32946	120172	54105	66066
2010	60814	30385	30429	57789	26019	31770	118603	56404	62199
2020	62145	33140	29005	59055	27882	31173	121200	61022	60178
2030	59883	38423	21460	56905	32565	24340	116788	70987	45800
2040	60822	47179	13643	57797	41498	16299	118619	88677	29941
2050	61027	54253	6775	57992	49035	8958	119020	103287	15732
2060	60856	58681	2175	57830	54404	3426	118686	113085	5601
2070	61161	61137	24	58119	57938	181	119280	119075	205
2080	61253	60671	583	58207	57973	235	119461	118643	817
2090	61348	60040	1308	58297	56930	1366	119645	116970	2674
2100	61506	60738	769	58448	57663	785	119954	118400	1554
2110	61620	60733	887	58556	57729	826	120176	118463	1713
2120	61746	60803	943	58676	57686	990	120422	118489	1933
2130	61878	61024	854	58801	57936	865	120679	118960	1719
2140	62003	61102	900	58919	58013	906	120922	119115	1806
2150	62131	61232	899	59041	58122	919	121172	119354	1818
2160	62259	61370	890	59163	58262	901	121422	119632	1791
2170	62387	61487	900	59284	58371	913	121672	119858	1813
2180	62516	61617	899	59407	58493	914	121923	120109	1813
2190	62645	61744	900	59529	58615	914	122174	120360	1814
2200	62774	61870	904	59652	58734	918	122425	120604	1821

Table 3
Demographic Indicators
World Population Projection No. 2010.R.L
Decline to Replacement Fertility Level (2.13); Mortality Level: Low

Year	1990	2000	2010	2020	2030	2040	2050	2060	2070	2080	2090
Birth Rate ‰	27.9	19.8	17.7	16.5	14.8	14.4	14.0	13.8	13.8	13.9	13.8
Death Rate ‰	11.0	8.9	8.4	8.3	9.0	10.7	12.2	13.2	13.8	13.8	13.5
Growth Rate %	1.69	1.09	0.93	0.82	0.58	0.36	0.19	0.07	0.00	0.01	0.03
Total Fertility Rate	3.400	2.506	2.130	2.130	2.130	2.130	2.130	2.130	2.130	2.130	2.130
GRR	1.684	1.203	1.051	1.035	1.038	1.041	1.038	1.039	1.039	1.039	1.039
NRR	1.5	1.1	1.0	1.0	1.0	1.0	1.0	1.0	1.0	1.0	1.0
IMR - Males	67.2	49.5	34.0	21.0	18.2	18.2	18.2	18.2	18.2	18.2	18.2
IMR - Females	62.8	44.4	27.4	15.0	12.6	12.6	12.6	12.6	12.6	12.6	12.6
IMR - Both Sexes	65.0	47.0	30.7	18.0	15.4	15.4	15.4	15.4	15.4	15.4	15.4
E(0) - Males	65.36	67.19	69.03	70.84	72.06	72.06	72.06	72.06	72.06	72.06	72.06
E(0) - Females	68.43	70.71	73.00	75.08	76.51	76.51	76.51	76.51	76.51	76.51	76.51
E(0) - Both Sexes	66.90	68.95	71.02	72.96	74.28	74.28	74.28	74.28	74.28	74.28	74.28

Year	2100	2110	2120	2130	2140	2150	2160	2170	2180	2190	2200
Birth Rate ‰	13.8	13.8	13.8	13.8	13.8	13.8	13.8	13.8	13.8	13.8	13.8
Death Rate ‰	13.7	13.6	13.6	13.6	13.6	13.6	13.6	13.6	13.6	13.6	13.6
Growth Rate %	0.02	0.02	0.02	0.02	0.02	0.02	0.02	0.02	0.02	0.02	0.02
Total Fertility Rate	2.130	2.130	2.130	2.130	2.130	2.130	2.130	2.130	2.130	2.130	2.130
GRR	1.039	1.039	1.039	1.039	1.039	1.039	1.039	1.039	1.039	1.039	1.039
NRR	1.0	1.0	1.0	1.0	1.0	1.0	1.0	1.0	1.0	1.0	1.0
IMR - Males	18.2	18.2	18.2	18.2	18.2	18.2	18.2	18.2	18.2	18.2	18.2
IMR - Females	12.6	12.6	12.6	12.6	12.6	12.6	12.6	12.6	12.6	12.6	12.6
IMR - Both Sexes	15.4	15.4	15.4	15.4	15.4	15.4	15.4	15.4	15.4	15.4	15.4
E(0) - Males	72.06	72.06	72.06	72.06	72.06	72.06	72.06	72.06	72.06	72.06	72.06
E(0) - Females	76.51	76.51	76.51	76.51	76.51	76.51	76.51	76.51	76.51	76.51	76.51
E(0) - Both Sexes	74.28	74.28	74.28	74.28	74.28	74.28	74.28	74.28	74.28	74.28	74.28

Graph 1

Projected Total Population
World Population Projection No. 2010.R.L
Decline to Replacement Fertility Level (2.13)
Mortality Level: Low

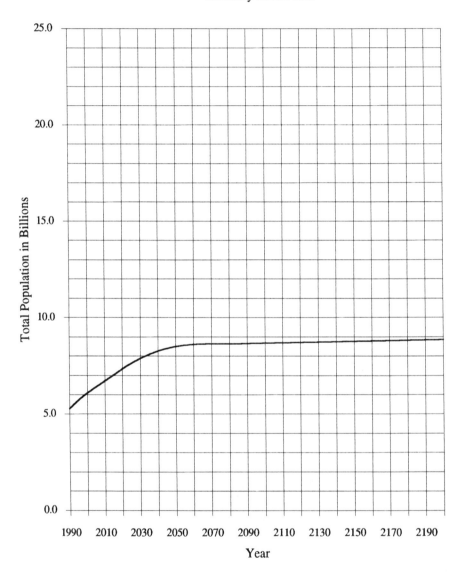

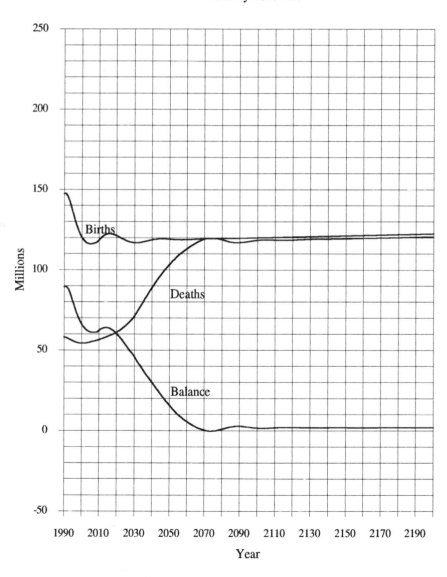

Graph 3

Age Structure of World Population 1990, 2050 and 2100

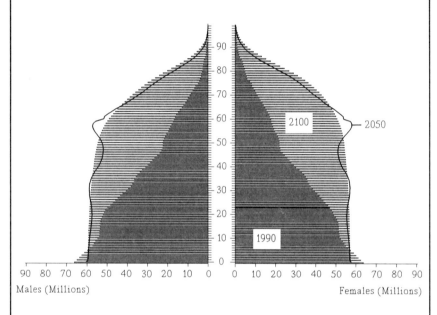

Population Projection No. 2010.R.L.

Target year for replacement fertility
level (TFR = 2.13): 2010
Form of fertility decline: Hyperbolic
Mortality level: Low

Total population: 1990 5 275 Million
2050 8 490 Million
2100 8 666 Million

Table 1
Projected Total Population
World Population Projection No. 2010.B.H
Decline Below Replacement Fertility Level; Mortality Level: High

- Millions -

Age Year	0-4	5-9	10-14	15-19	20-24	25-29	30-34	35-39	40-44	45-49	50-54	55-59	60-64	65-69	70-74	75+	Total
1990	625	563	528	519	490	436	380	342	282	230	214	186	160	123	87	108	5275
2000	590	645	609	555	518	508	479	424	367	327	264	209	184	149	113	121	6062
2010	548	540	578	637	599	545	508	496	464	406	345	298	229	168	131	149	6639
2020	562	556	539	535	570	628	589	533	494	477	438	372	300	240	163	169	7164
2030	530	544	556	552	534	529	562	617	575	515	468	438	382	301	214	225	7541
2040	516	517	525	541	551	546	527	520	549	595	544	473	409	355	273	289	7729
2050	503	507	511	514	521	534	543	537	515	502	520	547	477	384	292	351	7757
2060	485	490	499	504	506	508	514	526	531	518	487	461	455	443	341	383	7650
2070	470	474	480	487	494	498	499	499	502	507	503	476	427	374	324	439	7454
2080	455	460	466	471	476	482	487	490	488	482	475	466	440	386	305	401	7229
2090	440	444	451	457	461	465	470	474	476	473	462	443	416	378	314	393	7017
2100	426	430	436	442	447	451	455	458	459	457	451	435	405	359	297	393	6799
2110	412	416	422	427	432	437	441	444	445	442	434	420	395	352	289	374	6581
2120	398	402	408	413	418	422	426	429	431	429	421	406	380	341	282	365	6371
2130	385	389	395	400	404	409	412	415	416	414	408	394	369	329	271	354	6165
2140	372	376	382	387	391	395	399	402	403	401	394	381	357	319	263	342	5964
2150	360	364	369	374	378	382	386	389	390	388	382	368	345	309	255	332	5769
2160	348	352	357	362	366	370	373	376	377	375	369	356	334	299	246	321	5580
2170	337	340	345	350	354	357	361	363	364	363	357	345	323	289	238	310	5396
2180	326	329	334	338	342	346	349	351	352	351	345	333	312	279	231	300	5218
2190	315	318	323	327	331	334	337	340	341	339	334	322	302	270	223	290	5046
2200	304	307	312	316	320	323	326	329	330	328	323	312	292	261	216	281	4879

Table 2
Components of Population Change
World Population Projection No. 2010.B.H
Decline Below Replacement Fertility Level; Mortality Level: High

Year	Males Births	Males Deaths - Thousands -	Males Balance	Females Births	Females Deaths - Thousands -	Females Balance	Births	Total Deaths - Thousands -	Balance
1990	75539	29422	46117	71783	28562	43221	147322	57985	89338
2000	61579	30308	31272	58517	27162	31354	120096	57470	62626
2010	60223	33558	26665	57228	28572	28656	117451	62130	55321
2020	58789	37362	21426	55865	31192	24673	114654	68554	46099
2030	55299	44051	11248	52549	37091	15458	107848	81142	26706
2040	54270	51204	3066	51571	44909	6662	105842	96113	9729
2050	52621	56675	-4053	50004	51294	-1290	102626	107969	-5343
2060	50748	59665	-8917	48224	55612	-7388	98972	115277	-16305
2070	49246	60487	-11241	46796	57953	-11156	96042	118440	-22398
2080	47634	58321	-10687	45265	56275	-11010	92900	114596	-21697
2090	46064	56706	-10641	43773	54498	-10725	89838	111204	-21366
2100	44581	55438	-10857	42364	53595	-11231	86945	109032	-22087
2110	43114	53563	-10449	40970	51765	-10795	84083	105328	-21244
2120	41696	51952	-10255	39623	50179	-10556	81319	102130	-20811
2130	40327	50343	-10017	38321	48681	-10360	78648	99024	-20377
2140	38995	48699	-9704	37056	47083	-10027	76051	95782	-19731
2150	37708	47141	-9434	35832	45580	-9748	73540	92721	-19181
2160	36461	45612	-9150	34648	44111	-9463	71109	89722	-18613
2170	35254	44119	-8865	33501	42667	-9166	68755	86785	-18030
2180	34086	42677	-8590	32391	41275	-8884	66477	83951	-17474
2190	32956	41275	-8318	31317	39921	-8604	64274	81196	-16922
2200	31863	39915	-8053	30278	38607	-8329	62141	78522	-16381

Table 3
Demographic Indicators
World Population Projection No. 2010.B.H
Decline Below Replacement Fertility Level; Mortality Level: High

Year	1990	2000	2010	2020	2030	2040	2050	2060	2070	2080	2090
Birth Rate ‰	27.9	19.8	17.7	16.0	14.3	13.7	13.2	12.9	12.9	12.9	12.8
Death Rate ‰	11.0	9.5	9.4	9.6	10.8	12.4	13.9	15.1	15.9	15.9	15.8
Growth Rate %	1.69	1.03	0.83	0.64	0.35	0.13	-0.07	-0.21	-0.30	-0.30	-0.30
Total Fertility Rate	3.400	2.506	2.130	2.034	1.998	1.982	1.974	1.969	1.965	1.963	1.962
GRR	1.684	1.203	1.043	0.986	0.972	0.965	0.959	0.957	0.956	0.954	0.954
NRR	1.5	1.1	1.0	1.0	0.9	0.9	0.9	0.9	0.9	0.9	0.9
IMR - Males	67.2	53.4	39.5	26.3	24.6	24.6	24.6	24.6	24.6	24.6	24.6
IMR - Females	62.8	47.9	31.8	18.8	17.0	17.0	17.0	17.0	17.0	17.0	17.0
IMR - Both Sexes	65.0	50.6	35.7	22.5	20.8	20.8	20.8	20.8	20.8	20.8	20.8
E(0) - Males	65.36	66.12	67.01	67.99	68.39	68.39	68.39	68.39	68.39	68.39	68.39
E(0) - Females	68.43	69.71	71.16	72.53	73.25	73.25	73.25	73.25	73.25	73.25	73.25
E(0) - Both Sexes	66.90	67.91	69.08	70.26	70.82	70.82	70.82	70.82	70.82	70.82	70.82

Year	2100	2110	2120	2130	2140	2150	2160	2170	2180	2190	2200
Birth Rate ‰	12.8	12.8	12.8	12.8	12.8	12.7	12.7	12.7	12.7	12.7	12.7
Death Rate ‰	16.0	16.0	16.0	16.1	16.1	16.1	16.1	16.1	16.1	16.1	16.1
Growth Rate %	-0.32	-0.32	-0.33	-0.33	-0.33	-0.33	-0.33	-0.33	-0.33	-0.34	-0.34
Total Fertility Rate	1.960	1.960	1.959	1.958	1.958	1.958	1.957	1.957	1.957	1.957	1.957
GRR	0.953	0.953	0.952	0.952	0.952	0.952	0.952	0.951	0.951	0.951	0.954
NRR	0.9	0.9	0.9	0.9	0.9	0.9	0.9	0.9	0.9	0.9	0.9
IMR - Males	24.6	24.6	24.6	24.6	24.6	24.6	24.6	24.6	24.6	24.6	24.6
IMR - Females	17.0	17.0	17.0	17.0	17.0	17.0	17.0	17.0	17.0	17.0	17.0
IMR - Both Sexes	20.8	20.8	20.8	20.8	20.8	20.8	20.8	20.8	20.8	20.8	20.8
E(0) - Males	68.39	68.39	68.39	68.39	68.39	68.39	68.39	68.39	68.39	68.39	68.39
E(0) - Females	73.25	73.25	73.25	73.25	73.25	73.25	73.25	73.25	73.25	73.25	73.25
E(0) - Both Sexes	70.82	70.82	70.82	70.82	70.82	70.82	70.82	70.82	70.82	70.82	70.82

Graph 1

Projected Total Population
World Population Projection No. 2010.B.H
Decline Below Replacement Fertility Level
Mortality Level: High

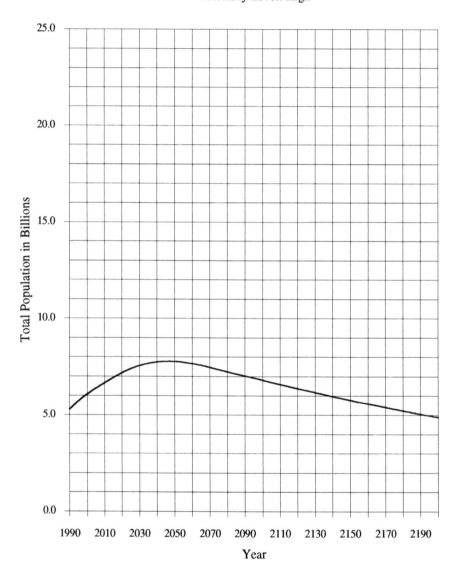

Graph 2

Components of Population Change
World Population Projection No. 2010.B.H
Decline Below Replacement Fertility Level
Mortality Level: High

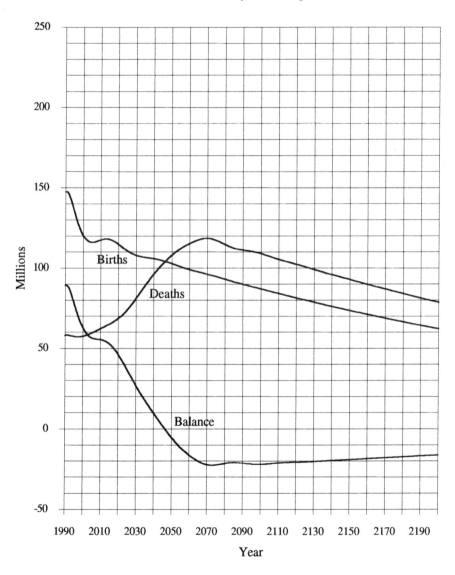

233

Graph 3

Age Structure of World Population 1990, 2050 and 2100

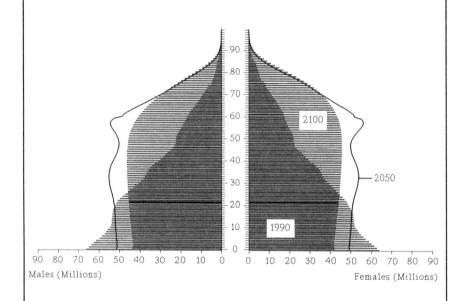

Population Projection No. 2010.B.H.

Decline below replacement fertility level by the year:	2010
Form of fertility decline:	Hyperbolic
Mortality level:	High

Total population: 1990   5 275 Million
                   2050   7 757 Million
                   2100   6 799 Million

Table 1
Projected Total Population
World Population Projection No. 2010.B.M
Decline Below Replacement Fertility Level; Mortality Level: Medium
- Millions -

Age Year	0-4	5-9	10-14	15-19	20-24	25-29	30-34	35-39	40-44	45-49	50-54	55-59	60-64	65-69	70-74	75+	Total
1990	625	563	528	519	490	436	380	342	282	230	214	186	160	123	87	108	5275
2000	591	646	609	555	519	508	479	424	367	327	264	209	185	149	114	124	6071
2010	550	543	580	638	600	545	508	496	465	408	346	299	231	170	133	157	6671
2020	565	559	543	538	573	629	590	535	496	479	441	375	305	246	169	186	7230
2030	535	548	560	556	538	532	566	620	578	518	472	444	391	312	226	257	7653
2040	521	522	531	545	556	550	531	524	554	601	551	482	421	370	292	339	7891
2050	510	514	517	520	526	540	549	542	521	509	528	558	491	401	314	417	7957
2060	492	498	506	511	513	514	520	532	538	526	497	472	470	465	366	459	7880
2070	478	482	488	495	502	506	507	507	510	516	513	489	442	393	350	527	7705
2080	464	468	474	479	484	490	496	499	497	492	486	479	457	407	330	488	7490
2090	449	454	460	466	470	474	479	483	486	484	474	457	433	399	341	476	7285
2100	436	440	446	451	457	461	465	468	469	468	463	449	422	380	323	477	7075
2110	422	427	432	438	442	447	451	455	456	453	447	435	413	374	315	457	6863
2120	409	413	419	424	429	433	437	440	442	441	435	421	398	362	308	445	6658
2130	397	401	406	411	416	420	424	427	428	427	422	410	387	351	297	434	6456
2140	384	388	394	399	403	407	411	414	415	414	409	397	376	341	289	420	6259
2150	373	376	381	386	391	395	398	401	403	401	396	385	364	330	280	407	6067
2160	361	365	370	374	378	382	386	389	390	389	384	373	353	320	271	395	5881
2170	350	353	358	363	367	370	374	377	378	377	372	361	342	311	263	383	5699
2180	339	342	347	351	355	359	362	365	366	365	361	350	331	301	255	371	5523
2190	328	332	336	340	344	348	351	354	355	354	350	339	321	292	247	360	5352
2200	318	321	326	330	334	337	340	343	344	343	339	329	311	283	240	349	5186

Table 2
Components of Population Change
World Population Projection No. 2010.B.M
Decline Below Replacement Fertility Level; Mortality Level: Medium

Year	Males Births	Males Deaths - Thousands -	Males Balance	Females Births	Females Deaths - Thousands -	Females Balance	Births	Total Deaths - Thousands -	Balance
1990	75539	29422	46117	71783	28562	43221	147322	57985	89338
2000	61599	29409	32190	58535	26390	32145	120134	55799	64335
2010	60296	31999	28298	57297	27320	29977	117594	59319	58275
2020	58986	35288	23698	56053	29575	26478	115038	64862	50176
2030	55614	41362	14252	52848	34940	17908	108461	76301	32160
2040	54674	49265	5410	51955	43286	8670	106630	92550	14079
2050	53121	55442	-2321	50480	50180	300	103601	105622	-2021
2060	51344	59020	-7676	48791	54937	-6147	100135	113957	-13823
2070	49924	60482	-10558	47442	57774	-10332	97366	118256	-20890
2080	48392	58778	-10386	45986	56697	-10711	94378	115475	-21097
2090	46896	57100	-10203	44564	54828	-10264	91460	111927	-20467
2100	45481	56047	-10567	43219	54059	-10840	88699	110106	-21407
2110	44076	54310	-10235	41884	52410	-10526	85960	106720	-20760
2120	42716	52760	-10044	40592	50865	-10273	83308	103624	-20317
2130	41399	51256	-9857	39340	49468	-10127	80740	100724	-19985
2140	40116	49688	-9571	38121	47953	-9832	78237	97641	-19403
2150	38873	48197	-9324	36939	46514	-9574	75812	94710	-18898
2160	37666	46735	-9069	35793	45113	-9320	73459	91848	-18389
2170	36496	45300	-8805	34681	43729	-9048	71176	89029	-17853
2180	35360	43912	-8551	33602	42390	-8788	68962	86302	-17340
2190	34260	42559	-8299	32556	41087	-8531	66816	83646	-16831
2200	33192	41244	-8052	31541	39818	-8277	64734	81062	-16328

Table 3
Demographic Indicators
World Population Projection No. 2010.B.M
Decline Below Replacement Fertility Level; Mortality Level: Medium

Year	1990	2000	2010	2020	2030	2040	2050	2060	2070	2080	2090
Birth Rate ‰	27.9	19.8	17.6	15.9	14.2	13.5	13.0	12.7	12.6	12.6	12.6
Death Rate ‰	11.0	9.2	8.9	9.0	10.0	11.7	13.3	14.5	15.3	15.4	15.4
Growth Rate %	1.69	1.06	0.87	0.69	0.42	0.18	-0.03	-0.18	-0.27	-0.28	-0.28
Total Fertility Rate	3.400	2.506	2.130	2.034	1.998	1.982	1.974	1.969	1.965	1.963	1.962
GRR	1.684	1.203	1.044	0.986	0.972	0.965	0.959	0.957	0.956	0.954	0.954
NRR	1.5	1.1	1.0	1.0	0.9	0.9	0.9	0.9	0.9	0.9	0.9
IMR - Males	67.2	51.4	36.8	23.7	21.4	21.4	21.4	21.4	21.4	21.4	21.4
IMR - Females	62.8	46.2	29.6	16.9	14.8	14.8	14.8	14.8	14.8	14.8	14.8
IMR - Both Sexes	65.0	48.8	33.2	20.3	18.1	18.1	18.1	18.1	18.1	18.1	18.1
E(0) - Males	65.36	66.65	67.98	69.34	70.09	70.09	70.09	70.09	70.09	70.09	70.09
E(0) - Females	68.43	70.20	72.05	73.74	74.76	74.76	74.76	74.76	74.76	74.76	74.76
E(0) - Both Sexes	66.90	68.43	70.02	71.54	72.43	72.43	72.43	72.43	72.43	72.43	72.43

Year	2100	2110	2120	2130	2140	2150	2160	2170	2180	2190	2200
Birth Rate ‰	12.5	12.5	12.5	12.5	12.5	12.5	12.5	12.5	12.5	12.5	12.5
Death Rate ‰	15.6	15.5	15.6	15.6	15.6	15.6	15.6	15.6	15.6	15.6	15.6
Growth Rate %	-0.30	-0.30	-0.31	-0.31	-0.31	-0.31	-0.31	-0.31	-0.31	-0.31	-0.31
Total Fertility Rate	1.960	1.960	1.959	1.958	1.958	1.958	1.957	1.957	1.957	1.957	1.957
GRR	0.953	0.953	0.952	0.952	0.952	0.952	0.952	0.952	0.951	0.951	0.954
NRR	0.9	0.9	0.9	0.9	0.9	0.9	0.9	0.9	0.9	0.9	0.9
IMR - Males	21.4	21.4	21.4	21.4	21.4	21.4	21.4	21.4	21.4	21.4	21.4
IMR - Females	14.8	14.8	14.8	14.8	14.8	14.8	14.8	14.8	14.8	14.8	14.8
IMR - Both Sexes	18.1	18.1	18.1	18.1	18.1	18.1	18.1	18.1	18.1	18.1	18.1
E(0) - Males	70.09	70.09	70.09	70.09	70.09	70.09	70.09	70.09	70.09	70.09	70.09
E(0) - Females	74.76	74.76	74.76	74.76	74.76	74.76	74.76	74.76	74.76	74.76	74.76
E(0) - Both Sexes	72.43	72.43	72.43	72.43	72.43	72.43	72.43	72.43	72.43	72.43	72.43

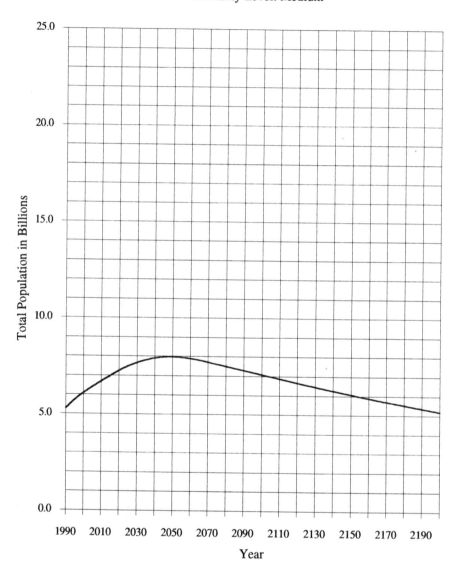

Graph 2

Components of Population Change
World Population Projection No. 2010.B.M
Decline Below Replacement Fertility Level
Mortality Level: Medium

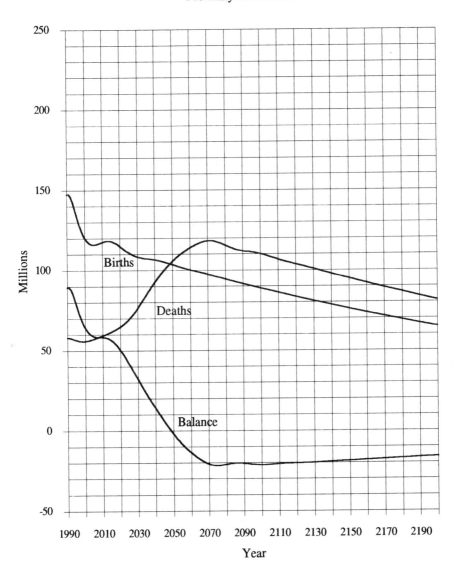

Graph 3

Age Structure of World Population 1990, 2050 and 2100

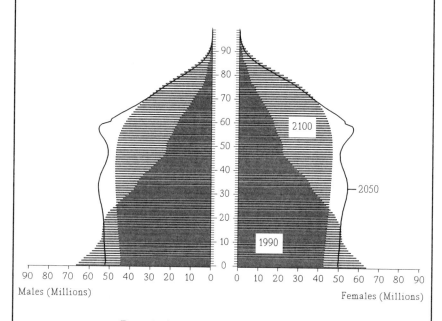

Population Projection No. 2010.B.M.

Decline below replacement fertility level
by the year: 2010
Form of fertility decline: Hyperbolic
Mortality level: Medium

Total population:
1990 5 275 Million
2050 7 957 Million
2100 7 075 Million

Table 1
Projected Total Population
World Population Projection No. 2010.B.L
Decline Below Replacement Fertility Level; Mortality Level: Low
- Millions -

Age Year	0-4	5-9	10-14	15-19	20-24	25-29	30-34	35-39	40-44	45-49	50-54	55-59	60-64	65-69	70-74	75+	Total
1990	625	563	528	519	490	436	380	342	282	230	214	186	160	123	87	108	5275
2000	593	647	609	555	519	508	479	425	367	328	265	210	185	150	115	126	6079
2010	553	545	582	640	600	546	509	497	466	409	347	301	233	172	136	166	6703
2020	569	563	546	541	575	631	592	537	498	481	444	379	310	252	176	205	7299
2030	539	553	564	560	541	536	569	623	581	522	477	451	400	323	239	295	7773
2040	527	528	536	550	560	555	536	529	559	607	558	491	432	386	312	401	8068
2050	516	520	523	526	532	546	555	548	527	515	537	570	506	420	337	500	8179
2060	499	505	513	518	520	521	527	539	545	534	506	484	487	488	394	555	8136
2070	486	490	496	503	509	514	515	515	518	525	524	502	459	414	379	638	7986
2080	473	477	483	488	493	499	504	507	506	502	498	493	475	430	357	599	7783
2090	459	463	470	475	480	484	488	492	496	494	486	471	451	422	370	584	7585
2100	446	450	456	461	467	471	475	478	479	480	476	464	440	403	351	586	7384
2110	433	437	443	448	453	457	462	465	467	465	461	451	431	397	343	563	7178
2120	421	425	430	436	440	444	448	452	454	453	448	437	417	386	336	550	6978
2130	409	413	418	423	428	432	436	439	441	440	436	426	406	374	325	537	6781
2140	397	401	406	411	415	419	423	426	428	428	423	413	395	364	316	521	6588
2150	385	389	394	399	403	407	411	414	416	415	411	402	384	354	308	507	6400
2160	374	378	383	387	392	396	399	402	404	403	400	390	373	344	299	492	6216
2170	363	367	372	376	380	384	388	391	392	392	388	379	362	334	290	478	6036
2180	353	356	361	365	369	373	376	379	381	381	377	368	352	324	282	465	5862
2190	342	346	350	355	358	362	366	368	370	370	366	357	341	315	274	451	5692
2200	332	336	340	344	348	352	355	358	359	359	355	347	332	306	266	438	5527

241

Table 2
Components of Population Change
World Population Projection No. 2010.B.L
Decline Below Replacement Fertility Level; Mortality Level: Low

Year	Births	Males Deaths - Thousands -	Balance	Births	Females Deaths - Thousands -	Balance	Births	Total Deaths - Thousands -	Balance
1990	75539	29422	46117	71783	28562	43221	147322	57985	89338
2000	61618	28498	33120	58554	25607	32946	120172	54105	66066
2010	60369	30370	29999	57367	26008	31359	117736	56378	61359
2020	59184	33033	26151	56241	27809	28432	115425	60841	54583
2030	55930	38284	17646	53148	32475	20673	109078	70759	38319
2040	55081	46951	8130	52342	41355	10987	107423	88306	19117
2050	53626	53913	-287	50959	48821	2138	104585	102734	1851
2060	51946	58173	-6227	49363	54088	-4725	101309	112261	-10952
2070	50612	60312	-9700	48095	57436	-9341	98707	117748	-19041
2080	49162	59233	-10071	46717	57092	-10374	95879	116325	-20446
2090	47742	57498	-9755	45368	55199	-9831	93110	112696	-19586
2100	46397	56623	-10226	44090	54484	-10394	90487	111107	-20619
2110	45058	55072	-10014	42818	53067	-10249	87876	108139	-20263
2120	43760	53576	-9816	41583	51561	-9977	85343	105137	-19794
2130	42499	52181	-9681	40386	50260	-9875	82885	102441	-19556
2140	41268	50697	-9429	39216	48841	-9625	80484	99537	-19053
2150	40073	49274	-9201	38080	47465	-9386	78152	96739	-18587
2160	38910	47885	-8975	36975	46137	-9162	75885	94022	-18137
2170	37779	46513	-8733	35901	44817	-8917	73680	91330	-17650
2180	36681	45181	-8501	34857	43536	-8679	71538	88717	-17180
2190	35613	43883	-8269	33842	42287	-8445	69456	86170	-16714
2200	34576	42616	-8040	32856	41067	-8211	67432	83683	-16251

Table 3
Demographic Indicators
World Population Projection No. 2010.B.L
Decline Below Replacement Fertility Level; Mortality Level: Low

Year	1990	2000	2010	2020	2030	2040	2050	2060	2070	2080	2090
Birth Rate ‰	27.9	19.8	17.6	15.8	14.0	13.3	12.8	12.5	12.4	12.3	12.3
Death Rate ‰	11.0	8.9	8.4	8.3	9.1	10.9	12.6	13.8	14.7	14.9	14.9
Growth Rate %	1.69	1.09	0.92	0.75	0.49	0.24	0.02	-0.13	-0.24	-0.26	-0.26
Total Fertility Rate	3.400	2.506	2.130	2.034	1.998	1.982	1.974	1.969	1.965	1.963	1.962
GRR	1.684	1.203	1.044	0.986	0.972	0.965	0.959	0.957	0.956	0.954	0.954
NRR	1.5	1.1	1.0	1.0	1.0	0.9	0.9	0.9	0.9	0.9	0.9
IMR - Males	67.2	49.5	34.0	21.0	18.2	18.2	18.2	18.2	18.2	18.2	18.2
IMR - Females	62.8	44.4	27.4	15.0	12.6	12.6	12.6	12.6	12.6	12.6	12.6
IMR - Both Sexes	65.0	47.0	30.7	18.0	15.4	15.4	15.4	15.4	15.4	15.4	15.4
E(0) - Males	65.36	67.19	69.03	70.84	72.06	72.06	72.06	72.06	72.06	72.06	72.06
E(0) - Females	68.43	70.71	73.00	75.08	76.51	76.51	76.51	76.51	76.51	76.51	76.51
E(0) - Both Sexes	66.90	68.95	71.02	72.96	74.28	74.28	74.28	74.28	74.28	74.28	74.28

Year	2100	2110	2120	2130	2140	2150	2160	2170	2180	2190	2200
Birth Rate ‰	12.3	12.2	12.2	12.2	12.2	12.2	12.2	12.2	12.2	12.2	12.2
Death Rate ‰	15.0	15.1	15.1	15.1	15.1	15.1	15.1	15.1	15.1	15.1	15.1
Growth Rate %	-0.28	-0.28	-0.28	-0.29	-0.29	-0.29	-0.29	-0.29	-0.29	-0.29	-0.29
Total Fertility Rate	1.960	1.960	1.959	1.958	1.958	1.958	1.957	1.957	1.957	1.957	1.957
GRR	0.953	0.953	0.953	0.952	0.952	0.952	0.952	0.952	0.952	0.951	0.954
NRR	0.9	0.9	0.9	0.9	0.9	0.9	0.9	0.9	0.9	0.9	0.9
IMR - Males	18.2	18.2	18.2	18.2	18.2	18.2	18.2	18.2	18.2	18.2	18.2
IMR - Females	12.6	12.6	12.6	12.6	12.6	12.6	12.6	12.6	12.6	12.6	12.6
IMR - Both Sexes	15.4	15.4	15.4	15.4	15.4	15.4	15.4	15.4	15.4	15.4	15.4
E(0) - Males	72.06	72.06	72.06	72.06	72.06	72.06	72.06	72.06	72.06	72.06	72.06
E(0) - Females	76.51	76.51	76.51	76.51	76.51	76.51	76.51	76.51	76.51	76.51	76.51
E(0) - Both Sexes	74.28	74.28	74.28	74.28	74.28	74.28	74.28	74.28	74.28	74.28	74.28

Graph 1

Projected Total Population
World Population Projection No. 2010.B.L
Decline Below Replacement Fertility Level
Mortality Level: Low

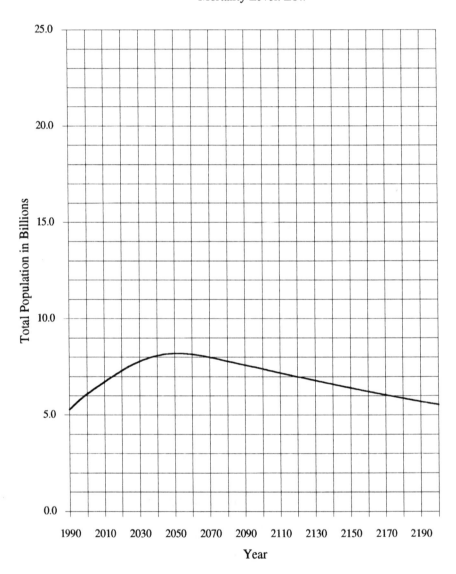

Graph 2

Components of Population Change
World Population Projection No. 2010.B.L
Decline Below Replacement Fertility Level
Mortality Level: Low

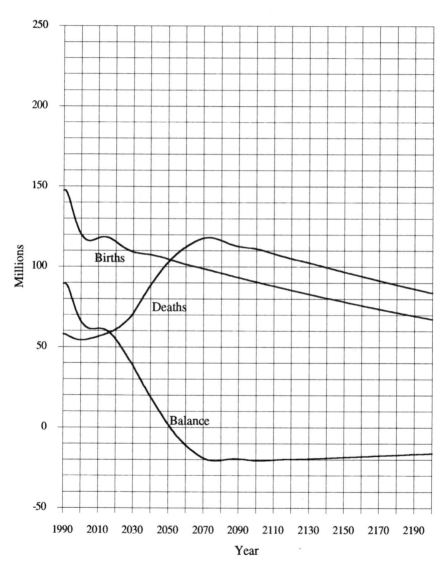

245

Graph 3

Age Structure of World Population 1990, 2050 and 2100

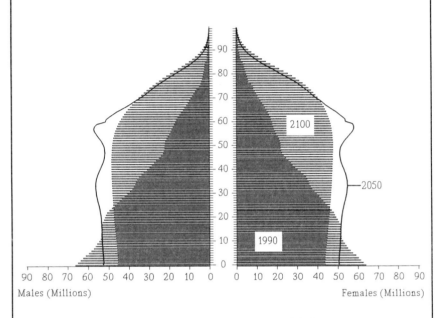

Population Projection No. 2010.B.L.

Decline below replacement fertility level
by the year: 2010
Form of fertility decline: Hyperbolic
Mortality level: Low

Total population: 1990   5 275 Million
2050   8 179 Million
2100   7 384 Million

Table 1
Projected Total Population
World Population Projection No. 2020.R.H
Decline to Replacement Fertility Level (2.13); Mortality Level: High

- Millions -

Age Year	0-4	5-9	10-14	15-19	20-24	25-29	30-34	35-39	40-44	45-49	50-54	55-59	60-64	65-69	70-74	75+	Total
1990	625	563	528	519	490	436	380	342	282	230	214	186	160	123	87	108	5275
2000	630	654	609	555	518	508	479	424	367	327	264	209	184	149	113	121	6112
2010	592	588	617	646	599	545	508	496	464	406	345	298	229	168	131	149	6779
2020	606	596	583	583	609	636	589	533	494	477	438	372	300	240	163	169	7387
2030	599	601	600	592	577	576	600	625	575	515	468	438	382	301	214	225	7887
2040	596	592	594	597	594	585	569	566	587	603	544	473	409	355	273	289	8227
2050	598	593	591	589	589	590	586	576	556	546	555	555	477	384	292	351	8427
2060	595	593	592	590	585	582	581	580	573	556	526	502	486	449	341	383	8514
2070	594	590	590	589	587	583	578	572	567	560	542	511	461	407	347	443	8521
2080	593	590	589	587	584	582	579	573	564	552	537	515	475	414	329	430	8493
2090	591	588	588	586	583	580	577	573	566	553	534	507	470	417	339	423	8477
2100	590	587	586	585	582	579	575	570	563	553	536	509	468	411	336	429	8460
2110	589	586	585	583	581	578	575	570	562	550	533	508	469	412	334	425	8441
2120	588	584	584	582	580	577	573	568	561	550	532	506	467	412	335	424	8423
2130	587	583	583	581	579	576	572	567	560	549	532	505	466	410	333	424	8405
2140	585	582	582	580	577	574	571	566	559	547	530	504	465	410	333	423	8387
2150	584	581	581	579	576	573	569	565	557	546	529	503	464	409	332	422	8370
2160	583	580	580	577	575	572	568	564	556	545	528	502	463	408	331	421	8352
2170	582	578	578	576	574	571	567	562	555	544	527	501	462	407	331	420	8334
2180	580	577	576	575	572	569	566	561	554	543	526	500	461	406	330	419	8316
2190	579	576	575	574	571	568	565	560	553	542	525	499	460	405	329	418	8299
2200	578	575	574	572	570	567	563	559	552	540	524	498	459	404	329	417	8281

Table 2
Components of Population Change
World Population Projection No. 2020.R.H
Decline to Replacement Fertility Level (2.13); Mortality Level: High

Year	Births	Males Deaths - Thousands -	Balance	Births	Females Deaths - Thousands -	Balance	Births	Total Deaths - Thousands -	Balance
1990	75539	29422	46117	71783	28562	43221	147322	57985	89338
2000	66985	30788	36197	63654	27574	36079	130639	58363	72276
2010	64644	33922	30722	61429	28848	32581	126073	62770	63303
2020	64142	37714	26428	60952	31421	29531	125095	69135	55960
2030	63118	44559	18560	59979	37410	22570	123098	81968	41129
2040	63140	51942	11198	60000	45371	14629	123141	97313	25828
2050	63167	57909	5258	60026	52047	7979	123193	109956	13237
2060	62878	61847	1031	59751	56955	2796	122629	118803	3827
2070	62803	64194	-1391	59680	60586	-906	122482	124780	-2298
2080	62676	63759	-1083	59559	60777	-1218	122235	124537	-2302
2090	62521	63258	-738	59411	60075	-664	121932	123333	-1401
2100	62401	63366	-965	59298	60298	-1000	121699	123664	-1965
2110	62266	63140	-874	59169	60090	-921	121436	123231	-1795
2120	62131	62999	-868	59042	59917	-875	121173	122916	-1743
2130	62002	62897	-896	58918	59843	-925	120920	122741	-1821
2140	61869	62744	-875	58792	59694	-901	120661	122437	-1776
2150	61738	62614	-877	58667	59566	-898	120405	122180	-1775
2160	61607	62485	-878	58543	59447	-904	120150	121932	-1782
2170	61476	62348	-873	58418	59316	-897	119894	121664	-1770
2180	61345	62217	-872	58294	59191	-896	119639	121408	-1769
2190	61215	62085	-871	58170	59066	-895	119385	121151	-1766
2200	61085	61953	-868	58047	58939	-892	119132	120892	-1761

Table 3
Demographic Indicators
World Population Projection No. 2020.R.H
Decline to Replacement Fertility Level (2.13); Mortality Level: High

Year	1990	2000	2010	2020	2030	2040	2050	2060	2070	2080	2090
Birth Rate ‰	27.9	21.4	18.6	16.9	15.6	15.0	14.6	14.4	14.4	14.4	14.4
Death Rate ‰	11.0	9.5	9.3	9.4	10.4	11.8	13.0	14.0	14.6	14.7	14.5
Growth Rate %	1.69	1.18	0.93	0.76	0.52	0.31	0.16	0.04	-0.03	-0.03	-0.02
Total Fertility Rate	3.400	2.717	2.287	2.130	2.130	2.130	2.130	2.130	2.130	2.130	2.130
GRR	1.684	1.309	1.118	1.040	1.038	1.039	1.039	1.039	1.039	1.039	1.039
NRR	1.5	1.2	1.1	1.0	1.0	1.0	1.0	1.0	1.0	1.0	1.0
IMR - Males	67.2	53.4	39.5	26.3	24.6	24.6	24.6	24.6	24.6	24.6	24.6
IMR - Females	62.8	47.9	31.8	18.8	17.0	17.0	17.0	17.0	17.0	17.0	17.0
IMR - Both Sexes	65.0	50.6	35.7	22.5	20.8	20.8	20.8	20.8	20.8	20.8	20.8
E(0) - Males	65.36	66.12	67.01	67.99	68.39	68.39	68.39	68.39	68.39	68.39	68.39
E(0) - Females	68.43	69.71	71.16	72.53	73.25	73.25	73.25	73.25	73.25	73.25	73.25
E(0) - Both Sexes	66.90	67.91	69.08	70.26	70.82	70.82	70.82	70.82	70.82	70.82	70.82

Year	2100	2110	2120	2130	2140	2150	2160	2170	2180	2190	2200
Birth Rate ‰	14.4	14.4	14.4	14.4	14.4	14.4	14.4	14.4	14.4	14.4	14.4
Death Rate ‰	14.6	14.6	14.6	14.6	14.6	14.6	14.6	14.6	14.6	14.6	14.6
Growth Rate %	-0.02	-0.02	-0.02	-0.02	-0.02	-0.02	-0.02	-0.02	-0.02	-0.02	-0.02
Total Fertility Rate	2.130	2.130	2.130	2.130	2.130	2.130	2.130	2.130	2.130	2.130	2.130
GRR	1.039	1.039	1.039	1.039	1.039	1.039	1.039	1.039	1.039	1.039	1.039
NRR	1.0	1.0	1.0	1.0	1.0	1.0	1.0	1.0	1.0	1.0	1.0
IMR - Males	24.6	24.6	24.6	24.6	24.6	24.6	24.6	24.6	24.6	24.6	24.6
IMR - Females	17.0	17.0	17.0	17.0	17.0	17.0	17.0	17.0	17.0	17.0	17.0
IMR - Both Sexes	20.8	20.8	20.8	20.8	20.8	20.8	20.8	20.8	20.8	20.8	20.8
E(0) - Males	68.39	68.39	68.39	68.39	68.39	68.39	68.39	68.39	68.39	68.39	68.39
E(0) - Females	73.25	73.25	73.25	73.25	73.25	73.25	73.25	73.25	73.25	73.25	73.25
E(0) - Both Sexes	70.82	70.82	70.82	70.82	70.82	70.82	70.82	70.82	70.82	70.82	70.82

Graph 1

Projected Total Population
World Population Projection No. 2020.R.H
Decline to Replacement Fertility Level (2.13)
Mortality Level: High

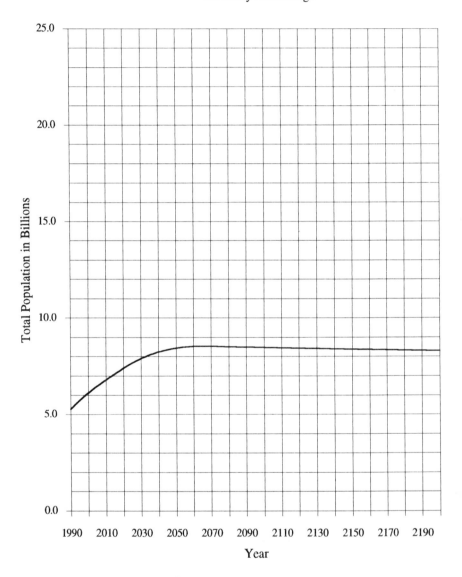

Graph 2

Components of Population Change
World Population Projection No. 2020.R.H
Decline to Replacement Fertility Level (2.13)
Mortality Level: High

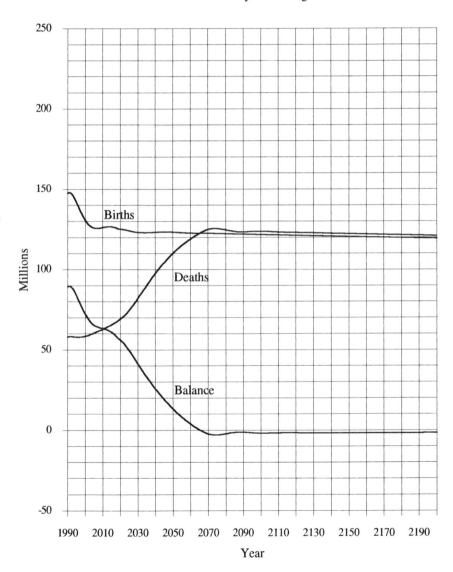

Graph 3

Age Structure of World Population 1990, 2050 and 2100

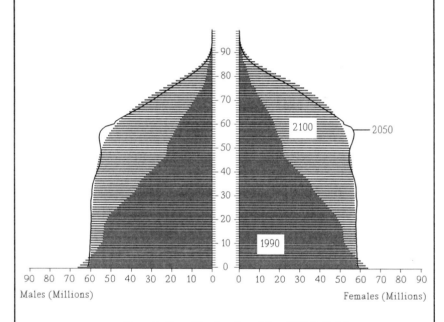

Population Projection No. 2020.R.H.

Target year for replacement fertility
level (TFR = 2.13): 2020
Form of fertility decline: Hyperbolic
Mortality level: High

Total population: 1990 5 275 Million
2050 8 427 Million
2100 8 460 Million

Table 1
Projected Total Population
World Population Projection No. 2020.R.M
Decline to Replacement Fertility Level (2.13); Mortality Level: Medium
- Millions -

Age Year	0-4	5-9	10-14	15-19	20-24	25-29	30-34	35-39	40-44	45-49	50-54	55-59	60-64	65-69	70-74	75+	Total
1990	625	563	528	519	490	436	380	342	282	230	214	186	160	123	87	108	5275
2000	632	655	609	555	519	508	479	424	367	327	264	209	185	149	114	124	6120
2010	594	591	619	647	600	545	508	496	465	408	346	299	231	170	133	157	6811
2020	610	600	586	586	612	638	590	535	496	479	441	375	305	246	169	186	7454
2030	605	606	604	596	581	579	604	628	578	518	472	444	391	312	226	257	8002
2040	603	599	600	602	599	590	574	571	592	609	551	482	421	370	292	339	8394
2050	605	601	598	596	595	596	592	582	562	554	565	566	491	401	314	417	8636
2060	604	601	601	598	593	590	588	588	580	564	536	514	503	471	366	459	8758
2070	604	600	599	598	596	592	586	581	576	570	554	524	478	428	374	531	8794
2080	605	601	599	597	595	592	589	583	575	563	550	530	493	437	356	521	8786
2090	604	601	600	598	595	591	588	584	577	566	548	523	490	441	368	513	8786
2100	604	601	600	598	595	592	588	583	576	566	551	526	488	436	365	521	8788
2110	604	601	600	598	595	592	588	583	576	565	549	526	490	438	364	518	8786
2120	604	601	600	598	595	592	588	583	576	566	549	525	489	438	366	517	8786
2130	604	601	600	598	595	592	588	583	576	566	550	526	489	437	365	518	8786
2140	604	601	600	598	595	592	588	583	576	565	549	525	490	438	365	518	8786
2150	604	601	600	598	595	592	588	583	576	565	549	525	489	438	365	518	8785
2160	604	601	599	598	595	592	588	583	576	565	549	525	489	438	365	518	8785
2170	604	601	599	598	595	592	588	583	576	565	549	525	489	438	365	518	8785
2180	604	601	599	598	595	592	588	583	576	565	549	525	489	438	365	518	8785
2190	604	601	599	598	595	592	588	583	576	565	549	525	489	438	365	518	8784
2200	604	601	599	598	595	591	588	583	576	565	549	525	489	438	365	518	8784

Table 2
Components of Population Change
World Population Projection No. 2020.R.M
Decline to Replacement Fertility Level (2.13); Mortality Level: Medium

Year	Males Births	Males Deaths - Thousands -	Males Balance	Females Births	Females Deaths - Thousands -	Females Balance	Total Births	Total Deaths - Thousands -	Total Balance
1990	75539	29422	46117	71783	28562	43221	147322	57985	89338
2000	67006	29872	37134	63674	26788	36886	130680	56660	74020
2010	64723	32338	32385	61504	27578	33926	126226	59915	66311
2020	64360	35606	28754	61159	29781	31378	125519	65387	60132
2030	63478	41807	21671	60321	35219	25102	123799	77025	46774
2040	63612	49913	13699	60448	43691	16757	124060	93604	30456
2050	63770	56531	7239	60598	50841	9757	124368	107372	16995
2060	63618	60966	2652	60454	56126	4328	124072	117092	6981
2070	63671	63868	-197	60504	60148	356	124175	124016	159
2080	63676	63951	-275	60510	60937	-428	124186	124889	-703
2090	63652	63461	191	60487	60265	222	124139	123726	412
2100	63663	63725	-62	60497	60564	-67	124160	124289	-129
2110	63658	63675	-16	60493	60540	-47	124151	124214	-63
2120	63654	63646	8	60488	60467	21	124142	124113	29
2130	63654	63682	-28	60489	60518	-30	124143	124201	-58
2140	63651	63663	-12	60486	60502	-16	124137	124165	-28
2150	63649	63661	-12	60484	60493	-10	124132	124154	-22
2160	63647	63664	-17	60482	60500	-18	124129	124164	-35
2170	63645	63658	-14	60480	60494	-14	124124	124152	-28
2180	63643	63657	-15	60478	60492	-14	124120	124149	-29
2190	63641	63656	-15	60476	60491	-15	124116	124147	-30
2200	63638	63653	-14	60474	60488	-15	124112	124141	-29

Table 3
Demographic Indicators
World Population Projection No. 2020.R.M
Decline to Replacement Fertility Level (2.13); Mortality Level: Medium

Year	1990	2000	2010	2020	2030	2040	2050	2060	2070	2080	2090
Birth Rate ‰	27.9	21.4	18.5	16.8	15.5	14.8	14.4	14.2	14.1	14.1	14.1
Death Rate ‰	11.0	9.3	8.8	8.8	9.6	11.2	12.4	13.4	14.1	14.2	14.1
Growth Rate %	1.69	1.21	0.97	0.81	0.58	0.36	0.20	0.08	0.00	-0.01	0.00
Total Fertility Rate	3.400	2.717	2.287	2.130	2.130	2.130	2.130	2.130	2.130	2.130	2.130
GRR	1.684	1.309	1.118	1.040	1.038	1.040	1.039	1.039	1.039	1.039	1.039
NRR	1.5	1.2	1.1	1.0	1.0	1.0	1.0	1.0	1.0	1.0	1.0
IMR - Males	67.2	51.4	36.8	23.7	21.4	21.4	21.4	21.4	21.4	21.4	21.4
IMR - Females	62.8	46.2	29.6	16.9	14.8	14.8	14.8	14.8	14.8	14.8	14.8
IMR - Both Sexes	65.0	48.8	33.2	20.3	18.1	18.1	18.1	18.1	18.1	18.1	18.1
E(0) - Males	65.36	66.65	67.98	69.34	70.09	70.09	70.09	70.09	70.09	70.09	70.09
E(0) - Females	68.43	70.20	72.05	73.74	74.76	74.76	74.76	74.76	74.76	74.76	74.76
E(0) - Both Sexes	66.90	68.43	70.02	71.54	72.43	72.43	72.43	72.43	72.43	72.43	72.43

Year	2100	2110	2120	2130	2140	2150	2160	2170	2180	2190	2200
Birth Rate ‰	14.1	14.1	14.1	14.1	14.1	14.1	14.1	14.1	14.1	14.1	14.1
Death Rate ‰	14.1	14.1	14.1	14.1	14.1	14.1	14.1	14.1	14.1	14.1	14.1
Growth Rate %	0.00	0.00	0.00	0.00	0.00	0.00	0.00	0.00	0.00	0.00	0.00
Total Fertility Rate	2.130	2.130	2.130	2.130	2.130	2.130	2.130	2.130	2.130	2.130	2.130
GRR	1.039	1.039	1.039	1.039	1.039	1.039	1.039	1.039	1.039	1.039	1.039
NRR	1.0	1.0	1.0	1.0	1.0	1.0	1.0	1.0	1.0	1.0	1.0
IMR - Males	21.4	21.4	21.4	21.4	21.4	21.4	21.4	21.4	21.4	21.4	21.4
IMR - Females	14.8	14.8	14.8	14.8	14.8	14.8	14.8	14.8	14.8	14.8	14.8
IMR - Both Sexes	18.1	18.1	18.1	18.1	18.1	18.1	18.1	18.1	18.1	18.1	18.1
E(0) - Males	70.09	70.09	70.09	70.09	70.09	70.09	70.09	70.09	70.09	70.09	70.09
E(0) - Females	74.76	74.76	74.76	74.76	74.76	74.76	74.76	74.76	74.76	74.76	74.76
E(0) - Both Sexes	72.43	72.43	72.43	72.43	72.43	72.43	72.43	72.43	72.43	72.43	72.43

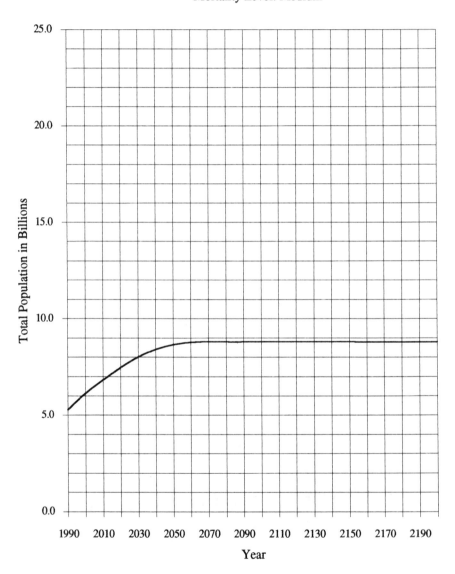

Graph 1

Projected Total Population
World Population Projection No. 2020.R.M
Decline to Replacement Fertility Level (2.13)
Mortality Level: Medium

Graph 2

Components of Population Change
World Population Projection No. 2020.R.M
Decline to Replacement Fertility Level (2.13)
Mortality Level: Medium

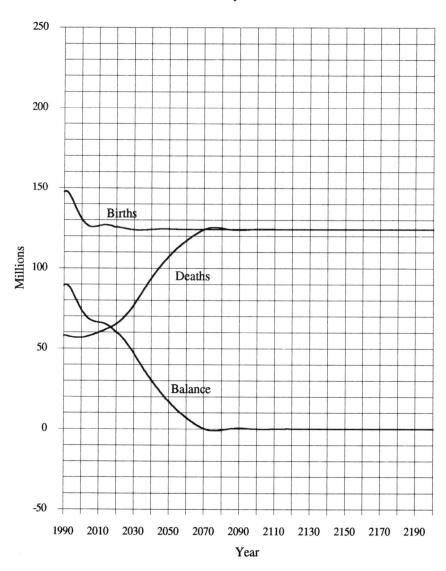

Graph 3

Age Structure of World Population 1990, 2050 and 2100

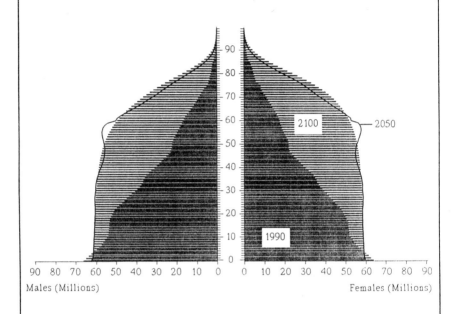

Population Projection No. 2020.R.M.

Target year for replacement fertility
level (TFR = 2.13): 2020
Form of fertility decline: Hyperbolic
Mortality level: Medium

Total population: 1990 5 275 Million
2050 8 636 Million
2100 8 788 Million

Table 1
Projected Total Population
World Population Projection No. 2020.R.L
Decline to Replacement Fertility Level (2.13); Mortality Level: Low

- Millions -

Age Year	0-4	5-9	10-14	15-19	20-24	25-29	30-34	35-39	40-44	45-49	50-54	55-59	60-64	65-69	70-74	75+	Total
1990	625	563	528	519	490	436	380	342	282	230	214	186	160	123	87	108	5275
2000	633	656	609	555	519	508	479	425	367	328	265	210	185	150	115	126	6129
2010	597	594	621	649	600	546	509	497	466	409	347	301	233	172	136	166	6844
2020	613	604	589	589	615	640	592	537	498	481	444	379	310	252	176	205	7524
2030	610	610	609	601	585	583	608	632	581	522	477	451	400	323	239	295	8125
2040	609	605	606	608	604	595	579	576	597	615	558	491	432	386	312	401	8576
2050	613	609	605	603	602	603	598	588	569	561	574	578	506	420	337	500	8866
2060	613	611	609	606	601	597	596	595	588	573	547	527	520	495	394	555	9028
2070	615	611	609	608	605	601	595	590	586	580	565	538	495	451	405	643	9096
2080	616	613	611	608	605	603	599	593	585	575	563	545	512	461	386	638	9112
2090	617	614	612	610	606	603	599	595	589	578	562	540	510	466	399	629	9129
2100	619	615	613	611	608	605	600	595	589	580	566	543	509	462	397	639	9151
2110	620	616	615	612	609	606	602	597	590	580	566	545	513	465	397	637	9169
2120	621	617	616	614	610	607	603	598	592	582	567	545	513	466	399	638	9188
2130	622	619	617	615	612	608	604	599	593	583	568	546	514	466	399	641	9207
2140	624	620	618	616	613	609	606	601	594	584	569	548	515	468	400	641	9226
2150	625	621	620	617	614	611	607	602	595	585	571	549	516	469	401	643	9245
2160	626	623	621	619	615	612	608	603	596	586	572	550	517	469	402	644	9264
2170	628	624	622	620	617	613	609	604	598	588	573	551	518	471	403	646	9283
2180	629	625	623	621	618	615	611	606	599	589	574	552	519	471	404	647	9302
2190	630	626	625	622	619	616	612	607	600	590	575	553	520	472	404	648	9321
2200	632	628	626	624	621	617	613	608	601	591	576	554	521	473	405	650	9341

Table 2
Components of Population Change
World Population Projection No. 2020.R.L
Decline to Replacement Fertility Level (2.13); Mortality Level: Low

Year	Births	Males Deaths - Thousands -	Balance	Births	Females Deaths - Thousands -	Balance	Births	Total Deaths - Thousands -	Balance
1990	75539	29422	46117	71783	28562	43221	147322	57985	89338
2000	67027	28945	38082	63694	25990	37704	130721	54935	75786
2010	64801	30685	34117	61579	26246	35332	126380	56931	69449
2020	64578	33317	31261	61366	27993	33373	125944	61309	64635
2030	63839	38665	25175	60665	32714	27951	124504	71379	53125
2040	64086	47507	16579	60899	41702	19197	124985	89210	35776
2050	64377	54852	9526	61176	49390	11786	125553	104241	21312
2060	64366	59869	4497	61165	55116	6049	125531	114985	10546
2070	64550	63339	1211	61340	59530	1810	125890	122869	3021
2080	64691	64074	618	61474	61012	463	126166	125085	1080
2090	64803	63635	1168	61580	60459	1121	126383	124094	2289
2100	64949	64010	939	61719	60767	952	126668	124777	1891
2110	65081	64160	921	61844	60947	897	126925	125106	1818
2120	65212	64247	965	61969	60981	988	127181	125229	1953
2130	65349	64420	929	62099	61152	947	127448	125572	1876
2140	65483	64542	941	62226	61275	951	127709	125816	1892
2150	65617	64670	948	62354	61389	965	127971	126059	1912
2160	65753	64809	943	62483	61525	958	128236	126334	1901
2170	65888	64940	948	62611	61649	962	128499	126589	1911
2180	66024	65074	950	62740	61775	965	128764	126849	1915
2190	66160	65209	951	62870	61904	966	129029	127112	1917
2200	66296	65342	954	62999	62030	969	129295	127373	1922

Table 3
Demographic Indicators
World Population Projection No. 2020.R.L
Decline to Replacement Fertility Level (2.13); Mortality Level: Low

Year	1990	2000	2010	2020	2030	2040	2050	2060	2070	2080	2090
Birth Rate ‰	27.9	21.3	18.5	16.7	15.3	14.6	14.2	13.9	13.8	13.8	13.8
Death Rate ‰	11.0	9.0	8.3	8.1	8.8	10.4	11.8	12.7	13.5	13.7	13.6
Growth Rate %	1.69	1.24	1.01	0.86	0.65	0.42	0.24	0.12	0.03	0.01	0.03
Total Fertility Rate	3.400	2.717	2.287	2.130	2.130	2.130	2.130	2.130	2.130	2.130	2.130
GRR	1.684	1.309	1.118	1.040	1.038	1.040	1.039	1.039	1.039	1.039	1.039
NRR	1.5	1.2	1.1	1.0	1.0	1.0	1.0	1.0	1.0	1.0	1.0
IMR - Males	67.2	49.5	34.0	21.0	18.2	18.2	18.2	18.2	18.2	18.2	18.2
IMR - Females	62.8	44.4	27.4	15.0	12.6	12.6	12.6	12.6	12.6	12.6	12.6
IMR - Both Sexes	65.0	47.0	30.7	18.0	15.4	15.4	15.4	15.4	15.4	15.4	15.4
E(0) - Males	65.36	67.19	69.03	70.84	72.06	72.06	72.06	72.06	72.06	72.06	72.06
E(0) - Females	68.43	70.71	73.00	75.08	76.51	76.51	76.51	76.51	76.51	76.51	76.51
E(0) - Both Sexes	66.90	68.95	71.02	72.96	74.28	74.28	74.28	74.28	74.28	74.28	74.28

Year	2100	2110	2120	2130	2140	2150	2160	2170	2180	2190	2200
Birth Rate ‰	13.8	13.8	13.8	13.8	13.8	13.8	13.8	13.8	13.8	13.8	13.8
Death Rate ‰	13.6	13.6	13.6	13.6	13.6	13.6	13.6	13.6	13.6	13.6	13.6
Growth Rate %	0.02	0.02	0.02	0.02	0.02	0.02	0.02	0.02	0.02	0.02	0.02
Total Fertility Rate	2.130	2.130	2.130	2.130	2.130	2.130	2.130	2.130	2.130	2.130	2.130
GRR	1.039	1.039	1.039	1.039	1.039	1.039	1.039	1.039	1.039	1.039	1.039
NRR	1.0	1.0	1.0	1.0	1.0	1.0	1.0	1.0	1.0	1.0	1.0
IMR - Males	18.2	18.2	18.2	18.2	18.2	18.2	18.2	18.2	18.2	18.2	18.2
IMR - Females	12.6	12.6	12.6	12.6	12.6	12.6	12.6	12.6	12.6	12.6	12.6
IMR - Both Sexes	15.4	15.4	15.4	15.4	15.4	15.4	15.4	15.4	15.4	15.4	15.4
E(0) - Males	72.06	72.06	72.06	72.06	72.06	72.06	72.06	72.06	72.06	72.06	72.06
E(0) - Females	76.51	76.51	76.51	76.51	76.51	76.51	76.51	76.51	76.51	76.51	76.51
E(0) - Both Sexes	74.28	74.28	74.28	74.28	74.28	74.28	74.28	74.28	74.28	74.28	74.28

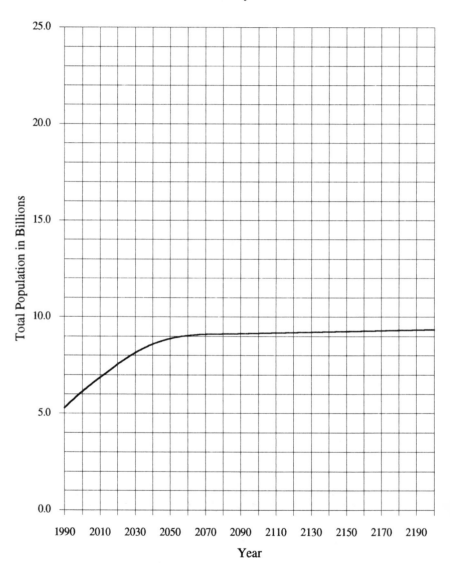

Graph 1

Projected Total Population
World Population Projection No. 2020.R.L
Decline to Replacement Fertility Level (2.13)
Mortality Level: Low

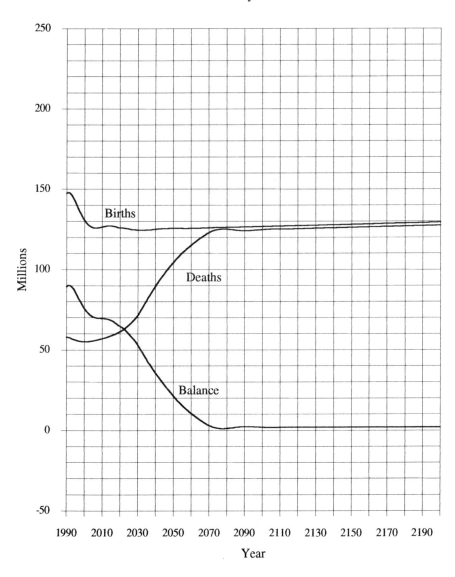

Graph 3

Age Structure of World Population 1990, 2050 and 2100

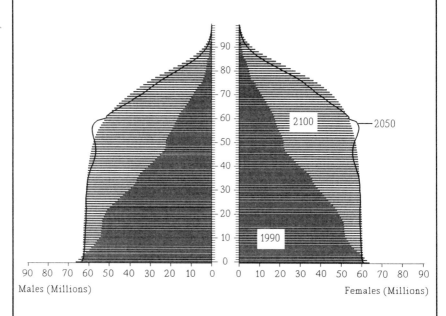

Population Projection No. 2020.R.L.

Target year for replacement fertility level (TFR = 2.13):	2020
Form of fertility decline:	Hyperbolic
Mortality level:	Low

Total population:	1990	5 275 Million
	2050	8 866 Million
	2100	9 151 Million

Table 1
Projected Total Population
World Population Projection No. 2020.B.H
Decline Below Replacement Fertility Level; Mortality Level: High
- Millions -

Age Year	0-4	5-9	10-14	15-19	20-24	25-29	30-34	35-39	40-44	45-49	50-54	55-59	60-64	65-69	70-74	75+	Total
1990	625	563	528	519	490	436	380	342	282	230	214	186	160	123	87	108	5275
2000	630	654	609	555	518	508	479	424	367	327	264	209	184	149	113	121	6112
2010	592	588	617	646	599	545	508	496	464	406	345	298	229	168	131	149	6779
2020	606	596	583	583	609	636	589	533	494	477	438	372	300	240	163	169	7387
2030	583	594	600	592	577	576	600	625	575	515	468	438	382	301	214	225	7864
2040	569	570	578	590	594	585	569	566	587	603	544	473	409	355	273	289	8154
2050	557	560	563	566	573	583	586	576	556	546	555	555	477	384	292	351	8280
2060	540	545	552	557	558	560	565	573	573	556	526	502	486	449	341	383	8266
2070	524	528	535	541	547	550	551	550	552	554	542	511	461	407	347	443	8144
2080	509	514	520	525	530	535	540	541	538	531	523	509	475	414	329	430	7962
2090	493	498	505	510	515	519	523	526	527	522	510	488	458	412	339	423	7769
2100	478	483	489	495	500	505	508	510	511	508	499	480	446	396	327	426	7561
2110	464	468	474	480	485	489	493	496	496	493	484	467	437	389	318	412	7344
2120	449	453	459	465	470	474	478	481	482	479	470	453	423	378	312	403	7130
2130	435	439	445	450	455	460	464	466	467	464	456	440	411	367	302	393	6915
2140	421	425	431	436	441	445	449	452	453	450	442	427	400	357	294	381	6703
2150	407	411	417	422	427	431	435	438	439	436	429	414	387	346	285	370	6495
2160	394	398	404	409	413	417	421	424	425	423	416	401	375	335	276	359	6291
2170	382	385	391	396	400	404	408	411	411	409	402	388	364	325	268	348	6092
2180	369	373	378	383	387	391	395	397	398	396	390	376	352	315	260	338	5898
2190	357	361	366	371	375	379	382	385	386	384	377	364	341	305	251	327	5710
2200	346	349	354	359	363	366	370	372	373	371	365	353	330	295	243	317	5526

Table 2
Components of Population Change
World Population Projection No. 2020.B.H
Decline Below Replacement Fertility Level; Mortality Level: High

Year	Males Births	Males Deaths - Thousands -	Males Balance	Females Births	Females Deaths - Thousands -	Females Balance	Total Births	Total Deaths - Thousands -	Total Balance
1990	75539	29422	46117	71783	28562	43221	147322	57985	89338
2000	66985	30788	36197	63654	27574	36079	130639	58363	72276
2010	64644	33922	30722	61429	28848	32581	126073	62770	63303
2020	63860	37707	26153	60684	31416	29269	124545	69123	55422
2030	60962	44470	16492	57930	37351	20579	118892	81821	37071
2040	59875	51791	8084	56898	45273	11624	116773	97064	19708
2050	58392	57659	732	55488	51889	3599	113880	109548	4331
2060	56559	61469	-4911	53746	56717	-2971	110305	118187	-7882
2070	55004	63628	-8624	52268	60232	-7963	107272	123859	-16587
2080	53356	62859	-9503	50703	60223	-9520	104059	123081	-19023
2090	51709	61737	-10027	49138	59130	-9992	100847	120866	-20019
2100	50130	60794	-10664	47637	58538	-10901	97767	119332	-21564
2110	48561	59183	-10622	46146	57055	-10909	94707	116239	-21531
2120	47030	57640	-10610	44691	55567	-10876	91721	113207	-21486
2130	45541	56068	-10527	43276	54122	-10846	88817	110189	-21372
2140	44087	54413	-10326	41894	52538	-10644	85981	106952	-20970
2150	42673	52801	-10128	40551	50995	-10444	83224	103796	-20572
2160	41300	51200	-9900	39246	49466	-10220	80545	100666	-20120
2170	39965	49617	-9652	37977	47944	-9966	77942	97560	-19618
2180	38670	48071	-9401	36747	46457	-9711	75416	94528	-19112
2190	37413	46558	-9144	35553	45001	-9449	72966	91559	-18593
2200	36194	45080	-8886	34394	43577	-9183	70589	88658	-18069

Table 3
Demographic Indicators
World Population Projection No. 2020.B.H
Decline Below Replacement Fertility Level; Mortality Level: High

Year	1990	2000	2010	2020	2030	2040	2050	2060	2070	2080	2090
Birth Rate ‰	27.9	21.4	18.6	16.9	15.1	14.3	13.8	13.3	13.2	13.1	13.0
Death Rate ‰	11.0	9.5	9.3	9.4	10.4	11.9	13.2	14.3	15.2	15.5	15.6
Growth Rate %	1.69	1.18	0.93	0.75	0.47	0.24	0.05	-0.10	-0.20	-0.24	-0.26
Total Fertility Rate	3.400	2.717	2.287	2.130	2.062	2.027	2.007	1.994	1.985	1.980	1.975
GRR	1.684	1.309	1.118	1.035	1.003	0.987	0.976	0.970	0.966	0.963	0.961
NRR	1.5	1.2	1.1	1.0	1.0	1.0	0.9	0.9	0.9	0.9	0.9
IMR - Males	67.2	53.4	39.5	26.3	24.6	24.6	24.6	24.6	24.6	24.6	24.6
IMR - Females	62.8	47.9	31.8	18.8	17.0	17.0	17.0	17.0	17.0	17.0	17.0
IMR - Both Sexes	65.0	50.6	35.7	22.5	20.8	20.8	20.8	20.8	20.8	20.8	20.8
E(0) - Males	65.36	66.12	67.01	67.99	68.39	68.39	68.39	68.39	68.39	68.39	68.39
E(0) - Females	68.43	69.71	71.16	72.53	73.25	73.25	73.25	73.25	73.25	73.25	73.25
E(0) - Both Sexes	66.90	67.91	69.08	70.26	70.82	70.82	70.82	70.82	70.82	70.82	70.82

Year	2100	2110	2120	2130	2140	2150	2160	2170	2180	2190	2200
Birth Rate ‰	12.9	12.9	12.9	12.8	12.8	12.8	12.8	12.8	12.8	12.8	12.8
Death Rate ‰	15.8	15.8	15.9	15.9	16.0	16.0	16.0	16.0	16.0	16.0	16.0
Growth Rate %	-0.29	-0.29	-0.30	-0.31	-0.31	-0.32	-0.32	-0.32	-0.32	-0.33	-0.33
Total Fertility Rate	1.972	1.970	1.968	1.966	1.965	1.964	1.963	1.962	1.961	1.961	1.960
GRR	0.959	0.958	0.957	0.956	0.955	0.955	0.954	0.954	0.954	0.953	0.956
NRR	0.9	0.9	0.9	0.9	0.9	0.9	0.9	0.9	0.9	0.9	0.9
IMR - Males	24.6	24.6	24.6	24.6	24.6	24.6	24.6	24.6	24.6	24.6	24.6
IMR - Females	17.0	17.0	17.0	17.0	17.0	17.0	17.0	17.0	17.0	17.0	17.0
IMR - Both Sexes	20.8	20.8	20.8	20.8	20.8	20.8	20.8	20.8	20.8	20.8	20.8
E(0) - Males	68.39	68.39	68.39	68.39	68.39	68.39	68.39	68.39	68.39	68.39	68.39
E(0) - Females	73.25	73.25	73.25	73.25	73.25	73.25	73.25	73.25	73.25	73.25	73.25
E(0) - Both Sexes	70.82	70.82	70.82	70.82	70.82	70.82	70.82	70.82	70.82	70.82	70.82

Graph 1

Projected Total Population
World Population Projection No. 2020.B.H
Decline Below Replacement Fertility Level
Mortality Level: High

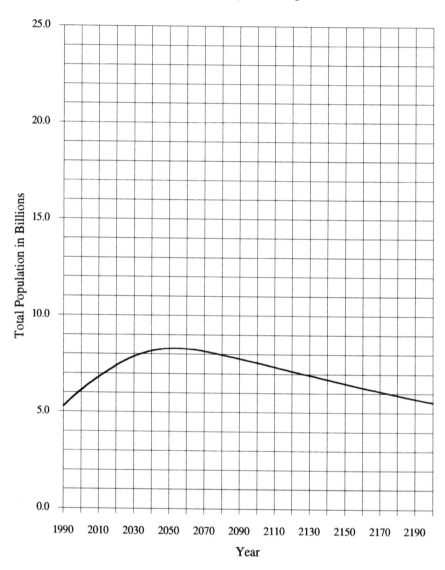

Graph 2

Components of Population Change
World Population Projection No. 2020.B.H
Decline Below Replacement Fertility Level
Mortality Level: High

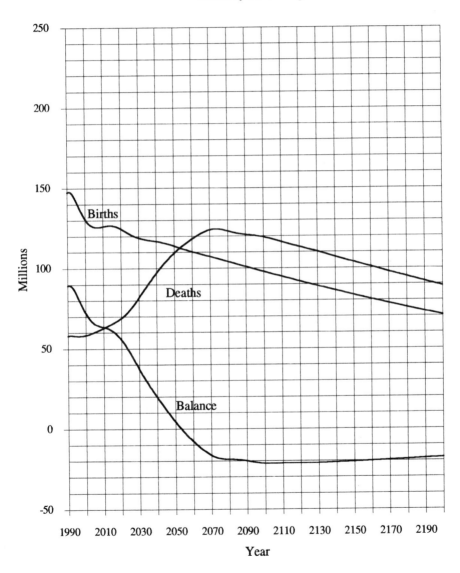

Graph 3

Age Structure of World Population 1990, 2050 and 2100

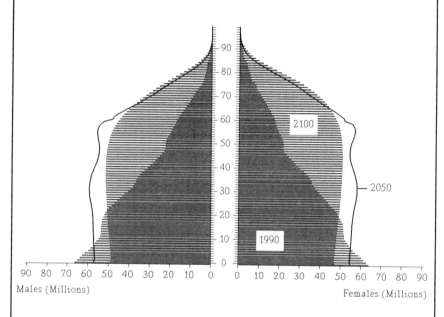

Population Projection No. 2020.B.H.

Decline below replacement fertility level
by the year: 2020
Form of fertility decline: Hyperbolic
Mortality level: High

Total population: 1990 5 275 Million
2050 8 280 Million
2100 7 561 Million

Table 1
Projected Total Population
World Population Projection No. 2020.B.M
Decline Below Replacement Fertility Level; Mortality Level: Medium

- Millions -

Age Year	0-4	5-9	10-14	15-19	20-24	25-29	30-34	35-39	40-44	45-49	50-54	55-59	60-64	65-69	70-74	75+	Total
1990	625	563	528	519	490	436	380	342	282	230	214	186	160	123	87	108	5275
2000	632	655	609	555	519	508	479	424	367	327	264	209	185	149	114	124	6120
2010	594	591	619	647	600	545	508	496	465	408	346	299	231	170	133	157	6811
2020	610	600	586	586	612	638	590	535	496	479	441	375	305	246	169	186	7454
2030	588	598	604	596	581	579	604	628	578	518	472	444	391	312	226	257	7979
2040	575	576	584	595	599	590	574	571	592	609	551	482	421	370	292	339	8320
2050	564	567	570	573	579	589	592	582	562	554	565	566	491	401	314	417	8487
2060	548	553	560	564	566	567	572	581	580	564	536	514	503	471	366	459	8506
2070	533	537	544	550	556	559	559	559	561	563	554	524	478	428	374	531	8410
2080	519	523	529	534	539	544	549	551	548	542	535	523	493	437	356	521	8245
2090	504	509	515	521	525	529	533	537	538	534	523	504	476	436	368	513	8063
2100	490	494	500	506	511	515	519	521	522	520	513	496	465	419	355	517	7866
2110	476	480	486	491	496	501	505	508	509	506	498	483	457	413	347	502	7658
2120	462	466	472	477	482	486	490	494	495	493	485	470	444	403	341	491	7450
2130	448	452	458	463	468	473	476	479	481	479	472	458	432	391	331	481	7241
2140	434	439	444	450	454	459	463	466	467	465	458	445	420	381	322	467	7034
2150	421	425	431	436	441	445	449	452	453	452	445	432	408	370	313	455	6830
2160	409	413	418	423	428	432	436	439	440	438	432	420	397	360	304	442	6630
2170	396	400	406	411	415	419	423	426	427	425	420	407	385	349	296	430	6434
2180	384	388	393	398	402	406	410	413	414	413	407	395	374	339	287	418	6242
2190	373	376	381	386	390	394	398	400	402	400	395	383	363	329	279	405	6055
2200	361	365	370	374	378	382	386	388	390	388	383	372	352	319	270	393	5873

Table 2
Components of Population Change
World Population Projection No. 2020.B.M
Decline Below Replacement Fertility Level; Mortality Level: Medium

Year	Births	Males Deaths - Thousands -	Balance	Births	Females Deaths - Thousands -	Balance	Births	Total Deaths - Thousands -	Balance
1990	75539	29422	46117	71783	28562	43221	147322	57985	89338
2000	67006	29872	37134	63674	26788	36886	130680	56660	74020
2010	64723	32338	32385	61504	27578	33926	126226	59915	66311
2020	64077	35599	28478	60890	29777	31113	124967	65376	59591
2030	61309	41729	19580	58260	35168	23093	119569	76896	42673
2040	60322	49780	10542	57322	43605	13717	117644	93385	24259
2050	58948	56311	2637	56017	50703	5314	114965	107014	7951
2060	57224	60632	-3408	54378	55916	-1538	111602	116549	-4947
2070	55763	63368	-7604	52990	59835	-6845	108753	123203	-14450
2080	54207	63152	-8945	51511	60447	-8936	105717	123599	-17882
2090	52644	62099	-9454	50026	59424	-9398	102670	121523	-18852
2100	51143	61376	-10234	48599	58972	-10373	99742	120349	-20607
2110	49646	59951	-10306	47177	57704	-10527	96823	117655	-20833
2120	48181	58500	-10319	45785	56296	-10511	93966	114796	-20830
2130	46753	57049	-10296	44428	54964	-10536	91181	112014	-20832
2140	45355	55492	-10137	43100	53485	-10385	88455	108977	-20522
2150	43993	53963	-9970	41805	52021	-10216	85798	105984	-20187
2160	42666	52443	-9777	40544	50574	-10030	83210	103017	-19808
2170	41373	50931	-9558	39316	49124	-9809	80689	100056	-19367
2180	40116	49450	-9334	38121	47703	-9581	78237	97153	-18916
2190	38894	47996	-9102	36960	46307	-9347	75854	94303	-18450
2200	37706	46572	-8867	35830	44937	-9107	73536	91509	-17973

Table 3
Demographic Indicators
World Population Projection No. 2020.B.M
Decline Below Replacement Fertility Level; Mortality Level: Medium

Year	1990	2000	2010	2020	2030	2040	2050	2060	2070	2080	2090
Birth Rate ‰	27.9	21.4	18.5	16.8	15.0	14.1	13.5	13.1	12.9	12.8	12.7
Death Rate ‰	11.0	9.3	8.8	8.8	9.6	11.2	12.6	13.7	14.6	15.0	15.1
Growth Rate %	1.69	1.21	0.97	0.80	0.53	0.29	0.09	-0.06	-0.17	-0.22	-0.23
Total Fertility Rate	3.400	2.717	2.287	2.130	2.062	2.027	2.007	1.994	1.985	1.980	1.975
GRR	1.684	1.309	1.118	1.035	1.003	0.987	0.976	0.970	0.966	0.963	0.961
NRR	1.5	1.2	1.1	1.0	1.0	1.0	1.0	0.9	0.9	0.9	0.9
IMR - Males	67.2	51.4	36.8	23.7	21.4	21.4	21.4	21.4	21.4	21.4	21.4
IMR - Females	62.8	46.2	29.6	16.9	14.8	14.8	14.8	14.8	14.8	14.8	14.8
IMR - Both Sexes	65.0	48.8	33.2	20.3	18.1	18.1	18.1	18.1	18.1	18.1	18.1
E(0) - Males	65.36	66.65	67.98	69.34	70.09	70.09	70.09	70.09	70.09	70.09	70.09
E(0) - Females	68.43	70.20	72.05	73.74	74.76	74.76	74.76	74.76	74.76	74.76	74.76
E(0) - Both Sexes	66.90	68.43	70.02	71.54	72.43	72.43	72.43	72.43	72.43	72.43	72.43

Year	2100	2110	2120	2130	2140	2150	2160	2170	2180	2190	2200
Birth Rate ‰	12.7	12.6	12.6	12.6	12.6	12.6	12.6	12.5	12.5	12.5	12.5
Death Rate ‰	15.3	15.4	15.4	15.5	15.5	15.5	15.5	15.6	15.6	15.6	15.6
Growth Rate %	-0.26	-0.27	-0.28	-0.29	-0.29	-0.30	-0.30	-0.30	-0.30	-0.30	-0.31
Total Fertility Rate	1.972	1.970	1.968	1.966	1.965	1.964	1.963	1.962	1.961	1.961	1.960
GRR	0.959	0.958	0.957	0.956	0.955	0.955	0.954	0.954	0.954	0.953	0.956
NRR	0.9	0.9	0.9	0.9	0.9	0.9	0.9	0.9	0.9	0.9	0.9
IMR - Males	21.4	21.4	21.4	21.4	21.4	21.4	21.4	21.4	21.4	21.4	21.4
IMR - Females	14.8	14.8	14.8	14.8	14.8	14.8	14.8	14.8	14.8	14.8	14.8
IMR - Both Sexes	18.1	18.1	18.1	18.1	18.1	18.1	18.1	18.1	18.1	18.1	18.1
E(0) - Males	70.09	70.09	70.09	70.09	70.09	70.09	70.09	70.09	70.09	70.09	70.09
E(0) - Females	74.76	74.76	74.76	74.76	74.76	74.76	74.76	74.76	74.76	74.76	74.76
E(0) - Both Sexes	72.43	72.43	72.43	72.43	72.43	72.43	72.43	72.43	72.43	72.43	72.43

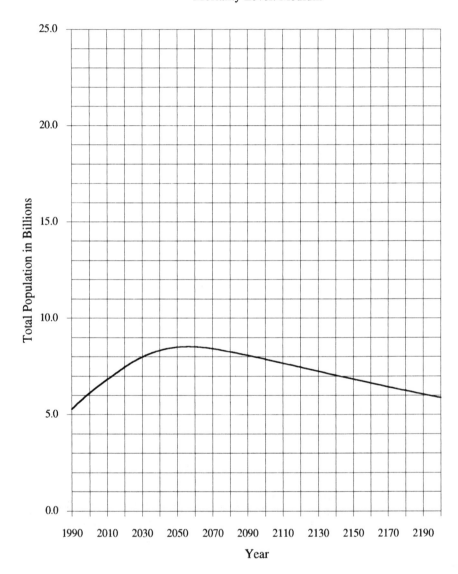

Graph 1

Projected Total Population
World Population Projection No. 2020.B.M
Decline Below Replacement Fertility Level
Mortality Level: Medium

Graph 2

Components of Population Change
World Population Projection No. 2020.B.M
Decline Below Replacement Fertility Level
Mortality Level: Medium

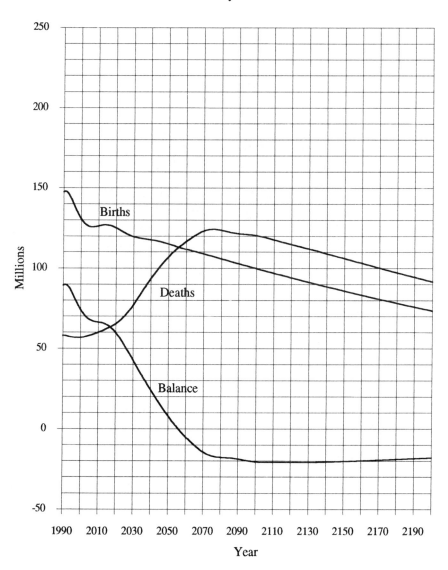

Graph 3

Age Structure of World Population 1990, 2050 and 2100

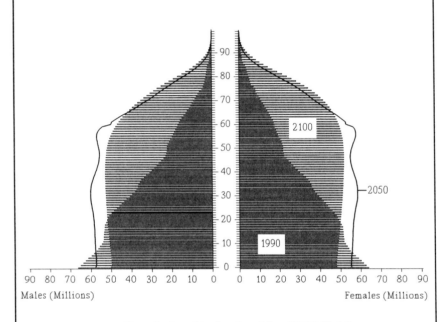

90 80 70 60 50 40 30 20 10 0   0 10 20 30 40 50 60 70 80 90
Males (Millions)   Females (Millions)

Population Projection No. 2020.B.M.

Decline below replacement fertility level by the year:	2020
Form of fertility decline:	Hyperbolic
Mortality level:	Medium

Total population:	1990	5 275 Million
	2050	8 487 Million
	2100	7 866 Million

Table 1
Projected Total Population
World Population Projection No. 2020.B.L
Decline Below Replacement Fertility Level; Mortality Level: Low

Age Year	0-4	5-9	10-14	15-19	20-24	25-29	30-34	35-39	40-44	45-49	50-54	55-59	60-64	65-69	70-74	75+	Total
1990	625	563	528	519	490	436	380	342	282	230	214	186	160	123	87	108	5275
2000	633	656	609	555	519	508	479	425	367	328	265	210	185	150	115	126	6129
2010	597	594	621	649	600	546	509	497	466	409	347	301	233	172	136	166	6844
2020	613	604	589	589	615	640	592	537	498	481	444	379	310	252	176	205	7524
2030	594	603	609	601	585	583	608	632	581	522	477	451	400	323	239	295	8101
2040	581	582	590	601	604	595	579	576	597	615	558	491	432	386	312	401	8501
2050	572	575	577	580	586	595	598	588	569	561	574	578	506	420	337	500	8716
2060	556	561	568	572	573	575	580	588	588	573	547	527	520	495	394	555	8772
2070	543	546	552	559	564	567	568	568	570	573	565	538	495	451	405	643	8707
2080	529	533	539	544	549	554	558	560	558	553	547	538	512	461	386	638	8561
2090	515	519	526	531	535	539	543	547	549	546	536	519	496	460	399	629	8391
2100	501	506	512	517	522	527	530	533	534	533	527	513	486	445	386	635	8206
2110	488	492	498	503	508	513	517	520	521	519	513	501	478	439	378	619	8007
2120	474	479	485	490	495	499	503	506	508	507	501	487	465	428	372	607	7806
2130	461	466	471	477	481	486	490	493	494	493	488	476	454	417	362	595	7604
2140	449	453	458	463	468	472	477	480	481	480	475	463	442	407	353	580	7402
2150	436	440	446	451	455	459	463	467	468	467	462	451	430	397	344	566	7203
2160	424	428	433	438	443	447	451	454	455	455	450	439	419	386	335	551	7007
2170	412	416	421	426	430	434	438	441	443	442	438	427	408	376	326	537	6814
2180	400	404	409	414	418	422	426	429	431	430	425	415	396	365	318	522	6625
2190	389	392	397	402	406	410	414	417	419	418	414	404	386	355	309	508	6440
2200	378	381	386	391	395	399	402	405	407	406	402	393	375	346	300	494	6259

- Millions -

Table 2
Components of Population Change
World Population Projection No. 2020.B.L
Decline Below Replacement Fertility Level; Mortality Level: Low

Year	Males Births	Males Deaths - Thousands -	Males Balance	Females Births	Females Deaths - Thousands -	Females Balance	Total Births	Total Deaths - Thousands -	Total Balance
1990	75539	29422	46117	71783	28562	43221	147322	57985	89338
2000	67027	28945	38082	63694	25990	37704	130721	54935	75786
2010	64801	30685	34117	61579	26246	35332	126380	56931	69449
2020	64294	33311	30983	61097	27989	33108	125391	61299	64091
2030	61658	38598	23060	58592	32670	25922	120250	71268	48982
2040	60772	47393	13379	57750	41629	16121	118522	89022	29499
2050	59510	54663	4847	56550	49271	7279	116060	103933	12126
2060	57896	59582	-1686	55017	54935	82	112913	114517	-1604
2070	56533	62907	-6374	53721	59260	-5539	110254	122167	-11913
2080	55070	63380	-8310	52331	60588	-8256	107401	123968	-16567
2090	53595	62442	-8847	50930	59728	-8799	104525	122170	-17645
2100	52175	61910	-9735	49580	59360	-9780	101755	121270	-19515
2110	50754	60716	-9962	48230	58347	-10117	98984	119063	-20079
2120	49359	59362	-10002	46905	57028	-10123	96264	116390	-20125
2130	47996	58036	-10039	45610	55807	-10198	93606	113843	-20237
2140	46659	56587	-9928	44338	54444	-10106	90997	111031	-20034
2150	45352	55144	-9793	43096	53064	-9968	88448	108208	-19760
2160	44076	53712	-9636	41884	51703	-9819	85959	105414	-19455
2170	42830	52277	-9447	40700	50331	-9632	83529	102608	-19079
2180	41615	50866	-9250	39546	48979	-9433	81161	99844	-18684
2190	40432	49477	-9045	38421	47648	-9227	78852	97124	-18272
2200	39278	48111	-8833	37325	46337	-9012	76603	94448	-17845

Table 3
Demographic Indicators
World Population Projection No. 2020.B.L
Decline Below Replacement Fertility Level; Mortality Level: Low

Year	1990	2000	2010	2020	2030	2040	2050	2060	2070	2080	2090
Birth Rate ‰	27.9	21.3	18.5	16.7	14.8	13.9	13.3	12.9	12.7	12.5	12.5
Death Rate ‰	11.0	9.0	8.3	8.1	8.8	10.5	11.9	13.1	14.0	14.5	14.6
Growth Rate %	1.69	1.24	1.01	0.85	0.60	0.35	0.14	-0.02	-0.14	-0.19	-0.21
Total Fertility Rate	3.400	2.717	2.287	2.130	2.062	2.027	2.007	1.994	1.985	1.980	1.975
GRR	1.684	1.309	1.118	1.035	1.003	0.987	0.976	0.970	0.966	0.963	0.961
NRR	1.5	1.2	1.1	1.0	1.0	1.0	1.0	1.0	0.9	0.9	0.9
IMR - Males	67.2	49.5	34.0	21.0	18.2	18.2	18.2	18.2	18.2	18.2	18.2
IMR - Females	62.8	44.4	27.4	15.0	12.6	12.6	12.6	12.6	12.6	12.6	12.6
IMR - Both Sexes	65.0	47.0	30.7	18.0	15.4	15.4	15.4	15.4	15.4	15.4	15.4
E(0) - Males	65.36	67.19	69.03	70.84	72.06	72.06	72.06	72.06	72.06	72.06	72.06
E(0) - Females	68.43	70.71	73.00	75.08	76.51	76.51	76.51	76.51	76.51	76.51	76.51
E(0) - Both Sexes	66.90	68.95	71.02	72.96	74.28	74.28	74.28	74.28	74.28	74.28	74.28

Year	2100	2110	2120	2130	2140	2150	2160	2170	2180	2190	2200
Birth Rate ‰	12.4	12.4	12.3	12.3	12.3	12.3	12.3	12.3	12.3	12.2	12.2
Death Rate ‰	14.8	14.9	14.9	15.0	15.0	15.0	15.0	15.1	15.1	15.1	15.1
Growth Rate %	-0.24	-0.25	-0.26	-0.27	-0.27	-0.27	-0.28	-0.28	-0.28	-0.28	-0.29
Total Fertility Rate	1.972	1.970	1.968	1.966	1.965	1.964	1.963	1.962	1.961	1.961	1.960
GRR	0.959	0.958	0.957	0.956	0.955	0.955	0.954	0.954	0.954	0.953	0.956
NRR	0.9	0.9	0.9	0.9	0.9	0.9	0.9	0.9	0.9	0.9	0.9
IMR - Males	18.2	18.2	18.2	18.2	18.2	18.2	18.2	18.2	18.2	18.2	18.2
IMR - Females	12.6	12.6	12.6	12.6	12.6	12.6	12.6	12.6	12.6	12.6	12.6
IMR - Both Sexes	15.4	15.4	15.4	15.4	15.4	15.4	15.4	15.4	15.4	15.4	15.4
E(0) - Males	72.06	72.06	72.06	72.06	72.06	72.06	72.06	72.06	72.06	72.06	72.06
E(0) - Females	76.51	76.51	76.51	76.51	76.51	76.51	76.51	76.51	76.51	76.51	76.51
E(0) - Both Sexes	74.28	74.28	74.28	74.28	74.28	74.28	74.28	74.28	74.28	74.28	74.28

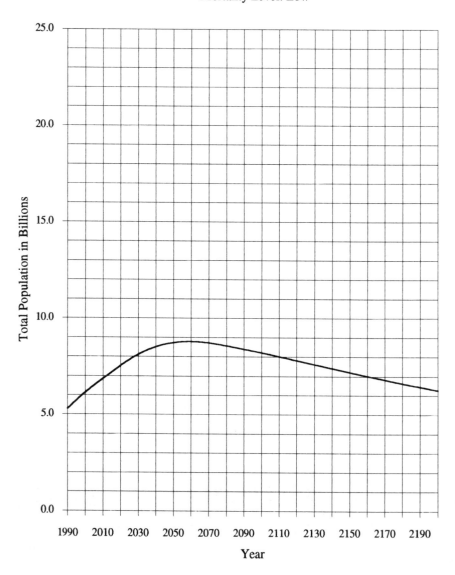

Graph 1

Projected Total Population
World Population Projection No. 2020.B.L
Decline Below Replacement Fertility Level
Mortality Level: Low

Graph 2

Components of Population Change
World Population Projection No. 2020.B.L
Decline Below Replacement Fertility Level
Mortality Level: Low

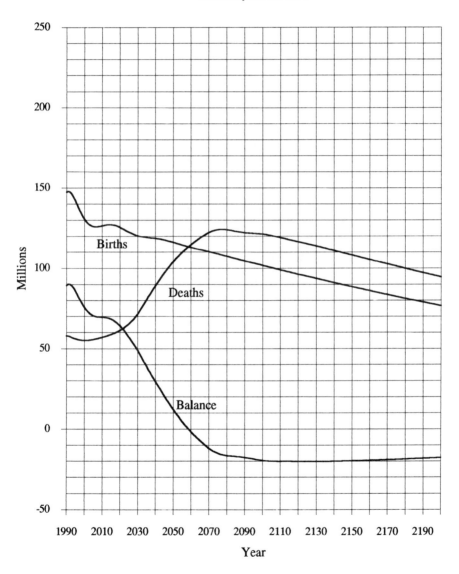

281

Graph 3

Age Structure of World Population 1990, 2050 and 2100

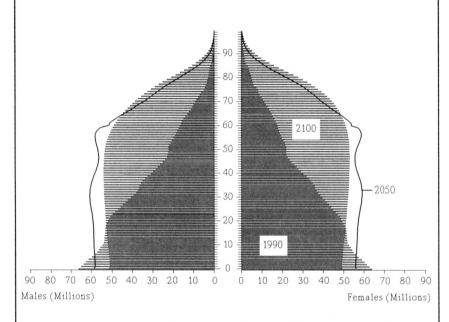

Population Projection No. 2020.B.L.

Decline below replacement fertility level
by the year: 2020
Form of fertility decline: Hyperbolic
Mortality level: Low

Total population: 1990 5 275 Million
2050 8 716 Million
2100 8 206 Million

Table 1
Projected Total Population
World Population Projection No. 2030.R.H
Decline to Replacement Fertility Level (2.13); Mortality Level: High

- Millions -

Age Year	0-4	5-9	10-14	15-19	20-24	25-29	30-34	35-39	40-44	45-49	50-54	55-59	60-64	65-69	70-74	75+	Total
1990	625	563	528	519	490	436	380	342	282	230	214	186	160	123	87	108	5275
2000	652	658	609	555	518	508	479	424	367	327	264	209	184	149	113	121	6137
2010	625	619	638	650	599	545	508	496	464	406	345	298	229	168	131	149	6869
2020	642	630	616	614	630	640	589	533	494	477	438	372	300	240	163	169	7546
2030	628	634	636	626	609	606	621	629	575	515	468	438	382	301	214	225	8106
2040	629	621	622	630	630	618	601	596	606	607	544	473	409	355	273	289	8505
2050	630	627	623	617	616	623	622	608	587	575	574	558	477	384	292	351	8765
2060	626	623	624	623	617	610	608	613	607	587	556	529	503	452	341	383	8903
2070	626	622	620	620	619	616	609	600	594	592	575	539	487	428	359	445	8950
2080	625	621	620	618	615	613	610	606	595	579	563	544	504	437	348	447	8943
2090	623	619	619	618	615	611	607	602	596	585	564	532	492	441	360	447	8929
2100	622	618	617	616	613	610	606	601	592	581	565	537	493	431	351	454	8909
2110	620	617	616	614	612	609	605	600	592	580	561	534	494	436	352	446	8889
2120	619	616	615	613	611	607	603	598	591	579	561	533	491	433	353	447	8871
2130	618	614	613	612	609	606	602	597	589	578	560	532	491	432	351	447	8852
2140	616	613	612	611	608	605	601	596	588	576	558	531	490	432	351	445	8833
2150	615	612	611	609	607	603	600	595	587	575	557	530	489	430	350	444	8815
2160	614	610	610	608	605	602	599	593	586	574	556	529	488	429	349	443	8796
2170	613	609	608	607	604	601	597	592	585	573	555	528	487	429	348	442	8777
2180	611	608	607	605	603	600	596	591	583	572	554	526	486	428	348	441	8758
2190	610	606	606	604	602	598	595	590	582	570	553	525	485	427	347	441	8740
2200	609	605	604	603	600	597	593	588	581	569	551	524	484	426	346	440	8721

283

Table 2
Components of Population Change
World Population Projection No. 2030.R.H
Decline to Replacement Fertility Level (2.13); Mortality Level: High

Year	Males Births	Males Deaths - Thousands -	Males Balance	Females Births	Females Deaths - Thousands -	Females Balance	Total Births	Total Deaths - Thousands -	Total Balance
1990	75539	29422	46117	71783	28562	43221	147322	57985	89338
2000	70220	31067	39153	66728	27813	38914	136947	58880	78067
2010	68262	34201	34060	64867	29061	35806	133129	63263	69866
2020	68017	37970	30048	64635	31588	33047	132652	69558	63094
2030	66004	44802	21202	62722	37558	25163	128726	82361	46365
2040	66699	52318	14380	63382	45604	17777	130081	97923	32158
2050	66492	58518	7974	63185	52416	10769	129677	110934	18743
2060	66184	62981	3203	62893	57645	5248	129077	120626	8451
2070	66176	66230	-54	62885	62023	862	129062	128253	809
2080	65995	66809	-814	62713	63387	-674	128709	130197	-1488
2090	65843	66704	-861	62568	63339	-771	128411	130043	-1632
2100	65724	66770	-1046	62455	63579	-1124	128179	130349	-2170
2110	65573	66453	-879	62312	63229	-916	127886	129681	-1795
2120	65435	66366	-931	62181	63111	-931	127616	129477	-1861
2130	65299	66244	-946	62051	63038	-987	127350	129282	-1932
2140	65158	66072	-914	61917	62854	-937	127075	128926	-1851
2150	65020	65948	-928	61786	62738	-951	126806	128686	-1879
2160	64882	65806	-924	61655	62607	-952	126537	128413	-1876
2170	64744	65662	-919	61524	62467	-943	126268	128130	-1862
2180	64606	65526	-919	61393	62339	-945	126000	127864	-1864
2190	64469	65386	-916	61263	62205	-942	125732	127591	-1859
2200	64332	65247	-914	61133	62072	-940	125465	127319	-1854

Table 3
Demographic Indicators
World Population Projection No. 2030.R.H
Decline to Replacement Fertility Level (2.13); Mortality Level: High

Year	1990	2000	2010	2020	2030	2040	2050	2060	2070	2080	2090
Birth Rate ‰	27.9	22.3	19.4	17.6	15.9	15.3	14.8	14.5	14.4	14.4	14.4
Death Rate ‰	11.0	9.6	9.2	9.2	10.2	11.5	12.7	13.5	14.3	14.6	14.6
Growth Rate %	1.69	1.27	1.02	0.84	0.57	0.38	0.21	0.09	0.01	-0.02	-0.02
Total Fertility Rate	3.400	2.838	2.414	2.224	2.130	2.130	2.130	2.130	2.130	2.130	2.130
GRR	1.684	1.372	1.180	1.082	1.040	1.040	1.038	1.039	1.039	1.039	1.039
NRR	1.5	1.3	1.1	1.0	1.0	1.0	1.0	1.0	1.0	1.0	1.0
IMR - Males	67.2	53.4	39.5	26.3	24.6	24.6	24.6	24.6	24.6	24.6	24.6
IMR - Females	62.8	47.9	31.8	18.8	17.0	17.0	17.0	17.0	17.0	17.0	17.0
IMR - Both Sexes	65.0	50.6	35.7	22.5	20.8	20.8	20.8	20.8	20.8	20.8	20.8
E(0) - Males	65.36	66.12	67.01	67.99	68.39	68.39	68.39	68.39	68.39	68.39	68.39
E(0) - Females	68.43	69.71	71.16	72.53	73.25	73.25	73.25	73.25	73.25	73.25	73.25
E(0) - Both Sexes	66.90	67.91	69.08	70.26	70.82	70.82	70.82	70.82	70.82	70.82	70.82

Year	2100	2110	2120	2130	2140	2150	2160	2170	2180	2190	2200
Birth Rate ‰	14.4	14.4	14.4	14.4	14.4	14.4	14.4	14.4	14.4	14.4	14.4
Death Rate ‰	14.6	14.6	14.6	14.6	14.6	14.6	14.6	14.6	14.6	14.6	14.6
Growth Rate %	-0.02	-0.02	-0.02	-0.02	-0.02	-0.02	-0.02	-0.02	-0.02	-0.02	-0.02
Total Fertility Rate	2.130	2.130	2.130	2.130	2.130	2.130	2.130	2.130	2.130	2.130	2.130
GRR	1.039	1.039	1.039	1.039	1.039	1.039	1.039	1.039	1.039	1.039	1.039
NRR	1.0	1.0	1.0	1.0	1.0	1.0	1.0	1.0	1.0	1.0	1.0
IMR - Males	24.6	24.6	24.6	24.6	24.6	24.6	24.6	24.6	24.6	24.6	24.6
IMR - Females	17.0	17.0	17.0	17.0	17.0	17.0	17.0	17.0	17.0	17.0	17.0
IMR - Both Sexes	20.8	20.8	20.8	20.8	20.8	20.8	20.8	20.8	20.8	20.8	20.8
E(0) - Males	68.39	68.39	68.39	68.39	68.39	68.39	68.39	68.39	68.39	68.39	68.39
E(0) - Females	73.25	73.25	73.25	73.25	73.25	73.25	73.25	73.25	73.25	73.25	73.25
E(0) - Both Sexes	70.82	70.82	70.82	70.82	70.82	70.82	70.82	70.82	70.82	70.82	70.82

Graph 1

Projected Total Population
World Population Projection No. 2030.R.H
Decline to Replacement Fertility Level (2.13)
Mortality Level: High

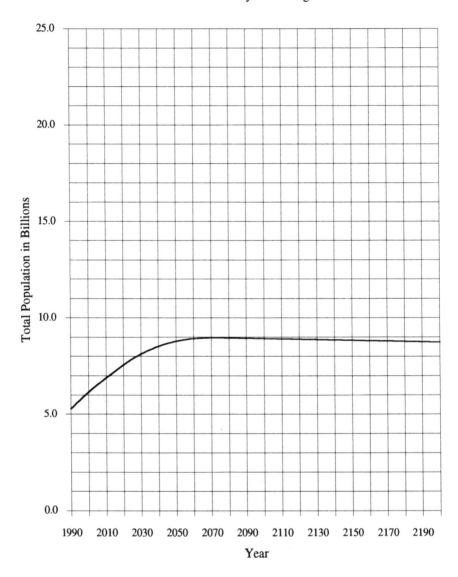

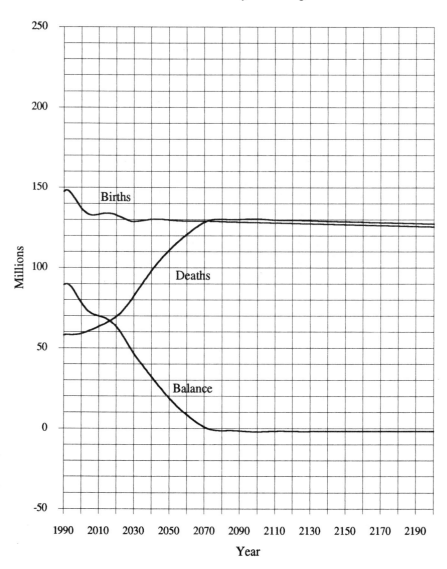

Graph 2

Components of Population Change
World Population Projection No. 2030.R.H
Decline to Replacement Fertility Level (2.13)
Mortality Level: High

Graph 3

Age Structure of World Population 1990, 2050 and 2100

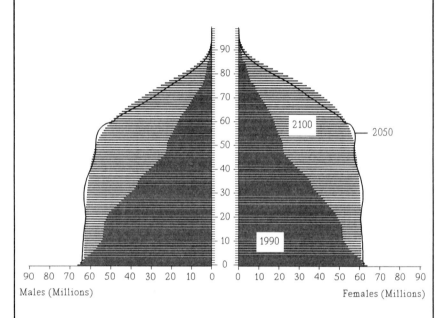

Population Projection No. 2030.R.H.

Target year for replacement fertility
level (TFR = 2.13):   2030
Form of fertility decline: Hyperbolic
Mortality level: High

Total population: 1990   5 275 Million
                                            2050   8 765 Million
                                            2100   8 909 Million

Table 1
Projected Total Population
World Population Projection No. 2030.R.M
Decline to Replacement Fertility Level (2.13); Mortality Level: Medium

- Millions -

Age Year	0-4	5-9	10-14	15-19	20-24	25-29	30-34	35-39	40-44	45-49	50-54	55-59	60-64	65-69	70-74	75+	Total
1990	625	563	528	519	490	436	380	342	282	230	214	186	160	123	87	108	5275
2000	653	659	609	555	519	508	479	424	367	327	264	209	185	149	114	124	6146
2010	628	622	640	652	600	545	508	496	465	408	346	299	231	170	133	157	6901
2020	646	634	619	617	633	642	590	535	496	479	441	375	305	246	169	186	7614
2030	633	639	641	630	614	610	625	633	578	518	472	444	391	312	226	257	8223
2040	636	628	628	636	636	624	606	601	612	613	551	482	421	370	292	339	8674
2050	638	635	631	625	632	630	628	615	594	583	584	570	491	401	314	417	8978
2060	636	633	633	632	626	618	616	621	615	596	567	542	520	475	366	459	9153
2070	637	632	631	630	628	625	618	609	604	602	587	554	505	451	387	533	9233
2080	637	633	632	629	626	623	621	616	606	591	576	559	523	461	377	541	9250
2090	636	633	632	630	627	623	618	614	608	597	578	549	513	466	390	541	9255
2100	637	633	631	629	627	624	619	614	606	596	580	555	515	457	382	550	9255
2110	636	633	632	629	626	623	619	615	607	595	578	553	517	462	384	543	9253
2120	636	633	631	630	627	623	619	614	607	596	579	553	515	461	385	545	9254
2130	636	633	631	629	626	623	619	614	607	595	579	554	516	460	384	546	9253
2140	636	633	631	629	626	623	619	614	607	595	579	553	516	461	384	545	9253
2150	636	633	631	629	626	623	619	614	607	596	579	553	515	461	384	545	9253
2160	636	633	631	629	626	623	619	614	607	595	579	553	515	461	384	545	9252
2170	636	633	631	629	626	623	619	614	607	595	579	553	515	461	384	545	9252
2180	636	633	631	629	626	623	619	614	607	595	579	553	515	461	384	545	9252
2190	636	633	631	629	626	623	619	614	607	595	579	553	515	461	384	545	9251
2200	636	633	631	629	626	623	619	614	607	595	579	553	515	461	384	545	9251

Table 2
Components of Population Change
World Population Projection No. 2030.R.M
Decline to Replacement Fertility Level (2.13); Mortality Level: Medium

Year	Males Births	Males Deaths - Thousands -	Males Balance	Females Births	Females Deaths - Thousands -	Females Balance	Births	Total Deaths - Thousands -	Balance
1990	75539	29422	46117	71783	28562	43221	147322	57985	89338
2000	70242	30141	40101	66749	27018	39730	136991	57160	79831
2010	68345	32599	35746	64946	27776	37170	133291	60375	72916
2020	68249	35837	32413	64855	29932	34923	133104	65769	67336
2030	66381	42020	24361	63080	35349	27731	129460	77369	52092
2040	67197	50243	16954	63855	43895	19960	131053	94139	36914
2050	67127	57068	10059	63788	51166	12622	130915	108234	22681
2060	66964	61978	4986	63634	56736	6897	130598	118714	11883
2070	67091	65732	1359	63755	61445	2310	130846	127177	3670
2080	67049	66875	174	63715	63400	315	130764	130275	489
2090	67035	66900	135	63701	63496	205	130736	130396	340
2100	67053	67166	-113	63718	63874	-155	130772	131040	-268
2110	67040	67017	24	63706	63712	-5	130747	130728	19
2120	67039	67041	-1	63705	63680	26	130745	130720	24
2130	67039	67077	-38	63705	63755	-50	130745	130832	-87
2140	67035	67039	-4	63701	63705	-4	130737	130744	-8
2150	67034	67050	-17	63700	63714	-14	130733	130764	-31
2160	67032	67049	-18	63698	63718	-21	130729	130768	-38
2170	67029	67042	-13	63695	63708	-13	130724	130751	-26
2180	67027	67043	-16	63693	63710	-16	130720	130753	-32
2190	67025	67040	-16	63691	63708	-16	130716	130748	-32
2200	67022	67037	-15	63689	63704	-15	130711	130742	-30

Table 3
Demographic Indicators
World Population Projection No. 2030.R.M
Decline to Replacement Fertility Level (2.13); Mortality Level: Medium

Year	1990	2000	2010	2020	2030	2040	2050	2060	2070	2080	2090
Birth Rate ‰	27.9	22.3	19.3	17.5	15.7	15.1	14.6	14.3	14.2	14.1	14.1
Death Rate ‰	11.0	9.3	8.7	8.6	9.4	10.9	12.1	13.0	13.8	14.1	14.1
Growth Rate %	1.69	1.30	1.06	0.88	0.63	0.43	0.25	0.13	0.04	0.01	0.00
Total Fertility Rate	3.400	2.838	2.414	2.224	2.130	2.130	2.130	2.130	2.130	2.130	2.130
GRR	1.684	1.372	1.180	1.082	1.040	1.040	1.038	1.039	1.039	1.039	1.039
NRR	1.5	1.3	1.1	1.0	1.0	1.0	1.0	1.0	1.0	1.0	1.0
IMR - Males	67.2	51.4	36.8	23.7	21.4	21.4	21.4	21.4	21.4	21.4	21.4
IMR - Females	62.8	46.2	29.6	16.9	14.8	14.8	14.8	14.8	14.8	14.8	14.8
IMR - Both Sexes	65.0	48.8	33.2	20.3	18.1	18.1	18.1	18.1	18.1	18.1	18.1
E(0) - Males	65.36	66.65	67.98	69.34	70.09	70.09	70.09	70.09	70.09	70.09	70.09
E(0) - Females	68.43	70.20	72.05	73.74	74.76	74.76	74.76	74.76	74.76	74.76	74.76
E(0) - Both Sexes	66.90	68.43	70.02	71.54	72.43	72.43	72.43	72.43	72.43	72.43	72.43

Year	2100	2110	2120	2130	2140	2150	2160	2170	2180	2190	2200
Birth Rate ‰	14.1	14.1	14.1	14.1	14.1	14.1	14.1	14.1	14.1	14.1	14.1
Death Rate ‰	14.2	14.1	14.1	14.1	14.1	14.1	14.1	14.1	14.1	14.1	14.1
Growth Rate %	0.00	0.00	0.00	0.00	0.00	0.00	0.00	0.00	0.00	0.00	0.00
Total Fertility Rate	2.130	2.130	2.130	2.130	2.130	2.130	2.130	2.130	2.130	2.130	2.130
GRR	1.039	1.039	1.039	1.039	1.039	1.039	1.039	1.039	1.039	1.039	1.039
NRR	1.0	1.0	1.0	1.0	1.0	1.0	1.0	1.0	1.0	1.0	1.0
IMR - Males	21.4	21.4	21.4	21.4	21.4	21.4	21.4	21.4	21.4	21.4	21.4
IMR - Females	14.8	14.8	14.8	14.8	14.8	14.8	14.8	14.8	14.8	14.8	14.8
IMR - Both Sexes	18.1	18.1	18.1	18.1	18.1	18.1	18.1	18.1	18.1	18.1	18.1
E(0) - Males	70.09	70.09	70.09	70.09	70.09	70.09	70.09	70.09	70.09	70.09	70.09
E(0) - Females	74.76	74.76	74.76	74.76	74.76	74.76	74.76	74.76	74.76	74.76	74.76
E(0) - Both Sexes	72.43	72.43	72.43	72.43	72.43	72.43	72.43	72.43	72.43	72.43	72.43

Graph 1

Projected Total Population
World Population Projection No. 2030.R.M
Decline to Replacement Fertility Level (2.13)
Mortality Level: Medium

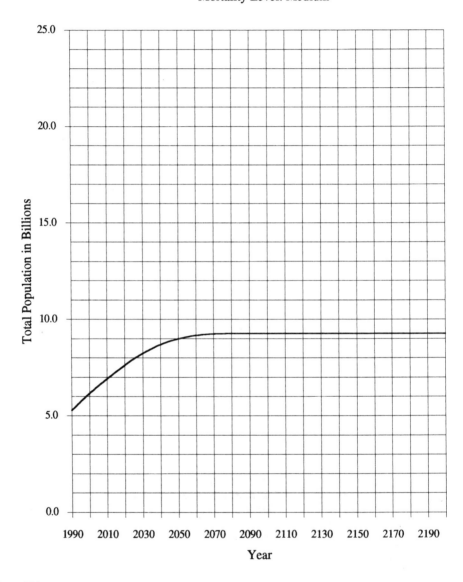

Graph 2

Components of Population Change
World Population Projection No. 2030.R.M
Decline to Replacement Fertility Level (2.13)
Mortality Level: Medium

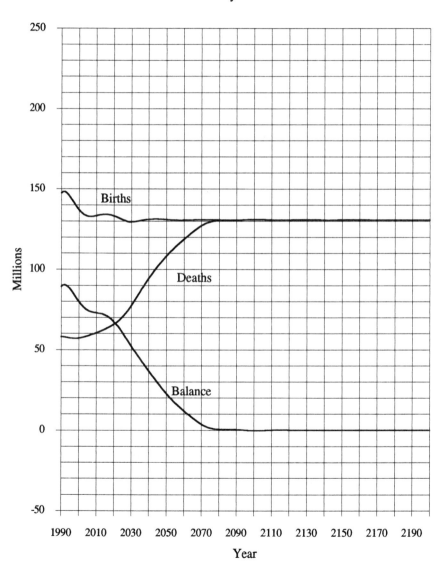

Graph 3

Age Structure of World Population 1990, 2050 and 2100

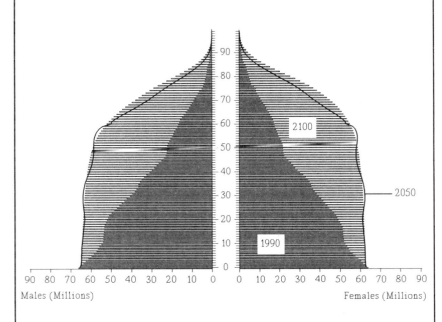

Population Projection No. 2030.R.M.

Target year for replacement fertility level (TFR = 2.13):	2030
Form of fertility decline:	Hyperbolic
Mortality level:	Medium

Total population: 1990 5 275 Million
                   2050 8 978 Million
                   2100 9 255 Million

Table 1
Projected Total Population
World Population Projection No. 2030.R.L
Decline to Replacement Fertility Level (2.13); Mortality Level: Low
- Millions -

Age Year	0-4	5-9	10-14	15-19	20-24	25-29	30-34	35-39	40-44	45-49	50-54	55-59	60-64	65-69	70-74	75+	Total
1990	625	563	528	519	490	436	380	342	282	230	214	186	160	123	87	108	5275
2000	655	660	609	555	519	508	479	425	367	328	265	210	185	150	115	126	6154
2010	631	625	642	653	600	546	509	497	466	409	347	301	233	172	136	166	6934
2020	650	638	623	620	635	644	592	537	498	481	444	379	310	252	176	205	7685
2030	639	645	645	634	618	614	628	636	581	522	477	451	400	323	239	295	8347
2040	643	635	635	642	641	629	612	607	618	619	558	491	432	386	312	401	8859
2050	647	643	638	632	630	636	635	621	601	591	593	582	506	420	337	500	9212
2060	645	642	642	640	634	627	624	628	624	605	578	555	537	498	394	555	9429
2070	648	643	641	639	638	635	628	619	613	612	599	568	523	475	419	645	9545
2080	649	645	643	640	637	634	632	627	617	603	589	575	543	487	408	662	9591
2090	650	646	645	643	639	635	630	626	621	611	593	566	534	492	423	663	9616
2100	652	648	646	643	640	637	633	627	620	610	596	574	537	485	416	675	9638
2110	653	649	647	645	641	638	634	629	622	611	595	573	540	491	418	669	9656
2120	654	650	649	646	643	639	635	630	623	613	597	574	539	490	421	673	9677
2130	656	652	650	647	644	641	637	631	624	614	599	576	541	491	420	675	9697
2140	657	653	651	649	646	642	638	633	626	615	600	577	542	493	422	675	9717
2150	658	654	653	650	647	643	639	634	627	616	601	578	543	493	423	677	9737
2160	660	656	654	651	648	645	640	635	628	618	602	579	545	494	423	679	9757
2170	661	657	655	653	650	646	642	637	629	619	603	580	546	496	424	680	9777
2180	662	658	657	654	651	647	643	638	631	620	605	581	547	497	425	681	9797
2190	664	660	658	655	652	649	644	639	632	621	606	583	548	498	426	683	9817
2200	665	661	659	657	654	650	646	641	633	623	607	584	549	499	427	684	9837

Table 2
Components of Population Change
World Population Projection No. 2030.R.L
Decline to Replacement Fertility Level (2.13); Mortality Level: Low

Year	Males Births	Males Deaths - Thousands -	Males Balance	Females Births	Females Deaths - Thousands -	Females Balance	Total Births	Total Deaths - Thousands -	Total Balance
1990	75539	29422	46117	71783	28562	43221	147322	57985	89338
2000	70264	29204	41060	66770	26212	40558	137034	55417	81617
2010	68428	30927	37501	65025	26430	38595	133453	57357	76096
2020	68482	33522	34959	65076	28127	36949	133558	61650	71908
2030	66760	38848	27912	63439	32825	30614	130199	71673	58526
2040	67699	47791	19908	64332	41878	22455	132031	89668	42363
2050	67767	55315	12453	64397	49669	14728	132164	104984	27180
2060	67752	60752	7000	64383	55644	8739	132135	116396	15738
2070	68018	65009	3010	64636	60674	3962	132654	125683	6972
2080	68119	66828	1291	64731	63290	1441	132850	130118	2732
2090	68248	67042	1206	64854	63627	1226	133102	130669	2433
2100	68408	67484	924	65006	64102	904	133414	131587	1828
2110	68539	67534	1005	65130	64157	974	133669	131691	1978
2120	68681	67663	1018	65265	64208	1057	133947	131871	2076
2130	68825	67860	965	65402	64428	975	134227	132288	1939
2140	68965	67964	1001	65535	64522	1013	134500	132486	2014
2150	69107	68112	995	65671	64655	1015	134778	132767	2010
2160	69250	68257	992	65806	64800	1006	135056	133057	1999
2170	69392	68392	1000	65941	64925	1016	135333	133317	2016
2180	69535	68535	1000	66077	65061	1016	135612	133597	2016
2190	69678	68677	1002	66213	65196	1017	135892	133873	2019
2200	69822	68817	1005	66350	65329	1020	136172	134146	2025

Table 3
Demographic Indicators
World Population Projection No. 2030.R.L
Decline to Replacement Fertility Level (2.13); Mortality Level: Low

Year	1990	2000	2010	2020	2030	2040	2050	2060	2070	2080	2090
Birth Rate ‰	27.9	22.3	19.2	17.4	15.6	14.9	14.3	14.0	13.9	13.9	13.8
Death Rate ‰	11.0	9.0	8.3	8.0	8.6	10.1	11.4	12.3	13.2	13.6	13.6
Growth Rate %	1.69	1.33	1.10	0.94	0.70	0.48	0.30	0.17	0.07	0.03	0.03
Total Fertility Rate	3.400	2.838	2.414	2.224	2.130	2.130	2.130	2.130	2.130	2.130	2.130
GRR	1.684	1.372	1.180	1.082	1.040	1.040	1.038	1.039	1.039	1.039	1.039
NRR	1.5	1.3	1.1	1.1	1.0	1.0	1.0	1.0	1.0	1.0	1.0
IMR - Males	67.2	49.5	34.0	21.0	18.2	18.2	18.2	18.2	18.2	18.2	18.2
IMR - Females	62.8	44.4	27.4	15.0	12.6	12.6	12.6	12.6	12.6	12.6	12.6
IMR - Both Sexes	65.0	47.0	30.7	18.0	15.4	15.4	15.4	15.4	15.4	15.4	15.4
E(0) - Males	65.36	67.19	69.03	70.84	72.06	72.06	72.06	72.06	72.06	72.06	72.06
E(0) - Females	68.43	70.71	73.00	75.08	76.51	76.51	76.51	76.51	76.51	76.51	76.51
E(0) - Both Sexes	66.90	68.95	71.02	72.96	74.28	74.28	74.28	74.28	74.28	74.28	74.28

Year	2100	2110	2120	2130	2140	2150	2160	2170	2180	2190	2200
Birth Rate ‰	13.8	13.8	13.8	13.8	13.8	13.8	13.8	13.8	13.8	13.8	13.8
Death Rate ‰	13.7	13.6	13.6	13.6	13.6	13.6	13.6	13.6	13.6	13.6	13.6
Growth Rate %	0.02	0.02	0.02	0.02	0.02	0.02	0.02	0.02	0.02	0.02	0.02
Total Fertility Rate	2.130	2.130	2.130	2.130	2.130	2.130	2.130	2.130	2.130	2.130	2.130
GRR	1.039	1.039	1.039	1.039	1.039	1.039	1.039	1.039	1.039	1.039	1.039
NRR	1.0	1.0	1.0	1.0	1.0	1.0	1.0	1.0	1.0	1.0	1.0
IMR - Males	18.2	18.2	18.2	18.2	18.2	18.2	18.2	18.2	18.2	18.2	18.2
IMR - Females	12.6	12.6	12.6	12.6	12.6	12.6	12.6	12.6	12.6	12.6	12.6
IMR - Both Sexes	15.4	15.4	15.4	15.4	15.4	15.4	15.4	15.4	15.4	15.4	15.4
E(0) - Males	72.06	72.06	72.06	72.06	72.06	72.06	72.06	72.06	72.06	72.06	72.06
E(0) - Females	76.51	76.51	76.51	76.51	76.51	76.51	76.51	76.51	76.51	76.51	76.51
E(0) - Both Sexes	74.28	74.28	74.28	74.28	74.28	74.28	74.28	74.28	74.28	74.28	74.28

Graph 1

Projected Total Population
World Population Projection No. 2030.R.L
Decline to Replacement Fertility Level (2.13)
Mortality Level: Low

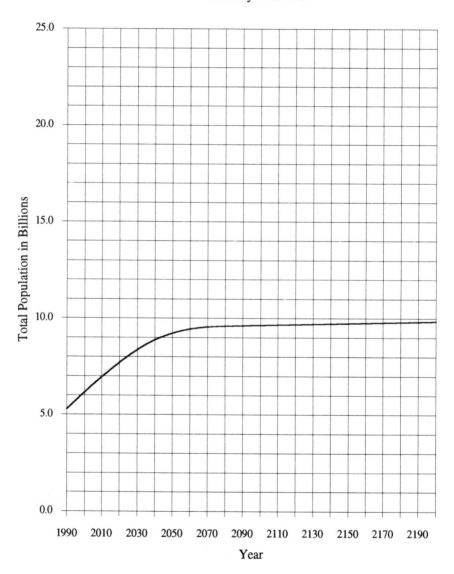

Graph 2

Components of Population Change
World Population Projection No. 2030.R.L
Decline to Replacement Fertility Level (2.13)
Mortality Level: Low

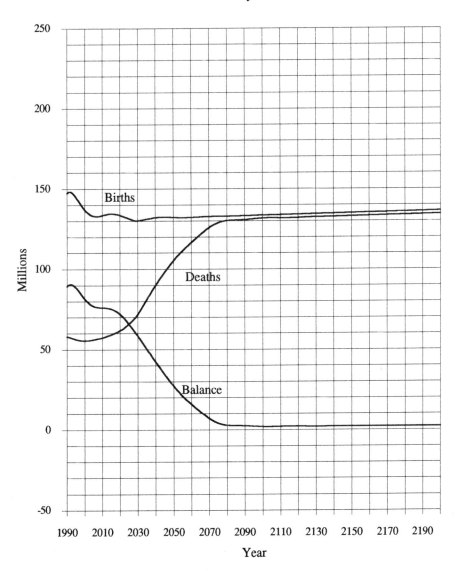

Graph 3

Age Structure of World Population 1990, 2050 and 2100

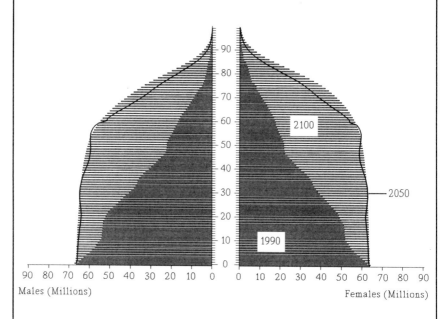

Population Projection No. 2030.R.L.

Target year for replacement fertility
level (TFR = 2.13): 2030
Form of fertility decline: Hyperbolic
Mortality level: Low

Total population: 1990   5 275 Million
2050   9 212 Million
2100   9 638 Million

Table 1
Projected Total Population
World Population Projection No. 2030.B.H
Decline Below Replacement Fertility Level; Mortality Level: High

- Millions -

Age Year	0-4	5-9	10-14	15-19	20-24	25-29	30-34	35-39	40-44	45-49	50-54	55-59	60-64	65-69	70-74	75+	Total
1990	625	563	528	519	490	436	380	342	282	230	214	186	160	123	87	108	5275
2000	652	658	609	555	518	508	479	424	367	327	264	209	184	149	113	121	6137
2010	625	619	638	650	599	545	508	496	464	406	345	298	229	168	131	149	6869
2020	642	630	616	614	630	640	589	533	494	477	438	372	300	240	163	169	7546
2030	628	634	636	626	609	606	621	629	575	515	468	438	382	301	214	225	8106
2040	616	616	622	630	630	618	601	596	606	607	544	473	409	355	273	289	8487
2050	607	608	610	612	616	623	622	608	587	575	574	558	477	384	292	351	8705
2060	591	595	601	605	605	605	608	613	607	587	556	529	503	452	341	383	8781
2070	577	580	586	592	596	598	597	595	594	592	575	539	487	428	359	445	8738
2080	562	566	572	576	581	585	588	588	583	574	563	544	504	437	348	447	8616
2090	546	551	557	562	566	570	573	575	574	567	552	528	492	441	360	447	8461
2100	531	535	542	547	552	556	559	560	559	555	544	521	483	428	351	454	8278
2110	516	520	526	532	537	541	545	547	546	541	530	510	476	423	345	444	8078
2120	501	505	511	517	522	526	529	532	532	528	517	497	464	413	340	437	7870
2130	486	490	496	502	507	511	515	517	517	513	504	485	453	403	331	428	7658
2140	471	475	482	487	492	496	500	503	503	499	490	472	441	393	323	418	7444
2150	457	461	467	473	477	481	485	488	488	485	476	459	429	382	315	408	7231
2160	443	447	453	458	463	467	471	473	474	471	463	446	417	372	306	397	7019
2170	429	433	439	444	449	453	457	459	460	457	449	433	405	361	298	386	6810
2180	416	420	425	430	435	439	443	445	446	443	436	420	393	351	289	375	6605
2190	403	406	412	417	421	425	429	432	432	430	422	407	381	340	280	364	6404
2200	390	394	399	404	408	412	416	418	419	417	410	395	370	330	272	353	6207

Table 2
Components of Population Change
World Population Projection No. 2030.B.H
Decline Below Replacement Fertility Level; Mortality Level: High

Year	Males Births	Males Deaths - Thousands -	Males Balance	Females Births	Females Deaths - Thousands -	Females Balance	Births	Total Deaths - Thousands -	Balance
1990	75539	29422	46117	71783	28562	43221	147322	57985	89338
2000	70220	31067	39153	66728	27813	38914	136947	58880	78067
2010	68262	34201	34060	64867	29061	35806	133129	63263	69866
2020	68017	37970	30048	64635	31588	33047	132652	69558	63094
2030	65801	44797	21004	62529	37555	24974	128330	82352	45978
2040	64956	52247	12709	61726	45557	16168	126682	97805	28877
2050	63717	58390	5326	60548	52334	8214	124264	110724	13540
2060	62049	62768	-719	58963	57510	1452	121011	120278	733
2070	60564	65901	-5337	57552	61816	-4264	118116	127717	-9601
2080	58958	66314	-7356	56026	63077	-7051	114985	129392	-14407
2090	57315	65919	-8605	54464	62855	-8391	111779	128774	-16996
2100	55707	65453	-9746	52937	62762	-9825	108644	128215	-19571
2110	54091	64230	-10140	51401	61723	-10322	105492	125953	-20462
2120	52495	62914	-10419	49884	60500	-10616	102378	123414	-21035
2130	50927	61492	-10565	48394	59225	-10831	99321	120717	-21396
2140	49384	59928	-10544	46928	57757	-10828	96313	117685	-21372
2150	47874	58354	-10479	45493	56268	-10775	93368	114622	-21254
2160	46398	56755	-10357	44091	54756	-10666	90489	111511	-21022
2170	44957	55147	-10190	42721	53222	-10501	87678	108369	-20691
2180	43551	53553	-10002	41385	51699	-10314	84937	105252	-20315
2190	42183	51975	-9793	40085	50189	-10104	82267	102164	-19897
2200	40850	50420	-9570	38818	48696	-9878	79668	99117	-19448

Table 3
Demographic Indicators
World Population Projection No. 2030.B.H
Decline Below Replacement Fertility Level; Mortality Level: High

Year	1990	2000	2010	2020	2030	2040	2050	2060	2070	2080	2090
Birth Rate ‰	27.9	22.3	19.4	17.6	15.8	14.9	14.3	13.8	13.5	13.3	13.2
Death Rate ‰	11.0	9.6	9.2	9.2	10.2	11.5	12.7	13.7	14.6	15.0	15.2
Growth Rate %	1.69	1.27	1.02	0.84	0.57	0.34	0.16	0.01	-0.11	-0.17	-0.20
Total Fertility Rate	3.400	2.838	2.414	2.224	2.130	2.078	2.047	2.026	2.012	2.002	1.994
GRR	1.684	1.372	1.180	1.082	1.037	1.013	0.996	0.986	0.979	0.974	0.970
NRR	1.5	1.3	1.1	1.0	1.0	1.0	1.0	1.0	1.0	0.9	0.9
IMR - Males	67.2	53.4	39.5	26.3	24.6	24.6	24.6	24.6	24.6	24.6	24.6
IMR - Females	62.8	47.9	31.8	18.8	17.0	17.0	17.0	17.0	17.0	17.0	17.0
IMR - Both Sexes	65.0	50.6	35.7	22.5	20.8	20.8	20.8	20.8	20.8	20.8	20.8
E(0) - Males	65.36	66.12	67.01	67.99	68.39	68.39	68.39	68.39	68.39	68.39	68.39
E(0) - Females	68.43	69.71	71.16	72.53	73.25	73.25	73.25	73.25	73.25	73.25	73.25
E(0) - Both Sexes	66.90	67.91	69.08	70.26	70.82	70.82	70.82	70.82	70.82	70.82	70.82

Year	2100	2110	2120	2130	2140	2150	2160	2170	2180	2190	2200
Birth Rate ‰	13.1	13.1	13.0	13.0	12.9	12.9	12.9	12.9	12.9	12.8	12.8
Death Rate ‰	15.5	15.6	15.7	15.8	15.8	15.9	15.9	15.9	15.9	16.0	16.0
Growth Rate %	-0.24	-0.25	-0.27	-0.28	-0.29	-0.29	-0.30	-0.30	-0.31	-0.31	-0.31
Total Fertility Rate	1.988	1.984	1.980	1.977	1.975	1.973	1.971	1.970	1.968	1.967	1.966
GRR	0.967	0.965	0.963	0.961	0.960	0.959	0.958	0.958	0.957	0.956	0.959
NRR	0.9	0.9	0.9	0.9	0.9	0.9	0.9	0.9	0.9	0.9	0.9
IMR - Males	24.6	24.6	24.6	24.6	24.6	24.6	24.6	24.6	24.6	24.6	24.6
IMR - Females	17.0	17.0	17.0	17.0	17.0	17.0	17.0	17.0	17.0	17.0	17.0
IMR - Both Sexes	20.8	20.8	20.8	20.8	20.8	20.8	20.8	20.8	20.8	20.8	20.8
E(0) - Males	68.39	68.39	68.39	68.39	68.39	68.39	68.39	68.39	68.39	68.39	68.39
E(0) - Females	73.25	73.25	73.25	73.25	73.25	73.25	73.25	73.25	73.25	73.25	73.25
E(0) - Both Sexes	70.82	70.82	70.82	70.82	70.82	70.82	70.82	70.82	70.82	70.82	70.82

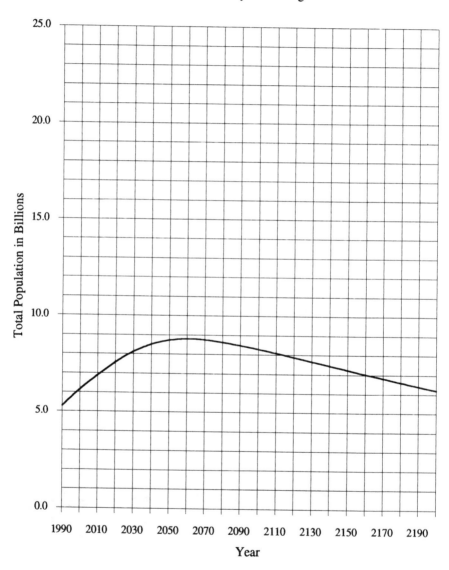

Graph 1

Projected Total Population
World Population Projection No. 2030.B.H
Decline Below Replacement Fertility Level
Mortality Level: High

Graph 2

Components of Population Change
World Population Projection No. 2030.B.H
Decline Below Replacement Fertility Level
Mortality Level: High

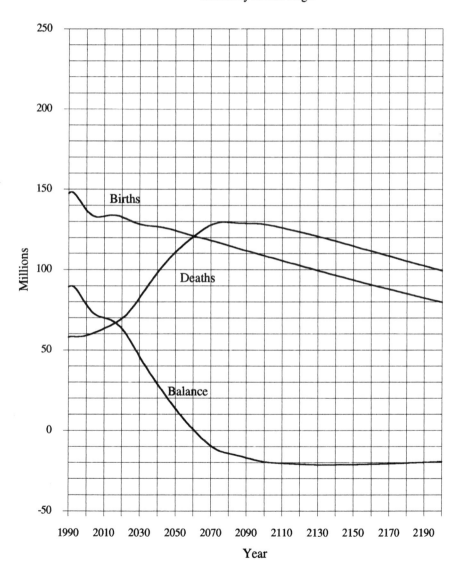

Graph 3

Age Structure of World Population 1990, 2050 and 2100

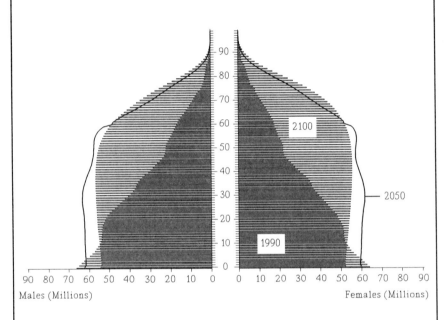

Males (Millions) Females (Millions)

Population Projection No. 2030.B.H.

Decline below replacement fertility level
by the year: 2030
Form of fertility decline: Hyperbolic
Mortality level: High

Total population: 1990 5 275 Million
2050 8 705 Million
2100 8 278 Million

Table 1
Projected Total Population
World Population Projection No. 2030.B.M
Decline Below Replacement Fertility Level; Mortality Level: Medium
- Millions -

Age Year	0-4	5-9	10-14	15-19	20-24	25-29	30-34	35-39	40-44	45-49	50-54	55-59	60-64	65-69	70-74	75+	Total
1990	625	563	528	519	490	436	380	342	282	230	214	186	160	123	87	108	5275
2000	653	659	609	555	519	508	479	424	367	327	264	209	185	149	114	124	6146
2010	628	622	640	652	600	545	508	496	465	408	346	299	231	170	133	157	6901
2020	646	634	619	617	633	642	590	535	496	479	441	375	305	246	169	186	7614
2030	633	639	641	630	614	610	625	633	578	518	472	444	391	312	226	257	8223
2040	623	622	628	636	636	624	606	601	612	613	551	482	421	370	292	339	8656
2050	615	616	618	619	623	630	628	615	594	583	584	570	491	401	314	417	8918
2060	600	604	610	613	613	613	616	621	615	596	567	542	520	475	366	459	9029
2070	587	590	595	601	605	607	606	604	604	602	587	554	505	451	387	533	9017
2080	573	577	582	587	591	595	598	598	594	586	576	559	523	461	377	541	8917
2090	558	562	569	574	578	581	584	586	586	580	566	544	513	466	390	541	8777
2100	544	548	554	559	564	568	571	572	572	569	559	539	504	453	382	550	8609
2110	529	533	540	545	550	554	557	560	559	555	546	528	498	449	376	541	8419
2120	515	519	525	531	535	539	543	546	546	543	534	516	486	440	371	533	8222
2130	501	505	511	516	521	525	529	532	532	529	521	504	475	430	362	524	8017
2140	486	491	497	502	507	511	515	518	518	516	508	492	464	420	354	512	7810
2150	473	477	483	488	493	497	501	504	505	502	494	479	452	410	346	501	7603
2160	459	463	469	474	479	483	487	490	491	488	481	466	440	399	337	489	7396
2170	446	450	455	461	465	469	473	476	477	475	468	454	429	388	328	476	7191
2180	433	437	442	447	452	456	460	463	464	462	455	441	417	378	320	464	6989
2190	420	424	429	434	439	443	447	449	450	449	442	429	405	368	311	451	6791
2200	408	411	417	422	426	430	434	436	438	436	430	417	394	357	302	439	6596

Table 2
Components of Population Change
World Population Projection No. 2030.B.M
Decline Below Replacement Fertility Level; Mortality Level: Medium

Year	Males Births	Males Deaths - Thousands -	Males Balance	Females Births	Females Deaths - Thousands -	Females Balance	Total Births	Total Deaths - Thousands -	Total Balance
1990	75539	29422	46117	71783	28562	43221	147322	57985	89338
2000	70242	30141	40101	66749	27018	39730	136991	57160	79831
2010	68345	32599	35746	64946	27776	37170	133291	60375	72916
2020	68249	35837	32413	64855	29932	34923	133104	65769	67336
2030	66177	42016	24161	62886	35346	27540	129062	77362	51701
2040	65442	50181	15261	62187	43854	18333	127629	94035	33593
2050	64325	56956	7369	61126	51094	10032	125451	108050	17401
2060	62779	61790	989	59657	56618	3039	122436	118407	4029
2070	61401	65442	-4040	58348	61262	-2914	119749	126704	-6955
2080	59899	66437	-6538	56920	63126	-6205	116819	129563	-12743
2090	58352	66202	-7851	55450	63067	-7617	113802	129270	-15468
2100	56833	65985	-9152	54007	63146	-9139	110840	129131	-18291
2110	55300	64987	-9687	52550	62350	-9800	107850	127337	-19487
2120	53780	63797	-10017	51106	61243	-10137	104886	125040	-20154
2130	52283	62520	-10236	49683	60104	-10420	101967	122623	-20657
2140	50806	61077	-10271	48279	58761	-10482	99085	119838	-20752
2150	49356	59605	-10250	46901	57372	-10471	96257	116977	-20720
2160	47934	58105	-10171	45550	55958	-10408	93484	114063	-20579
2170	46542	56584	-10042	44227	54511	-10284	90769	111096	-20327
2180	45181	55069	-9888	42934	53067	-10133	88116	108136	-20021
2190	43853	53564	-9711	41672	51629	-9957	85525	105193	-19668
2200	42556	52074	-9517	40440	50202	-9762	82996	102276	-19280

Table 3
Demographic Indicators
World Population Projection No. 2030.B.M
Decline Below Replacement Fertility Level; Mortality Level: Medium

Year	1990	2000	2010	2020	2030	2040	2050	2060	2070	2080	2090
Birth Rate ‰	27.9	22.3	19.3	17.5	15.7	14.7	14.1	13.6	13.3	13.1	13.0
Death Rate ‰	11.0	9.3	8.7	8.6	9.4	10.9	12.1	13.1	14.1	14.5	14.7
Growth Rate %	1.69	1.30	1.06	0.88	0.63	0.39	0.20	0.04	-0.08	-0.14	-0.18
Total Fertility Rate	3.400	2.838	2.414	2.224	2.130	2.078	2.047	2.026	2.012	2.002	1.994
GRR	1.684	1.372	1.180	1.082	1.037	1.013	0.996	0.986	0.979	0.974	0.970
NRR	1.5	1.3	1.1	1.0	1.0	1.0	1.0	1.0	1.0	1.0	0.9
IMR - Males	67.2	51.4	36.8	23.7	21.4	21.4	21.4	21.4	21.4	21.4	21.4
IMR - Females	62.8	46.2	29.6	16.9	14.8	14.8	14.8	14.8	14.8	14.8	14.8
IMR - Both Sexes	65.0	48.8	33.2	20.3	18.1	18.1	18.1	18.1	18.1	18.1	18.1
E(0) - Males	65.36	66.65	67.98	69.34	70.09	70.09	70.09	70.09	70.09	70.09	70.09
E(0) - Females	68.43	70.20	72.05	73.74	74.76	74.76	74.76	74.76	74.76	74.76	74.76
E(0) - Both Sexes	66.90	68.43	70.02	71.54	72.43	72.43	72.43	72.43	72.43	72.43	72.43

Year	2100	2110	2120	2130	2140	2150	2160	2170	2180	2190	2200
Birth Rate ‰	12.9	12.8	12.8	12.7	12.7	12.7	12.6	12.6	12.6	12.6	12.6
Death Rate ‰	15.0	15.1	15.2	15.3	15.3	15.4	15.4	15.4	15.5	15.5	15.5
Growth Rate %	-0.21	-0.23	-0.25	-0.26	-0.27	-0.27	-0.28	-0.28	-0.29	-0.29	-0.29
Total Fertility Rate	1.988	1.984	1.980	1.977	1.975	1.973	1.971	1.970	1.968	1.967	1.966
GRR	0.967	0.965	0.963	0.962	0.960	0.959	0.958	0.958	0.957	0.957	0.959
NRR	0.9	0.9	0.9	0.9	0.9	0.9	0.9	0.9	0.9	0.9	0.9
IMR - Males	21.4	21.4	21.4	21.4	21.4	21.4	21.4	21.4	21.4	21.4	21.4
IMR - Females	14.8	14.8	14.8	14.8	14.8	14.8	14.8	14.8	14.8	14.8	14.8
IMR - Both Sexes	18.1	18.1	18.1	18.1	18.1	18.1	18.1	18.1	18.1	18.1	18.1
E(0) - Males	70.09	70.09	70.09	70.09	70.09	70.09	70.09	70.09	70.09	70.09	70.09
E(0) - Females	74.76	74.76	74.76	74.76	74.76	74.76	74.76	74.76	74.76	74.76	74.76
E(0) - Both Sexes	72.43	72.43	72.43	72.43	72.43	72.43	72.43	72.43	72.43	72.43	72.43

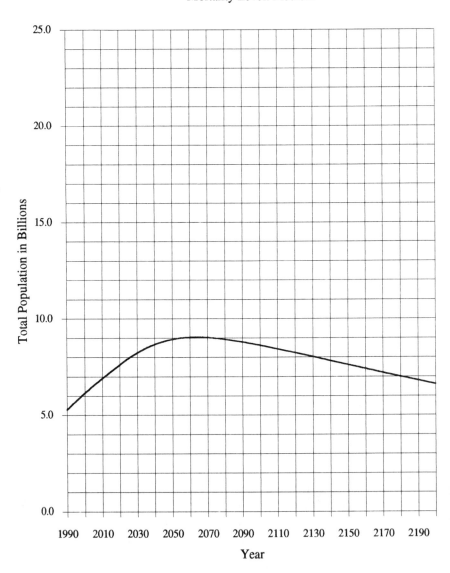

Graph 1

Projected Total Population
World Population Projection No. 2030.B.M
Decline Below Replacement Fertility Level
Mortality Level: Medium

Graph 2

Components of Population Change
World Population Projection No. 2030.B.M
Decline Below Replacement Fertility Level
Mortality Level: Medium

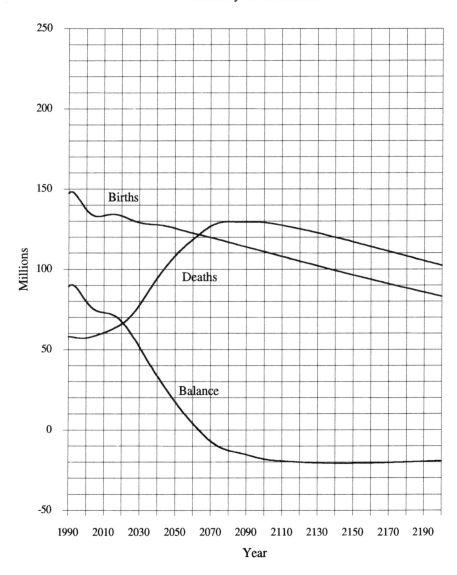

Graph 3

Age Structure of World Population 1990, 2050 and 2100

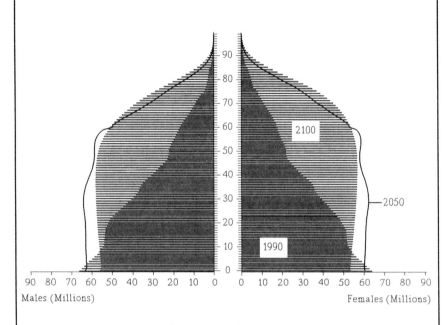

Population Projection No. 2030.B.M.

Decline below replacement fertility level by the year:	2030
Form of fertility decline:	Hyperbolic
Mortality level:	Medium

Total population:	1990	5 275 Million
	2050	8 918 Million
	2100	8 609 Million

Table 1
Projected Total Population
World Population Projection No. 2030.B.L
Decline Below Replacement Fertility Level; Mortality Level: Low

- Millions -

Age Year	0-4	5-9	10-14	15-19	20-24	25-29	30-34	35-39	40-44	45-49	50-54	55-59	60-64	65-69	70-74	75+	Total
1990	625	563	528	519	490	436	380	342	282	230	214	186	160	123	87	108	5275
2000	655	660	609	555	519	508	479	425	367	328	265	210	185	150	115	126	6154
2010	631	625	642	653	600	546	509	497	466	409	347	301	233	172	136	166	6934
2020	650	638	623	620	635	644	592	537	498	481	444	379	310	252	176	205	7685
2030	639	645	645	634	618	614	628	636	581	522	477	451	400	323	239	295	8347
2040	630	629	635	642	641	629	612	607	618	619	558	491	432	386	312	401	8840
2050	623	624	625	627	630	636	635	621	601	591	593	582	506	420	337	500	9151
2060	609	613	619	621	621	621	624	628	624	605	578	555	537	498	394	555	9303
2070	597	600	605	610	614	616	615	614	613	612	599	568	523	475	419	645	9326
2080	584	588	593	597	601	605	608	608	604	598	589	575	543	487	408	662	9251
2090	570	574	580	585	589	592	595	598	598	593	581	561	534	492	423	663	9129
2100	557	561	567	572	576	580	583	585	585	582	574	557	526	481	416	675	8977
2110	543	547	553	558	563	567	571	573	573	570	562	547	520	476	410	666	8800
2120	529	533	539	545	549	553	557	560	561	558	551	535	509	468	405	658	8612
2130	516	520	526	531	536	540	544	547	548	546	539	524	499	458	397	649	8417
2140	502	506	512	518	522	527	530	533	534	533	526	512	488	449	389	635	8217
2150	489	493	499	504	509	513	517	520	521	520	513	500	477	439	380	622	8016
2160	476	480	486	491	496	500	504	507	508	507	501	488	465	428	371	609	7815
2170	463	467	473	478	482	487	491	494	495	494	488	476	454	418	362	595	7615
2180	450	454	460	465	470	474	478	481	482	481	476	464	442	407	353	580	7417
2190	438	442	447	452	457	461	465	468	469	468	463	452	431	397	344	566	7221
2200	426	430	435	440	444	449	452	455	457	456	451	440	420	387	336	552	7029

Table 2
Components of Population Change
World Population Projection No. 2030.B.L
Decline Below Replacement Fertility Level; Mortality Level: Low

Year	Males Births	Males Deaths - Thousands -	Males Balance	Females Births	Females Deaths - Thousands -	Females Balance	Total Births	Total Deaths - Thousands -	Total Balance
1990	75539	29422	46117	71783	28562	43221	147322	57985	89338
2000	70264	29204	41060	66770	26212	40558	137034	55417	81617
2010	68428	30927	37501	65025	26430	38595	133453	57357	76096
2020	68482	33522	34959	65076	28127	36949	133558	61650	71908
2030	66554	38844	27710	63244	32823	30422	129799	71666	58132
2040	65930	47737	18193	62651	41842	20809	128582	89580	39002
2050	64939	55218	9720	61709	49607	12102	126648	104825	21822
2060	63518	60590	2927	60359	55542	4817	123876	116132	7744
2070	62249	64758	-2509	59153	60516	-1363	121403	125274	-3872
2080	60854	66449	-5594	57828	63053	-5225	118682	129501	-10820
2090	59407	66436	-7029	56452	63256	-6803	115859	129691	-13832
2100	57981	66449	-8468	55097	63468	-8371	113078	129918	-16839
2110	56535	65720	-9185	53723	62952	-9229	110258	128672	-18414
2120	55096	64669	-9572	52356	61977	-9621	107453	126646	-19193
2130	53675	63542	-9867	51005	60974	-9968	104680	124516	-19836
2140	52267	62233	-9966	49668	59770	-10102	101935	122003	-20068
2150	50881	60870	-9989	48351	58487	-10136	99232	119357	-20125
2160	49519	59477	-9958	47056	57177	-10121	96575	116653	-20079
2170	48181	58050	-9869	45785	55825	-10040	93966	113875	-19909
2180	46870	56621	-9750	44539	54465	-9925	91410	111085	-19675
2190	45587	55194	-9607	43320	53105	-9785	88907	108299	-19392
2200	44332	53775	-9443	42127	51750	-9623	86459	105525	-19066

Table 3
Demographic Indicators
World Population Projection No. 2030.B.L
Decline Below Replacement Fertility Level; Mortality Level: Low

Year	1990	2000	2010	2020	2030	2040	2050	2060	2070	2080	2090
Birth Rate ‰	27.9	22.3	19.2	17.4	15.6	14.5	13.8	13.3	13.0	12.8	12.7
Death Rate ‰	11.0	9.0	8.3	8.0	8.6	10.1	11.5	12.5	13.4	14.0	14.2
Growth Rate %	1.69	1.33	1.10	0.94	0.70	0.44	0.24	0.08	-0.04	-0.12	-0.15
Total Fertility Rate	3.400	2.838	2.414	2.224	2.130	2.078	2.047	2.026	2.012	2.002	1.994
GRR	1.684	1.372	1.180	1.082	1.037	1.013	0.996	0.986	0.979	0.974	0.970
NRR	1.5	1.3	1.1	1.1	1.0	1.0	1.0	1.0	1.0	1.0	1.0
IMR - Males	67.2	49.5	34.0	21.0	18.2	18.2	18.2	18.2	18.2	18.2	18.2
IMR - Females	62.8	44.4	27.4	15.0	12.6	12.6	12.6	12.6	12.6	12.6	12.6
IMR - Both Sexes	65.0	47.0	30.7	18.0	15.4	15.4	15.4	15.4	15.4	15.4	15.4
E(0) - Males	65.36	67.19	69.03	70.84	72.06	72.06	72.06	72.06	72.06	72.06	72.06
E(0) - Females	68.43	70.71	73.00	75.08	76.51	76.51	76.51	76.51	76.51	76.51	76.51
E(0) - Both Sexes	66.90	68.95	71.02	72.96	74.28	74.28	74.28	74.28	74.28	74.28	74.28

Year	2100	2110	2120	2130	2140	2150	2160	2170	2180	2190	2200
Birth Rate ‰	12.6	12.5	12.5	12.4	12.4	12.4	12.4	12.3	12.3	12.3	12.3
Death Rate ‰	14.5	14.6	14.7	14.8	14.8	14.9	14.9	15.0	15.0	15.0	15.0
Growth Rate %	-0.19	-0.21	-0.22	-0.24	-0.24	-0.25	-0.26	-0.26	-0.27	-0.27	-0.27
Total Fertility Rate	1.988	1.984	1.980	1.977	1.975	1.973	1.971	1.970	1.968	1.967	1.966
GRR	0.967	0.965	0.963	0.962	0.960	0.959	0.959	0.958	0.957	0.957	0.959
NRR	0.9	0.9	0.9	0.9	0.9	0.9	0.9	0.9	0.9	0.9	0.9
IMR - Males	18.2	18.2	18.2	18.2	18.2	18.2	18.2	18.2	18.2	18.2	18.2
IMR - Females	12.6	12.6	12.6	12.6	12.6	12.6	12.6	12.6	12.6	12.6	12.6
IMR - Both Sexes	15.4	15.4	15.4	15.4	15.4	15.4	15.4	15.4	15.4	15.4	15.4
E(0) - Males	72.06	72.06	72.06	72.06	72.06	72.06	72.06	72.06	72.06	72.06	72.06
E(0) - Females	76.51	76.51	76.51	76.51	76.51	76.51	76.51	76.51	76.51	76.51	76.51
E(0) - Both Sexes	74.28	74.28	74.28	74.28	74.28	74.28	74.28	74.28	74.28	74.28	74.28

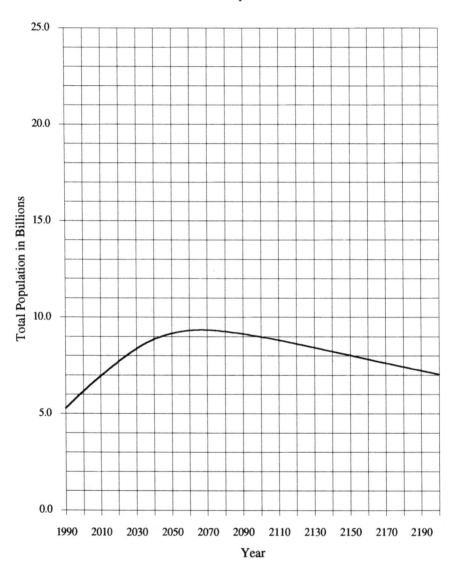

Graph 1

Projected Total Population
World Population Projection No. 2030.B.L
Decline Below Replacement Fertility Level
Mortality Level: Low

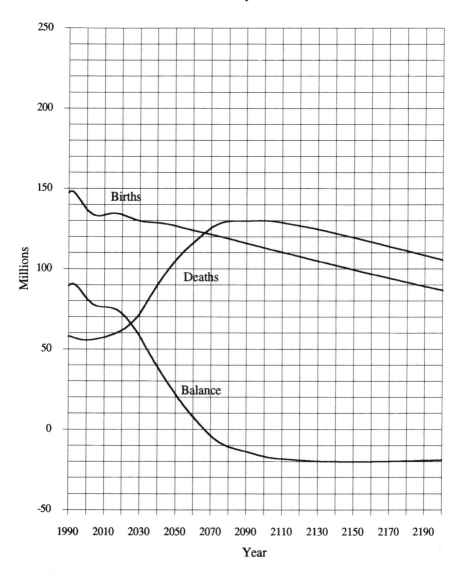

Graph 3

Age Structure of World Population 1990, 2050 and 2100

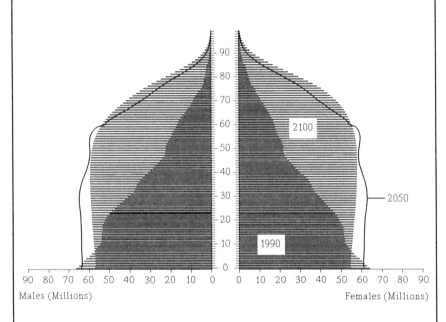

Population Projection No. 2030.B.L.

Decline below replacement fertility level
by the year: 2030
Form of fertility decline: Hyperbolic
Mortality level: Low

Total population: 1990   5 275 Million
2050   9 151 Million
2100   8 977 Million

Table 1
Projected Total Population
World Population Projection No. 2040.R.H
Decline to Replacement Fertility Level (2.13); Mortality Level: High

- Millions -

Age Year	0-4	5-9	10-14	15-19	20-24	25-29	30-34	35-39	40-44	45-49	50-54	55-59	60-64	65-69	70-74	75+	Total
1990	625	563	528	519	490	436	380	342	282	230	214	186	160	123	87	108	5275
2000	665	661	609	555	518	508	479	424	367	327	264	209	184	149	113	121	6153
2010	650	641	651	653	599	545	508	496	464	406	345	298	229	168	131	149	6931
2020	672	657	640	635	643	643	589	533	494	477	438	372	300	240	163	169	7664
2030	665	668	666	652	634	627	633	632	575	515	468	438	382	301	214	225	8294
2040	658	655	659	664	660	645	625	616	619	610	544	473	409	355	273	289	8753
2050	662	656	652	651	653	656	651	634	611	595	586	560	477	384	292	351	9070
2060	659	657	656	652	646	644	644	645	636	612	579	547	513	454	341	383	9267
2070	657	653	653	653	650	644	637	633	629	623	602	562	507	443	366	446	9359
2080	656	653	651	649	647	645	642	634	622	611	596	572	527	456	362	459	9382
2090	655	651	651	649	645	641	638	635	627	612	589	562	522	464	376	465	9381
2100	653	649	649	647	645	641	636	631	623	613	594	562	516	455	372	476	9363
2110	652	648	647	646	643	640	636	631	622	609	591	563	520	456	368	471	9341
2120	650	647	646	644	642	638	634	629	621	609	589	559	517	456	371	469	9322
2130	649	645	645	643	640	637	633	627	619	607	588	559	516	454	369	470	9302
2140	648	644	643	642	639	636	632	626	618	606	587	558	515	453	368	468	9282
2150	646	643	642	640	637	634	630	625	617	605	586	557	514	452	368	467	9263
2160	645	641	641	639	636	633	629	624	616	603	584	556	513	451	367	466	9243
2170	644	640	639	638	635	631	628	622	614	602	583	554	512	450	366	465	9223
2180	642	639	638	636	633	630	626	621	613	601	582	553	510	449	365	464	9204
2190	641	637	637	635	632	629	625	620	612	599	581	552	509	448	364	463	9184
2200	640	636	635	634	631	627	624	618	610	598	579	551	508	448	364	462	9165

Table 2
Components of Population Change
World Population Projection No. 2040.R.H
Decline to Replacement Fertility Level (2.13); Mortality Level: High

Year	Births	Males Deaths - Thousands -	Balance	Births	Females Deaths - Thousands -	Balance	Births	Total Deaths - Thousands -	Balance
1990	75539	29422	46117	71783	28562	43221	147322	57985	89338
2000	72324	31246	41078	68727	27966	40760	141050	59213	81838
2010	71107	34415	36693	67571	29224	38347	138678	63638	75040
2020	71449	38177	33272	67896	31724	36172	139345	69901	69444
2030	69920	45061	24859	66443	37719	28724	136363	82780	53583
2040	69634	52621	17014	66171	45790	20381	135805	98411	37394
2050	70024	59027	10997	66542	52727	13815	136566	111753	24812
2060	69554	63878	5676	66095	58192	7903	135649	122070	13579
2070	69493	67834	1660	66037	63123	2914	135530	130957	4573
2080	69382	69328	54	65932	65432	499	135314	134761	553
2090	69184	69839	-655	65743	66146	-403	134927	135985	-1059
2100	69061	70184	-1123	65626	66785	-1159	134687	136969	-2282
2110	68913	69889	-976	65486	66538	-1052	134399	136427	-2028
2120	68760	69699	-939	65340	66275	-935	134100	135974	-1874
2130	68619	69622	-1003	65206	66241	-1035	133825	135862	-2038
2140	68472	69438	-967	65066	66067	-1001	133538	135506	-1968
2150	68326	69293	-967	64928	65916	-988	133253	135209	-1956
2160	68181	69155	-974	64790	65794	-1004	132971	134949	-1978
2170	68036	69001	-965	64652	65645	-992	132688	134646	-1958
2180	67891	68857	-965	64515	65506	-991	132406	134363	-1957
2190	67747	68711	-964	64378	65369	-991	132125	134080	-1955
2200	67603	68564	-961	64241	65229	-987	131844	133792	-1948

Table 3
Demographic Indicators
World Population Projection No. 2040.R.H
Decline to Replacement Fertility Level (2.13); Mortality Level: High

Year	1990	2000	2010	2020	2030	2040	2050	2060	2070	2080	2090
Birth Rate ‰	27.9	22.9	20.0	18.2	16.4	15.5	15.1	14.6	14.5	14.4	14.4
Death Rate ‰	11.0	9.6	9.2	9.1	10.0	11.2	12.3	13.2	14.0	14.4	14.5
Growth Rate %	1.69	1.33	1.08	0.91	0.65	0.43	0.27	0.15	0.05	0.01	-0.01
Total Fertility Rate	3.400	2.915	2.512	2.306	2.195	2.130	2.130	2.130	2.130	2.130	2.130
GRR	1.684	1.413	1.229	1.124	1.069	1.041	1.039	1.038	1.039	1.039	1.039
NRR	1.5	1.3	1.2	1.1	1.0	1.0	1.0	1.0	1.0	1.0	1.0
IMR - Males	67.2	53.4	39.5	26.3	24.6	24.6	24.6	24.6	24.6	24.6	24.6
IMR - Females	62.8	47.9	31.8	18.8	17.0	17.0	17.0	17.0	17.0	17.0	17.0
IMR - Both Sexes	65.0	50.6	35.7	22.5	20.8	20.8	20.8	20.8	20.8	20.8	20.8
E(0) - Males	65.36	66.12	67.01	67.99	68.39	68.39	68.39	68.39	68.39	68.39	68.39
E(0) - Females	68.43	69.71	71.16	72.53	73.25	73.25	73.25	73.25	73.25	73.25	73.25
E(0) - Both Sexes	66.90	67.91	69.08	70.26	70.82	70.82	70.82	70.82	70.82	70.82	70.82

Year	2100	2110	2120	2130	2140	2150	2160	2170	2180	2190	2200
Birth Rate ‰	14.4	14.4	14.4	14.4	14.4	14.4	14.4	14.4	14.4	14.4	14.4
Death Rate ‰	14.6	14.6	14.6	14.6	14.6	14.6	14.6	14.6	14.6	14.6	14.6
Growth Rate %	-0.02	-0.02	-0.02	-0.02	-0.02	-0.02	-0.02	-0.02	-0.02	-0.02	-0.02
Total Fertility Rate	2.130	2.130	2.130	2.130	2.130	2.130	2.130	2.130	2.130	2.130	2.130
GRR	1.039	1.039	1.039	1.039	1.039	1.039	1.039	1.039	1.039	1.039	1.039
NRR	1.0	1.0	1.0	1.0	1.0	1.0	1.0	1.0	1.0	1.0	1.0
IMR - Males	24.6	24.6	24.6	24.6	24.6	24.6	24.6	24.6	24.6	24.6	24.6
IMR - Females	17.0	17.0	17.0	17.0	17.0	17.0	17.0	17.0	17.0	17.0	17.0
IMR - Both Sexes	20.8	20.8	20.8	20.8	20.8	20.8	20.8	20.8	20.8	20.8	20.8
E(0) - Males	68.39	68.39	68.39	68.39	68.39	68.39	68.39	68.39	68.39	68.39	68.39
E(0) - Females	73.25	73.25	73.25	73.25	73.25	73.25	73.25	73.25	73.25	73.25	73.25
E(0) - Both Sexes	70.82	70.82	70.82	70.82	70.82	70.82	70.82	70.82	70.82	70.82	70.82

Graph 1

Projected Total Population
World Population Projection No. 2040.R.H
Decline to Replacement Fertility Level (2.13)
Mortality Level: High

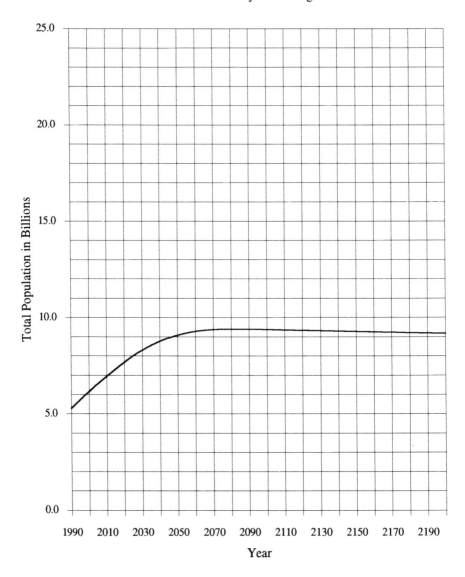

Graph 2

Components of Population Change
World Population Projection No. 2040.R.H
Decline to Replacement Fertility Level (2.13)
Mortality Level: High

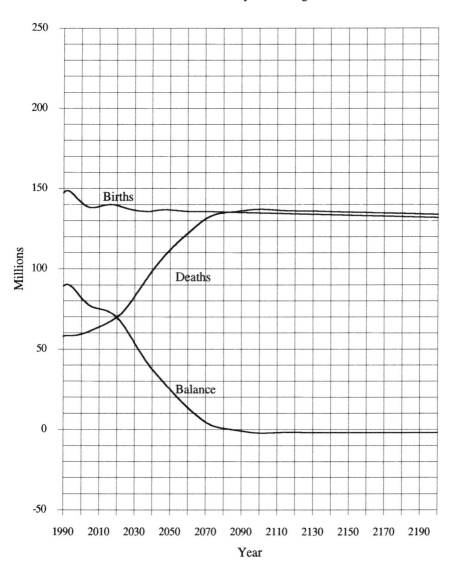

Graph 3

Age Structure of World Population 1990, 2050 and 2100

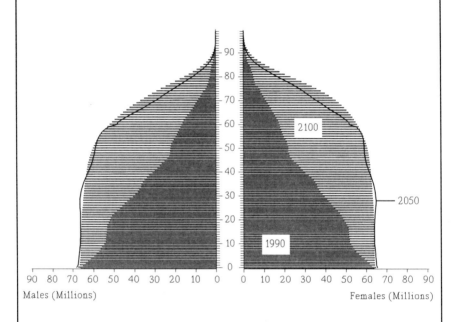

Population Projection No. 2040.R.H.

Target year for replacement fertility
level (TFR = 2.13):   2040
Form of fertility decline: Hyperbolic
Mortality level: High

Total population: 1990   5 275 Million
                                    2050   9 070 Million
                                    2100   9 363 Million

Table 1
Projected Total Population
World Population Projection No. 2040.R.M
Decline to Replacement Fertility Level (2.13); Mortality Level: Medium

- Millions -

Age Year	0-4	5-9	10-14	15-19	20-24	25-29	30-34	35-39	40-44	45-49	50-54	55-59	60-64	65-69	70-74	75+	Total
1990	625	563	528	519	490	436	380	342	282	230	214	186	160	123	87	108	5275
2000	666	662	609	555	519	508	479	424	367	327	264	209	185	149	114	124	6162
2010	653	643	653	654	600	545	508	496	465	408	346	299	231	170	133	157	6963
2020	677	661	644	638	645	645	590	535	496	479	441	375	305	246	169	186	7732
2030	671	673	671	657	638	631	637	635	578	518	472	444	391	312	226	257	8412
2040	665	662	666	670	665	650	631	622	624	616	551	482	421	370	292	339	8925
2050	671	664	660	659	660	663	658	641	618	603	596	572	491	401	314	417	9287
2060	669	667	666	661	655	652	653	654	644	621	590	560	530	477	366	459	9522
2070	668	664	664	663	660	654	647	643	639	634	615	577	525	467	395	534	9650
2080	669	665	663	661	658	656	653	645	634	623	610	589	547	481	392	555	9701
2090	669	665	664	662	658	654	651	647	640	625	605	579	543	490	408	563	9722
2100	669	665	663	662	659	655	650	644	638	627	610	581	538	482	405	578	9727
2110	669	665	664	661	658	655	651	646	637	625	608	583	543	484	402	573	9724
2120	669	665	664	662	658	655	651	645	638	626	608	581	542	486	405	571	9724
2130	669	665	664	661	658	655	651	645	637	626	609	582	541	484	404	574	9724
2140	669	665	664	661	658	655	651	645	637	626	608	582	542	484	404	573	9723
2150	669	665	664	661	658	655	651	645	638	626	608	581	542	484	404	573	9723
2160	669	665	663	661	658	655	651	645	637	626	608	581	542	484	404	573	9723
2170	669	665	663	661	658	655	651	645	637	626	608	581	542	484	404	573	9722
2180	669	665	663	661	658	655	651	645	637	626	608	581	542	484	404	573	9722
2190	669	665	663	661	658	655	651	645	637	626	608	581	542	484	404	573	9722
2200	669	665	663	661	658	655	651	645	637	626	608	581	542	484	404	573	9721

Table 2
Components of Population Change
World Population Projection No. 2040.R.M
Decline to Replacement Fertility Level (2.13); Mortality Level: Medium

Year	Males Births	Males Deaths - Thousands -	Males Balance	Females Births	Females Deaths - Thousands -	Females Balance	Total Births	Total Deaths - Thousands -	Total Balance
1990	75539	29422	46117	71783	28562	43221	147322	57985	89338
2000	72346	30314	42032	68748	27166	41582	141095	57480	83615
2010	71194	32797	38396	67653	27928	39725	138847	60725	78122
2020	71694	36024	35670	68128	30055	38073	139822	66079	73743
2030	70320	42246	28073	66823	35489	31333	137143	77736	59407
2040	70155	50509	19646	66666	44058	22608	136821	94567	42254
2050	70694	57517	13177	67178	51439	15739	137871	108956	28916
2060	70374	62776	7597	66874	57220	9654	137247	119996	17251
2070	70455	67192	3262	66951	62434	4517	137406	129626	7780
2080	70491	69261	1230	66985	65311	1674	137476	134572	2904
2090	70437	69975	462	66934	66231	703	137371	136206	1165
2100	70458	70573	-115	66954	67057	-103	137413	137630	-218
2110	70455	70494	-39	66951	67049	-98	137406	137543	-137
2120	70446	70413	33	66943	66887	55	137389	137300	88
2130	70449	70489	-40	66945	66983	-38	137394	137472	-78
2140	70445	70460	-15	66942	66966	-25	137387	137426	-40
2150	70442	70451	-9	66939	66943	-4	137381	137394	-13
2160	70440	70462	-21	66937	66960	-23	137378	137422	-44
2170	70438	70452	-15	66935	66951	-16	137372	137403	-30
2180	70435	70451	-16	66932	66947	-15	137368	137398	-31
2190	70433	70450	-17	66930	66948	-18	137363	137398	-35
2200	70431	70446	-16	66928	66944	-16	137359	137390	-32

Table 3
Demographic Indicators
World Population Projection No. 2040.R.M
Decline to Replacement Fertility Level (2.13); Mortality Level: Medium

Year	1990	2000	2010	2020	2030	2040	2050	2060	2070	2080	2090
Birth Rate ‰	27.9	22.9	19.9	18.1	16.3	15.3	14.8	14.4	14.2	14.2	14.1
Death Rate ‰	11.0	9.3	8.7	8.5	9.2	10.6	11.7	12.6	13.4	13.9	14.0
Growth Rate %	1.69	1.36	1.12	0.95	0.71	0.47	0.31	0.18	0.08	0.03	0.01
Total Fertility Rate	3.400	2.915	2.512	2.306	2.195	2.130	2.130	2.130	2.130	2.130	2.130
GRR	1.684	1.413	1.229	1.124	1.069	1.041	1.039	1.039	1.039	1.039	1.039
NRR	1.5	1.3	1.2	1.1	1.0	1.0	1.0	1.0	1.0	1.0	1.0
IMR - Males	67.2	51.4	36.8	23.7	21.4	21.4	21.4	21.4	21.4	21.4	21.4
IMR - Females	62.8	46.2	29.6	16.9	14.8	14.8	14.8	14.8	14.8	14.8	14.8
IMR - Both Sexes	65.0	48.8	33.2	20.3	18.1	18.1	18.1	18.1	18.1	18.1	18.1
E(0) - Males	65.36	66.65	67.98	69.34	70.09	70.09	70.09	70.09	70.09	70.09	70.09
E(0) - Females	68.43	70.20	72.05	73.74	74.76	74.76	74.76	74.76	74.76	74.76	74.76
E(0) - Both Sexes	66.90	68.43	70.02	71.54	72.43	72.43	72.43	72.43	72.43	72.43	72.43

Year	2100	2110	2120	2130	2140	2150	2160	2170	2180	2190	2200
Birth Rate ‰	14.1	14.1	14.1	14.1	14.1	14.1	14.1	14.1	14.1	14.1	14.1
Death Rate ‰	14.2	14.1	14.1	14.1	14.1	14.1	14.1	14.1	14.1	14.1	14.1
Growth Rate %	0.00	0.00	0.00	0.00	0.00	0.00	0.00	0.00	0.00	0.00	0.00
Total Fertility Rate	2.130	2.130	2.130	2.130	2.130	2.130	2.130	2.130	2.130	2.130	2.130
GRR	1.039	1.039	1.039	1.039	1.039	1.039	1.039	1.039	1.039	1.039	1.039
NRR	1.0	1.0	1.0	1.0	1.0	1.0	1.0	1.0	1.0	1.0	1.0
IMR - Males	21.4	21.4	21.4	21.4	21.4	21.4	21.4	21.4	21.4	21.4	21.4
IMR - Females	14.8	14.8	14.8	14.8	14.8	14.8	14.8	14.8	14.8	14.8	14.8
IMR - Both Sexes	18.1	18.1	18.1	18.1	18.1	18.1	18.1	18.1	18.1	18.1	18.1
E(0) - Males	70.09	70.09	70.09	70.09	70.09	70.09	70.09	70.09	70.09	70.09	70.09
E(0) - Females	74.76	74.76	74.76	74.76	74.76	74.76	74.76	74.76	74.76	74.76	74.76
E(0) - Both Sexes	72.43	72.43	72.43	72.43	72.43	72.43	72.43	72.43	72.43	72.43	72.43

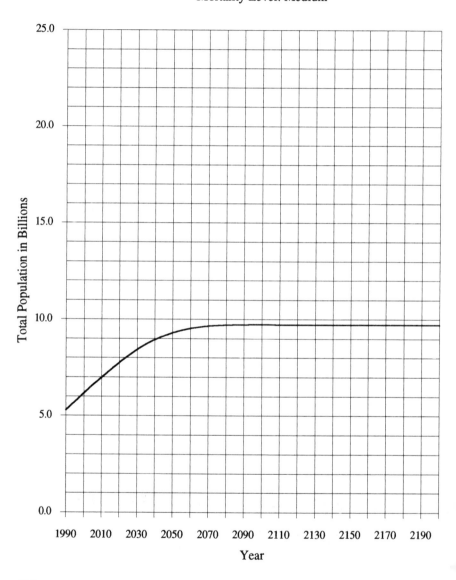

Graph 1

Projected Total Population
World Population Projection No. 2040.R.M
Decline to Replacement Fertility Level (2.13)
Mortality Level: Medium

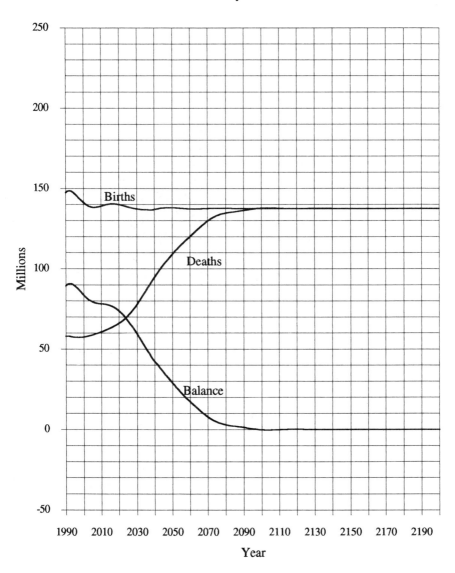

Graph 3

Age Structure of World Population 1990, 2050 and 2100

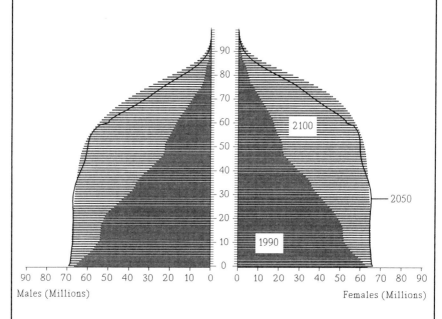

Population Projection No. 2040.R.M.

Target year for replacement fertility
level (TFR = 2.13): 2040
Form of fertility decline: Hyperbolic
Mortality level: Medium

Total population: 1990 5 275 Million
2050 9 287 Million
2100 9 727 Million

Table 1
Projected Total Population
World Population Projection No. 2040.R.L
Decline to Replacement Fertility Level (2.13); Mortality Level: Low

- Millions -

Age Year	0-4	5-9	10-14	15-19	20-24	25-29	30-34	35-39	40-44	45-49	50-54	55-59	60-64	65-69	70-74	75+	Total
1990	625	563	528	519	490	436	380	342	282	230	214	186	160	123	87	108	5275
2000	668	662	609	555	519	508	479	425	367	328	265	210	185	150	115	126	6170
2010	656	646	655	655	600	546	509	497	466	409	347	301	233	172	136	166	6996
2020	681	665	648	641	648	647	592	537	498	481	444	379	310	252	176	205	7804
2030	677	679	676	661	643	635	641	638	581	522	477	451	400	323	239	295	8538
2040	672	670	672	676	671	656	636	627	630	622	558	491	432	386	312	401	9112
2050	680	673	668	667	668	670	664	648	625	611	605	584	506	420	337	500	9526
2060	679	677	675	670	663	661	661	662	653	631	601	574	548	500	394	555	9804
2070	680	675	675	674	671	664	657	653	656	645	627	593	544	491	427	646	9971
2080	682	678	675	672	670	668	664	656	645	636	624	606	568	507	424	678	10055
2090	683	679	678	675	671	667	663	660	652	639	620	598	566	518	443	689	10101
2100	685	680	679	676	673	669	664	658	652	643	627	600	562	511	441	709	10129
2110	686	682	680	677	674	671	667	661	653	642	626	604	568	514	438	707	10148
2120	687	683	682	679	676	672	667	662	655	644	627	603	567	517	442	705	10169
2130	689	685	683	680	677	673	669	663	656	645	629	605	568	516	442	710	10190
2140	690	686	684	682	678	675	670	665	657	646	630	606	570	518	443	710	10211
2150	692	688	686	683	680	676	672	666	659	648	631	607	571	519	444	711	10232
2160	693	689	687	685	681	677	673	668	660	649	633	608	572	520	445	713	10253
2170	695	690	689	686	683	679	674	669	661	650	634	610	573	521	446	714	10274
2180	696	692	690	687	684	680	676	670	663	652	635	611	575	522	447	716	10295
2190	697	693	691	689	685	682	677	672	664	653	637	612	576	523	448	717	10317
2200	699	695	693	690	687	683	679	673	666	654	638	613	577	524	449	719	10338

Table 2
Components of Population Change
World Population Projection No. 2040.R.L
Decline to Replacement Fertility Level (2.13); Mortality Level: Low

Year	Births	Males Deaths - Thousands -	Balance	Births	Females Deaths - Thousands -	Balance	Births	Total Deaths - Thousands -	Balance
1990	75539	29422	46117	71783	28562	43221	147322	57985	89338
2000	72369	29371	42999	68770	26355	42416	141139	55725	85414
2010	71280	31111	40170	67736	26571	41165	139016	57682	81334
2020	71939	33689	38250	68361	28237	40124	140300	61927	78374
2030	70722	39041	31680	67204	32945	34259	137926	71987	65939
2040	70679	48019	22661	67164	42017	25147	137843	90036	47808
2050	71369	55701	15667	67820	49903	17916	139189	105605	33584
2060	71202	61448	9755	67661	56062	11599	138863	117509	21354
2070	71429	66310	5119	67877	61543	6333	139306	127853	11453
2080	71616	69046	2569	68054	65041	3013	139670	134087	5583
2090	71712	70029	1683	68145	66261	1884	139857	136291	3567
2100	71883	70869	1014	68308	67248	1060	140191	138117	2075
2110	72030	71046	984	68448	67513	935	140479	138559	1920
2120	72172	71079	1093	68583	67464	1119	140755	138543	2211
2130	72326	71301	1024	68729	67678	1051	141054	138979	2075
2140	72473	71437	1036	68869	67827	1042	141342	139264	2078
2150	72622	71568	1054	69010	67936	1074	141632	139503	2129
2160	72772	71730	1042	69153	68094	1059	141925	139825	2101
2170	72922	71872	1049	69295	68231	1064	142217	140103	2113
2180	73072	72020	1052	69438	68368	1070	142510	140388	2122
2190	73223	72170	1052	69581	68513	1069	142804	140683	2121
2200	73373	72318	1056	69724	68652	1072	143098	140970	2128

Table 3
Demographic Indicators
World Population Projection No. 2040.R.L
Decline to Replacement Fertility Level (2.13); Mortality Level: Low

Year	1990	2000	2010	2020	2030	2040	2050	2060	2070	2080	2090
Birth Rate ‰	27.9	22.9	19.9	18.0	16.2	15.1	14.6	14.2	14.0	13.9	13.8
Death Rate ‰	11.0	9.0	8.2	7.9	8.4	9.9	11.1	12.0	12.8	13.3	13.5
Growth Rate %	1.69	1.38	1.16	1.00	0.77	0.52	0.35	0.22	0.11	0.06	0.04
Total Fertility Rate	3.400	2.915	2.512	2.306	2.195	2.130	2.130	2.130	2.130	2.130	2.130
GRR	1.684	1.413	1.229	1.124	1.069	1.041	1.039	1.039	1.039	1.039	1.039
NRR	1.5	1.3	1.2	1.1	1.0	1.0	1.0	1.0	1.0	1.0	1.0
IMR - Males	67.2	49.5	34.0	21.0	18.2	18.2	18.2	18.2	18.2	18.2	18.2
IMR - Females	62.8	44.4	27.4	15.0	12.6	12.6	12.6	12.6	12.6	12.6	12.6
IMR - Both Sexes	65.0	47.0	30.7	18.0	15.4	15.4	15.4	15.4	15.4	15.4	15.4
E(0) - Males	65.36	67.19	69.03	70.84	72.06	72.06	72.06	72.06	72.06	72.06	72.06
E(0) - Females	68.43	70.71	73.00	75.08	76.51	76.51	76.51	76.51	76.51	76.51	76.51
E(0) - Both Sexes	66.90	68.95	71.02	72.96	74.28	74.28	74.28	74.28	74.28	74.28	74.28

Year	2100	2110	2120	2130	2140	2150	2160	2170	2180	2190	2200
Birth Rate ‰	13.8	13.8	13.8	13.8	13.8	13.8	13.8	13.8	13.8	13.8	13.8
Death Rate ‰	13.6	13.7	13.6	13.6	13.6	13.6	13.6	13.6	13.6	13.6	13.6
Growth Rate %	0.02	0.02	0.02	0.02	0.02	0.02	0.02	0.02	0.02	0.02	0.02
Total Fertility Rate	2.130	2.130	2.130	2.130	2.130	2.130	2.130	2.130	2.130	2.130	2.130
GRR	1.039	1.039	1.039	1.039	1.039	1.039	1.039	1.039	1.039	1.039	1.039
NRR	1.0	1.0	1.0	1.0	1.0	1.0	1.0	1.0	1.0	1.0	1.0
IMR - Males	18.2	18.2	18.2	18.2	18.2	18.2	18.2	18.2	18.2	18.2	18.2
IMR - Females	12.6	12.6	12.6	12.6	12.6	12.6	12.6	12.6	12.6	12.6	12.6
IMR - Both Sexes	15.4	15.4	15.4	15.4	15.4	15.4	15.4	15.4	15.4	15.4	15.4
E(0) - Males	72.06	72.06	72.06	72.06	72.06	72.06	72.06	72.06	72.06	72.06	72.06
E(0) - Females	76.51	76.51	76.51	76.51	76.51	76.51	76.51	76.51	76.51	76.51	76.51
E(0) - Both Sexes	74.28	74.28	74.28	74.28	74.28	74.28	74.28	74.28	74.28	74.28	74.28

Graph 1

Projected Total Population
World Population Projection No. 2040.R.L
Decline to Replacement Fertility Level (2.13)
Mortality Level: Low

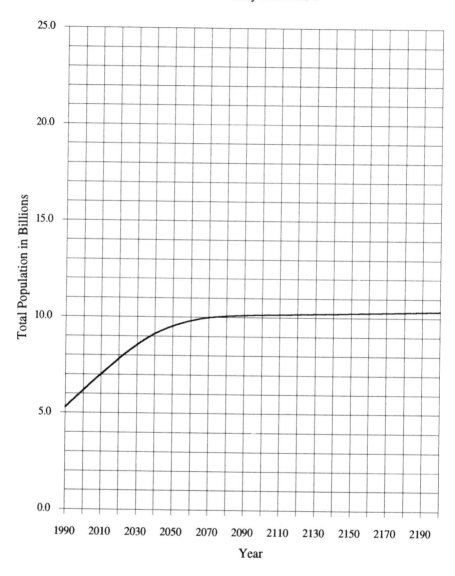

Graph 2

Components of Population Change
World Population Projection No. 2040.R.L
Decline to Replacement Fertility Level (2.13)
Mortality Level: Low

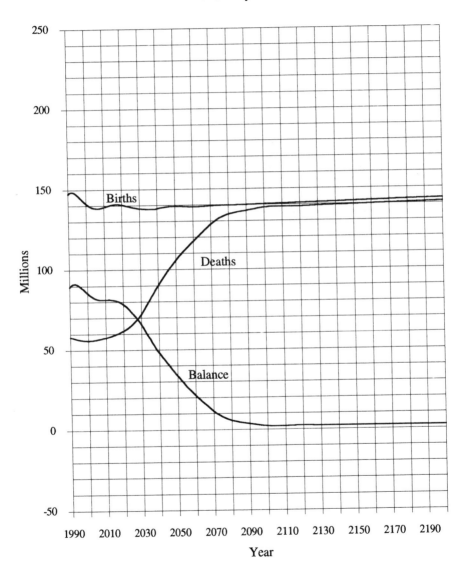

335

Graph 3

Age Structure of World Population 1990, 2050 and 2100

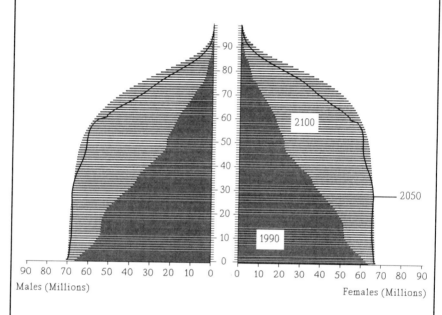

Males (Millions)   Females (Millions)

Population Projection No. 2040.R.L.

Target year for replacement fertility
level (TFR = 2.13):   2040
Form of fertility decline: Hyperbolic
Mortality level: Low

Total population: 1990   5 275 Million
     2050   9 526 Million
     2100   10 129 Million

Table 1
Projected Total Population
World Population Projection No. 2040.B.H
Decline Below Replacement Fertility Level; Mortality Level: High

- Millions -

Age Year	0-4	5-9	10-14	15-19	20-24	25-29	30-34	35-39	40-44	45-49	50-54	55-59	60-64	65-69	70-74	75+	Total
1990	625	563	528	519	490	436	380	342	282	230	214	186	160	123	87	108	5275
2000	665	661	609	555	518	508	479	424	367	327	264	209	184	149	113	121	6153
2010	650	641	651	653	599	545	508	496	464	406	345	298	229	168	131	149	6931
2020	672	657	640	635	643	643	589	533	494	477	438	372	300	240	163	169	7664
2030	665	668	666	652	634	627	633	632	575	515	468	438	382	301	214	225	8294
2040	658	655	659	664	660	645	625	616	619	610	544	473	409	355	273	289	8753
2050	652	651	652	651	653	656	651	634	611	595	586	560	477	384	292	351	9055
2060	639	641	646	648	646	644	644	645	636	612	579	547	513	454	341	383	9216
2070	626	628	633	637	640	640	637	633	629	623	602	562	507	443	366	446	9253
2080	613	615	620	624	627	630	631	629	622	611	596	572	527	456	362	459	9197
2090	598	601	607	612	615	617	619	619	617	608	589	562	522	464	376	465	9090
2100	583	586	592	598	602	605	607	607	604	598	584	558	516	455	372	476	8944
2110	568	572	578	583	587	591	594	595	593	586	573	549	511	453	368	471	8769
2120	553	556	563	568	573	576	579	581	580	574	561	538	501	445	365	467	8580
2130	537	541	548	553	558	562	565	567	566	561	549	527	491	436	358	461	8379
2140	522	526	533	538	543	547	550	552	552	547	536	515	481	428	351	452	8172
2150	507	511	518	523	528	532	535	538	537	533	523	503	469	418	343	443	7960
2160	493	497	503	508	513	517	521	523	523	519	509	490	457	407	335	433	7747
2170	478	482	488	494	498	502	506	508	509	505	495	477	446	397	327	422	7535
2180	464	468	474	479	484	488	492	494	494	491	482	464	434	387	318	412	7323
2190	450	454	460	465	470	474	477	480	480	477	468	451	422	376	310	401	7114
2200	436	440	446	451	456	460	463	466	466	463	455	438	410	366	301	390	6907

Table 2
Components of Population Change
World Population Projection No. 2040.B.H
Decline Below Replacement Fertility Level; Mortality Level: High

Year	Males Births	Males Deaths - Thousands -	Males Balance	Females Births	Females Deaths - Thousands -	Females Balance	Total Births	Total Deaths - Thousands -	Total Balance
1990	75539	29422	46117	71783	28562	43221	147322	57985	89338
2000	72324	31246	41078	68727	27966	40760	141050	59213	81838
2010	71107	34415	36693	67571	29224	38347	138678	63638	75040
2020	71449	38177	33272	67896	31724	36172	139345	69901	69444
2030	69920	45061	24859	66443	37719	28724	136363	82780	53583
2040	69472	52617	16855	66017	45787	20229	135488	98404	37084
2050	68558	58967	9591	65149	52687	12462	133707	111654	22053
2060	67141	63768	3374	63802	58121	5681	130944	121889	9055
2070	65821	67646	-1825	62548	63004	-457	128369	130651	-2282
2080	64331	69036	-4705	61132	65248	-4117	125463	134285	-8822
2090	62760	69397	-6637	59639	65869	-6230	122398	135266	-12867
2100	61187	69483	-8297	58144	66352	-8209	119331	135836	-16505
2110	59578	68718	-9141	56615	65812	-9197	116193	134530	-18337
2120	57965	67727	-9762	55082	64947	-9865	113047	132674	-19626
2130	56362	66542	-10180	53559	63933	-10374	109921	130475	-20554
2140	54769	65151	-10382	52045	62658	-10613	106813	127809	-20995
2150	53195	63690	-10495	50550	61301	-10751	103745	124990	-21246
2160	51646	62161	-10516	49077	59874	-10797	100723	122035	-21312
2170	50122	60588	-10466	47630	58388	-10758	97752	118976	-21224
2180	48629	59000	-10372	46210	56883	-10673	94839	115883	-21044
2190	47166	57405	-10239	44821	55366	-10545	91987	112771	-20784
2200	45736	55815	-10078	43462	53848	-10386	89198	109662	-20465

Table 3
Demographic Indicators
World Population Projection No. 2040.B.H
Decline Below Replacement Fertility Level; Mortality Level: High

Year	1990	2000	2010	2020	2030	2040	2050	2060	2070	2080	2090
Birth Rate ‰	27.9	22.9	20.0	18.2	16.4	15.5	14.8	14.2	13.9	13.6	13.5
Death Rate ‰	11.0	9.6	9.2	9.1	10.0	11.2	12.3	13.2	14.1	14.6	14.9
Growth Rate %	1.69	1.33	1.08	0.91	0.65	0.42	0.24	0.10	-0.02	-0.10	-0.14
Total Fertility Rate	3.400	2.915	2.512	2.306	2.195	2.130	2.089	2.061	2.041	2.027	2.016
GRR	1.684	1.413	1.229	1.124	1.069	1.038	1.017	1.003	0.994	0.986	0.981
NRR	1.5	1.3	1.2	1.1	1.0	1.0	1.0	1.0	1.0	1.0	1.0
IMR - Males	67.2	53.4	39.5	26.3	24.6	24.6	24.6	24.6	24.6	24.6	24.6
IMR - Females	62.8	47.9	31.8	18.8	17.0	17.0	17.0	17.0	17.0	17.0	17.0
IMR - Both Sexes	65.0	50.6	35.7	22.5	20.8	20.8	20.8	20.8	20.8	20.8	20.8
E(0) - Males	65.36	66.12	67.01	67.99	68.39	68.39	68.39	68.39	68.39	68.39	68.39
E(0) - Females	68.43	69.71	71.16	72.53	73.25	73.25	73.25	73.25	73.25	73.25	73.25
E(0) - Both Sexes	66.90	67.91	69.08	70.26	70.82	70.82	70.82	70.82	70.82	70.82	70.82

Year	2100	2110	2120	2130	2140	2150	2160	2170	2180	2190	2200
Birth Rate ‰	13.3	13.2	13.2	13.1	13.1	13.0	13.0	13.0	13.0	12.9	12.9
Death Rate ‰	15.2	15.3	15.5	15.6	15.6	15.7	15.8	15.8	15.8	15.9	15.9
Growth Rate %	-0.18	-0.21	-0.23	-0.25	-0.26	-0.27	-0.28	-0.28	-0.29	-0.29	-0.30
Total Fertility Rate	2.007	2.001	1.995	1.991	1.987	1.984	1.981	1.979	1.977	1.975	1.974
GRR	0.977	0.973	0.970	0.968	0.966	0.965	0.964	0.962	0.961	0.961	0.963
NRR	1.0	0.9	0.9	0.9	0.9	0.9	0.9	0.9	0.9	0.9	0.9
IMR - Males	24.6	24.6	24.6	24.6	24.6	24.6	24.6	24.6	24.6	24.6	24.6
IMR - Females	17.0	17.0	17.0	17.0	17.0	17.0	17.0	17.0	17.0	17.0	17.0
IMR - Both Sexes	20.8	20.8	20.8	20.8	20.8	20.8	20.8	20.8	20.8	20.8	20.8
E(0) - Males	68.39	68.39	68.39	68.39	68.39	68.39	68.39	68.39	68.39	68.39	68.39
E(0) - Females	73.25	73.25	73.25	73.25	73.25	73.25	73.25	73.25	73.25	73.25	73.25
E(0) - Both Sexes	70.82	70.82	70.82	70.82	70.82	70.82	70.82	70.82	70.82	70.82	70.82

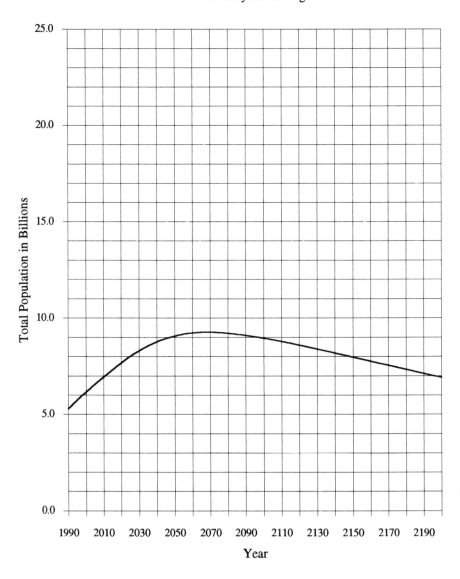

Graph 2

Components of Population Change
World Population Projection No. 2040.B.H
Decline Below Replacement Fertility Level
Mortality Level: High

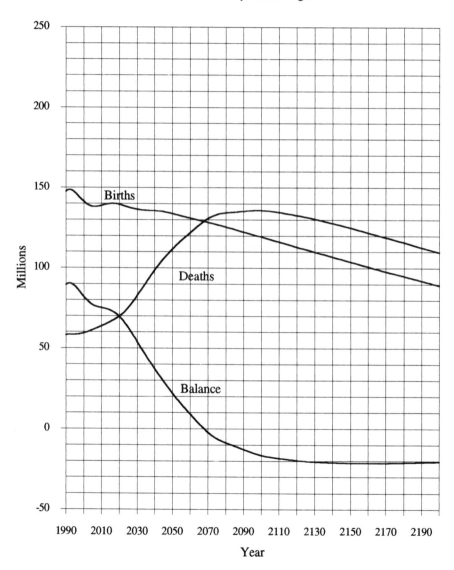

Graph 3

Age Structure of World Population 1990, 2050 and 2100

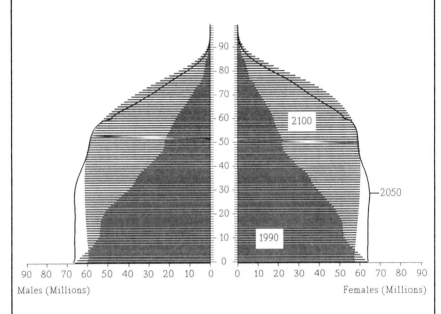

Population Projection No. 2040.B.H.

Decline below replacement fertility level
by the year: 2040
Form of fertility decline: Hyperbolic
Mortality level: High

Total population: 1990 5 275 Million
2050 9 055 Million
2100 8 944 Million

Table 1
Projected Total Population
World Population Projection No. 2040.B.M
Decline Below Replacement Fertility Level; Mortality Level: Medium

- Millions -

Age Year	0-4	5-9	10-14	15-19	20-24	25-29	30-34	35-39	40-44	45-49	50-54	55-59	60-64	65-69	70-74	75+	Total
1990	625	563	528	519	490	436	380	342	282	230	214	186	160	123	87	108	5275
2000	666	662	609	555	519	508	479	424	367	327	264	209	185	149	114	124	6162
2010	653	643	653	654	600	545	508	496	465	408	346	299	231	170	133	157	6963
2020	677	661	644	638	645	645	590	535	496	479	441	375	305	246	169	186	7732
2030	671	673	671	657	638	631	637	635	578	518	472	444	391	312	226	257	8412
2040	665	662	666	670	665	650	631	622	624	616	551	482	421	370	292	339	8925
2050	660	660	660	659	660	663	658	641	618	603	596	572	491	401	314	417	9272
2060	648	651	655	656	655	652	653	654	644	621	590	560	530	477	366	459	9471
2070	637	639	643	647	650	650	647	643	639	634	615	577	525	467	395	534	9542
2080	625	627	632	636	638	641	642	640	634	623	610	589	547	481	392	555	9512
2090	611	614	620	624	627	629	631	632	629	621	605	579	543	490	408	563	9426
2100	597	600	606	611	615	618	620	620	618	612	600	577	538	482	405	578	9297
2110	583	586	592	597	601	605	608	609	607	601	590	569	535	481	402	573	9137
2120	568	572	578	583	587	591	594	596	595	590	579	559	525	474	399	569	8960
2130	554	558	564	569	573	577	581	583	582	578	568	549	516	465	392	564	8770
2140	539	543	549	555	559	563	567	569	569	565	555	537	506	457	385	554	8572
2150	525	529	535	540	545	549	553	555	555	552	543	525	495	447	377	544	8368
2160	511	515	521	526	531	535	539	541	541	538	530	513	483	437	369	533	8162
2170	497	501	507	512	517	521	525	527	528	525	517	500	472	427	360	521	7955
2180	483	487	493	498	503	507	511	513	514	511	503	488	460	417	352	509	7748
2190	469	473	479	484	489	493	497	500	500	498	490	475	448	406	343	497	7543
2200	456	460	466	471	475	480	483	486	487	484	477	462	437	396	334	485	7339

Table 2
Components of Population Change
World Population Projection No. 2040.B.M
Decline Below Replacement Fertility Level; Mortality Level: Medium

Year	Males			Females			Total		
	Births	Deaths	Balance	Births	Deaths	Balance	Births	Deaths	Balance
		- Thousands -			- Thousands -			- Thousands -	
1990	75539	29422	46117	71783	28562	43221	147322	57985	89338
2000	72346	30314	42032	68748	27166	41582	141095	57480	83615
2010	71194	32797	38396	67653	27928	39725	138847	60725	78122
2020	71694	36024	35670	68128	30055	38073	139822	66079	73743
2030	70320	42246	28073	66823	35489	31333	137143	77736	59407
2040	69991	50505	19486	66510	44056	22454	136501	94561	41940
2050	69214	57464	11750	65772	51405	14367	134986	108869	26117
2060	67933	62679	5253	64554	57157	7397	132487	119837	12650
2070	66732	67027	-295	63413	62329	1084	130145	129356	789
2080	65359	69002	-3644	62108	65148	-3040	127467	134150	-6683
2090	63896	69583	-5686	60719	65985	-5267	124615	135568	-10953
2100	62425	69949	-7525	59320	66673	-7353	121745	136622	-14878
2110	60910	69443	-8533	57881	66401	-8520	118792	135844	-17052
2120	59386	68611	-9225	56432	65685	-9252	115818	134295	-18477
2130	57864	67597	-9733	54986	64830	-9843	112850	132426	-19576
2140	56346	66350	-10004	53544	63703	-10159	109890	130053	-20163
2150	54842	65014	-10172	52114	62466	-10352	106956	127480	-20524
2160	53356	63604	-10248	50702	61156	-10454	104058	124760	-20702
2170	51890	62136	-10245	49310	59775	-10465	101200	121910	-20711
2180	50449	60643	-10194	47940	58364	-10423	98389	119007	-20617
2190	49035	59135	-10101	46596	56934	-10338	95630	116069	-20439
2200	47647	57623	-9976	45278	55494	-10217	92925	113118	-20193

Table 3
Demographic Indicators
World Population Projection No. 2040.B.M
Decline Below Replacement Fertility Level; Mortality Level: Medium

Year	1990	2000	2010	2020	2030	2040	2050	2060	2070	2080	2090
Birth Rate ‰	27.9	22.9	19.9	18.1	16.3	15.3	14.6	14.0	13.6	13.4	13.2
Death Rate ‰	11.0	9.3	8.7	8.5	9.2	10.6	11.7	12.7	13.6	14.1	14.4
Growth Rate %	1.69	1.36	1.12	0.95	0.71	0.47	0.28	0.13	0.01	-0.07	-0.12
Total Fertility Rate	3.400	2.915	2.512	2.306	2.195	2.130	2.089	2.061	2.041	2.027	2.016
GRR	1.684	1.413	1.229	1.124	1.069	1.038	1.017	1.003	0.994	0.986	0.981
NRR	1.5	1.3	1.2	1.1	1.0	1.0	1.0	1.0	1.0	1.0	1.0
IMR - Males	67.2	51.4	36.8	23.7	21.4	21.4	21.4	21.4	21.4	21.4	21.4
IMR - Females	62.8	46.2	29.6	16.9	14.8	14.8	14.8	14.8	14.8	14.8	14.8
IMR - Both Sexes	65.0	48.8	33.2	20.3	18.1	18.1	18.1	18.1	18.1	18.1	18.1
E(0) - Males	65.36	66.65	67.98	69.34	70.09	70.09	70.09	70.09	70.09	70.09	70.09
E(0) - Females	68.43	70.20	72.05	73.74	74.76	74.76	74.76	74.76	74.76	74.76	74.76
E(0) - Both Sexes	66.90	68.43	70.02	71.54	72.43	72.43	72.43	72.43	72.43	72.43	72.43

Year	2100	2110	2120	2130	2140	2150	2160	2170	2180	2190	2200
Birth Rate ‰	13.1	13.0	12.9	12.9	12.8	12.8	12.7	12.7	12.7	12.7	12.7
Death Rate ‰	14.7	14.9	15.0	15.1	15.2	15.2	15.3	15.3	15.4	15.4	15.4
Growth Rate %	-0.16	-0.19	-0.21	-0.22	-0.24	-0.25	-0.25	-0.26	-0.27	-0.27	-0.28
Total Fertility Rate	2.007	2.001	1.995	1.991	1.987	1.984	1.981	1.979	1.977	1.975	1.974
GRR	0.977	0.973	0.971	0.968	0.966	0.965	0.964	0.962	0.961	0.961	0.963
NRR	1.0	1.0	0.9	0.9	0.9	0.9	0.9	0.9	0.9	0.9	0.9
IMR - Males	21.4	21.4	21.4	21.4	21.4	21.4	21.4	21.4	21.4	21.4	21.4
IMR - Females	14.8	14.8	14.8	14.8	14.8	14.8	14.8	14.8	14.8	14.8	14.8
IMR - Both Sexes	18.1	18.1	18.1	18.1	18.1	18.1	18.1	18.1	18.1	18.1	18.1
E(0) - Males	70.09	70.09	70.09	70.09	70.09	70.09	70.09	70.09	70.09	70.09	70.09
E(0) - Females	74.76	74.76	74.76	74.76	74.76	74.76	74.76	74.76	74.76	74.76	74.76
E(0) - Both Sexes	72.43	72.43	72.43	72.43	72.43	72.43	72.43	72.43	72.43	72.43	72.43

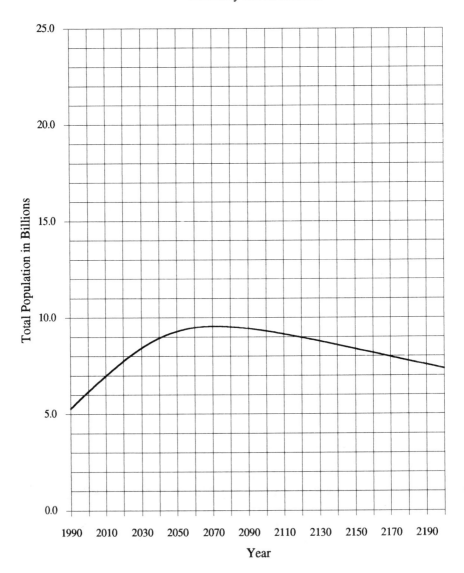

Graph 2

Components of Population Change
World Population Projection No. 2040.B.M
Decline Below Replacement Fertility Level
Mortality Level: Medium

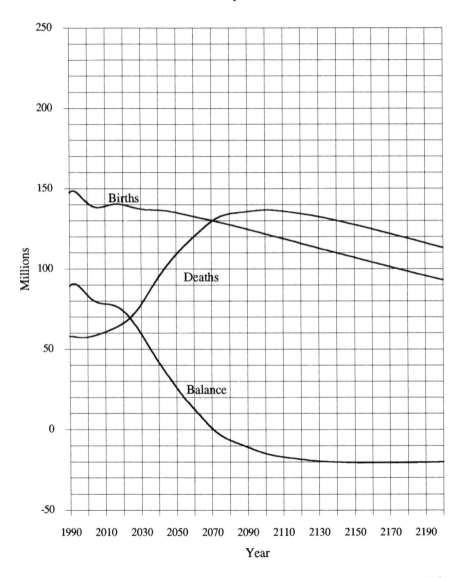

347

Graph 3

Age Structure of World Population 1990, 2050 and 2100

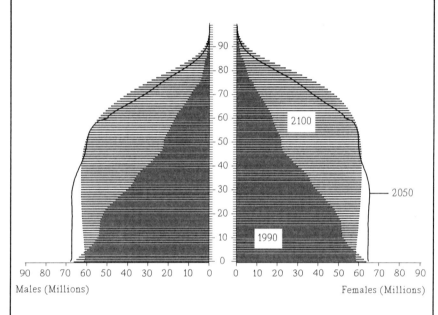

Population Projection No. 2040.B.M.

Decline below replacement fertility level
by the year: 2040
Form of fertility decline: Hyperbolic
Mortality level: Medium

Total population: 1990   5 275 Million
2050   9 272 Million
2100   9 297 Million

Table 1
Projected Total Population
World Population Projection No. 2040.B.L
Decline Below Replacement Fertility Level; Mortality Level: Low

- Millions -

Age Year	0-4	5-9	10-14	15-19	20-24	25-29	30-34	35-39	40-44	45-49	50-54	55-59	60-64	65-69	70-74	75+	Total
1990	625	563	528	519	490	436	380	342	282	230	214	186	160	123	87	108	5275
2000	668	662	609	555	519	508	479	425	367	328	265	210	185	150	115	126	6170
2010	656	646	655	655	600	546	509	497	466	409	347	301	233	172	136	166	6996
2020	681	665	648	641	648	647	592	537	498	481	444	379	310	252	176	205	7804
2030	677	679	676	661	643	635	641	638	581	522	477	451	400	323	239	295	8538
2040	672	670	672	676	671	656	636	627	630	622	558	491	432	386	312	401	9112
2050	669	668	668	667	668	670	664	648	625	611	605	584	506	420	337	500	9510
2060	658	661	664	665	663	661	661	662	653	631	601	574	548	500	394	555	9752
2070	648	650	654	658	660	660	657	653	650	645	627	593	544	491	427	646	9862
2080	637	639	644	647	650	652	653	651	645	636	624	606	568	507	424	678	9862
2090	624	627	632	637	639	641	643	644	642	635	620	598	566	518	443	689	9798
2100	611	614	620	624	628	631	633	634	632	627	617	596	562	511	441	709	9690
2110	598	601	607	612	616	619	622	623	622	617	607	589	559	510	438	707	9546
2120	584	588	594	599	603	606	609	611	611	607	598	580	550	504	435	703	9383
2130	570	574	580	585	590	594	597	599	599	596	587	570	542	496	429	697	9205
2140	557	561	567	572	576	580	584	586	587	584	575	560	532	488	422	687	9016
2150	543	547	553	558	563	567	570	573	574	571	563	548	521	479	414	676	8821
2160	529	534	539	545	549	553	557	560	561	558	551	536	511	469	406	664	8623
2170	516	520	526	531	536	540	544	547	548	545	539	524	499	459	398	651	8422
2180	503	507	513	518	522	527	530	533	534	532	526	512	488	449	389	637	8221
2190	490	494	499	505	509	513	517	520	521	520	513	500	477	438	380	623	8020
2200	477	481	486	492	496	500	504	507	508	507	501	488	465	428	371	609	7820

Table 2
Components of Population Change
World Population Projection No. 2040.B.L
Decline Below Replacement Fertility Level; Mortality Level: Low

Year	Males Births	Males Deaths - Thousands -	Males Balance	Females Births	Females Deaths - Thousands -	Females Balance	Total Births	Total Deaths - Thousands -	Total Balance
1990	75539	29422	46117	71783	28562	43221	147322	57985	89338
2000	72369	29371	42999	68770	26355	42416	141139	55725	85414
2010	71280	31111	40170	67736	26571	41165	139016	57682	81334
2020	71939	33689	38250	68361	28237	40124	140300	61927	78374
2030	70722	39041	31680	67204	32945	34259	137926	71987	65939
2040	70514	48016	22499	67007	42015	24992	137521	90031	47491
2050	69875	55656	14219	66400	49874	16526	136275	105530	30745
2060	68732	61364	7368	65314	56008	9307	134047	117372	16675
2070	67654	66167	1487	64289	61453	2836	131944	127620	4324
2080	66401	68823	-2421	63099	64900	-1801	129501	133723	-4222
2090	65052	69689	-4636	61817	66049	-4232	126869	135737	-8868
2100	63686	70326	-6640	60519	66914	-6395	124205	137240	-13035
2110	62271	70123	-7852	59175	66947	-7773	121446	137070	-15624
2120	60840	69467	-8628	57814	66399	-8585	118654	135866	-17213
2130	59405	68632	-9228	56450	65707	-9256	115855	134339	-18484
2140	57967	67547	-9579	55084	64743	-9658	113051	132289	-19238
2150	56538	66344	-9806	53726	63635	-9909	110263	129979	-19716
2160	55120	65061	-9941	52379	62449	-10070	107499	127510	-20011
2170	53719	63708	-9989	51047	61181	-10134	104766	124889	-20123
2180	52336	62318	-9982	49733	59872	-10138	102069	122190	-20121
2190	50975	60906	-9931	48440	58536	-10096	99414	119442	-20027
2200	49636	59481	-9844	47168	57182	-10015	96804	116663	-19859

Table 3
Demographic Indicators
World Population Projection No. 2040.B.L
Decline Below Replacement Fertility Level; Mortality Level: Low

Year	1990	2000	2010	2020	2030	2040	2050	2060	2070	2080	2090
Birth Rate ‰	27.9	22.9	19.9	18.0	16.2	15.1	14.3	13.7	13.4	13.1	12.9
Death Rate ‰	11.0	9.0	8.2	7.9	8.4	9.9	11.1	12.0	12.9	13.6	13.9
Growth Rate %	1.69	1.38	1.16	1.00	0.77	0.52	0.32	0.17	0.04	-0.04	-0.09
Total Fertility Rate	3.400	2.915	2.512	2.306	2.195	2.130	2.089	2.061	2.041	2.027	2.016
GRR	1.684	1.413	1.229	1.124	1.069	1.039	1.017	1.003	0.994	0.986	0.981
NRR	1.5	1.3	1.2	1.1	1.0	1.0	1.0	1.0	1.0	1.0	1.0
IMR - Males	67.2	49.5	34.0	21.0	18.2	18.2	18.2	18.2	18.2	18.2	18.2
IMR - Females	62.8	44.4	27.4	15.0	12.6	12.6	12.6	12.6	12.6	12.6	12.6
IMR - Both Sexes	65.0	47.0	30.7	18.0	15.4	15.4	15.4	15.4	15.4	15.4	15.4
E(0) - Males	65.36	67.19	69.03	70.84	72.06	72.06	72.06	72.06	72.06	72.06	72.06
E(0) - Females	68.43	70.71	73.00	75.08	76.51	76.51	76.51	76.51	76.51	76.51	76.51
E(0) - Both Sexes	66.90	68.95	71.02	72.96	74.28	74.28	74.28	74.28	74.28	74.28	74.28

Year	2100	2110	2120	2130	2140	2150	2160	2170	2180	2190	2200
Birth Rate ‰	12.8	12.7	12.6	12.6	12.5	12.5	12.5	12.4	12.4	12.4	12.4
Death Rate ‰	14.2	14.4	14.5	14.6	14.7	14.7	14.8	14.8	14.9	14.9	14.9
Growth Rate %	-0.13	-0.16	-0.18	-0.20	-0.21	-0.22	-0.23	-0.24	-0.24	-0.25	-0.25
Total Fertility Rate	2.007	2.001	1.995	1.991	1.987	1.984	1.981	1.979	1.977	1.975	1.974
GRR	0.977	0.973	0.971	0.968	0.967	0.965	0.964	0.962	0.962	0.961	0.962
NRR	1.0	1.0	1.0	0.9	0.9	0.9	0.9	0.9	0.9	0.9	0.9
IMR - Males	18.2	18.2	18.2	18.2	18.2	18.2	18.2	18.2	18.2	18.2	18.2
IMR - Females	12.6	12.6	12.6	12.6	12.6	12.6	12.6	12.6	12.6	12.6	12.6
IMR - Both Sexes	15.4	15.4	15.4	15.4	15.4	15.4	15.4	15.4	15.4	15.4	15.4
E(0) - Males	72.06	72.06	72.06	72.06	72.06	72.06	72.06	72.06	72.06	72.06	72.06
E(0) - Females	76.51	76.51	76.51	76.51	76.51	76.51	76.51	76.51	76.51	76.51	76.51
E(0) - Both Sexes	74.28	74.28	74.28	74.28	74.28	74.28	74.28	74.28	74.28	74.28	74.28

Graph 1

Projected Total Population
World Population Projection No. 2040.B.L
Decline Below Replacement Fertility Level
Mortality Level: Low

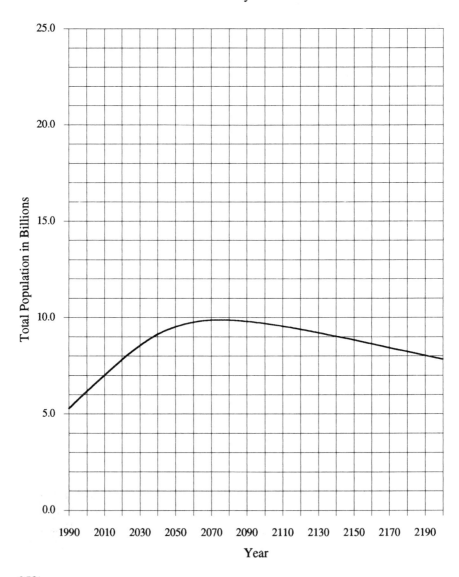

Graph 2

Components of Population Change
World Population Projection No. 2040.B.L
Decline Below Replacement Fertility Level
Mortality Level: Low

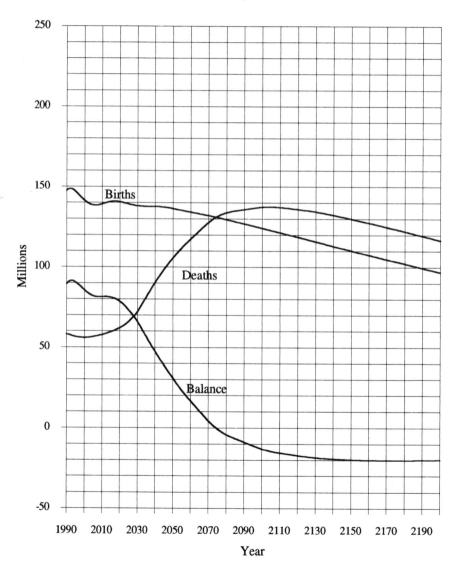

Graph 3

Age Structure of World Population 1990, 2050 and 2100

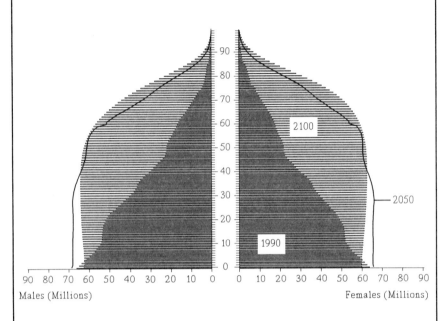

Population Projection No. 2040.B.L.

Decline below replacement fertility level by the year:	2040
Form of fertility decline:	Hyperbolic
Mortality level:	Low

Total population:	1990	5 275 Million
	2050	9 510 Million
	2100	9 690 Million

Table 1
Projected Total Population
World Population Projection No. 2050.R.H
Decline to Replacement Fertility Level (2.13); Mortality Level: High

- Millions -

Age Year	0-4	5-9	10-14	15-19	20-24	25-29	30-34	35-39	40-44	45-49	50-54	55-59	60-64	65-69	70-74	75+	Total
1990	625	563	528	519	490	436	380	342	282	230	214	186	160	123	87	108	5275
2000	674	662	609	555	518	508	479	424	367	327	264	209	184	149	113	121	6164
2010	670	656	660	655	599	545	508	496	464	406	345	298	229	168	131	149	6976
2020	697	678	659	650	651	645	589	533	494	477	438	372	300	240	163	169	7754
2030	697	696	690	674	653	642	642	633	575	515	468	438	382	301	214	225	8443
2040	694	689	690	692	684	666	644	631	627	609	544	473	409	355	273	289	8972
2050	692	690	688	685	684	684	675	655	629	611	594	562	477	384	292	351	9350
2060	691	687	686	686	682	677	675	673	659	632	596	560	520	455	341	383	9602
2070	690	686	685	683	680	678	673	666	659	649	624	581	522	454	371	447	9747
2080	688	684	684	682	679	675	671	666	657	643	624	597	547	471	373	467	9807
2090	687	683	682	680	677	674	670	663	655	643	622	591	547	484	390	479	9828
2100	685	682	681	679	676	672	668	663	654	640	620	591	545	479	390	495	9821
2110	684	680	679	677	675	671	667	661	653	640	620	589	543	479	389	494	9800
2120	682	679	678	676	673	670	665	660	651	638	618	588	543	477	388	493	9779
2130	681	677	676	675	672	668	664	658	650	637	617	586	541	477	387	492	9759
2140	680	676	675	673	670	667	663	657	649	636	616	585	540	475	386	491	9738
2150	678	674	673	672	669	665	661	656	647	634	614	584	539	474	386	490	9717
2160	677	673	672	670	667	664	660	654	646	633	613	583	538	474	385	489	9696
2170	675	671	671	669	666	662	658	653	644	632	612	582	537	472	384	488	9676
2180	674	670	669	667	665	661	657	651	643	630	610	580	536	471	383	487	9655
2190	672	669	668	666	663	660	656	650	642	629	609	579	534	470	382	486	9635
2200	671	667	666	665	662	658	654	649	640	628	608	578	533	469	382	485	9614

Table 2
Components of Population Change
World Population Projection No. 2050.R.H
Decline to Replacement Fertility Level (2.13); Mortality Level: High

Year	Males Births	Males Deaths - Thousands -	Males Balance	Females Births	Females Deaths - Thousands -	Females Balance	Total Births	Total Deaths - Thousands -	Total Balance
1990	75539	29422	46117	71783	28562	43221	147322	57985	89338
2000	73795	31370	42424	70125	28073	42052	143920	59443	84476
2010	73358	34580	38778	69710	29350	40360	143067	63930	79137
2020	74307	38344	35963	70612	31835	38777	144919	70179	74740
2030	73447	45277	28170	69795	37854	31940	143242	83132	60110
2040	73470	52923	20547	69816	45979	23837	143286	98902	44384
2050	73079	59443	13636	69445	52980	16464	142523	112423	30100
2060	73105	64624	8481	69469	58647	10822	142574	123271	19303
2070	72899	69140	3759	69273	64005	5268	142172	133146	9027
2080	72748	71415	1333	69130	67075	2055	141878	138490	3388
2090	72606	72588	17	68995	68518	477	141600	141106	495
2100	72442	73387	-945	68839	69677	-838	141281	143064	-1783
2110	72291	73348	-1057	68696	69797	-1101	140987	143145	-2158
2120	72138	73163	-1025	68551	69606	-1055	140689	142769	-2080
2130	71983	73001	-1018	68404	69449	-1045	140387	142450	-2063
2140	71831	72855	-1024	68259	69310	-1051	140090	142165	-2075
2150	71679	72698	-1019	68114	69164	-1050	139792	141862	-2069
2160	71526	72542	-1016	67969	69012	-1043	139495	141553	-2058
2170	71374	72390	-1016	67825	68869	-1044	139199	141259	-2060
2180	71223	72235	-1012	67681	68721	-1041	138903	140956	-2053
2190	71071	72082	-1010	67537	68575	-1038	138608	140657	-2049
2200	70920	71929	-1008	67393	68430	-1037	138313	140358	-2045

Table 3
Demographic Indicators
World Population Projection No. 2050.R.H
Decline to Replacement Fertility Level (2.13); Mortality Level: High

Year	1990	2000	2010	2020	2030	2040	2050	2060	2070	2080	2090
Birth Rate ‰	27.9	23.3	20.5	18.7	17.0	16.0	15.2	14.8	14.6	14.5	14.4
Death Rate ‰	11.0	9.6	9.2	9.1	9.8	11.0	12.0	12.8	13.7	14.1	14.4
Growth Rate %	1.69	1.37	1.13	0.96	0.71	0.49	0.32	0.20	0.09	0.03	0.01
Total Fertility Rate	3.400	2.968	2.590	2.377	2.255	2.179	2.130	2.130	2.130	2.130	2.130
GRR	1.684	1.442	1.267	1.159	1.099	1.063	1.040	1.039	1.039	1.039	1.039
NRR	1.5	1.3	1.2	1.1	1.1	1.0	1.0	1.0	1.0	1.0	1.0
IMR - Males	67.2	53.4	39.5	26.3	24.6	24.6	24.6	24.6	24.6	24.6	24.6
IMR - Females	62.8	47.9	31.8	18.8	17.0	17.0	17.0	17.0	17.0	17.0	17.0
IMR - Both Sexes	65.0	50.6	35.7	22.5	20.8	20.8	20.8	20.8	20.8	20.8	20.8
E(0) - Males	65.36	66.12	67.01	67.99	68.39	68.39	68.39	68.39	68.39	68.39	68.39
E(0) - Females	68.43	69.71	71.16	72.53	73.25	73.25	73.25	73.25	73.25	73.25	73.25
E(0) - Both Sexes	66.90	67.91	69.08	70.26	70.82	70.82	70.82	70.82	70.82	70.82	70.82

Year	2100	2110	2120	2130	2140	2150	2160	2170	2180	2190	2200
Birth Rate ‰	14.4	14.4	14.4	14.4	14.4	14.4	14.4	14.4	14.4	14.4	14.4
Death Rate ‰	14.6	14.6	14.6	14.6	14.6	14.6	14.6	14.6	14.6	14.6	14.6
Growth Rate %	-0.02	-0.02	-0.02	-0.02	-0.02	-0.02	-0.02	-0.02	-0.02	-0.02	-0.02
Total Fertility Rate	2.130	2.130	2.130	2.130	2.130	2.130	2.130	2.130	2.130	2.130	2.130
GRR	1.039	1.039	1.039	1.039	1.039	1.039	1.039	1.039	1.039	1.039	1.039
NRR	1.0	1.0	1.0	1.0	1.0	1.0	1.0	1.0	1.0	1.0	1.0
IMR - Males	24.6	24.6	24.6	24.6	24.6	24.6	24.6	24.6	24.6	24.6	24.6
IMR - Females	17.0	17.0	17.0	17.0	17.0	17.0	17.0	17.0	17.0	17.0	17.0
IMR - Both Sexes	20.8	20.8	20.8	20.8	20.8	20.8	20.8	20.8	20.8	20.8	20.8
E(0) - Males	68.39	68.39	68.39	68.39	68.39	68.39	68.39	68.39	68.39	68.39	68.39
E(0) - Females	73.25	73.25	73.25	73.25	73.25	73.25	73.25	73.25	73.25	73.25	73.25
E(0) - Both Sexes	70.82	70.82	70.82	70.82	70.82	70.82	70.82	70.82	70.82	70.82	70.82

Graph 1

Projected Total Population
World Population Projection No. 2050.R.H
Decline to Replacement Fertility Level (2.13)
Mortality Level: High

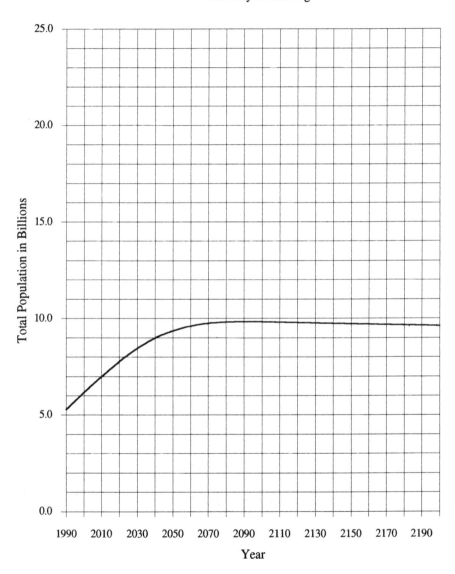

Graph 2

Components of Population Change
World Population Projection No. 2050.R.H
Decline to Replacement Fertility Level (2.13)
Mortality Level: High

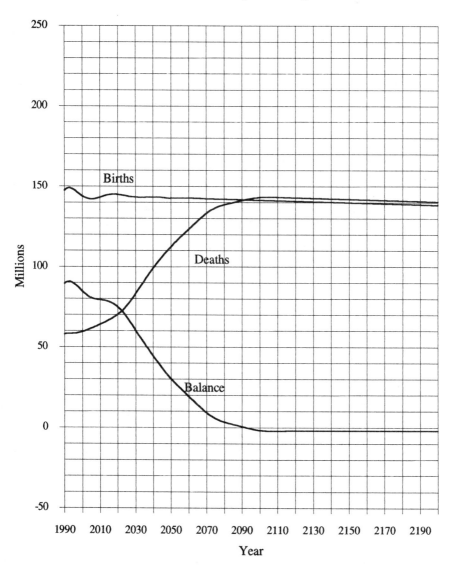

Graph 3

Age Structure of World Population 1990, 2050 and 2100

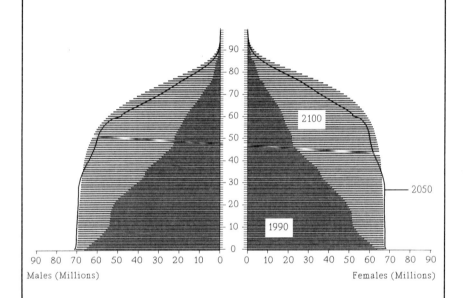

Population Projection No. 2050.R.H.

Target year for replacement fertility
level (TFR = 2.13): 2050
Form of fertility decline: Hyperbolic
Mortality level: High

Total population: 1990 5 275 Million
2050 9 350 Million
2100 9 821 Million

Table 1
Projected Total Population
World Population Projection No. 2050.R.M
Decline to Replacement Fertility Level (2.13); Mortality Level: Medium

Age Year	0-4	5-9	10-14	15-19	20-24	25-29	30-34	35-39	40-44	45-49	50-54	55-59	60-64	65-69	70-74	75+	Total
1990	625	563	528	519	490	436	380	342	282	230	214	186	160	123	87	108	5275
2000	675	663	609	555	519	508	479	424	367	327	264	209	185	149	114	124	6172
2010	673	659	662	656	600	545	508	496	465	408	346	299	231	170	133	157	7008
2020	702	683	663	653	654	647	590	535	496	479	441	375	305	246	169	186	7824
2030	703	702	695	678	657	646	646	637	578	518	472	444	391	312	226	257	8563
2040	702	697	697	698	690	672	650	637	633	617	551	482	421	370	292	339	9146
2050	701	699	696	693	692	691	682	662	636	617	604	574	491	401	314	417	9570
2060	702	697	696	695	691	686	684	681	668	642	607	573	537	478	366	459	9862
2070	702	698	696	693	690	688	683	676	670	661	637	596	541	478	401	535	10045
2080	702	697	696	694	691	686	682	678	669	656	639	614	568	497	403	564	10137
2090	702	698	696	694	691	687	683	676	668	657	638	609	569	511	423	580	10183
2100	702	698	696	694	691	687	683	677	669	656	637	611	568	508	424	600	10201
2110	702	698	696	694	691	687	682	677	669	657	638	609	568	509	424	602	10202
2120	702	698	696	694	691	687	683	677	669	656	638	610	568	508	423	602	10201
2130	702	697	696	694	691	687	683	677	669	657	638	610	568	508	424	601	10201
2140	702	697	696	694	691	687	683	677	669	657	638	610	568	508	424	601	10201
2150	702	697	696	694	691	687	683	677	669	656	638	610	568	508	424	601	10200
2160	701	697	696	694	691	687	683	677	669	656	638	610	568	508	424	601	10200
2170	701	697	696	694	691	687	682	677	669	656	638	610	568	508	424	601	10200
2180	701	697	696	694	691	687	682	677	669	656	638	610	568	508	424	601	10199
2190	701	697	696	694	691	687	682	677	669	656	638	610	568	508	424	601	10199
2200	701	697	696	694	690	687	682	677	669	656	638	610	568	508	424	601	10199

- Millions -

Table 2
Components of Population Change
World Population Projection No. 2050.R.M
Decline to Replacement Fertility Level (2.13); Mortality Level: Medium

Year	Males Births	Males Deaths - Thousands -	Males Balance	Females Births	Females Deaths - Thousands -	Females Balance	Total Births	Total Deaths - Thousands -	Total Balance
1990	75539	29422	46117	71783	28562	43221	147322	57985	89338
2000	73818	30434	43384	70147	27269	42878	143965	57703	86262
2010	73447	32952	40495	69795	28046	41749	143242	60997	82244
2020	74562	36175	38387	70854	30155	40699	145416	66330	79086
2030	73868	42436	31431	70194	35608	34586	144062	78044	66018
2040	74020	50775	23245	70339	44224	26115	144358	94998	49360
2050	73778	57884	15894	70109	51662	18447	143887	109546	34342
2060	73967	63440	10527	70288	57622	12667	144255	121062	23194
2070	73908	68378	5530	70233	63225	7008	144141	131603	12538
2080	73911	71222	2689	70235	66836	3399	144146	138058	6087
2090	73921	72643	1279	70245	68519	1726	144167	141162	3005
2100	73909	73734	175	70233	69900	333	144142	143634	508
2110	73909	73959	-50	70234	70296	-62	144143	144255	-112
2120	73908	73926	-18	70232	70255	-23	144140	144180	-41
2130	73904	73915	-11	70228	70239	-11	144132	144154	-22
2140	73902	73921	-19	70227	70243	-17	144129	144164	-35
2150	73899	73918	-18	70224	70245	-21	144124	144163	-39
2160	73897	73912	-15	70222	70236	-15	144119	144148	-30
2170	73894	73912	-18	70220	70238	-18	144114	144150	-36
2180	73892	73909	-17	70217	70235	-17	144109	144143	-34
2190	73889	73906	-17	70215	70232	-17	144104	144138	-34
2200	73887	73904	-17	70212	70230	-18	144099	144134	-35

Table 3
Demographic Indicators
World Population Projection No. 2050.R.M
Decline to Replacement Fertility Level (2.13); Mortality Level: Medium

Year	1990	2000	2010	2020	2030	2040	2050	2060	2070	2080	2090
Birth Rate ‰	27.9	23.3	20.4	18.6	16.8	15.8	15.0	14.6	14.3	14.2	14.2
Death Rate ‰	11.0	9.3	8.7	8.5	9.1	10.4	11.4	12.3	13.1	13.6	13.9
Growth Rate %	1.69	1.40	1.17	1.01	0.77	0.54	0.36	0.24	0.12	0.06	0.03
Total Fertility Rate	3.400	2.968	2.590	2.377	2.255	2.179	2.130	2.130	2.130	2.130	2.130
GRR	1.684	1.442	1.267	1.160	1.099	1.063	1.040	1.039	1.039	1.039	1.039
NRR	1.5	1.3	1.2	1.1	1.1	1.0	1.0	1.0	1.0	1.0	1.0
IMR - Males	67.2	51.4	36.8	23.7	21.4	21.4	21.4	21.4	21.4	21.4	21.4
IMR - Females	62.8	46.2	29.6	16.9	14.8	14.8	14.8	14.8	14.8	14.8	14.8
IMR - Both Sexes	65.0	48.8	33.2	20.3	18.1	18.1	18.1	18.1	18.1	18.1	18.1
E(0) - Males	65.36	66.65	67.98	69.34	70.09	70.09	70.09	70.09	70.09	70.09	70.09
E(0) - Females	68.43	70.20	72.05	73.74	74.76	74.76	74.76	74.76	74.76	74.76	74.76
E(0) - Both Sexes	66.90	68.43	70.02	71.54	72.43	72.43	72.43	72.43	72.43	72.43	72.43

Year	2100	2110	2120	2130	2140	2150	2160	2170	2180	2190	2200
Birth Rate ‰	14.1	14.1	14.1	14.1	14.1	14.1	14.1	14.1	14.1	14.1	14.1
Death Rate ‰	14.1	14.1	14.1	14.1	14.1	14.1	14.1	14.1	14.1	14.1	14.1
Growth Rate %	0.00	0.00	0.00	0.00	0.00	0.00	0.00	0.00	0.00	0.00	0.00
Total Fertility Rate	2.130	2.130	2.130	2.130	2.130	2.130	2.130	2.130	2.130	2.130	2.130
GRR	1.039	1.039	1.039	1.039	1.039	1.039	1.039	1.039	1.039	1.039	1.039
NRR	1.0	1.0	1.0	1.0	1.0	1.0	1.0	1.0	1.0	1.0	1.0
IMR - Males	21.4	21.4	21.4	21.4	21.4	21.4	21.4	21.4	21.4	21.4	21.4
IMR - Females	14.8	14.8	14.8	14.8	14.8	14.8	14.8	14.8	14.8	14.8	14.8
IMR - Both Sexes	18.1	18.1	18.1	18.1	18.1	18.1	18.1	18.1	18.1	18.1	18.1
E(0) - Males	70.09	70.09	70.09	70.09	70.09	70.09	70.09	70.09	70.09	70.09	70.09
E(0) - Females	74.76	74.76	74.76	74.76	74.76	74.76	74.76	74.76	74.76	74.76	74.76
E(0) - Both Sexes	72.43	72.43	72.43	72.43	72.43	72.43	72.43	72.43	72.43	72.43	72.43

Graph 1

Projected Total Population
World Population Projection No. 2050.R.M
Decline to Replacement Fertility Level (2.13)
Mortality Level: Medium

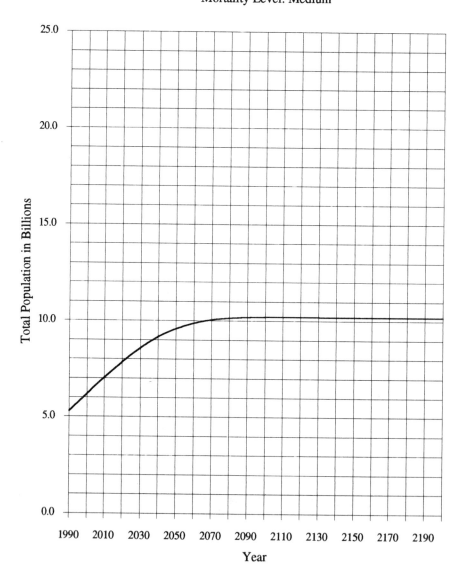

Graph 2

Components of Population Change
World Population Projection No. 2050.R.M
Decline to Replacement Fertility Level (2.13)
Mortality Level: Medium

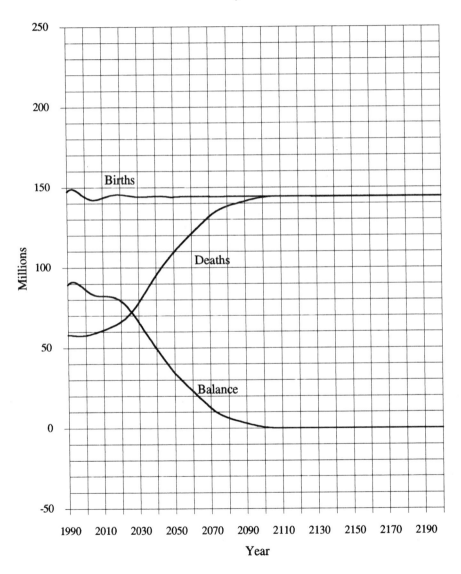

Graph 3

Age Structure of World Population 1990, 2050 and 2100

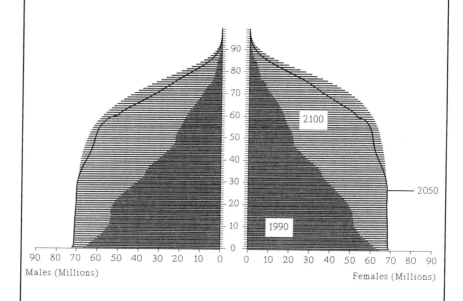

Population Projection No. 2050.R.M.

Target year for replacement fertility level (TFR = 2.13):	2050
Form of fertility decline:	Hyperbolic
Mortality level:	Medium
Total population:	1990 5 275 Million
	2050 9 570 Million
	2100 10 201 Million

Table 1
Projected Total Population
World Population Projection No. 2050.R.L
Decline to Replacement Fertility Level (2.13); Mortality Level: Low

- Millions -

Age Year	0-4	5-9	10-14	15-19	20-24	25-29	30-34	35-39	40-44	45-49	50-54	55-59	60-64	65-69	70-74	75+	Total
1990	625	563	528	519	490	436	380	342	282	230	214	186	160	123	87	108	5275
2000	677	664	609	555	519	508	479	425	367	328	265	210	185	150	115	126	6181
2010	676	662	664	657	600	546	509	497	466	409	347	301	233	172	136	166	7042
2020	706	687	667	656	657	649	592	537	498	481	444	379	310	252	176	205	7896
2030	709	708	701	683	662	650	650	640	581	522	477	451	400	323	239	295	8690
2040	710	705	704	704	696	677	655	642	639	623	558	491	432	386	312	401	9335
2050	710	708	705	702	700	698	689	669	644	626	613	586	506	420	337	500	9812
2060	713	707	705	704	700	696	693	690	677	652	619	588	556	501	394	555	10150
2070	714	710	708	704	701	698	693	687	681	672	650	612	561	503	433	647	10375
2080	715	711	709	707	703	698	694	690	681	669	654	631	589	524	437	689	10502
2090	717	713	710	708	704	701	696	690	682	672	655	629	593	540	459	709	10577
2100	718	714	712	709	706	702	697	692	684	672	655	631	593	538	462	736	10622
2110	720	715	714	711	707	703	699	693	685	674	657	631	594	540	462	741	10647
2120	721	717	715	712	709	705	700	695	687	675	659	633	596	540	462	742	10668
2130	723	718	716	714	710	706	702	696	688	677	660	634	597	542	464	743	10690
2140	724	720	718	715	712	708	703	697	690	678	661	636	598	543	465	745	10712
2150	726	721	719	717	713	709	705	699	691	679	662	637	599	544	466	746	10734
2160	727	723	721	718	715	711	706	700	692	681	664	638	600	545	467	748	10756
2170	729	724	722	720	716	712	707	702	694	682	665	640	602	546	468	750	10778
2180	730	726	724	721	718	713	709	703	695	684	667	641	603	547	469	751	10801
2190	732	727	725	723	719	715	710	705	697	685	668	642	604	549	470	753	10823
2200	733	729	727	724	720	716	712	706	698	687	669	644	605	550	471	754	10845

Table 2
Components of Population Change
World Population Projection No. 2050.R.L
Decline to Replacement Fertility Level (2.13); Mortality Level: Low

Year	Males Births	Males Deaths - Thousands -	Males Balance	Females Births	Females Deaths - Thousands -	Females Balance	Births	Total Deaths - Thousands -	Balance
1990	75539	29422	46117	71783	28562	43221	147322	57985	89338
2000	73841	29486	44355	70169	26453	43716	144010	55940	88071
2010	73537	31254	42283	69880	26680	43199	143416	57934	85482
2020	74818	33824	40994	71097	28326	42771	145915	62150	83765
2030	74290	39204	35086	70595	33047	37549	144886	72251	72635
2040	74573	48247	26326	70864	42159	28706	145438	90406	55032
2050	74484	56018	18466	70780	50095	20685	145263	106113	39151
2060	74838	62024	12814	71116	56409	14708	145955	118433	27522
2070	74930	67362	7568	71204	62237	8967	146134	129599	16535
2080	75091	70856	4235	71357	66430	4927	146448	137286	9162
2090	75260	72590	2670	71517	68442	3075	146777	141032	5745
2100	75404	73967	1436	71654	70023	1630	147057	143991	3067
2110	75562	74501	1062	71805	70731	1073	147367	145232	2135
2120	75719	74635	1084	71953	70861	1092	147672	145496	2176
2130	75873	74776	1098	72100	70985	1115	147973	145761	2212
2140	76030	74937	1094	72249	71136	1114	148280	146072	2207
2150	76187	75094	1093	72398	71290	1108	148585	146384	2201
2160	76344	75243	1100	72547	71429	1118	148890	146672	2218
2170	76501	75401	1100	72696	71579	1117	149197	146981	2217
2180	76658	75556	1103	72846	71727	1119	149505	147283	2222
2190	76816	75711	1105	72996	71873	1123	149812	147585	2228
2200	76975	75868	1107	73146	72022	1124	150121	147890	2231

Table 3
Demographic Indicators
World Population Projection No. 2050.R.L
Decline to Replacement Fertility Level (2.13); Mortality Level: Low

Year	1990	2000	2010	2020	2030	2040	2050	2060	2070	2080	2090
Birth Rate ‰	27.9	23.3	20.4	18.5	16.7	15.6	14.8	14.4	14.1	13.9	13.9
Death Rate ‰	11.0	9.1	8.2	7.9	8.3	9.7	10.8	11.7	12.5	13.1	13.3
Growth Rate %	1.69	1.42	1.21	1.06	0.84	0.59	0.40	0.27	0.16	0.09	0.05
Total Fertility Rate	3.400	2.968	2.590	2.377	2.255	2.179	2.130	2.130	2.130	2.130	2.130
GRR	1.684	1.442	1.267	1.160	1.099	1.063	1.040	1.039	1.039	1.039	1.039
NRR	1.5	1.4	1.2	1.1	1.1	1.0	1.0	1.0	1.0	1.0	1.0
IMR - Males	67.2	49.5	34.0	21.0	18.2	18.2	18.2	18.2	18.2	18.2	18.2
IMR - Females	62.8	44.4	27.4	15.0	12.6	12.6	12.6	12.6	12.6	12.6	12.6
IMR - Both Sexes	65.0	47.0	30.7	18.0	15.4	15.4	15.4	15.4	15.4	15.4	15.4
E(0) - Males	65.36	67.19	69.03	70.84	72.06	72.06	72.06	72.06	72.06	72.06	72.06
E(0) - Females	68.43	70.71	73.00	75.08	76.51	76.51	76.51	76.51	76.51	76.51	76.51
E(0) - Both Sexes	66.90	68.95	71.02	72.96	74.28	74.28	74.28	74.28	74.28	74.28	74.28

Year	2100	2110	2120	2130	2140	2150	2160	2170	2180	2190	2200
Birth Rate ‰	13.8	13.8	13.8	13.8	13.8	13.8	13.8	13.8	13.8	13.8	13.8
Death Rate ‰	13.6	13.6	13.6	13.6	13.6	13.6	13.6	13.6	13.6	13.6	13.6
Growth Rate %	0.03	0.02	0.02	0.02	0.02	0.02	0.02	0.02	0.02	0.02	0.02
Total Fertility Rate	2.130	2.130	2.130	2.130	2.130	2.130	2.130	2.130	2.130	2.130	2.130
GRR	1.039	1.039	1.039	1.039	1.039	1.039	1.039	1.039	1.039	1.039	1.039
NRR	1.0	1.0	1.0	1.0	1.0	1.0	1.0	1.0	1.0	1.0	1.0
IMR - Males	18.2	18.2	18.2	18.2	18.2	18.2	18.2	18.2	18.2	18.2	18.2
IMR - Females	12.6	12.6	12.6	12.6	12.6	12.6	12.6	12.6	12.6	12.6	12.6
IMR - Both Sexes	15.4	15.4	15.4	15.4	15.4	15.4	15.4	15.4	15.4	15.4	15.4
E(0) - Males	72.06	72.06	72.06	72.06	72.06	72.06	72.06	72.06	72.06	72.06	72.06
E(0) - Females	76.51	76.51	76.51	76.51	76.51	76.51	76.51	76.51	76.51	76.51	76.51
E(0) - Both Sexes	74.28	74.28	74.28	74.28	74.28	74.28	74.28	74.28	74.28	74.28	74.28

Graph 1

Projected Total Population
World Population Projection No. 2050.R.L
Decline to Replacement Fertility Level (2.13)
Mortality Level: Low

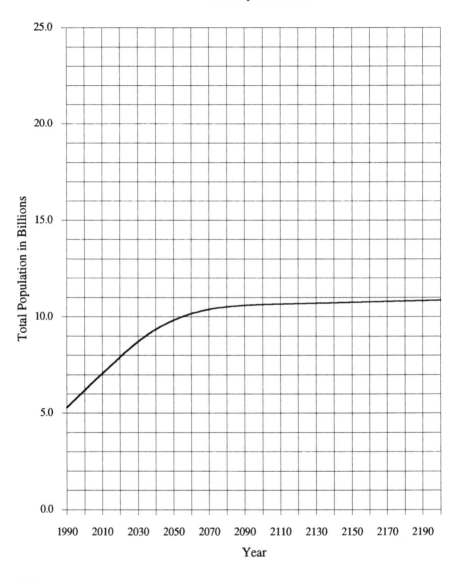

Graph 2

Components of Population Change
World Population Projection No. 2050.R.L
Decline to Replacement Fertility Level (2.13)
Mortality Level: Low

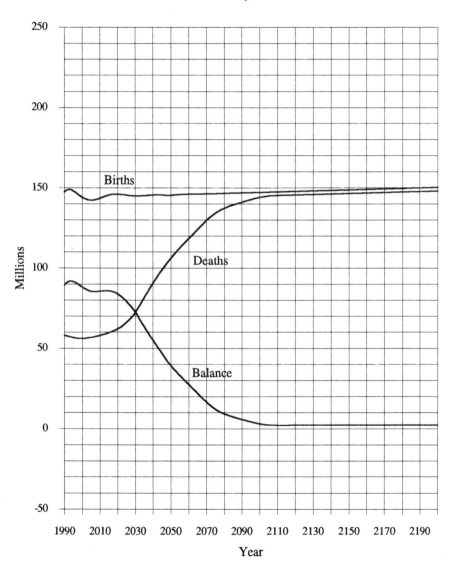

Graph 3

Age Structure of World Population 1990, 2050 and 2100

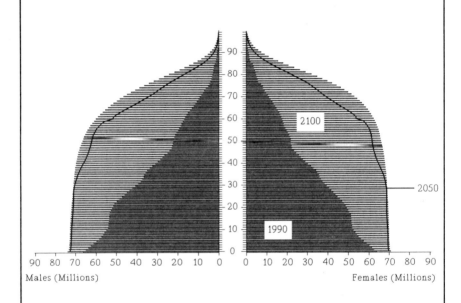

Males (Millions) Females (Millions)

Population Projection No. 2050.R.L.

Target year for replacement fertility
level (TFR = 2.13):   2050
Form of fertility decline: Hyperbolic
Mortality level: Low

Total population: 1990 5 275 Million
                             2050 9 812 Million
                             2100 10 622 Million

Table 1
Projected Total Population
World Population Projection No. 2050.B.H
Decline Below Replacement Fertility Level; Mortality Level: High

Age Year	0-4	5-9	10-14	15-19	20-24	25-29	30-34	35-39	40-44	45-49	50-54	55-59	60-64	65-69	70-74	75+	Total
1990	625	563	528	519	490	436	380	342	282	230	214	186	160	123	87	108	5275
2000	674	662	609	555	518	508	479	424	367	327	264	209	184	149	113	121	6164
2010	670	656	660	655	599	545	508	496	464	406	345	298	229	168	131	149	6976
2020	697	678	659	650	651	645	589	533	494	477	438	372	300	240	163	169	7754
2030	697	696	690	674	653	642	642	633	575	515	468	438	382	301	214	225	8443
2040	694	689	690	692	684	666	644	631	627	611	544	473	409	355	273	289	8972
2050	692	690	688	685	684	684	675	655	629	609	594	562	477	384	292	351	9350
2060	682	683	686	686	682	677	675	673	659	632	596	560	520	455	341	383	9589
2070	672	673	676	679	680	678	673	666	659	649	624	581	522	454	371	447	9703
2080	660	662	666	669	670	671	671	666	657	643	624	597	547	471	373	467	9713
2090	647	649	654	658	660	661	661	660	655	643	622	591	547	484	390	479	9662
2100	633	636	641	646	649	651	651	650	646	637	620	591	545	479	390	495	9559
2110	619	622	627	632	635	638	640	640	636	627	612	585	543	479	389	494	9418
2120	604	607	613	618	622	625	627	627	625	618	602	576	535	474	388	493	9255
2130	589	592	598	603	607	611	613	614	612	606	592	567	527	467	382	490	9073
2140	573	577	583	589	593	596	599	601	599	593	580	557	518	460	376	483	8878
2150	558	562	568	574	578	582	585	587	585	580	567	545	508	451	370	476	8676
2160	543	547	553	559	563	567	570	572	571	566	554	533	497	442	362	467	8467
2170	528	532	538	544	548	552	556	558	557	552	541	520	485	432	355	457	8256
2180	513	517	523	529	533	537	541	543	543	538	528	508	474	422	346	448	8043
2190	499	503	509	514	519	523	526	529	528	524	514	495	462	411	338	437	7830
2200	484	488	494	500	504	508	512	514	514	510	500	482	450	401	330	427	7618

Table 2
Components of Population Change
World Population Projection No. 2050.B.H
Decline Below Replacement Fertility Level; Mortality Level: High

Year	Males Births	Males Deaths - Thousands -	Males Balance	Females Births	Females Deaths - Thousands -	Females Balance	Total Births	Total Deaths - Thousands -	Total Balance
1990	75539	29422	46117	71783	28562	43221	147322	57985	89338
2000	73795	31370	42424	70125	28073	42052	143920	59443	84476
2010	73358	34580	38778	69710	29350	40360	143067	63930	79137
2020	74307	38344	35963	70612	31835	38777	144919	70179	74740
2030	73447	45277	28170	69795	37854	31940	143242	83132	60110
2040	73470	52923	20547	69816	45979	23837	143286	98902	44384
2050	72942	59440	13503	69315	52978	16337	142257	112418	29840
2060	71837	64573	7264	68264	58613	9651	140101	123186	16916
2070	70750	69043	1707	67231	63942	3289	137981	132985	4996
2080	69437	71247	-1810	65984	66968	-985	135420	138216	-2795
2090	67996	72324	-4328	64614	68351	-3737	132610	140676	-8065
2100	66512	72986	-6473	63204	69425	-6221	129717	142411	-12694
2110	64960	72712	-7752	61729	69403	-7674	126689	142115	-15427
2120	63376	72103	-8727	60224	68948	-8724	123600	141051	-17451
2130	61778	71218	-9439	58706	68253	-9547	120484	139471	-18986
2140	60171	70059	-9888	57179	67229	-10050	117350	137288	-19938
2150	58568	68772	-10205	55655	66063	-10407	114223	134835	-20612
2160	56975	67370	-10396	54141	64777	-10636	111116	132147	-21031
2170	55396	65885	-10488	52641	63391	-10750	108038	129276	-21238
2180	53838	64351	-10513	51161	61952	-10792	104999	126304	-21305
2190	52303	62784	-10480	49702	60473	-10771	102006	123257	-21251
2200	50794	61197	-10403	48268	58969	-10701	99063	120167	-21104

Table 3
Demographic Indicators
World Population Projection No. 2050.B.H
Decline Below Replacement Fertility Level; Mortality Level: High

Year	1990	2000	2010	2020	2030	2040	2050	2060	2070	2080	2090
Birth Rate ‰	27.9	23.3	20.5	18.7	17.0	16.0	15.2	14.6	14.2	13.9	13.7
Death Rate ‰	11.0	9.6	9.2	9.1	9.8	11.0	12.0	12.8	13.7	14.2	14.6
Growth Rate %	1.69	1.37	1.13	0.96	0.71	0.49	0.32	0.18	0.05	-0.03	-0.08
Total Fertility Rate	3.400	2.968	2.590	2.377	2.255	2.179	2.130	2.096	2.071	2.053	2.039
GRR	1.684	1.442	1.267	1.159	1.099	1.063	1.038	1.021	1.009	0.999	0.992
NRR	1.5	1.3	1.2	1.1	1.1	1.0	1.0	1.0	1.0	1.0	1.0
IMR - Males	67.2	53.4	39.5	26.3	24.6	24.6	24.6	24.6	24.6	24.6	24.6
IMR - Females	62.8	47.9	31.8	18.8	17.0	17.0	17.0	17.0	17.0	17.0	17.0
IMR - Both Sexes	65.0	50.6	35.7	22.5	20.8	20.8	20.8	20.8	20.8	20.8	20.8
E(0) - Males	65.36	66.12	67.01	67.99	68.39	68.39	68.39	68.39	68.39	68.39	68.39
E(0) - Females	68.43	69.71	71.16	72.53	73.25	73.25	73.25	73.25	73.25	73.25	73.25
E(0) - Both Sexes	66.90	67.91	69.08	70.26	70.82	70.82	70.82	70.82	70.82	70.82	70.82

Year	2100	2110	2120	2130	2140	2150	2160	2170	2180	2190	2200
Birth Rate ‰	13.6	13.5	13.4	13.3	13.2	13.2	13.1	13.1	13.1	13.0	13.0
Death Rate ‰	14.9	15.1	15.2	15.4	15.5	15.5	15.6	15.7	15.7	15.7	15.8
Growth Rate %	-0.13	-0.16	-0.19	-0.21	-0.22	-0.24	-0.25	-0.26	-0.26	-0.27	-0.28
Total Fertility Rate	2.028	2.019	2.012	2.006	2.001	1.996	1.993	1.990	1.987	1.984	1.982
GRR	0.987	0.982	0.979	0.976	0.973	0.971	0.969	0.968	0.966	0.965	0.967
NRR	1.0	1.0	1.0	0.9	0.9	0.9	0.9	0.9	0.9	0.9	0.9
IMR - Males	24.6	24.6	24.6	24.6	24.6	24.6	24.6	24.6	24.6	24.6	24.6
IMR - Females	17.0	17.0	17.0	17.0	17.0	17.0	17.0	17.0	17.0	17.0	17.0
IMR - Both Sexes	20.8	20.8	20.8	20.8	20.8	20.8	20.8	20.8	20.8	20.8	20.8
E(0) - Males	68.39	68.39	68.39	68.39	68.39	68.39	68.39	68.39	68.39	68.39	68.39
E(0) - Females	73.25	73.25	73.25	73.25	73.25	73.25	73.25	73.25	73.25	73.25	73.25
E(0) - Both Sexes	70.82	70.82	70.82	70.82	70.82	70.82	70.82	70.82	70.82	70.82	70.82

Graph 1

Projected Total Population
World Population Projection No. 2050.B.H
Decline Below Replacement Fertility Level
Mortality Level: High

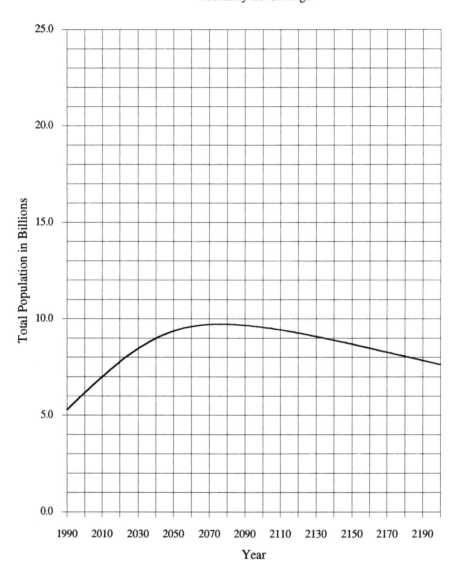

Graph 2

Components of Population Change
World Population Projection No. 2050.B.H
Decline Below Replacement Fertility Level
Mortality Level: High

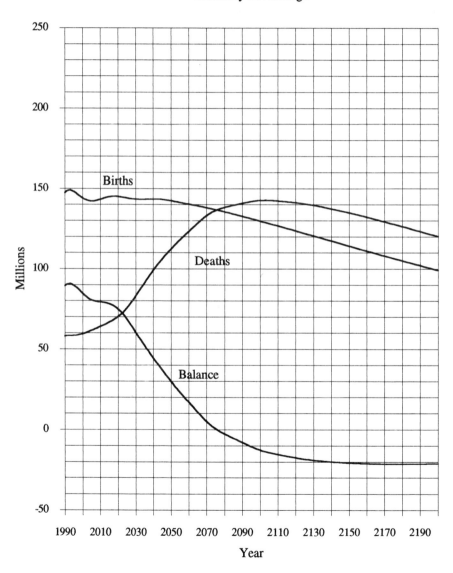

Graph 3

Age Structure of World Population 1990, 2050 and 2100

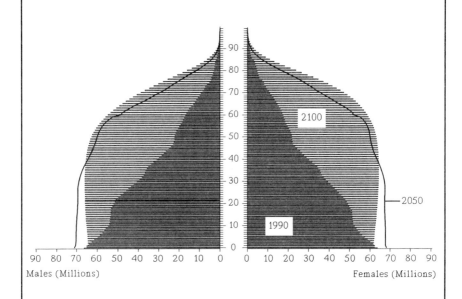

Population Projection No. 2050.B.H.

Decline below replacement fertility level by the year:	2050
Form of fertility decline:	Hyperbolic
Mortality level:	High
Total population:	1990 5 275 Million
	2050 9 350 Million
	2100 9 559 Million

Table 1
Projected Total Population
World Population Projection No. 2050.B.M
Decline Below Replacement Fertility Level; Mortality Level: Medium

- Millions -

Age Year	0-4	5-9	10-14	15-19	20-24	25-29	30-34	35-39	40-44	45-49	50-54	55-59	60-64	65-69	70-74	75+	Total
1990	625	563	528	519	490	436	380	342	282	230	214	186	160	123	87	108	5275
2000	675	663	609	555	519	508	479	424	367	327	264	209	185	149	114	124	6172
2010	673	659	662	656	600	545	508	496	465	408	346	299	231	170	133	157	7008
2020	702	683	663	653	654	647	590	535	496	479	441	375	305	246	169	186	7824
2030	703	702	695	678	657	646	646	637	578	518	472	444	391	312	226	257	8563
2040	702	697	697	698	690	672	650	637	633	617	551	482	421	370	292	339	9146
2050	701	699	696	693	692	691	682	662	636	617	604	574	491	401	314	417	9570
2060	693	693	696	695	691	686	684	681	668	642	607	573	537	478	366	459	9849
2070	684	684	687	690	690	688	683	676	670	661	637	596	541	478	401	535	10001
2080	673	675	678	681	682	683	682	678	669	656	639	614	568	497	403	564	10042
2090	661	663	668	671	673	674	674	673	668	657	638	609	569	511	423	580	10014
2100	648	651	656	660	663	665	665	664	660	652	637	611	568	508	424	600	9933
2110	635	638	643	647	651	653	655	655	652	644	630	606	568	509	424	602	9810
2120	621	624	630	634	638	641	643	644	642	635	622	598	561	505	423	602	9662
2130	606	610	616	621	625	628	631	632	630	624	612	590	554	498	418	599	9494
2140	592	596	602	607	611	614	617	619	618	612	601	580	545	491	413	592	9311
2150	578	581	587	593	597	601	604	606	605	600	589	569	535	483	407	584	9118
2160	563	567	573	578	583	587	590	592	592	587	577	558	525	474	399	575	8919
2170	549	553	559	564	568	572	576	578	578	574	564	546	514	464	391	564	8715
2180	534	538	544	550	554	558	562	564	564	561	551	533	503	454	383	553	8509
2190	520	524	530	536	540	544	548	550	550	547	538	521	491	444	375	542	8301
2200	506	510	516	522	526	530	534	536	537	534	525	508	479	434	366	530	8094

Table 2
Components of Population Change
World Population Projection No. 2050.B.M
Decline Below Replacement Fertility Level; Mortality Level: Medium

Year	Males Births	Males Deaths - Thousands -	Males Balance	Females Births	Females Deaths - Thousands -	Females Balance	Total Births	Total Deaths - Thousands -	Total Balance
1990	75539	29422	46117	71783	28562	43221	147322	57985	89338
2000	73818	30434	43384	70147	27269	42878	143965	57703	86262
2010	73447	32952	40495	69795	28046	41749	143242	60997	82244
2020	74562	36175	38387	70854	30155	40699	145416	66330	79086
2030	73868	42436	31431	70194	35608	34586	144062	78044	66018
2040	74020	50775	23245	70339	44224	26115	144358	94998	49360
2050	73641	57881	15759	69978	51660	18318	143619	109541	34078
2060	72684	63395	9290	69069	57592	11478	141753	120986	20767
2070	71729	68292	3437	68162	63169	4993	139891	131461	8430
2080	70546	71073	-527	67038	66742	296	137584	137816	-231
2090	69228	72409	-3181	65785	68372	-2587	135013	140781	-5768
2100	67858	73377	-5519	64484	69676	-5192	132342	143053	-10711
2110	66413	73391	-6978	63111	69946	-6835	129524	143337	-13813
2120	64930	72972	-8042	61701	69667	-7966	126631	142639	-16008
2130	63426	72283	-8857	60271	69154	-8883	123697	141437	-17740
2140	61905	71294	-9389	58826	68301	-9475	120731	139595	-18863
2150	60381	70154	-9773	57379	67277	-9898	117760	137431	-19671
2160	58862	68892	-10030	55934	66127	-10192	114796	135018	-20222
2170	57351	67530	-10179	54499	64864	-10365	111850	132395	-20545
2180	55854	66110	-10256	53077	63536	-10460	108931	129647	-20716
2190	54376	64646	-10271	51672	62160	-10488	106047	126806	-20759
2200	52918	63154	-10237	50286	60750	-10464	103203	123904	-20700

Table 3
Demographic Indicators
World Population Projection No. 2050.B.M
Decline Below Replacement Fertility Level; Mortality Level: Medium

Year	1990	2000	2010	2020	2030	2040	2050	2060	2070	2080	2090
Birth Rate ‰	27.9	23.3	20.4	18.6	16.8	15.8	15.0	14.4	14.0	13.7	13.5
Death Rate ‰	11.0	9.3	8.7	8.5	9.1	10.4	11.4	12.3	13.1	13.7	14.1
Growth Rate %	1.69	1.40	1.17	1.01	0.77	0.54	0.36	0.21	0.08	0.00	-0.06
Total Fertility Rate	3.400	2.968	2.590	2.377	2.255	2.179	2.130	2.096	2.071	2.053	2.039
GRR	1.684	1.442	1.267	1.160	1.099	1.063	1.038	1.021	1.009	0.999	0.992
NRR	1.5	1.3	1.2	1.1	1.1	1.0	1.0	1.0	1.0	1.0	1.0
IMR - Males	67.2	51.4	36.8	23.7	21.4	21.4	21.4	21.4	21.4	21.4	21.4
IMR - Females	62.8	46.2	29.6	16.9	14.8	14.8	14.8	14.8	14.8	14.8	14.8
IMR - Both Sexes	65.0	48.8	33.2	20.3	18.1	18.1	18.1	18.1	18.1	18.1	18.1
E(0) - Males	65.36	66.65	67.98	69.34	70.09	70.09	70.09	70.09	70.09	70.09	70.09
E(0) - Females	68.43	70.20	72.05	73.74	74.76	74.76	74.76	74.76	74.76	74.76	74.76
E(0) - Both Sexes	66.90	68.43	70.02	71.54	72.43	72.43	72.43	72.43	72.43	72.43	72.43

Year	2100	2110	2120	2130	2140	2150	2160	2170	2180	2190	2200
Birth Rate ‰	13.3	13.2	13.1	13.0	13.0	12.9	12.9	12.8	12.8	12.8	12.8
Death Rate ‰	14.4	14.6	14.8	14.9	15.0	15.1	15.1	15.2	15.2	15.3	15.3
Growth Rate %	-0.11	-0.14	-0.17	-0.19	-0.20	-0.22	-0.23	-0.24	-0.24	-0.25	-0.26
Total Fertility Rate	2.028	2.019	2.012	2.006	2.001	1.996	1.993	1.990	1.987	1.984	1.982
GRR	0.987	0.982	0.979	0.976	0.973	0.971	0.969	0.968	0.966	0.965	0.967
NRR	1.0	1.0	1.0	1.0	1.0	0.9	0.9	0.9	0.9	0.9	0.9
IMR - Males	21.4	21.4	21.4	21.4	21.4	21.4	21.4	21.4	21.4	21.4	21.4
IMR - Females	14.8	14.8	14.8	14.8	14.8	14.8	14.8	14.8	14.8	14.8	14.8
IMR - Both Sexes	18.1	18.1	18.1	18.1	18.1	18.1	18.1	18.1	18.1	18.1	18.1
E(0) - Males	70.09	70.09	70.09	70.09	70.09	70.09	70.09	70.09	70.09	70.09	70.09
E(0) - Females	74.76	74.76	74.76	74.76	74.76	74.76	74.76	74.76	74.76	74.76	74.76
E(0) - Both Sexes	72.43	72.43	72.43	72.43	72.43	72.43	72.43	72.43	72.43	72.43	72.43

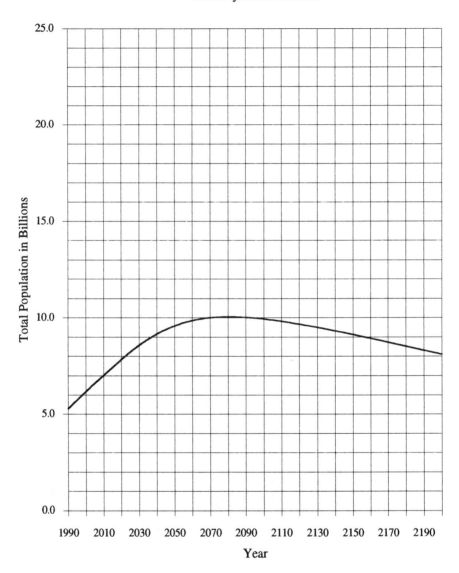

Graph 1

Projected Total Population
World Population Projection No. 2050.B.M
Decline Below Replacement Fertility Level
Mortality Level: Medium

Graph 2

Components of Population Change
World Population Projection No. 2050.B.M
Decline Below Replacement Fertility Level
Mortality Level: Medium

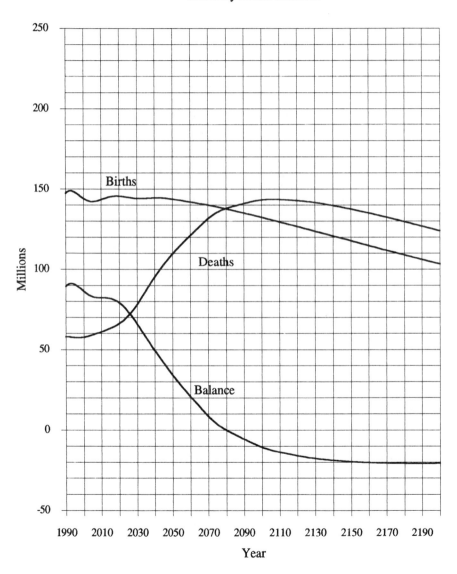

Graph 3

Age Structure of World Population 1990, 2050 and 2100

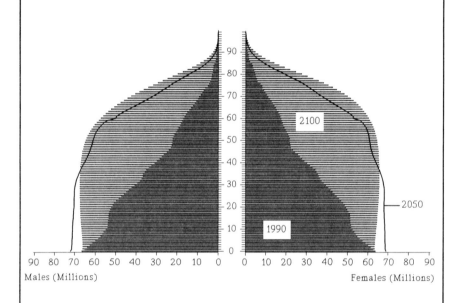

Population Projection No. 2050.B.M.

Decline below replacement fertility level by the year:	2050
Form of fertility decline:	Hyperbolic
Mortality level:	Medium
Total population:	1990 5 275 Million
	2050 9 570 Million
	2100 9 933 Million

Table 1
Projected Total Population
World Population Projection No. 2050.B.L
Decline Below Replacement Fertility Level; Mortality Level: Low

Age Year	0-4	5-9	10-14	15-19	20-24	25-29	30-34	35-39	40-44	45-49	50-54	55-59	60-64	65-69	70-74	75+	Total
							- Millions -										
1990	625	563	528	519	490	436	380	342	282	230	214	186	160	123	87	108	5275
2000	677	664	609	555	519	508	479	425	367	328	265	210	185	150	115	126	6181
2010	676	662	664	657	600	546	509	497	466	409	347	301	233	172	136	166	7042
2020	706	687	667	656	657	649	592	537	498	481	444	379	310	252	176	205	7896
2030	709	708	701	683	662	650	650	640	581	522	477	451	400	323	239	295	8690
2040	710	705	704	704	696	677	655	642	639	623	558	491	432	386	312	401	9335
2050	710	708	705	702	700	698	689	669	644	626	613	586	506	420	337	500	9812
2060	703	704	705	704	700	696	693	690	677	652	619	588	556	501	394	555	10136
2070	696	696	699	701	701	698	693	687	681	672	650	612	561	503	433	647	10329
2080	686	688	691	693	694	695	694	690	681	669	654	631	589	524	437	689	10405
2090	675	678	682	685	686	687	687	686	682	672	655	629	593	540	459	709	10404
2100	664	666	671	675	677	679	680	678	675	668	655	631	593	538	462	736	10347
2110	651	654	659	663	666	669	670	671	668	661	649	628	594	540	462	741	10245
2120	638	641	647	651	655	657	660	661	659	653	642	621	588	537	462	742	10114
2130	625	628	634	639	642	646	648	649	648	643	633	614	581	531	458	741	9961
2140	611	615	621	625	630	633	636	638	637	633	623	604	574	525	453	734	9791
2150	597	601	607	612	616	620	623	625	625	621	612	594	564	517	447	726	9610
2160	584	588	593	599	603	607	610	612	613	609	600	584	554	509	440	716	9420
2170	570	574	580	585	589	593	597	599	600	597	588	572	544	499	432	704	9225
2180	556	560	566	571	576	580	584	586	587	584	576	560	533	490	424	692	9026
2190	543	547	553	558	562	567	570	573	574	571	564	549	522	480	415	679	8825
2200	529	533	539	544	549	553	557	560	560	558	551	536	511	469	407	665	8623

Table 2
Components of Population Change
World Population Projection No. 2050.B.L
Decline Below Replacement Fertility Level; Mortality Level: Low

Year	Births	Males Deaths - Thousands -	Balance	Births	Females Deaths - Thousands -	Balance	Births	Total Deaths - Thousands -	Balance
1990	75539	29422	46117	71783	28562	43221	147322	57985	89338
2000	73841	29486	44355	70169	26453	43716	144010	55940	88071
2010	73537	31254	42283	69880	26680	43199	143416	57934	85482
2020	74818	33824	40994	71097	28326	42771	145915	62150	83765
2030	74290	39204	35086	70595	33047	37549	144886	72251	72635
2040	74573	48247	26326	70864	42159	28706	145438	90406	55032
2050	74345	56015	18329	70647	50093	20554	144992	106108	38884
2060	73540	61985	11555	69883	56383	13500	143423	118368	25055
2070	72721	67288	5433	69104	62189	6915	141826	129477	12349
2080	71673	70727	945	68108	66348	1760	139781	137076	2705
2090	70481	72387	-1906	66976	68314	-1339	137457	140701	-3244
2100	69230	73657	-4427	65787	69829	-4042	135018	143486	-8468
2110	67898	74006	-6107	64521	70427	-5905	132420	144432	-12013
2120	66520	73796	-7276	63212	70347	-7135	129733	144143	-14410
2130	65115	73315	-8200	61877	70023	-8147	126992	143338	-16346
2140	63687	72513	-8826	60520	69357	-8838	124206	141870	-17664
2150	62249	71532	-9282	59154	68485	-9331	121403	140017	-18614
2160	60809	70419	-9610	57785	67480	-9695	118595	137900	-19305
2170	59373	69194	-9821	56420	66351	-9931	115792	135545	-19752
2180	57944	67897	-9953	55062	65143	-10081	113007	133040	-20033
2190	56528	66546	-10018	53717	63878	-10161	110245	130424	-20180
2200	55127	65158	-10031	52386	62570	-10184	107513	127728	-20215

Table 3
Demographic Indicators
World Population Projection No. 2050.B.L
Decline Below Replacement Fertility Level; Mortality Level: Low

Year	1990	2000	2010	2020	2030	2040	2050	2060	2070	2080	2090
Birth Rate ‰	27.9	23.3	20.4	18.5	16.7	15.6	14.8	14.1	13.7	13.4	13.2
Death Rate ‰	11.0	9.1	8.2	7.9	8.3	9.7	10.8	11.7	12.5	13.2	13.5
Growth Rate %	1.69	1.42	1.21	1.06	0.84	0.59	0.40	0.25	0.12	0.03	-0.03
Total Fertility Rate	3.400	2.968	2.590	2.377	2.255	2.179	2.130	2.096	2.071	2.053	2.039
GRR	1.684	1.442	1.267	1.160	1.099	1.063	1.038	1.021	1.009	0.999	0.992
NRR	1.5	1.4	1.2	1.1	1.1	1.0	1.0	1.0	1.0	1.0	1.0
IMR - Males	67.2	49.5	34.0	21.0	18.2	18.2	18.2	18.2	18.2	18.2	18.2
IMR - Females	62.8	44.4	27.4	15.0	12.6	12.6	12.6	12.6	12.6	12.6	12.6
IMR - Both Sexes	65.0	47.0	30.7	18.0	15.4	15.4	15.4	15.4	15.4	15.4	15.4
E(0) - Males	65.36	67.19	69.03	70.84	72.06	72.06	72.06	72.06	72.06	72.06	72.06
E(0) - Females	68.43	70.71	73.00	75.08	76.51	76.51	76.51	76.51	76.51	76.51	76.51
E(0) - Both Sexes	66.90	68.95	71.02	72.96	74.28	74.28	74.28	74.28	74.28	74.28	74.28

Year	2100	2110	2120	2130	2140	2150	2160	2170	2180	2190	2200
Birth Rate ‰	13.0	12.9	12.8	12.7	12.7	12.6	12.6	12.6	12.5	12.5	12.5
Death Rate ‰	13.9	14.1	14.3	14.4	14.5	14.6	14.6	14.7	14.7	14.8	14.8
Growth Rate %	-0.08	-0.12	-0.14	-0.16	-0.18	-0.19	-0.20	-0.21	-0.22	-0.23	-0.23
Total Fertility Rate	2.028	2.019	2.012	2.006	2.001	1.996	1.993	1.990	1.987	1.984	1.982
GRR	0.987	0.982	0.979	0.976	0.973	0.971	0.969	0.968	0.966	0.965	0.967
NRR	1.0	1.0	1.0	1.0	1.0	1.0	1.0	0.9	0.9	0.9	0.9
IMR - Males	18.2	18.2	18.2	18.2	18.2	18.2	18.2	18.2	18.2	18.2	18.2
IMR - Females	12.6	12.6	12.6	12.6	12.6	12.6	12.6	12.6	12.6	12.6	12.6
IMR - Both Sexes	15.4	15.4	15.4	15.4	15.4	15.4	15.4	15.4	15.4	15.4	15.4
E(0) - Males	72.06	72.06	72.06	72.06	72.06	72.06	72.06	72.06	72.06	72.06	72.06
E(0) - Females	76.51	76.51	76.51	76.51	76.51	76.51	76.51	76.51	76.51	76.51	76.51
E(0) - Both Sexes	74.28	74.28	74.28	74.28	74.28	74.28	74.28	74.28	74.28	74.28	74.28

Graph 1

Projected Total Population
World Population Projection No. 2050.B.L
Decline Below Replacement Fertility Level
Mortality Level: Low

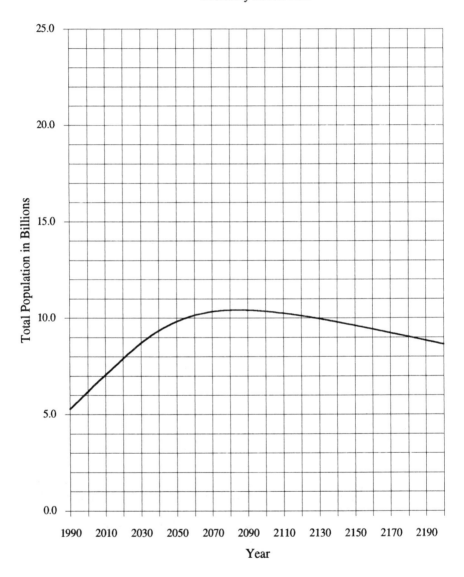

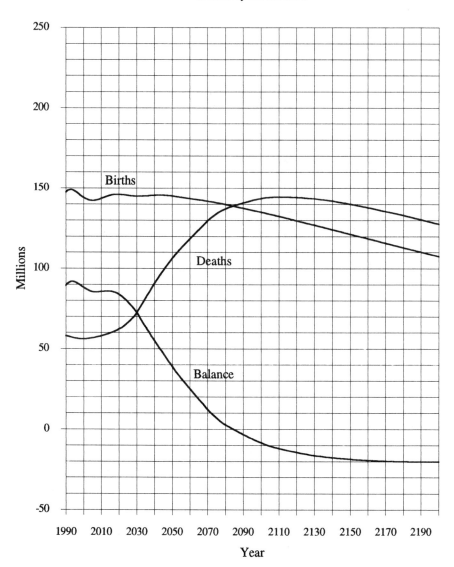

Graph 3

Age Structure of World Population 1990, 2050 and 2100

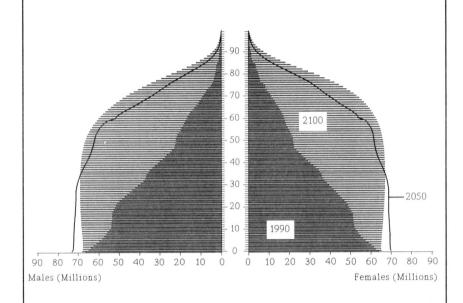

Population Projection No. 2050.B.L.

Decline below replacement fertility level by the year:	2050
Form of fertility decline:	Hyperbolic
Mortality level:	Low
Total population:	1990 5 275 Million
	2050 9 812 Million
	2100 10 347 Million

Table 1
Projected Total Population
World Population Projection No. 2060.R.H
Decline to Replacement Fertility Level (2.13); Mortality Level: High

- Millions -

Age Year	0-4	5-9	10-14	15-19	20-24	25-29	30-34	35-39	40-44	45-49	50-54	55-59	60-64	65-69	70-74	75+	Total
1990	625	563	528	519	490	436	380	342	282	230	214	186	160	123	87	108	5275
2000	680	664	609	555	518	508	479	424	367	327	264	209	184	149	113	121	6171
2010	685	667	666	656	599	545	508	496	464	406	345	298	229	168	131	149	7010
2020	718	696	674	661	657	646	589	533	494	477	438	372	300	240	163	169	7827
2030	724	720	711	691	667	653	648	589	575	515	468	438	382	301	214	225	8566
2040	726	719	717	716	704	683	658	635	633	613	544	473	409	355	273	289	9155
2050	729	724	720	715	711	707	695	642	643	620	600	563	477	384	292	351	9600
2060	722	721	722	720	713	706	701	672	679	649	609	569	525	456	341	383	9912
2070	723	717	716	717	715	711	704	696	685	672	643	596	533	462	375	447	10110
2080	721	718	716	713	714	708	706	695	687	671	649	617	563	483	381	473	10216
2090	719	715	715	714	710	704	700	699	689	675	651	616	568	500	402	490	10266
2100	718	714	713	711	710	705	700	697	683	672	653	620	570	500	405	511	10278
2110	717	713	712	710	706	703	699	693	684	669	647	618	572	503	407	514	10266
2120	715	711	710	708	705	701	697	694	683	670	648	615	567	501	408	517	10246
2130	713	709	708	707	704	700	696	691	683	667	647	615	567	498	405	516	10224
2140	712	708	707	705	702	698	694	690	681	666	645	613	566	499	405	513	10202
2150	710	706	706	704	701	697	693	688	680	665	644	612	564	497	404	513	10180
2160	709	705	704	702	699	696	691	687	678	663	642	611	564	496	403	512	10159
2170	707	703	703	701	698	694	690	685	677	662	641	609	562	495	402	511	10137
2180	706	702	701	699	696	693	688	684	675	660	640	608	561	494	401	511	10116
2190	704	700	700	698	695	691	687	683	674	659	638	607	560	493	401	510	10094
2200	703	699	698	696	693	690	685	681	672	657	637	605	559	492	400	508	10073

Table 2
Components of Population Change
World Population Projection No. 2060.R.H
Decline to Replacement Fertility Level (2.13); Mortality Level: High

Year	Males Births	Males Deaths - Thousands -	Males Balance	Females Births	Females Deaths - Thousands -	Females Balance	Total Births	Total Deaths - Thousands -	Total Balance
1990	75539	29422	46117	71783	28562	43221	147322	57985	89338
2000	74882	31462	43420	71158	28151	43007	146040	59613	86427
2010	75168	34711	40457	71430	29450	41979	146598	64162	82436
2020	76713	38482	38231	72898	31926	40972	149611	70407	79203
2030	76493	45459	31034	72689	37968	34721	149183	83427	65755
2040	77019	53183	23835	73188	46141	27047	150207	99325	50882
2050	76913	59838	17075	73088	53223	19865	150001	113061	36940
2060	76278	65244	11034	72484	59024	13460	148762	124268	24494
2070	76482	70241	6241	72679	64739	7940	149161	134980	14181
2080	76213	73176	3037	72423	68431	3992	148637	141607	7030
2090	76034	74977	1057	72253	70531	1723	148288	145508	2780
2100	75916	76295	-378	72141	72233	-92	148057	148528	-470
2110	75731	76651	-921	71964	72809	-845	147695	149461	-1766
2120	75573	76673	-1099	71815	72918	-1103	147389	149591	-2203
2130	75418	76516	-1099	71667	72821	-1154	147085	149337	-2253
2140	75253	76299	-1046	71511	72581	-1070	146764	148879	-2116
2150	75095	76170	-1075	71360	72460	-1100	146455	148630	-2175
2160	74935	76003	-1068	71209	72312	-1103	146144	148315	-2171
2170	74776	75834	-1059	71057	72143	-1086	145832	147977	-2145
2180	74617	75680	-1063	70906	71999	-1093	145523	147679	-2156
2190	74458	75517	-1058	70755	71844	-1089	145214	147361	-2147
2200	74300	75356	-1056	70605	71690	-1085	144905	147046	-2141

Table 3
Demographic Indicators
World Population Projection No. 2060.R.H
Decline to Replacement Fertility Level (2.13); Mortality Level: High

Year	1990	2000	2010	2020	2030	2040	2050	2060	2070	2080	2090
Birth Rate ‰	27.9	23.7	20.9	19.1	17.4	16.4	15.6	15.0	14.8	14.5	14.4
Death Rate ‰	11.0	9.7	9.2	9.0	9.7	10.8	11.8	12.5	13.4	13.9	14.2
Growth Rate %	1.69	1.40	1.18	1.01	0.77	0.56	0.38	0.25	0.14	0.07	0.03
Total Fertility Rate	3.400	3.007	2.651	2.437	2.308	2.225	2.169	2.130	2.130	2.130	2.130
GRR	1.684	1.463	1.298	1.190	1.126	1.086	1.057	1.040	1.039	1.039	1.039
NRR	1.5	1.4	1.2	1.2	1.1	1.1	1.0	1.0	1.0	1.0	1.0
IMR - Males	67.2	53.4	39.5	26.3	24.6	24.6	24.6	24.6	24.6	24.6	24.6
IMR - Females	62.8	47.9	31.8	18.8	17.0	17.0	17.0	17.0	17.0	17.0	17.0
IMR - Both Sexes	65.0	50.6	35.7	22.5	20.8	20.8	20.8	20.8	20.8	20.8	20.8
E(0) - Males	65.36	66.12	67.01	67.99	68.39	68.39	68.39	68.39	68.39	68.39	68.39
E(0) - Females	68.43	69.71	71.16	72.53	73.25	73.25	73.25	73.25	73.25	73.25	73.25
E(0) - Both Sexes	66.90	67.91	69.08	70.26	70.82	70.82	70.82	70.82	70.82	70.82	70.82

Year	2100	2110	2120	2130	2140	2150	2160	2170	2180	2190	2200
Birth Rate ‰	14.4	14.4	14.4	14.4	14.4	14.4	14.4	14.4	14.4	14.4	14.4
Death Rate ‰	14.5	14.6	14.6	14.6	14.6	14.6	14.6	14.6	14.6	14.6	14.6
Growth Rate %	0.00	-0.02	-0.02	-0.02	-0.02	-0.02	-0.02	-0.02	-0.02	-0.02	-0.02
Total Fertility Rate	2.130	2.130	2.130	2.130	2.130	2.130	2.130	2.130	2.130	2.130	2.130
GRR	1.039	1.039	1.039	1.039	1.039	1.039	1.039	1.039	1.039	1.039	1.039
NRR	1.0	1.0	1.0	1.0	1.0	1.0	1.0	1.0	1.0	1.0	1.0
IMR - Males	24.6	24.6	24.6	24.6	24.6	24.6	24.6	24.6	24.6	24.6	24.6
IMR - Females	17.0	17.0	17.0	17.0	17.0	17.0	17.0	17.0	17.0	17.0	17.0
IMR - Both Sexes	20.8	20.8	20.8	20.8	20.8	20.8	20.8	20.8	20.8	20.8	20.8
E(0) - Males	68.39	68.39	68.39	68.39	68.39	68.39	68.39	68.39	68.39	68.39	68.39
E(0) - Females	73.25	73.25	73.25	73.25	73.25	73.25	73.25	73.25	73.25	73.25	73.25
E(0) - Both Sexes	70.82	70.82	70.82	70.82	70.82	70.82	70.82	70.82	70.82	70.82	70.82

Graph 1

Projected Total Population
World Population Projection No. 2060.R.H
Decline to Replacement Fertility Level (2.13)
Mortality Level: High

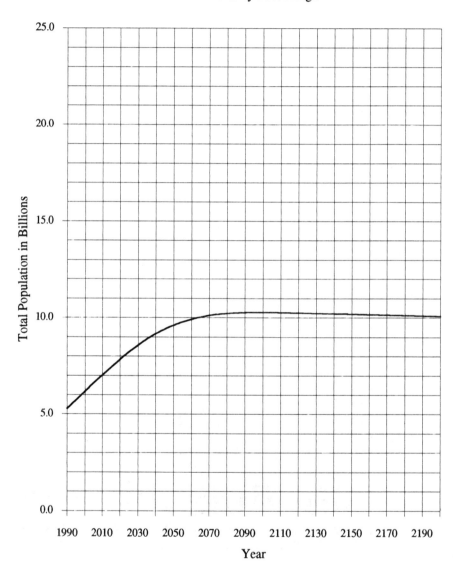

Graph 2

Components of Population Change
World Population Projection No. 2060.R.H
Decline to Replacement Fertility Level (2.13)
Mortality Level: High

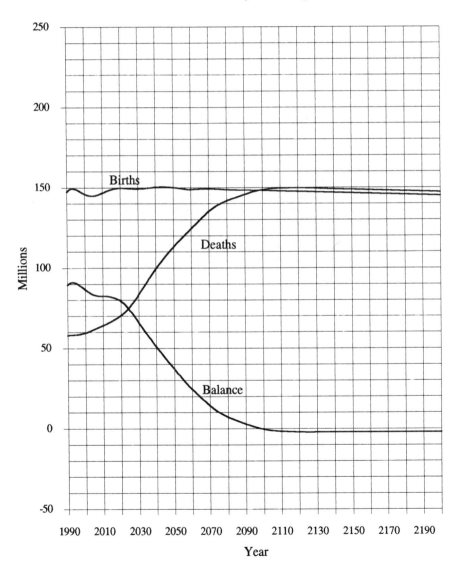

Graph 3

Age Structure of World Population 1990, 2050 and 2100

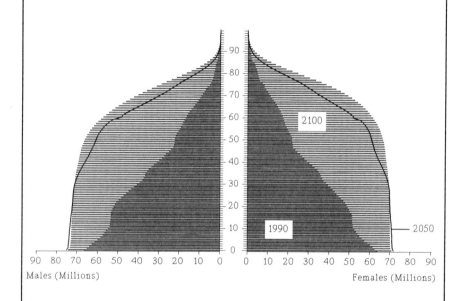

Population Projection No. 2060.R.H.

Target year for replacement fertility
level (TFR = 2.13):   2060
Form of fertility decline: Hyperbolic
Mortality level: High

Total population: 1990   5 275 Million
                                    2050   9 600 Million
                                    2100 10 278 Million

Table 1
Projected Total Population
World Population Projection No. 2060.R.M
Decline to Replacement Fertility Level (2.13); Mortality Level: Medium

- Millions -

Age Year	0-4	5-9	10-14	15-19	20-24	25-29	30-34	35-39	40-44	45-49	50-54	55-59	60-64	65-69	70-74	75+	Total
1990	625	563	528	519	490	436	380	342	282	230	214	186	160	123	87	108	5275
2000	682	665	609	555	519	508	479	424	367	327	264	209	185	149	114	124	6180
2010	688	670	668	657	600	545	508	496	465	408	346	299	231	170	133	157	7043
2020	723	700	678	664	660	648	590	535	496	479	441	375	305	246	169	186	7896
2030	730	726	716	696	672	657	652	638	578	518	472	444	391	312	226	257	8686
2040	734	727	724	722	710	689	664	648	639	619	551	482	421	370	292	339	9331
2050	738	733	729	723	719	715	702	679	651	628	609	575	491	401	314	417	9824
2060	733	732	732	729	723	716	710	704	688	659	621	584	543	479	366	459	10178
2070	735	729	728	728	726	722	715	705	696	683	656	612	553	486	405	536	10416
2080	736	732	730	726	722	721	718	712	700	684	664	635	585	510	413	571	10556
2090	735	731	730	728	724	718	713	710	703	690	668	636	591	529	436	593	10635
2100	735	731	729	727	724	721	716	708	699	689	671	641	595	529	441	619	10674
2110	735	731	729	727	723	719	716	710	701	686	667	640	598	534	444	626	10686
2120	735	731	729	727	724	720	715	709	701	689	669	638	594	533	446	630	10688
2130	735	731	729	727	724	720	715	709	700	688	669	640	596	531	443	631	10687
2140	735	731	729	727	723	720	715	709	701	688	668	639	596	533	444	629	10687
2150	735	731	729	727	724	720	715	709	701	688	669	639	595	532	444	630	10687
2160	735	731	729	727	723	720	715	709	701	688	668	639	595	532	444	630	10686
2170	735	731	729	727	723	720	715	709	701	688	668	639	595	532	444	630	10686
2180	735	731	729	727	723	720	715	709	701	688	668	639	595	532	444	630	10685
2190	735	731	729	727	723	720	715	709	701	688	668	639	595	532	444	630	10685
2200	735	731	729	727	723	719	715	709	701	688	668	639	595	532	444	630	10685

Table 2
Components of Population Change
World Population Projection No. 2060.R.M
Decline to Replacement Fertility Level (2.13); Mortality Level: Medium

Year	Males Births	Males Deaths - Thousands -	Males Balance	Females Births	Females Deaths - Thousands -	Females Balance	Total Births	Total Deaths - Thousands -	Total Balance
1990	75539	29422	46117	71783	28562	43221	147322	57985	89338
2000	74906	30522	44384	71180	27344	43836	146086	57866	88220
2010	75260	33074	42185	71517	28139	43378	146777	61214	85563
2020	76976	36299	40677	73148	30237	42911	150125	66536	83588
2030	76931	42596	34336	73105	35707	37398	150037	78303	71734
2040	77595	51003	26592	73736	44366	29370	151331	95369	55963
2050	77650	58232	19418	73788	51875	21913	151437	110107	41330
2060	77178	63991	13187	73340	57955	15385	150517	121945	28572
2070	77542	69374	8167	73685	63881	9804	151227	133256	17971
2080	77432	72869	4563	73581	68091	5490	151013	140959	10054
2090	77413	74945	2468	73563	70449	3114	150976	145394	5582
2100	77454	76581	873	73602	72395	1207	151056	148976	2079
2110	77427	77237	189	73576	73274	302	151003	150511	491
2120	77428	77453	-26	73577	73570	8	151005	151023	-18
2130	77430	77483	-53	73579	73654	-75	151009	151137	-128
2140	77423	77418	5	73573	73568	5	150995	150986	10
2150	77422	77443	-21	73572	73585	-14	150994	151028	-35
2160	77420	77443	-23	73569	73598	-29	150989	151041	-52
2170	77416	77429	-13	73566	73578	-12	150983	151007	-24
2180	77414	77434	-20	73564	73584	-19	150978	151017	-39
2190	77411	77429	-18	73562	73581	-19	150973	151010	-37
2200	77409	77426	-17	73559	73576	-17	150968	151002	-34

Table 3
Demographic Indicators
World Population Projection No. 2060.R.M
Decline to Replacement Fertility Level (2.13); Mortality Level: Medium

Year	1990	2000	2010	2020	2030	2040	2050	2060	2070	2080	2090
Birth Rate ‰	27.9	23.6	20.8	19.0	17.3	16.2	15.4	14.8	14.5	14.3	14.2
Death Rate ‰	11.0	9.4	8.7	8.4	9.0	10.2	11.2	12.0	12.8	13.4	13.7
Growth Rate %	1.69	1.43	1.21	1.06	0.83	0.60	0.42	0.28	0.17	0.10	0.05
Total Fertility Rate	3.400	3.007	2.651	2.437	2.308	2.225	2.169	2.130	2.130	2.130	2.130
GRR	1.684	1.463	1.298	1.190	1.126	1.086	1.058	1.040	1.039	1.039	1.039
NRR	1.5	1.4	1.2	1.2	1.1	1.1	1.0	1.0	1.0	1.0	1.0
IMR - Males	67.2	51.4	36.8	23.7	21.4	21.4	21.4	21.4	21.4	21.4	21.4
IMR - Females	62.8	46.2	29.6	16.9	14.8	14.8	14.8	14.8	14.8	14.8	14.8
IMR - Both Sexes	65.0	48.8	33.2	20.3	18.1	18.1	18.1	18.1	18.1	18.1	18.1
E(0) - Males	65.36	66.65	67.98	69.34	70.09	70.09	70.09	70.09	70.09	70.09	70.09
E(0) - Females	68.43	70.20	72.05	73.74	74.76	74.76	74.76	74.76	74.76	74.76	74.76
E(0) - Both Sexes	66.90	68.43	70.02	71.54	72.43	72.43	72.43	72.43	72.43	72.43	72.43

Year	2100	2110	2120	2130	2140	2150	2160	2170	2180	2190	2200
Birth Rate ‰	14.2	14.1	14.1	14.1	14.1	14.1	14.1	14.1	14.1	14.1	14.1
Death Rate ‰	14.0	14.1	14.1	14.1	14.1	14.1	14.1	14.1	14.1	14.1	14.1
Growth Rate %	0.02	0.00	0.00	0.00	0.00	0.00	0.00	0.00	0.00	0.00	0.00
Total Fertility Rate	2.130	2.130	2.130	2.130	2.130	2.130	2.130	2.130	2.130	2.130	2.130
GRR	1.039	1.039	1.039	1.039	1.039	1.039	1.039	1.039	1.039	1.039	1.039
NRR	1.0	1.0	1.0	1.0	1.0	1.0	1.0	1.0	1.0	1.0	1.0
IMR - Males	21.4	21.4	21.4	21.4	21.4	21.4	21.4	21.4	21.4	21.4	21.4
IMR - Females	14.8	14.8	14.8	14.8	14.8	14.8	14.8	14.8	14.8	14.8	14.8
IMR - Both Sexes	18.1	18.1	18.1	18.1	18.1	18.1	18.1	18.1	18.1	18.1	18.1
E(0) - Males	70.09	70.09	70.09	70.09	70.09	70.09	70.09	70.09	70.09	70.09	70.09
E(0) - Females	74.76	74.76	74.76	74.76	74.76	74.76	74.76	74.76	74.76	74.76	74.76
E(0) - Both Sexes	72.43	72.43	72.43	72.43	72.43	72.43	72.43	72.43	72.43	72.43	72.43

Graph 1

Projected Total Population
World Population Projection No. 2060.R.M
Decline to Replacement Fertility Level (2.13)
Mortality Level: Medium

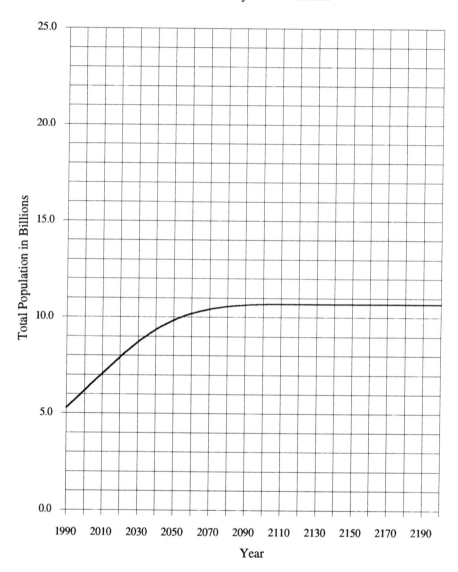

Graph 2

Components of Population Change
World Population Projection No. 2060.R.M
Decline to Replacement Fertility Level (2.13)
Mortality Level: Medium

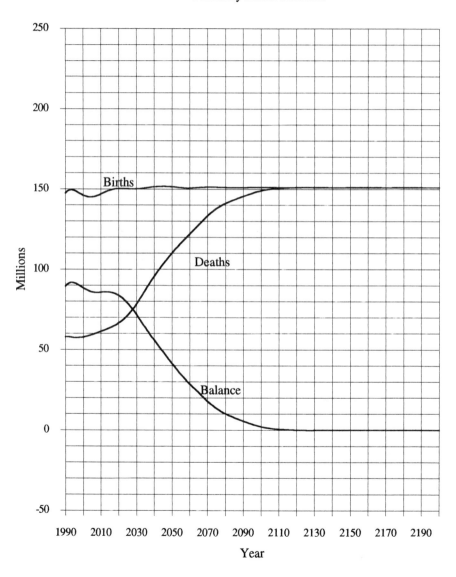

Graph 3

Age Structure of World Population 1990, 2050 and 2100

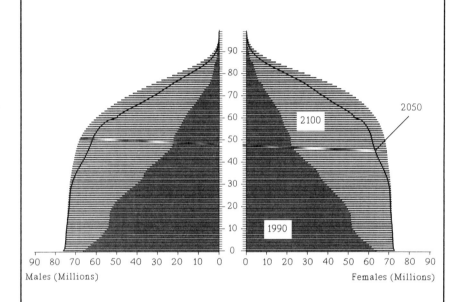

Population Projection No. 2060.R.M.

Target year for replacement fertility
level (TFR = 2.13):   2060
Form of fertility decline: Hyperbolic
Mortality level: Medium

Total population: 1990   5 275 Million
     2050   9 824 Million
     2100   10 674 Million

Table 1
Projected Total Population
World Population Projection No. 2060.R.L
Decline to Replacement Fertility Level (2.13); Mortality Level: Low
- Millions -

Age Year	0-4	5-9	10-14	15-19	20-24	25-29	30-34	35-39	40-44	45-49	50-54	55-59	60-64	65-69	70-74	75+	Total
1990	625	563	528	519	490	436	380	342	282	230	214	186	160	123	87	108	5275
2000	684	665	609	555	519	508	479	425	367	328	265	210	185	150	115	126	6189
2010	691	673	670	658	600	546	509	497	466	409	347	301	233	172	136	166	7076
2020	727	705	682	668	663	650	592	537	498	481	444	379	310	252	176	205	7969
2030	737	732	721	701	677	662	656	641	581	522	477	451	400	323	239	295	8814
2040	743	735	732	729	717	695	670	653	645	625	558	491	432	386	312	401	9522
2050	748	743	738	732	727	722	709	686	658	637	619	587	506	420	337	500	10068
2060	744	743	743	739	733	725	720	713	697	669	633	598	561	502	394	555	10469
2070	748	742	739	740	738	733	725	716	707	695	670	628	573	512	437	648	10752
2080	750	746	743	739	735	735	730	724	713	698	679	653	607	538	447	697	10931
2090	751	746	745	743	738	732	727	724	718	705	685	656	616	559	473	726	11043
2100	753	748	746	743	740	736	731	723	715	705	689	663	621	561	480	759	11112
2110	754	750	748	745	741	737	733	727	718	705	687	663	625	567	484	770	11151
2120	756	751	749	746	743	738	733	727	720	708	690	662	622	567	487	777	11177
2130	757	753	751	748	744	740	735	729	721	709	692	665	625	566	485	780	11200
2140	759	754	752	749	746	741	737	731	723	710	692	666	627	570	487	779	11223
2150	760	756	754	751	747	743	738	732	724	712	694	667	627	570	488	782	11246
2160	762	757	755	752	749	744	740	734	725	713	695	669	629	571	489	784	11269
2170	763	759	757	754	750	746	741	735	727	715	697	670	630	572	490	785	11292
2180	765	760	758	756	752	748	743	737	728	716	698	671	631	573	491	787	11316
2190	767	762	760	757	753	749	744	738	730	718	700	673	633	575	492	788	11339
2200	768	764	761	759	755	751	746	740	731	719	701	674	634	576	493	790	11362

Table 2
Components of Population Change
World Population Projection No. 2060.R.L
Decline to Replacement Fertility Level (2.13); Mortality Level: Low

Year	Males Births	Males Deaths - Thousands -	Males Balance	Females Births	Females Deaths - Thousands -	Females Balance	Births	Total Deaths - Thousands -	Balance
1990	75539	29422	46117	71783	28562	43221	147322	57985	89338
2000	74929	29571	45358	71203	26526	44677	146132	56097	90035
2010	75351	31368	43984	71604	26767	44837	146955	58135	88821
2020	77241	33935	43306	73399	28399	45000	150640	62334	88306
2030	77372	39340	38031	73524	33132	40392	150895	72472	78423
2040	78176	48443	29733	74288	42281	32007	152463	90724	61740
2050	78393	56317	22075	74494	50278	24216	152887	106596	46291
2060	78088	62503	15585	74204	56696	17508	152292	119199	33093
2070	78615	68244	10371	74705	62812	11893	153319	131056	22263
2080	78669	72367	6302	74757	67567	7190	153426	139934	13492
2090	78815	74782	4033	74895	70268	4628	153711	145050	8661
2100	79021	76734	2287	75091	72441	2650	154112	149175	4936
2110	79159	77735	1423	75222	73658	1564	154381	151394	2987
2120	79326	78168	1158	75381	74165	1216	154707	152332	2374
2130	79494	78393	1101	75541	74436	1104	155034	152829	2205
2140	79653	78490	1163	75692	74517	1175	155345	153006	2338
2150	79819	78668	1151	75849	74671	1178	155668	153339	2329
2160	79983	78841	1142	76006	74850	1156	155989	153691	2298
2170	80148	78990	1158	76162	74986	1176	156309	153975	2334
2180	80313	79159	1154	76319	75146	1173	156632	154304	2328
2190	80478	79322	1157	76476	75302	1174	156954	154624	2331
2200	80644	79483	1161	76633	75454	1179	157277	154937	2340

Table 3
Demographic Indicators
World Population Projection No. 2060.R.L
Decline to Replacement Fertility Level (2.13); Mortality Level: Low

Year	1990	2000	2010	2020	2030	2040	2050	2060	2070	2080	2090
Birth Rate ‰	27.9	23.6	20.8	18.9	17.1	16.0	15.2	14.5	14.3	14.0	13.9
Death Rate ‰	11.0	9.1	8.2	7.8	8.2	9.5	10.6	11.4	12.2	12.8	13.1
Growth Rate %	1.69	1.45	1.26	1.11	0.89	0.65	0.46	0.32	0.21	0.12	0.08
Total Fertility Rate	3.400	3.007	2.651	2.437	2.308	2.225	2.169	2.130	2.130	2.130	2.130
GRR	1.684	1.463	1.298	1.190	1.126	1.086	1.058	1.040	1.039	1.039	1.039
NRR	1.5	1.4	1.2	1.2	1.1	1.1	1.0	1.0	1.0	1.0	1.0
IMR - Males	67.2	49.5	34.0	21.0	18.2	18.2	18.2	18.2	18.2	18.2	18.2
IMR - Females	62.8	44.4	27.4	15.0	12.6	12.6	12.6	12.6	12.6	12.6	12.6
IMR - Both Sexes	65.0	47.0	30.7	18.0	15.4	15.4	15.4	15.4	15.4	15.4	15.4
E(0) - Males	65.36	67.19	69.03	70.84	72.06	72.06	72.06	72.06	72.06	72.06	72.06
E(0) - Females	68.43	70.71	73.00	75.08	76.51	76.51	76.51	76.51	76.51	76.51	76.51
E(0) - Both Sexes	66.90	68.95	71.02	72.96	74.28	74.28	74.28	74.28	74.28	74.28	74.28

Year	2100	2110	2120	2130	2140	2150	2160	2170	2180	2190	2200
Birth Rate ‰	13.9	13.8	13.8	13.8	13.8	13.8	13.8	13.8	13.8	13.8	13.8
Death Rate ‰	13.4	13.6	13.6	13.6	13.6	13.6	13.6	13.6	13.6	13.6	13.6
Growth Rate %	0.04	0.03	0.02	0.02	0.02	0.02	0.02	0.02	0.02	0.02	0.02
Total Fertility Rate	2.130	2.130	2.130	2.130	2.130	2.130	2.130	2.130	2.130	2.130	2.130
GRR	1.039	1.039	1.039	1.039	1.039	1.039	1.039	1.039	1.039	1.039	1.039
NRR	1.0	1.0	1.0	1.0	1.0	1.0	1.0	1.0	1.0	1.0	1.0
IMR - Males	18.2	18.2	18.2	18.2	18.2	18.2	18.2	18.2	18.2	18.2	18.2
IMR - Females	12.6	12.6	12.6	12.6	12.6	12.6	12.6	12.6	12.6	12.6	12.6
IMR - Both Sexes	15.4	15.4	15.4	15.4	15.4	15.4	15.4	15.4	15.4	15.4	15.4
E(0) - Males	72.06	72.06	72.06	72.06	72.06	72.06	72.06	72.06	72.06	72.06	72.06
E(0) - Females	76.51	76.51	76.51	76.51	76.51	76.51	76.51	76.51	76.51	76.51	76.51
E(0) - Both Sexes	74.28	74.28	74.28	74.28	74.28	74.28	74.28	74.28	74.28	74.28	74.28

Graph 1

Projected Total Population
World Population Projection No. 2060.R.L
Decline to Replacement Fertility Level (2.13)
Mortality Level: Low

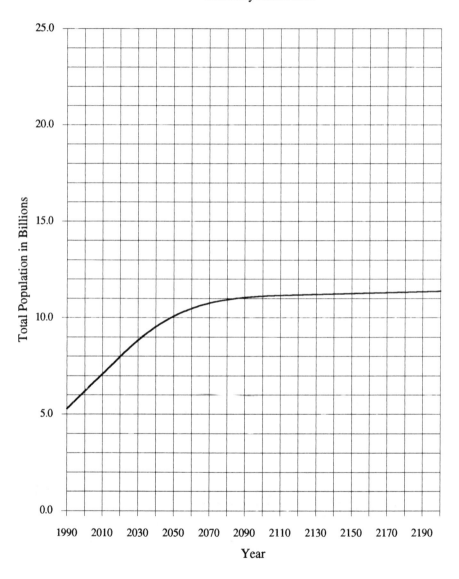

Graph 2

Components of Population Change
World Population Projection No. 2060.R.L
Decline to Replacement Fertility Level (2.13)
Mortality Level: Low

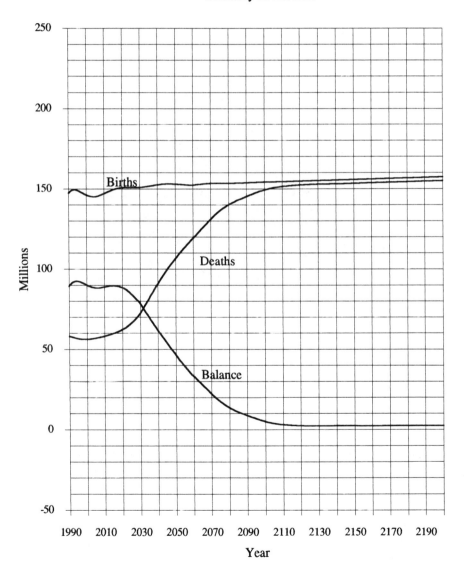

Graph 3

Age Structure of World Population 1990, 2050 and 2100

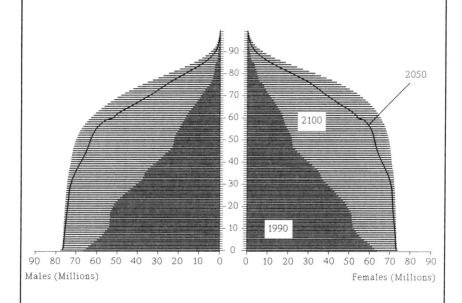

Population Projection No. 2060.R.L.

Target year for replacement fertility
level (TFR = 2.13):   2060
Form of fertility decline: Hyperbolic
Mortality level: Low

Total population: 1990   5 275 Million
                                            2050 10 068 Million
                                            2100 11 112 Million

Table 1
Projected Total Population
World Population Projection No. 2060.B.H
Decline Below Replacement Fertility Level; Mortality Level: High

Age Year	0-4	5-9	10-14	15-19	20-24	25-29	30-34	35-39	40-44	45-49	50-54	55-59	60-64	65-69	70-74	75+	Total
1990	625	563	528	519	490	436	380	342	282	230	214	186	160	123	87	108	5275
2000	680	664	609	555	518	508	479	424	367	327	264	209	184	149	113	121	6171
2010	685	667	666	656	599	545	508	496	464	406	345	298	229	168	131	149	7010
2020	718	696	674	661	657	646	589	533	494	477	438	372	300	240	163	169	7827
2030	724	720	711	691	667	653	648	635	575	515	468	438	382	301	214	225	8566
2040	726	719	717	716	704	683	658	642	633	613	544	473	409	355	273	289	9155
2050	729	724	720	715	711	707	695	672	643	620	600	563	477	384	292	351	9600
2060	722	721	722	720	713	706	701	696	679	649	609	569	525	456	341	383	9912
2070	715	714	716	717	715	711	704	695	685	672	643	596	533	462	375	447	10099
2080	705	706	708	710	709	708	706	699	687	671	649	617	563	483	381	473	10176
2090	694	695	699	702	702	701	700	697	689	675	651	616	568	500	402	490	10182
2100	681	683	688	691	693	693	693	690	683	672	653	620	570	500	405	511	10127
2110	668	670	675	679	681	683	684	682	677	666	647	618	572	503	407	514	10026
2120	654	656	662	666	669	671	672	672	668	658	641	612	567	501	408	517	9894
2130	639	642	648	653	656	659	660	660	657	648	632	605	561	496	405	516	9737
2140	624	628	633	638	642	645	647	648	645	637	622	596	554	490	400	512	9561
2150	609	613	619	624	628	631	633	634	632	625	611	585	544	483	395	506	9373
2160	594	598	604	609	613	617	619	620	619	612	599	574	535	475	389	499	9175
2170	579	582	589	594	598	602	605	606	605	599	586	563	524	466	382	491	8970
2180	564	567	574	579	583	587	590	592	591	585	573	550	513	456	374	482	8760
2190	549	552	559	564	568	572	575	577	576	571	560	538	502	446	366	472	8548
2200	534	538	544	549	554	557	561	563	562	557	546	525	490	436	358	462	8335

- Millions -

Table 2
Components of Population Change
World Population Projection No. 2060.B.H
Decline Below Replacement Fertility Level; Mortality Level: High

Year	Males Births	Males Deaths - Thousands -	Males Balance	Females Births	Females Deaths - Thousands -	Females Balance	Total Births	Total Deaths - Thousands -	Total Balance
1990	75539	29422	46117	71783	28562	43221	147322	57985	89338
2000	74882	31462	43420	71158	28151	43007	146040	59613	86427
2010	75168	34711	40457	71430	29450	41979	146598	64162	82436
2020	76713	38482	38231	72898	31926	40972	149611	70407	79203
2030	76493	45459	31034	72689	37968	34721	149183	83427	65755
2040	77019	53183	23835	73188	46141	27047	150207	99325	50882
2050	76913	59838	17075	73088	53223	19865	150001	113061	36940
2060	76160	65241	10919	72372	59022	13350	148532	124263	24269
2070	75355	70196	5159	71608	64709	6899	146963	134904	12058
2080	74268	73088	1179	70574	68374	2200	144842	141462	3379
2090	73005	74825	-1820	69374	70434	-1060	142379	145258	-2880
2100	71657	76053	-4396	68093	72080	-3987	139750	148133	-8383
2110	70204	76281	-6077	66713	72577	-5864	136917	148858	-11941
2120	68691	76087	-7396	65274	72556	-7281	133965	148643	-14678
2130	67137	75542	-8405	63798	72216	-8418	130934	147758	-16823
2140	65551	74660	-9109	62291	71485	-9194	127842	146145	-18303
2150	63950	73594	-9645	60769	70553	-9784	124719	144148	-19429
2160	62342	72365	-10023	59242	69453	-10211	121584	141818	-20234
2170	60735	71011	-10276	57715	68211	-10496	118450	139223	-20772
2180	59137	69575	-10438	56196	66880	-10684	115333	136455	-21122
2190	57552	68074	-10522	54690	65478	-10788	112241	133552	-21311
2200	55984	66529	-10545	53200	64025	-10826	109183	130554	-21371

Table 3
Demographic Indicators
World Population Projection No. 2060.B.H
Decline Below Replacement Fertility Level; Mortality Level: High

Year	1990	2000	2010	2020	2030	2040	2050	2060	2070	2080	2090
Birth Rate ‰	27.9	23.7	20.9	19.1	17.4	16.4	15.6	15.0	14.6	14.2	14.0
Death Rate ‰	11.0	9.7	9.2	9.0	9.7	10.8	11.8	12.5	13.4	13.9	14.3
Growth Rate %	1.69	1.40	1.18	1.01	0.77	0.56	0.38	0.24	0.12	0.03	-0.03
Total Fertility Rate	3.400	3.007	2.651	2.437	2.308	2.225	2.169	2.130	2.101	2.079	2.062
GRR	1.684	1.463	1.298	1.190	1.126	1.086	1.057	1.038	1.024	1.013	1.004
NRR	1.5	1.4	1.2	1.2	1.1	1.1	1.0	1.0	1.0	1.0	1.0
IMR - Males	67.2	53.4	39.5	26.3	24.6	24.6	24.6	24.6	24.6	24.6	24.6
IMR - Females	62.8	47.9	31.8	18.8	17.0	17.0	17.0	17.0	17.0	17.0	17.0
IMR - Both Sexes	65.0	50.6	35.7	22.5	20.8	20.8	20.8	20.8	20.8	20.8	20.8
E(0) - Males	65.36	66.12	67.01	67.99	68.39	68.39	68.39	68.39	68.39	68.39	68.39
E(0) - Females	68.43	69.71	71.16	72.53	73.25	73.25	73.25	73.25	73.25	73.25	73.25
E(0) - Both Sexes	66.90	67.91	69.08	70.26	70.82	70.82	70.82	70.82	70.82	70.82	70.82

Year	2100	2110	2120	2130	2140	2150	2160	2170	2180	2190	2200
Birth Rate ‰	13.8	13.7	13.5	13.4	13.4	13.3	13.3	13.2	13.2	13.1	13.1
Death Rate ‰	14.6	14.8	15.0	15.2	15.3	15.4	15.5	15.5	15.6	15.6	15.7
Growth Rate %	-0.08	-0.12	-0.15	-0.17	-0.19	-0.21	-0.22	-0.23	-0.24	-0.25	-0.26
Total Fertility Rate	2.049	2.038	2.029	2.021	2.015	2.010	2.005	2.001	1.998	1.994	1.992
GRR	0.997	0.992	0.987	0.984	0.980	0.978	0.975	0.973	0.972	0.970	0.972
NRR	1.0	1.0	1.0	1.0	1.0	1.0	0.9	0.9	0.9	0.9	0.9
IMR - Males	24.6	24.6	24.6	24.6	24.6	24.6	24.6	24.6	24.6	24.6	24.6
IMR - Females	17.0	17.0	17.0	17.0	17.0	17.0	17.0	17.0	17.0	17.0	17.0
IMR - Both Sexes	20.8	20.8	20.8	20.8	20.8	20.8	20.8	20.8	20.8	20.8	20.8
E(0) - Males	68.39	68.39	68.39	68.39	68.39	68.39	68.39	68.39	68.39	68.39	68.39
E(0) - Females	73.25	73.25	73.25	73.25	73.25	73.25	73.25	73.25	73.25	73.25	73.25
E(0) - Both Sexes	70.82	70.82	70.82	70.82	70.82	70.82	70.82	70.82	70.82	70.82	70.82

Graph 1

Projected Total Population
World Population Projection No. 2060.B.H
Decline Below Replacement Fertility Level
Mortality Level: High

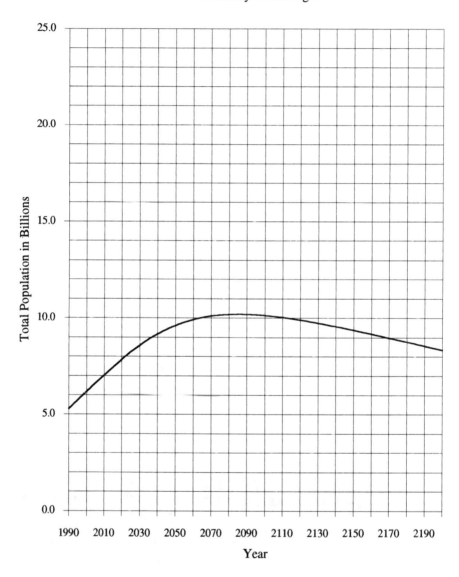

Graph 2

Components of Population Change
World Population Projection No. 2060.B.H
Decline Below Replacement Fertility Level
Mortality Level: High

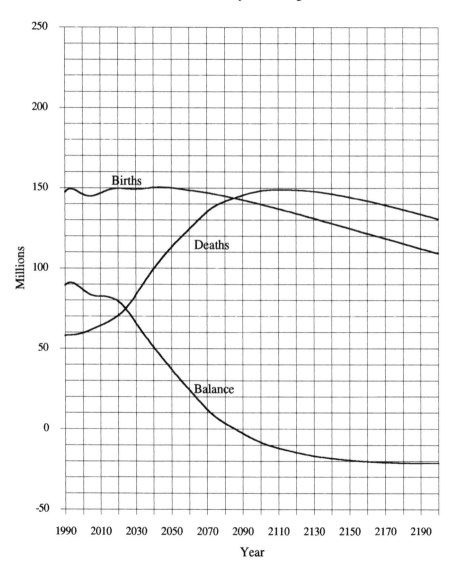

Graph 3

Age Structure of World Population 1990, 2050 and 2100

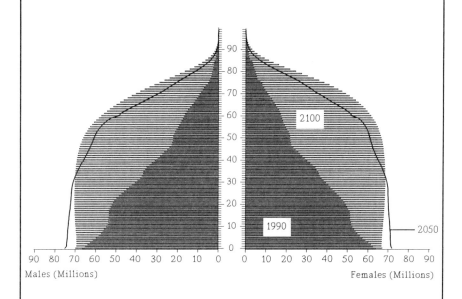

Population Projection No. 2060.B.H.

Decline below replacement fertility level by the year:	2060
Form of fertility decline:	Hyperbolic
Mortality level:	High
Total population:	1990 5 275 Million
	2050 9 600 Million
	2100 10 127 Million

Table 1
Projected Total Population
World Population Projection No. 2060.B.M
Decline Below Replacement Fertility Level; Mortality Level: Medium

- Millions -

Age Year	0-4	5-9	10-14	15-19	20-24	25-29	30-34	35-39	40-44	45-49	50-54	55-59	60-64	65-69	70-74	75+	Total
1990	625	563	528	519	490	436	380	342	282	230	214	186	160	123	87	108	5275
2000	682	665	609	555	519	508	479	424	367	327	264	209	185	149	114	124	6180
2010	688	670	668	657	600	545	508	496	465	408	346	299	231	170	133	157	7043
2020	723	700	678	664	660	648	590	535	496	479	441	375	305	246	169	186	7896
2030	730	726	716	696	672	657	652	638	578	518	472	444	391	312	226	257	8686
2040	734	727	724	722	710	689	664	648	639	619	551	482	421	370	292	339	9331
2050	738	733	729	723	719	715	702	679	651	628	609	575	491	401	314	417	9824
2060	733	732	732	729	723	716	710	704	688	659	621	584	543	479	366	459	10178
2070	727	726	728	728	726	722	715	705	696	683	656	612	553	486	405	536	10404
2080	719	719	722	722	722	721	718	712	700	684	664	635	585	510	413	571	10516
2090	709	710	714	716	716	715	713	710	703	690	668	636	591	529	436	593	10549
2100	698	699	703	706	708	708	708	705	699	689	671	641	595	529	441	619	10519
2110	685	688	692	696	698	699	700	698	693	683	667	640	598	534	444	626	10440
2120	672	675	680	684	687	689	690	689	686	677	661	635	594	533	446	630	10326
2130	658	661	667	671	675	677	679	679	676	668	654	629	589	529	443	631	10186
2140	644	648	653	658	662	664	667	667	665	658	645	621	582	524	439	627	10025
2150	630	634	639	644	648	651	654	655	653	647	634	611	574	517	434	622	9849
2160	616	619	625	630	634	638	641	642	641	635	623	601	565	509	428	615	9662
2170	601	605	611	616	620	624	627	629	628	623	611	590	555	501	421	606	9467
2180	587	591	597	602	606	610	613	615	614	610	599	578	544	491	414	596	9266
2190	572	576	582	587	592	596	599	601	601	596	586	566	533	482	406	585	9061
2200	558	562	568	573	578	582	585	587	587	583	573	554	522	472	398	574	8854

Table 2
Components of Population Change
World Population Projection No. 2060.B.M
Decline Below Replacement Fertility Level; Mortality Level: Medium

Year	Males Births	Males Deaths - Thousands -	Males Balance	Females Births	Females Deaths - Thousands -	Females Balance	Total Births	Total Deaths - Thousands -	Total Balance
1990	75539	29422	46117	71783	28562	43221	147322	57985	89338
2000	74906	30522	44384	71180	27344	43836	146086	57866	88220
2010	75260	33074	42185	71517	28139	43378	146777	61214	85563
2020	76976	36299	40677	73148	30237	42911	150125	66536	83588
2030	76931	42596	34336	73105	35707	37398	150037	78303	71734
2040	77595	51003	26592	73736	44366	29370	151331	95369	55963
2050	77650	58232	19418	73788	51875	21913	151437	110107	41330
2060	77058	63988	13070	73226	57953	15273	150285	121941	28344
2070	76399	69334	7065	72599	63855	8744	148998	133189	15809
2080	75455	72791	2664	71702	68040	3662	147157	140831	6326
2090	74328	74810	-482	70632	70363	268	144960	145173	-213
2100	73108	76366	-3259	69472	72260	-2788	142579	148626	-6046
2110	71776	76908	-5132	68207	73067	-4861	139983	149975	-9992
2120	70375	76929	-6554	66876	73246	-6371	137251	150176	-12925
2130	68927	76605	-7677	65499	73112	-7612	134427	149717	-15290
2140	67440	75917	-8476	64086	72573	-8487	131527	148490	-16963
2150	65931	75021	-9091	62652	71804	-9153	128582	146825	-18243
2160	64408	73953	-9545	61205	70860	-9655	125612	144812	-19200
2170	62879	72743	-9864	59752	69760	-10008	122631	142503	-19872
2180	61353	71439	-10087	58301	68558	-10256	119654	139997	-20343
2190	59833	70060	-10227	56857	67275	-10418	116690	137335	-20645
2200	58325	68626	-10302	55424	65932	-10508	113748	134558	-20809

Table 3
Demographic Indicators
World Population Projection No. 2060.B.M
Decline Below Replacement Fertility Level; Mortality Level: Medium

Year	1990	2000	2010	2020	2030	2040	2050	2060	2070	2080	2090
Birth Rate ‰	27.9	23.6	20.8	19.0	17.3	16.2	15.4	14.8	14.3	14.0	13.7
Death Rate ‰	11.0	9.4	8.7	8.4	9.0	10.2	11.2	12.0	12.8	13.4	13.8
Growth Rate %	1.69	1.43	1.21	1.06	0.83	0.60	0.42	0.28	0.15	0.06	0.00
Total Fertility Rate	3.400	3.007	2.651	2.437	2.308	2.225	2.169	2.130	2.101	2.079	2.062
GRR	1.684	1.463	1.298	1.190	1.126	1.086	1.058	1.038	1.024	1.013	1.004
NRR	1.5	1.4	1.2	1.2	1.1	1.1	1.0	1.0	1.0	1.0	1.0
IMR - Males	67.2	51.4	36.8	23.7	21.4	21.4	21.4	21.4	21.4	21.4	21.4
IMR - Females	62.8	46.2	29.6	16.9	14.8	14.8	14.8	14.8	14.8	14.8	14.8
IMR - Both Sexes	65.0	48.8	33.2	20.3	18.1	18.1	18.1	18.1	18.1	18.1	18.1
E(0) - Males	65.36	66.65	67.98	69.34	70.09	70.09	70.09	70.09	70.09	70.09	70.09
E(0) - Females	68.43	70.20	72.05	73.74	74.76	74.76	74.76	74.76	74.76	74.76	74.76
E(0) - Both Sexes	66.90	68.43	70.02	71.54	72.43	72.43	72.43	72.43	72.43	72.43	72.43

Year	2100	2110	2120	2130	2140	2150	2160	2170	2180	2190	2200
Birth Rate ‰	13.6	13.4	13.3	13.2	13.1	13.1	13.0	13.0	12.9	12.9	12.8
Death Rate ‰	14.1	14.4	14.5	14.7	14.8	14.9	15.0	15.1	15.1	15.2	15.2
Growth Rate %	-0.06	-0.10	-0.13	-0.15	-0.17	-0.19	-0.20	-0.21	-0.22	-0.23	-0.24
Total Fertility Rate	2.049	2.038	2.029	2.021	2.015	2.010	2.005	2.001	1.998	1.994	1.992
GRR	0.997	0.992	0.987	0.984	0.981	0.978	0.976	0.974	0.972	0.970	0.971
NRR	1.0	1.0	1.0	1.0	1.0	1.0	1.0	1.0	0.9	0.9	0.9
IMR - Males	21.4	21.4	21.4	21.4	21.4	21.4	21.4	21.4	21.4	21.4	21.4
IMR - Females	14.8	14.8	14.8	14.8	14.8	14.8	14.8	14.8	14.8	14.8	14.8
IMR - Both Sexes	18.1	18.1	18.1	18.1	18.1	18.1	18.1	18.1	18.1	18.1	18.1
E(0) - Males	70.09	70.09	70.09	70.09	70.09	70.09	70.09	70.09	70.09	70.09	70.09
E(0) - Females	74.76	74.76	74.76	74.76	74.76	74.76	74.76	74.76	74.76	74.76	74.76
E(0) - Both Sexes	72.43	72.43	72.43	72.43	72.43	72.43	72.43	72.43	72.43	72.43	72.43

Graph 1

Projected Total Population
World Population Projection No. 2060.B.M
Decline Below Replacement Fertility Level
Mortality Level: Medium

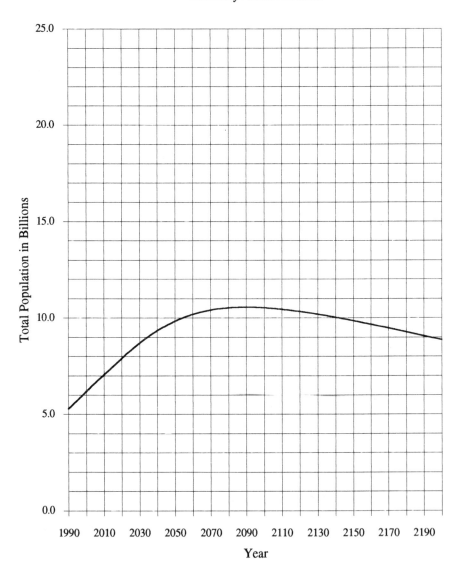

Graph 2

Components of Population Change
World Population Projection No. 2060.B.M
Decline Below Replacement Fertility Level
Mortality Level: Medium

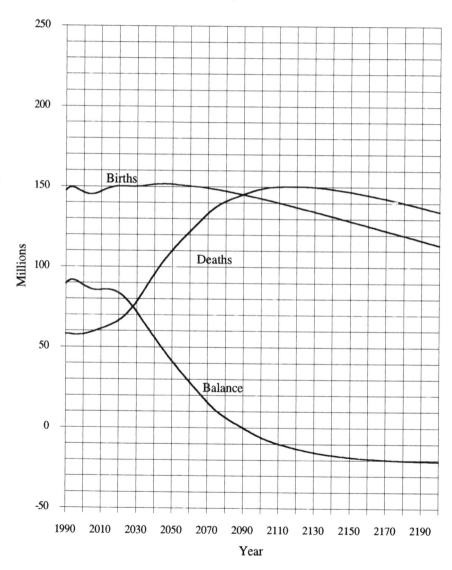

Graph 3

Age Structure of World Population 1990, 2050 and 2100

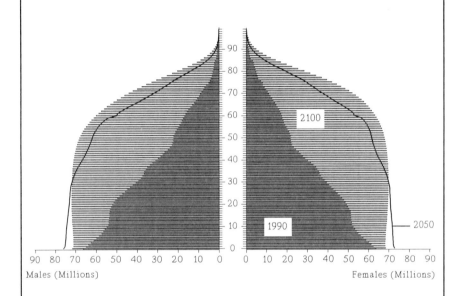

Population Projection No. 2060.B.M.

Decline below replacement fertility level by the year:	2060
Form of fertility decline:	Hyperbolic
Mortality level:	Medium

Total population:	1990	5 275 Million
	2050	9 824 Million
	2100	10 519 Million

Table 1
Projected Total Population
World Population Projection No. 2060.B.L
Decline Below Replacement Fertility Level; Mortality Level: Low

- Millions -

Age Year	0-4	5-9	10-14	15-19	20-24	25-29	30-34	35-39	40-44	45-49	50-54	55-59	60-64	65-69	70-74	75+	Total
1990	625	563	528	519	490	436	380	342	282	230	214	186	160	123	87	108	5275
2000	684	665	609	555	519	508	479	425	367	328	265	210	185	150	115	126	6189
2010	691	673	670	658	600	546	509	497	466	409	347	301	233	172	136	166	7076
2020	727	705	682	668	663	650	592	537	498	481	444	379	310	252	176	205	7969
2030	737	732	721	701	677	662	656	641	581	522	477	451	400	323	239	295	8814
2040	743	735	732	729	717	695	670	653	645	625	558	491	432	386	312	401	9522
2050	748	743	738	732	727	722	709	686	658	637	619	587	506	420	337	500	10068
2060	744	743	743	739	733	725	720	713	697	669	633	598	561	502	394	555	10469
2070	740	739	739	740	738	733	725	716	707	695	670	628	573	512	437	648	10740
2080	733	733	735	735	735	733	730	724	713	698	679	653	607	538	447	697	10890
2090	724	725	728	730	730	729	727	724	718	705	685	656	616	559	473	726	10955
2100	714	716	719	722	723	724	723	720	715	705	689	663	621	561	480	759	10954
2110	703	705	709	713	715	716	716	715	710	701	687	663	625	567	484	770	10898
2120	691	694	698	702	705	706	707	707	704	696	682	659	622	567	487	777	10805
2130	678	681	686	691	694	696	698	698	695	689	676	654	618	564	485	780	10683
2140	665	669	674	678	682	685	687	687	686	680	668	647	613	560	482	778	10539
2150	652	655	661	666	669	672	675	676	675	670	659	638	605	554	477	773	10377
2160	638	642	648	652	656	660	663	664	663	659	648	629	597	546	471	765	10203
2170	625	628	634	639	643	647	650	652	651	647	637	619	587	538	465	756	10019
2180	611	615	620	626	630	634	637	639	639	635	626	608	577	530	458	745	9827
2190	597	601	607	612	616	620	624	626	626	622	614	596	567	520	450	733	9631
2200	583	587	593	598	603	607	610	613	613	610	601	585	556	510	442	721	9431

Table 2
Components of Population Change
World Population Projection No. 2060.B.L
Decline Below Replacement Fertility Level; Mortality Level: Low

Year	Males Births	Males Deaths - Thousands -	Males Balance	Females Births	Females Deaths - Thousands -	Females Balance	Total Births	Total Deaths - Thousands -	Total Balance
1990	75539	29422	46117	71783	28562	43221	147322	57985	89338
2000	74929	29571	45358	71203	26526	44677	146132	56097	90035
2010	75351	31368	43984	71604	26767	44837	146955	58135	88821
2020	77241	33935	43306	73399	28399	45000	150640	62334	88306
2030	77372	39340	38031	73524	33132	40392	150895	72472	78423
2040	78176	48443	29733	74288	42281	32007	152463	90724	61740
2050	78393	56317	22075	74494	50278	24216	152887	106596	46291
2060	77967	62501	15466	74089	56695	17395	152056	119195	32861
2070	77456	68209	9247	73604	62789	10815	151060	130998	20062
2080	76660	72299	4361	72848	67523	5324	149508	139823	9685
2090	75674	74664	1010	71911	70193	1717	147585	144858	2727
2100	74586	76547	-1961	70877	72324	-1447	145463	148871	-3407
2110	73381	77448	-4067	69732	73479	-3747	143113	150927	-7813
2120	72100	77709	-5610	68514	73883	-5368	140614	151592	-10978
2130	70764	77619	-6855	67245	73961	-6717	138009	151581	-13572
2140	69382	77144	-7762	65932	73633	-7701	135314	150777	-15463
2150	67971	76432	-8461	64590	73039	-8449	132561	149471	-16910
2160	66540	75537	-8997	63230	72261	-9031	129770	147798	-18028
2170	65096	74485	-9389	61859	71315	-9456	126955	145800	-18845
2180	63649	73325	-9676	60483	70252	-9769	124132	143577	-19445
2190	62202	72079	-9877	59108	69099	-9991	121310	141178	-19868
2200	60761	70767	-10006	57739	67875	-10136	118499	138642	-20143

Table 3
Demographic Indicators
World Population Projection No. 2060.B.L
Decline Below Replacement Fertility Level; Mortality Level: Low

Year	1990	2000	2010	2020	2030	2040	2050	2060	2070	2080	2090
Birth Rate ‰	27.9	23.6	20.8	18.9	17.1	16.0	15.2	14.5	14.1	13.7	13.5
Death Rate ‰	11.0	9.1	8.2	7.8	8.2	9.5	10.6	11.4	12.2	12.8	13.2
Growth Rate %	1.69	1.45	1.26	1.11	0.89	0.65	0.46	0.31	0.19	0.09	0.02
Total Fertility Rate	3.400	3.007	2.651	2.437	2.308	2.225	2.169	2.130	2.101	2.079	2.062
GRR	1.684	1.463	1.298	1.190	1.126	1.086	1.058	1.038	1.024	1.013	1.004
NRR	1.5	1.4	1.2	1.2	1.1	1.1	1.0	1.0	1.0	1.0	1.0
IMR - Males	67.2	49.5	34.0	21.0	18.2	18.2	18.2	18.2	18.2	18.2	18.2
IMR - Females	62.8	44.4	27.4	15.0	12.6	12.6	12.6	12.6	12.6	12.6	12.6
IMR - Both Sexes	65.0	47.0	30.7	18.0	15.4	15.4	15.4	15.4	15.4	15.4	15.4
E(0) - Males	65.36	67.19	69.03	70.84	72.06	72.06	72.06	72.06	72.06	72.06	72.06
E(0) - Females	68.43	70.71	73.00	75.08	76.51	76.51	76.51	76.51	76.51	76.51	76.51
E(0) - Both Sexes	66.90	68.95	71.02	72.96	74.28	74.28	74.28	74.28	74.28	74.28	74.28

Year	2100	2110	2120	2130	2140	2150	2160	2170	2180	2190	2200
Birth Rate ‰	13.3	13.1	13.0	12.9	12.8	12.8	12.7	12.7	12.6	12.6	12.6
Death Rate ‰	13.6	13.8	14.0	14.2	14.3	14.4	14.5	14.6	14.6	14.7	14.7
Growth Rate %	-0.03	-0.07	-0.10	-0.13	-0.15	-0.16	-0.18	-0.19	-0.20	-0.21	-0.21
Total Fertility Rate	2.049	2.038	2.029	2.021	2.015	2.010	2.005	2.001	1.998	1.994	1.992
GRR	0.997	0.992	0.988	0.984	0.981	0.978	0.976	0.974	0.972	0.970	0.971
NRR	1.0	1.0	1.0	1.0	1.0	1.0	1.0	1.0	1.0	1.0	1.0
IMR - Males	18.2	18.2	18.2	18.2	18.2	18.2	18.2	18.2	18.2	18.2	18.2
IMR - Females	12.6	12.6	12.6	12.6	12.6	12.6	12.6	12.6	12.6	12.6	12.6
IMR - Both Sexes	15.4	15.4	15.4	15.4	15.4	15.4	15.4	15.4	15.4	15.4	15.4
E(0) - Males	72.06	72.06	72.06	72.06	72.06	72.06	72.06	72.06	72.06	72.06	72.06
E(0) - Females	76.51	76.51	76.51	76.51	76.51	76.51	76.51	76.51	76.51	76.51	76.51
E(0) - Both Sexes	74.28	74.28	74.28	74.28	74.28	74.28	74.28	74.28	74.28	74.28	74.28

Graph 1

Projected Total Population
World Population Projection No. 2060.B.L
Decline Below Replacement Fertility Level
Mortality Level: Low

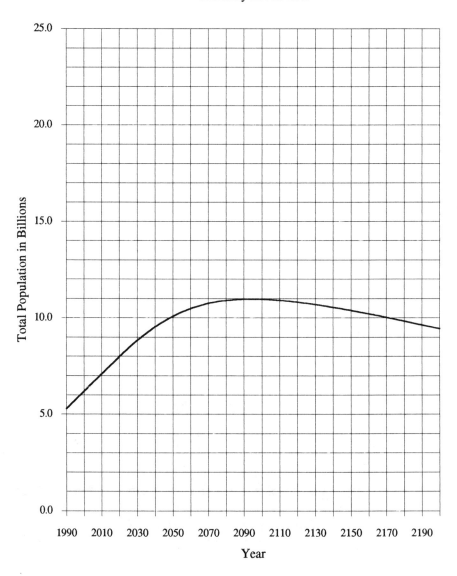

Graph 2

Components of Population Change
World Population Projection No. 2060.B.L
Decline Below Replacement Fertility Level
Mortality Level: Low

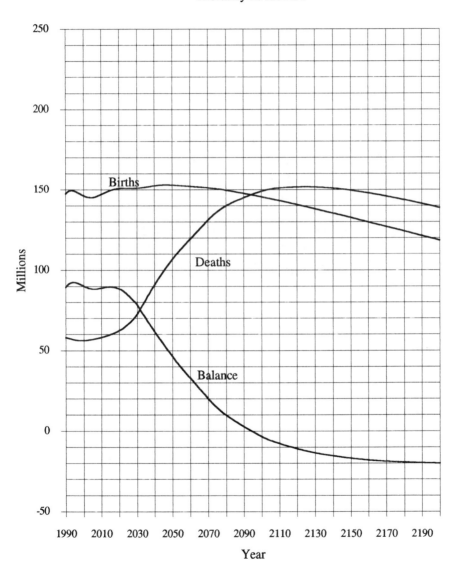

Graph 3

Age Structure of World Population 1990, 2050 and 2100

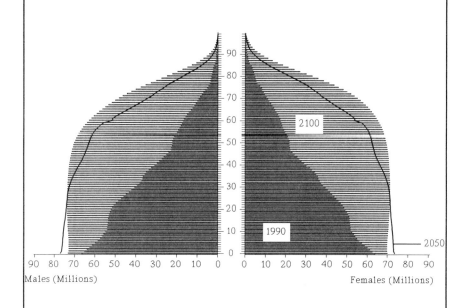

Population Projection No. 2060.B.L.

Decline below replacement fertility level
by the year: 2060
Form of fertility decline: Hyperbolic
Mortality level: Low

Total population: 1990   5 275 Million
                                      2050 10 068 Million
                                      2100 10 954 Million

Table 1
Projected Total Population
World Population Projection No. 2070.R.H
Decline to Replacement Fertility Level (2.13); Mortality Level: High

Age Year	0-4	5-9	10-14	15-19	20-24	25-29	30-34	35-39	40-44	45-49	50-54	55-59	60-64	65-69	70-74	75+	Total
								- Millions -									
1990	625	563	528	519	490	436	380	342	282	230	214	186	160	123	87	108	5275
2000	685	665	609	555	518	508	479	424	367	327	264	209	184	149	113	121	6177
2010	697	676	671	657	599	545	508	496	464	406	345	298	229	168	131	149	7037
2020	736	711	686	670	662	647	589	533	494	477	438	372	300	240	163	169	7885
2030	747	740	728	706	679	662	653	635	575	515	468	438	382	301	214	225	8668
2040	755	745	740	736	722	698	670	651	638	613	544	473	409	355	273	289	9310
2050	761	754	748	740	734	727	712	686	655	628	604	564	477	384	292	351	9817
2060	759	756	755	750	741	732	724	715	695	662	620	577	529	457	341	383	10195
2070	755	752	752	751	748	741	731	720	707	691	659	609	543	468	377	448	10451
2080	755	750	748	747	745	742	738	729	714	695	670	635	577	493	388	478	10604
2090	753	749	748	745	741	739	735	730	721	704	677	638	586	514	412	500	10693
2100	751	747	746	745	742	736	731	726	718	705	683	647	592	518	419	524	10730
2110	750	746	744	742	740	736	732	724	714	701	680	648	598	524	423	532	10734
2120	748	744	743	741	738	734	730	724	715	699	677	644	596	525	427	538	10721
2130	747	742	741	740	736	733	728	722	713	699	677	642	592	522	425	540	10700
2140	745	741	740	738	735	731	727	720	711	697	675	642	593	521	423	538	10676
2150	743	739	738	736	733	729	725	719	710	695	673	640	591	521	423	536	10653
2160	742	738	737	735	732	728	723	717	708	694	672	639	589	519	422	536	10631
2170	740	736	735	733	730	726	722	716	707	692	671	638	589	518	421	535	10608
2180	739	735	734	732	729	725	720	714	705	691	669	636	587	517	420	533	10586
2190	737	733	732	730	727	723	719	713	704	689	668	635	586	516	419	532	10563
2200	736	731	731	729	725	722	717	711	702	688	666	634	585	515	418	531	10541

Table 2
Components of Population Change
World Population Projection No. 2070.R.H
Decline to Replacement Fertility Level (2.13); Mortality Level: High

Year	Males Births	Males Deaths - Thousands -	Males Balance	Females Births	Females Deaths - Thousands -	Females Balance	Births	Total Deaths - Thousands -	Balance
1990	75539	29422	46117	71783	28562	43221	147322	57985	89338
2000	75720	31532	44188	71954	28211	43743	147674	59743	87931
2010	76651	34818	41833	72839	29532	43307	149490	64350	85140
2020	78761	38597	40164	74844	32002	42842	153605	70599	83006
2030	79147	45614	33533	75211	38065	37146	154358	83679	70678
2040	80182	53407	26775	76195	46281	29913	156377	99688	56688
2050	80517	60179	20338	76513	53434	23079	157030	113613	43416
2060	80143	65809	14334	76157	59370	16787	156300	125179	31121
2070	79761	71173	8588	75794	65354	10440	155554	136526	19028
2080	79850	74593	5156	75879	69578	6301	155729	144272	11457
2090	79570	77070	2501	75613	72262	3351	155183	149331	5852
2100	79417	78903	513	75467	74488	979	154884	153391	1493
2110	79270	79713	-443	75328	75542	-214	154598	155256	-658
2120	79082	80069	-987	75149	76037	-888	154231	156106	-1875
2130	78921	80090	-1169	74996	76197	-1201	153917	156287	-2370
2140	78754	79879	-1124	74838	76011	-1173	153592	155889	-2297
2150	78584	79685	-1101	74676	75800	-1124	153260	155486	-2226
2160	78419	79542	-1123	74519	75673	-1154	152938	155215	-2277
2170	78252	79364	-1112	74360	75507	-1146	152612	154870	-2258
2180	78085	79193	-1108	74202	75339	-1137	152287	154532	-2244
2190	77920	79029	-1110	74045	75186	-1141	151964	154215	-2251
2200	77754	78859	-1105	73887	75023	-1136	151641	153882	-2241

Table 3
Demographic Indicators
World Population Projection No. 2070.R.H
Decline to Replacement Fertility Level (2.13); Mortality Level: High

Year	1990	2000	2010	2020	2030	2040	2050	2060	2070	2080	2090
Birth Rate ‰	27.9	23.9	21.2	19.5	17.8	16.8	16.0	15.3	14.9	14.7	14.5
Death Rate ‰	11.0	9.7	9.1	9.0	9.7	10.7	11.6	12.3	13.1	13.6	14.0
Growth Rate %	1.69	1.42	1.21	1.05	0.82	0.61	0.44	0.31	0.18	0.11	0.05
Total Fertility Rate	3.400	3.037	2.702	2.490	2.356	2.267	2.206	2.163	2.130	2.130	2.130
GRR	1.684	1.480	1.324	1.216	1.150	1.107	1.076	1.054	1.040	1.039	1.039
NRR	1.5	1.4	1.3	1.2	1.1	1.1	1.0	1.0	1.0	1.0	1.0
IMR - Males	67.2	53.4	39.5	26.3	24.6	24.6	24.6	24.6	24.6	24.6	24.6
IMR - Females	62.8	47.9	31.8	18.8	17.0	17.0	17.0	17.0	17.0	17.0	17.0
IMR - Both Sexes	65.0	50.6	35.7	22.5	20.8	20.8	20.8	20.8	20.8	20.8	20.8
E(0) - Males	65.36	66.12	67.01	67.99	68.39	68.39	68.39	68.39	68.39	68.39	68.39
E(0) - Females	68.43	69.71	71.16	72.53	73.25	73.25	73.25	73.25	73.25	73.25	73.25
E(0) - Both Sexes	66.90	67.91	69.08	70.26	70.82	70.82	70.82	70.82	70.82	70.82	70.82

Year	2100	2110	2120	2130	2140	2150	2160	2170	2180	2190	2200
Birth Rate ‰	14.4	14.4	14.4	14.4	14.4	14.4	14.4	14.4	14.4	14.4	14.4
Death Rate ‰	14.3	14.5	14.6	14.6	14.6	14.6	14.6	14.6	14.6	14.6	14.6
Growth Rate %	0.01	-0.01	-0.02	-0.02	-0.02	-0.02	-0.02	-0.02	-0.02	-0.02	-0.02
Total Fertility Rate	2.130	2.130	2.130	2.130	2.130	2.130	2.130	2.130	2.130	2.130	2.130
GRR	1.039	1.039	1.039	1.039	1.039	1.039	1.039	1.039	1.039	1.039	1.039
NRR	1.0	1.0	1.0	1.0	1.0	1.0	1.0	1.0	1.0	1.0	1.0
IMR - Males	24.6	24.6	24.6	24.6	24.6	24.6	24.6	24.6	24.6	24.6	24.6
IMR - Females	17.0	17.0	17.0	17.0	17.0	17.0	17.0	17.0	17.0	17.0	17.0
IMR - Both Sexes	20.8	20.8	20.8	20.8	20.8	20.8	20.8	20.8	20.8	20.8	20.8
E(0) - Males	68.39	68.39	68.39	68.39	68.39	68.39	68.39	68.39	68.39	68.39	68.39
E(0) - Females	73.25	73.25	73.25	73.25	73.25	73.25	73.25	73.25	73.25	73.25	73.25
E(0) - Both Sexes	70.82	70.82	70.82	70.82	70.82	70.82	70.82	70.82	70.82	70.82	70.82

Graph 1

Projected Total Population
World Population Projection No. 2070.R.H
Decline to Replacement Fertility Level (2.13)
Mortality Level: High

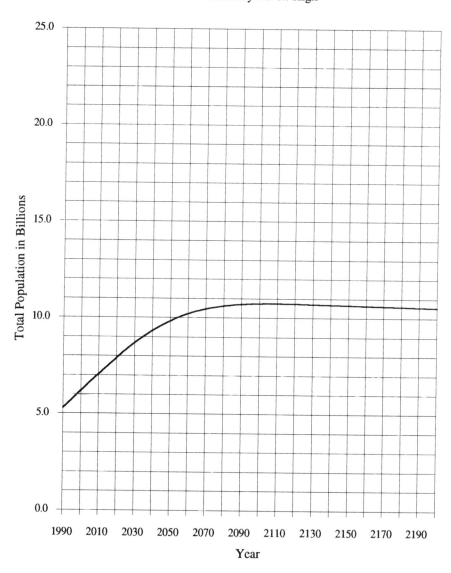

Graph 2

Components of Population Change
World Population Projection No. 2070.R.H
Decline to Replacement Fertility Level (2.13)
Mortality Level: High

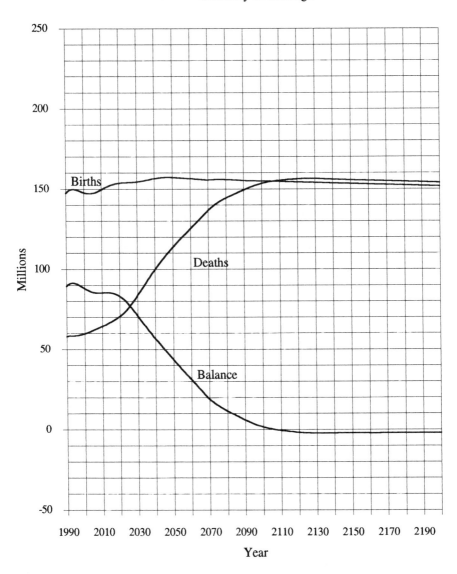

Graph 3

Age Structure of World Population 1990, 2050 and 2100

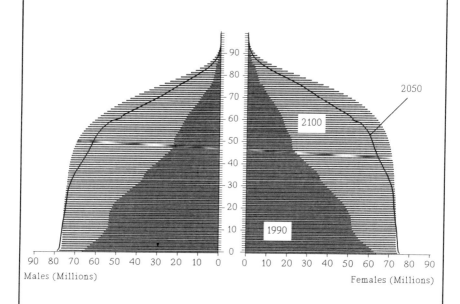

Population Projection No. 2070.R.H.

Target year for replacement fertility
level (TFR = 2.13): 2070
Form of fertility decline: Hyperbolic
Mortality level: High

Total population: 1990 5 275 Million
2050 9 817 Million
2100 10 730 Million

Table 1
Projected Total Population
World Population Projection No. 2070.R.M
Decline to Replacement Fertility Level (2.13); Mortality Level: Medium

- Millions -

Age Year	0-4	5-9	10-14	15-19	20-24	25-29	30-34	35-39	40-44	45-49	50-54	55-59	60-64	65-69	70-74	75+	Total
1990	625	563	528	519	490	436	380	342	282	230	214	186	160	123	87	108	5275
2000	687	665	609	555	519	508	479	424	367	327	264	209	185	149	114	124	6186
2010	700	679	673	658	600	545	508	496	465	408	346	299	231	170	133	157	7070
2020	740	715	690	673	665	649	590	535	496	479	441	375	305	246	169	186	7955
2030	754	746	734	711	684	666	657	639	578	518	472	444	391	312	226	257	8789
2040	763	753	748	743	728	703	676	656	643	619	551	482	421	370	292	339	9488
2050	771	764	757	749	742	735	719	693	662	636	614	576	491	401	314	417	10043
2060	770	767	765	760	751	742	733	724	705	672	632	591	547	479	366	459	10465
2070	768	765	764	763	759	753	743	731	718	703	672	625	563	493	408	536	10763
2080	770	764	762	761	758	755	750	742	728	709	685	653	599	521	420	577	10953
2090	769	766	764	760	756	753	750	744	735	719	694	659	610	544	447	604	11074
2100	769	764	763	762	758	752	747	742	734	722	701	668	618	549	455	635	11141
2110	769	765	763	761	757	754	749	742	732	720	701	671	625	557	461	647	11171
2120	769	765	763	761	757	753	749	743	734	719	698	669	624	559	466	656	11183
2130	769	765	763	761	757	753	748	742	733	720	700	668	622	557	465	660	11185
2140	769	765	763	761	757	753	748	742	733	719	700	669	623	556	464	660	11183
2150	769	765	763	761	757	753	748	742	733	720	699	668	623	558	465	658	11183
2160	769	765	763	761	757	753	748	742	733	720	700	669	623	557	465	659	11183
2170	769	765	763	761	757	753	748	742	733	720	699	669	623	557	464	659	11182
2180	769	765	763	761	757	753	748	742	733	720	699	669	623	557	465	659	11182
2190	769	765	763	761	757	753	748	742	733	720	699	669	623	557	465	659	11182
2200	769	765	763	761	757	753	748	742	733	720	699	669	623	557	464	659	11181

Table 2
Components of Population Change
World Population Projection No. 2070.R.M
Decline to Replacement Fertility Level (2.13); Mortality Level: Medium

Year	Births	Males Deaths - Thousands -	Balance	Births	Females Deaths - Thousands -	Balance	Births	Total Deaths - Thousands -	Balance
1990	75539	29422	46117	71783	28562	43221	147322	57985	89338
2000	75744	30590	45154	71977	27402	44574	147720	57992	89728
2010	76745	33174	43571	72928	28215	44713	149672	61389	88283
2020	79032	36403	42629	75101	30306	44795	154133	66709	87424
2030	79600	42731	36869	75642	35792	39849	155242	78524	76718
2040	80783	51199	29583	76765	44489	32277	157548	95688	61860
2050	81289	58533	22756	77246	52061	25186	158535	110593	47942
2060	81089	64492	16597	77056	58260	18796	158145	122752	35393
2070	80866	70215	10650	76844	64431	12413	157710	134647	23063
2080	81127	74281	6846	77093	69148	7944	158220	143430	14790
2090	81013	76950	4063	76984	72101	4884	157997	149051	8946
2100	81025	79122	1903	76996	74586	2410	158021	153709	4313
2110	81046	80257	788	77015	75963	1053	158061	156220	1841
2120	81023	80840	183	76993	76670	323	158016	157510	506
2130	81027	81085	-58	76998	77043	-45	158025	158128	-104
2140	81026	81059	-33	76996	77048	-52	158022	158107	-85
2150	81020	81021	-1	76991	76987	4	158011	158007	4
2160	81019	81044	-25	76990	77012	-22	158009	158056	-47
2170	81016	81036	-20	76987	77011	-25	158003	158048	-45
2180	81013	81028	-15	76984	76998	-14	157997	158026	-29
2190	81011	81031	-20	76982	77003	-21	157992	158034	-41
2200	81008	81026	-18	76979	76998	-19	157987	158024	-37

Table 3
Demographic Indicators
World Population Projection No. 2070.R.M
Decline to Replacement Fertility Level (2.13); Mortality Level: Medium

Year	1990	2000	2010	2020	2030	2040	2050	2060	2070	2080	2090
Birth Rate ‰	27.9	23.9	21.2	19.4	17.7	16.6	15.8	15.1	14.7	14.4	14.3
Death Rate ‰	11.0	9.4	8.7	8.4	8.9	10.1	11.0	11.7	12.5	13.1	13.5
Growth Rate %	1.69	1.45	1.25	1.10	0.87	0.65	0.48	0.34	0.21	0.14	0.08
Total Fertility Rate	3.400	3.037	2.702	2.490	2.356	2.267	2.206	2.163	2.130	2.130	2.130
GRR	1.684	1.480	1.324	1.217	1.150	1.107	1.076	1.054	1.040	1.039	1.039
NRR	1.5	1.4	1.3	1.2	1.1	1.1	1.1	1.0	1.0	1.0	1.0
IMR - Males	67.2	51.4	36.8	23.7	21.4	21.4	21.4	21.4	21.4	21.4	21.4
IMR - Females	62.8	46.2	29.6	16.9	14.8	14.8	14.8	14.8	14.8	14.8	14.8
IMR - Both Sexes	65.0	48.8	33.2	20.3	18.1	18.1	18.1	18.1	18.1	18.1	18.1
E(0) - Males	65.36	66.65	67.98	69.34	70.09	70.09	70.09	70.09	70.09	70.09	70.09
E(0) - Females	68.43	70.20	72.05	73.74	74.76	74.76	74.76	74.76	74.76	74.76	74.76
E(0) - Both Sexes	66.90	68.43	70.02	71.54	72.43	72.43	72.43	72.43	72.43	72.43	72.43

Year	2100	2110	2120	2130	2140	2150	2160	2170	2180	2190	2200
Birth Rate ‰	14.2	14.1	14.1	14.1	14.1	14.1	14.1	14.1	14.1	14.1	14.1
Death Rate ‰	13.8	14.0	14.1	14.1	14.1	14.1	14.1	14.1	14.1	14.1	14.1
Growth Rate %	0.04	0.02	0.00	0.00	0.00	0.00	0.00	0.00	0.00	0.00	0.00
Total Fertility Rate	2.130	2.130	2.130	2.130	2.130	2.130	2.130	2.130	2.130	2.130	2.130
GRR	1.039	1.039	1.039	1.039	1.039	1.039	1.039	1.039	1.039	1.039	1.039
NRR	1.0	1.0	1.0	1.0	1.0	1.0	1.0	1.0	1.0	1.0	1.0
IMR - Males	21.4	21.4	21.4	21.4	21.4	21.4	21.4	21.4	21.4	21.4	21.4
IMR - Females	14.8	14.8	14.8	14.8	14.8	14.8	14.8	14.8	14.8	14.8	14.8
IMR - Both Sexes	18.1	18.1	18.1	18.1	18.1	18.1	18.1	18.1	18.1	18.1	18.1
E(0) - Males	70.09	70.09	70.09	70.09	70.09	70.09	70.09	70.09	70.09	70.09	70.09
E(0) - Females	74.76	74.76	74.76	74.76	74.76	74.76	74.76	74.76	74.76	74.76	74.76
E(0) - Both Sexes	72.43	72.43	72.43	72.43	72.43	72.43	72.43	72.43	72.43	72.43	72.43

Graph 1

Projected Total Population
World Population Projection No. 2070.R.M
Decline to Replacement Fertility Level (2.13)
Mortality Level: Medium

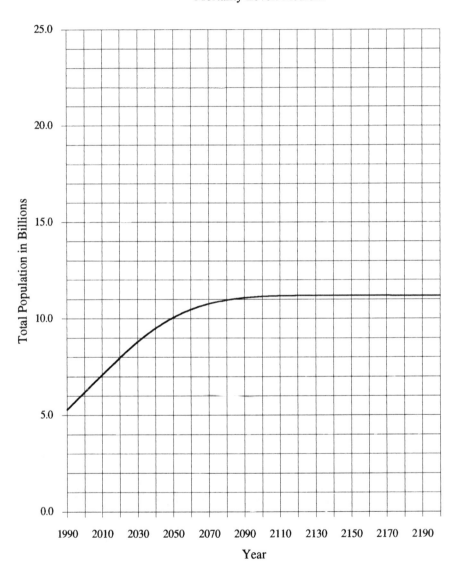

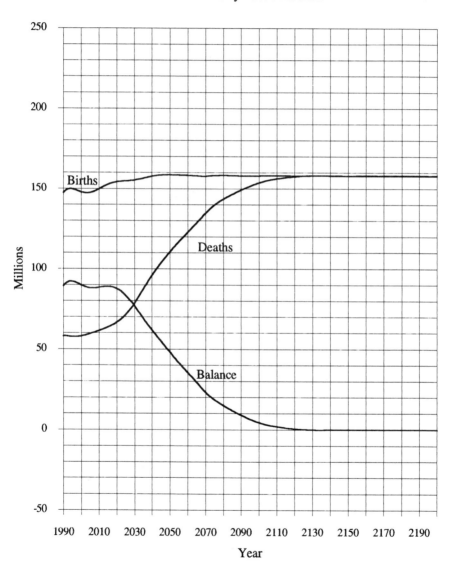

Graph 3

Age Structure of World Population 1990, 2050 and 2100

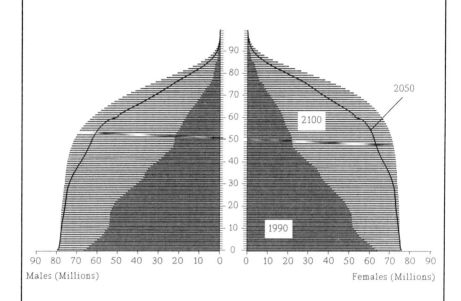

Population Projection No. 2070.R.M.

Target year for replacement fertility
level (TFR = 2.13):   2070
Form of fertility decline: Hyperbolic
Mortality level: Medium

Total population: 1990   5 275 Million
     2050   10 043 Million
     2100   11 141 Million

Table 1
Projected Total Population
World Population Projection No. 2070.R.L
Decline to Replacement Fertility Level (2.13); Mortality Level: Low
- Millions -

Age Year	0-4	5-9	10-14	15-19	20-24	25-29	30-34	35-39	40-44	45-49	50-54	55-59	60-64	65-69	70-74	75+	Total
1990	625	563	528	519	490	436	380	342	282	230	214	186	160	123	87	108	5275
2000	688	666	609	555	519	508	479	425	367	328	265	210	185	150	115	126	6195
2010	703	682	675	659	600	546	509	497	466	409	347	301	233	172	136	166	7103
2020	745	720	694	677	668	651	592	537	498	481	444	379	310	252	176	205	8028
2030	760	753	739	716	689	670	661	642	581	522	477	451	400	323	239	295	8918
2040	772	761	755	749	734	710	682	662	649	626	558	491	432	386	312	401	9680
2050	781	774	767	758	750	743	727	701	670	645	624	588	506	420	337	500	10290
2060	782	778	776	771	761	752	743	734	714	683	644	606	565	503	394	555	10761
2070	781	778	777	775	771	764	754	742	730	715	686	641	583	519	440	648	11105
2080	785	779	776	775	772	768	763	755	741	723	701	671	622	549	455	703	11338
2090	786	782	780	775	771	768	764	759	750	735	712	679	636	575	485	739	11495
2100	787	782	781	778	774	769	763	758	751	739	721	691	645	581	495	778	11595
2110	789	784	782	779	776	772	767	759	750	739	721	694	653	591	503	796	11655
2120	791	786	784	781	777	772	768	762	754	740	720	694	654	594	509	808	11694
2130	792	788	785	783	779	774	769	763	755	743	724	695	653	594	509	816	11721
2140	794	789	787	784	780	776	771	765	756	743	725	698	656	595	509	817	11745
2150	796	791	789	786	782	777	772	766	758	745	726	698	657	597	511	818	11769
2160	797	793	790	787	783	779	774	768	759	747	728	700	658	597	512	820	11793
2170	799	794	792	789	785	781	776	769	761	748	729	701	660	599	513	822	11817
2180	801	796	794	791	787	782	777	771	762	750	731	703	661	600	514	823	11842
2190	802	797	795	792	788	784	779	773	764	751	732	704	662	601	515	825	11866
2200	804	799	797	794	790	785	780	774	765	753	734	706	664	603	516	827	11891

Table 2
Components of Population Change
World Population Projection No. 2070.R.L
Decline to Replacement Fertility Level (2.13); Mortality Level: Low

Year	Males Births	Males Deaths - Thousands -	Males Balance	Females Births	Females Deaths - Thousands -	Females Balance	Total Births	Total Deaths - Thousands -	Total Balance
1990	75539	29422	46117	71783	28562	43221	147322	57985	89338
2000	75767	29636	46131	71999	26582	45417	147767	56218	91548
2010	76838	31460	45378	73017	26837	46179	149855	58297	91557
2020	79304	34028	45276	75360	28461	46899	154663	62489	92175
2030	80056	39457	40600	76075	33205	42870	156131	72661	83470
2040	81387	48611	32776	77340	42386	34954	158727	90997	67729
2050	82067	56576	25491	77986	50437	27549	160053	107014	53039
2060	82045	62938	19107	77965	56960	21005	160010	119897	40113
2070	81985	68987	12998	77908	63293	14615	159893	132280	27613
2080	82424	73657	8766	78325	68522	9802	160748	142180	18569
2090	82481	76679	5801	78379	71822	6557	160860	148502	12358
2100	82665	79189	3477	78554	74553	4001	161219	153742	7478
2110	82860	80695	2165	78739	76286	2453	161598	156981	4617
2120	83009	81529	1480	78881	77233	1649	161891	158761	3129
2130	83187	82012	1176	79050	77827	1224	162238	159838	2399
2140	83360	82187	1173	79215	78041	1174	162575	160228	2347
2150	83529	82309	1219	79375	78136	1239	162903	160445	2458
2160	83703	82501	1201	79540	78314	1225	163242	160815	2427
2170	83875	82673	1202	79703	78486	1217	163578	161159	2419
2180	84047	82834	1213	79867	78634	1233	163914	161468	2446
2190	84220	83011	1210	80032	78803	1229	164253	161813	2439
2200	84394	83180	1214	80197	78965	1232	164591	162145	2446

Table 3
Demographic Indicators
World Population Projection No. 2070.R.L
Decline to Replacement Fertility Level (2.13); Mortality Level: Low

Year	1990	2000	2010	2020	2030	2040	2050	2060	2070	2080	2090
Birth Rate ‰	27.9	23.9	21.1	19.3	17.5	16.4	15.6	14.9	14.4	14.2	14.0
Death Rate ‰	11.0	9.1	8.2	7.8	8.1	9.4	10.4	11.1	11.9	12.5	12.9
Growth Rate %	1.69	1.48	1.29	1.15	0.94	0.70	0.52	0.37	0.25	0.16	0.11
Total Fertility Rate	3.400	3.037	2.702	2.490	2.356	2.267	2.206	2.163	2.130	2.130	2.130
GRR	1.684	1.480	1.324	1.217	1.150	1.107	1.076	1.054	1.040	1.039	1.039
NRR	1.5	1.4	1.3	1.2	1.1	1.1	1.1	1.0	1.0	1.0	1.0
IMR - Males	67.2	49.5	34.0	21.0	18.2	18.2	18.2	18.2	18.2	18.2	18.2
IMR - Females	62.8	44.4	27.4	15.0	12.6	12.6	12.6	12.6	12.6	12.6	12.6
IMR - Both Sexes	65.0	47.0	30.7	18.0	15.4	15.4	15.4	15.4	15.4	15.4	15.4
E(0) - Males	65.36	67.19	69.03	70.84	72.06	72.06	72.06	72.06	72.06	72.06	72.06
E(0) - Females	68.43	70.71	73.00	75.08	76.51	76.51	76.51	76.51	76.51	76.51	76.51
E(0) - Both Sexes	66.90	68.95	71.02	72.96	74.28	74.28	74.28	74.28	74.28	74.28	74.28

Year	2100	2110	2120	2130	2140	2150	2160	2170	2180	2190	2200
Birth Rate ‰	13.9	13.9	13.8	13.8	13.8	13.8	13.8	13.8	13.8	13.8	13.8
Death Rate ‰	13.3	13.5	13.6	13.6	13.6	13.6	13.6	13.6	13.6	13.6	13.6
Growth Rate %	0.06	0.04	0.03	0.02	0.02	0.02	0.02	0.02	0.02	0.02	0.02
Total Fertility Rate	2.130	2.130	2.130	2.130	2.130	2.130	2.130	2.130	2.130	2.130	2.130
GRR	1.039	1.039	1.039	1.039	1.039	1.039	1.039	1.039	1.039	1.039	1.039
NRR	1.0	1.0	1.0	1.0	1.0	1.0	1.0	1.0	1.0	1.0	1.0
IMR - Males	18.2	18.2	18.2	18.2	18.2	18.2	18.2	18.2	18.2	18.2	18.2
IMR - Females	12.6	12.6	12.6	12.6	12.6	12.6	12.6	12.6	12.6	12.6	12.6
IMR - Both Sexes	15.4	15.4	15.4	15.4	15.4	15.4	15.4	15.4	15.4	15.4	15.4
E(0) - Males	72.06	72.06	72.06	72.06	72.06	72.06	72.06	72.06	72.06	72.06	72.06
E(0) - Females	76.51	76.51	76.51	76.51	76.51	76.51	76.51	76.51	76.51	76.51	76.51
E(0) - Both Sexes	74.28	74.28	74.28	74.28	74.28	74.28	74.28	74.28	74.28	74.28	74.28

Graph 1

Projected Total Population
World Population Projection No. 2070.R.L
Decline to Replacement Fertility Level (2.13)
Mortality Level: Low

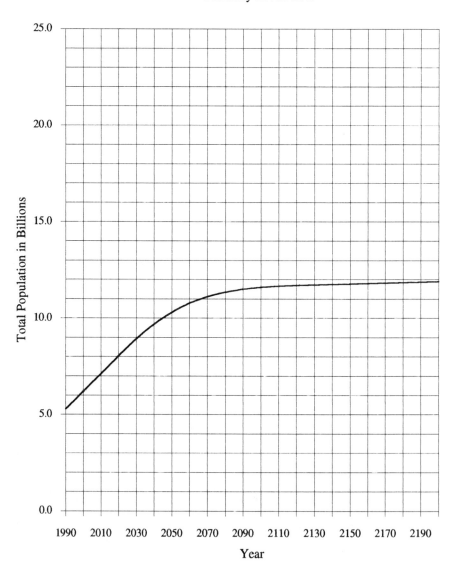

Graph 2

Components of Population Change
World Population Projection No. 2070.R.L
Decline to Replacement Fertility Level (2.13)
Mortality Level: Low

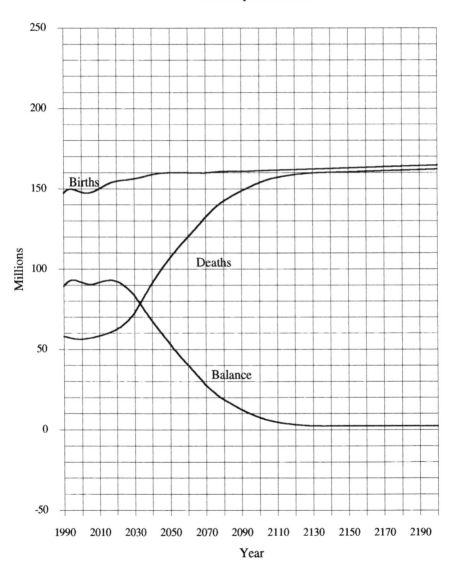

Graph 3

Age Structure of World Population 1990, 2050 and 2100

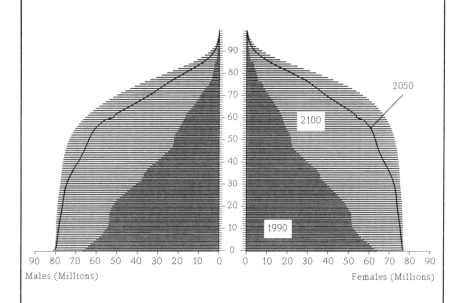

Males (Millions) Females (Millions)

Population Projection No. 2070.R.L.

Target year for replacement fertility
level (TFR = 2.13):   2070
Form of fertility decline: Hyperbolic
Mortality level: Low

Total population: 1990   5 275 Million
                                    2050 10 290 Million
                                    2100 11 595 Million

Table 1
Projected Total Population
World Population Projection No. 2070.B.H
Decline Below Replacement Fertility Level; Mortality Level: High

- Millions -

Age Year	0-4	5-9	10-14	15-19	20-24	25-29	30-34	35-39	40-44	45-49	50-54	55-59	60-64	65-69	70-74	75+	Total
1990	625	563	528	519	490	436	380	342	282	230	214	186	160	123	87	108	5275
2000	685	665	609	555	518	508	479	424	367	327	264	209	184	149	113	121	6177
2010	697	676	671	657	599	545	508	496	464	406	345	298	229	168	131	149	7037
2020	736	711	686	670	662	647	589	533	494	477	438	372	300	240	163	169	7885
2030	747	740	728	706	679	662	653	635	575	515	468	438	382	301	214	225	8668
2040	755	745	740	736	722	698	670	651	638	613	544	473	409	355	273	289	9310
2050	761	754	748	740	734	727	712	686	655	628	604	564	477	384	292	351	9817
2060	759	756	755	750	741	732	724	715	695	662	620	577	529	457	341	383	10195
2070	755	752	752	751	748	741	731	720	707	691	659	609	543	468	377	448	10451
2080	748	747	748	747	745	742	738	729	714	695	670	635	577	493	388	478	10594
2090	738	738	741	742	741	739	735	730	721	704	677	638	586	514	412	500	10657
2100	728	728	732	734	734	734	731	726	718	705	683	647	592	518	419	524	10653
2110	716	717	721	724	725	725	725	721	714	701	680	648	598	524	423	532	10594
2120	703	704	709	713	715	716	715	713	708	696	677	644	596	525	427	538	10498
2130	689	691	696	700	703	705	705	704	699	689	670	640	592	522	425	540	10371
2140	674	677	683	687	690	692	693	693	689	679	662	633	587	519	423	538	10220
2150	660	663	668	673	676	679	681	681	677	669	652	624	579	513	419	535	10050
2160	645	648	654	659	662	665	667	668	665	657	642	615	571	506	414	530	9867
2170	630	633	639	644	648	651	653	654	652	645	630	604	562	498	408	523	9673
2180	614	618	624	629	633	637	639	640	638	632	617	592	551	489	401	515	9471
2190	599	603	609	614	618	622	625	626	624	618	605	580	541	480	394	506	9263
2200	584	587	594	599	603	607	610	612	610	604	591	568	529	470	386	497	9052

Table 2
Components of Population Change
World Population Projection No. 2070.B.H
Decline Below Replacement Fertility Level; Mortality Level: High

Year	Males Births	Males Deaths - Thousands -	Males Balance	Females Births	Females Deaths - Thousands -	Females Balance	Total Births	Total Deaths - Thousands -	Total Balance
1990	75539	29422	46117	71783	28562	43221	147322	57985	89338
2000	75720	31532	44188	71954	28211	43743	147674	59743	87931
2010	76651	34818	41833	72839	29532	43307	149490	64350	85140
2020	78761	38597	40164	74844	32002	42842	153605	70599	83006
2030	79147	45614	33533	75211	38065	37146	154358	83679	70678
2040	80182	53407	26775	76195	46281	29913	156377	99688	56688
2050	80517	60179	20338	76513	53434	23079	157030	113613	43416
2060	80143	65809	14334	76157	59370	16787	156300	125179	31121
2070	79656	71170	8486	75694	65352	10342	155350	136522	18828
2080	78830	74652	4178	74910	69551	5359	153740	144203	9537
2090	77784	76989	795	73916	72210	1706	151700	149199	2501
2100	76610	78762	-2152	72800	74398	-1598	149411	153161	-3750
2110	75296	79489	-4193	71551	75401	-3850	146847	154890	-8043
2120	73888	79724	-5836	70213	75821	-5608	144101	155545	-11444
2130	72412	79544	-7132	68811	75859	-7048	141223	155403	-14180
2140	70880	78972	-8092	67355	75448	-8093	138235	154419	-16184
2150	69311	78162	-8851	65864	74784	-8920	135176	152946	-17770
2160	67718	77143	-9425	64350	73904	-9554	132068	151047	-18979
2170	66109	75958	-9849	62821	72842	-10020	128930	148800	-19869
2180	64494	74655	-10161	61287	71654	-10367	125781	146309	-20527
2190	62881	73256	-10375	59754	70363	-10609	122634	143619	-20984
2200	61274	71786	-10512	58227	68993	-10767	119500	140780	-21279

Table 3
Demographic Indicators
World Population Projection No. 2070.B.H
Decline Below Replacement Fertility Level; Mortality Level: High

Year	1990	2000	2010	2020	2030	2040	2050	2060	2070	2080	2090
Birth Rate ‰	27.9	23.9	21.2	19.5	17.8	16.8	16.0	15.3	14.9	14.5	14.2
Death Rate ‰	11.0	9.7	9.1	9.0	9.7	10.7	11.6	12.3	13.1	13.6	14.0
Growth Rate %	1.69	1.42	1.21	1.05	0.82	0.61	0.44	0.31	0.18	0.09	0.02
Total Fertility Rate	3.400	3.037	2.702	2.490	2.356	2.267	2.206	2.163	2.130	2.105	2.085
GRR	1.684	1.480	1.324	1.216	1.150	1.107	1.076	1.054	1.038	1.026	1.016
NRR	1.5	1.4	1.3	1.2	1.1	1.1	1.0	1.0	1.0	1.0	1.0
IMR - Males	67.2	53.4	39.5	26.3	24.6	24.6	24.6	24.6	24.6	24.6	24.6
IMR - Females	62.8	47.9	31.8	18.8	17.0	17.0	17.0	17.0	17.0	17.0	17.0
IMR - Both Sexes	65.0	50.6	35.7	22.5	20.8	20.8	20.8	20.8	20.8	20.8	20.8
E(0) - Males	65.36	66.12	67.01	67.99	68.39	68.39	68.39	68.39	68.39	68.39	68.39
E(0) - Females	68.43	69.71	71.16	72.53	73.25	73.25	73.25	73.25	73.25	73.25	73.25
E(0) - Both Sexes	66.90	67.91	69.08	70.26	70.82	70.82	70.82	70.82	70.82	70.82	70.82

Year	2100	2110	2120	2130	2140	2150	2160	2170	2180	2190	2200
Birth Rate ‰	14.0	13.9	13.7	13.6	13.5	13.4	13.4	13.3	13.3	13.2	13.2
Death Rate ‰	14.4	14.6	14.8	15.0	15.1	15.2	15.3	15.4	15.4	15.5	15.6
Growth Rate %	-0.04	-0.08	-0.11	-0.14	-0.16	-0.18	-0.19	-0.21	-0.22	-0.23	-0.24
Total Fertility Rate	2.070	2.057	2.046	2.037	2.030	2.023	2.018	2.013	2.009	2.005	2.002
GRR	1.008	1.001	0.996	0.992	0.988	0.985	0.982	0.979	0.977	0.975	0.976
NRR	1.0	1.0	1.0	1.0	1.0	1.0	1.0	1.0	1.0	0.9	1.0
IMR - Males	24.6	24.6	24.6	24.6	24.6	24.6	24.6	24.6	24.6	24.6	24.6
IMR - Females	17.0	17.0	17.0	17.0	17.0	17.0	17.0	17.0	17.0	17.0	17.0
IMR - Both Sexes	20.8	20.8	20.8	20.8	20.8	20.8	20.8	20.8	20.8	20.8	20.8
E(0) - Males	68.39	68.39	68.39	68.39	68.39	68.39	68.39	68.39	68.39	68.39	68.39
E(0) - Females	73.25	73.25	73.25	73.25	73.25	73.25	73.25	73.25	73.25	73.25	73.25
E(0) - Both Sexes	70.82	70.82	70.82	70.82	70.82	70.82	70.82	70.82	70.82	70.82	70.82

Graph 1

Projected Total Population
World Population Projection No. 2070.B.H
Decline Below Replacement Fertility Level
Mortality Level: High

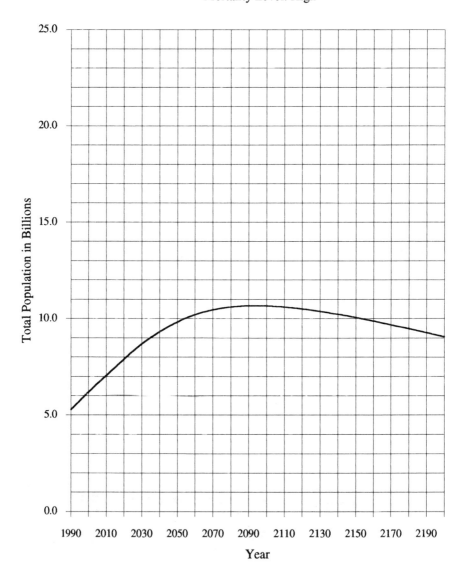

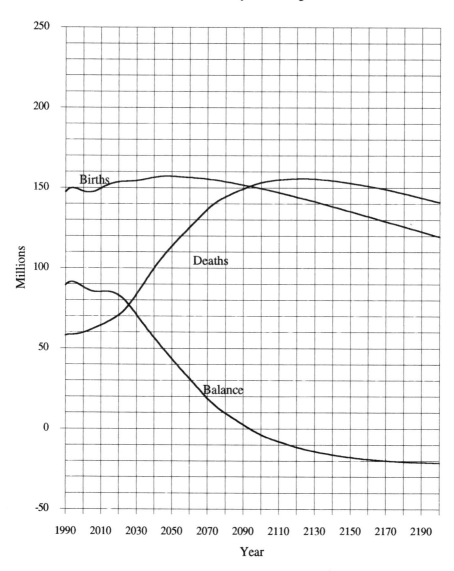

Graph 3

Age Structure of World Population 1990, 2050 and 2100

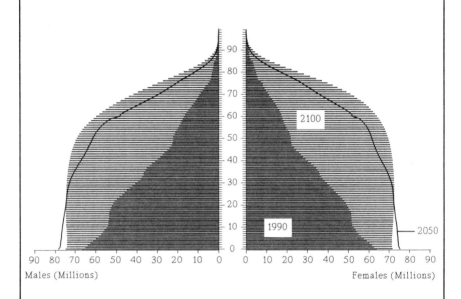

Population Projection No. 2070.B.H.

Decline below replacement fertility level
by the year: 2070
Form of fertility decline: Hyperbolic
Mortality level: High

Total population: 1990   5 275 Million
                                                2050   9 817 Million
                                                2100 10 653 Million

Table 1
Projected Total Population
World Population Projection No. 2070.B.M
Decline Below Replacement Fertility Level; Mortality Level: Medium

- Millions -

Age Year	0-4	5-9	10-14	15-19	20-24	25-29	30-34	35-39	40-44	45-49	50-54	55-59	60-64	65-69	70-74	75+	Total
1990	625	563	528	519	490	436	380	342	282	230	214	186	160	123	87	108	5275
2000	687	665	609	555	519	508	479	424	367	327	264	209	185	149	114	124	6186
2010	700	679	673	658	600	545	508	496	465	408	346	299	231	170	133	157	7070
2020	740	715	690	673	665	649	590	535	496	479	441	375	305	246	169	186	7955
2030	754	746	734	711	684	666	657	639	578	518	472	444	391	312	226	257	8789
2040	763	753	748	743	728	703	676	656	643	619	551	482	421	370	292	339	9488
2050	771	764	757	749	742	735	719	693	662	636	614	576	491	401	314	417	10043
2060	770	767	765	760	751	742	733	724	705	672	632	591	547	479	366	459	10465
2070	768	765	764	763	759	753	743	731	718	703	672	625	563	493	408	536	10763
2080	762	761	762	761	758	755	750	742	728	709	685	653	599	521	420	577	10943
2090	754	754	757	757	756	753	750	744	735	719	694	659	610	544	447	604	11037
2100	745	746	749	750	751	750	747	742	734	722	701	668	618	549	455	635	11062
2110	734	736	739	742	743	743	742	739	732	720	701	671	625	557	461	647	11028
2120	722	724	729	732	733	734	734	732	727	716	698	669	624	559	466	656	10954
2130	710	712	717	720	723	724	725	724	719	710	693	666	622	557	465	660	10846
2140	696	699	704	708	711	713	714	714	710	702	686	660	617	554	464	660	10712
2150	683	685	691	695	699	701	703	703	700	692	677	652	611	549	460	657	10559
2160	668	672	677	682	685	688	690	691	689	682	668	643	603	543	456	652	10389
2170	654	657	663	668	672	675	677	678	676	670	657	633	595	536	450	645	10207
2180	640	643	649	654	658	661	664	665	664	658	645	622	585	527	443	637	10016
2190	625	629	635	640	644	647	650	652	651	645	633	611	575	518	436	627	9818
2200	610	614	620	625	630	633	636	638	637	632	621	599	564	509	428	617	9614

Table 2
Components of Population Change
World Population Projection No. 2070.B.M
Decline Below Replacement Fertility Level; Mortality Level: Medium

Year	Births	Males Deaths - Thousands -	Balance	Births	Females Deaths - Thousands -	Balance	Births	Total Deaths - Thousands -	Balance
1990	75539	29422	46117	71783	28562	43221	147322	57985	89338
2000	75744	30590	45154	71977	27402	44574	147720	57992	89728
2010	76745	33174	43571	72928	28215	44713	149672	61389	88283
2020	79032	36403	42629	75101	30306	44795	154133	66709	87424
2030	79600	42731	36869	75642	35792	39849	155242	78524	76718
2040	80783	51199	29583	76765	44489	32277	157548	95688	61860
2050	81289	58533	22756	77246	52061	25186	158535	110593	47942
2060	81089	64492	16597	77056	58260	18796	158145	122752	35393
2070	80759	70213	10546	76743	64430	12313	157503	134643	22860
2080	80091	74245	5847	76108	69124	6984	156200	143369	12831
2090	79194	76879	2316	75256	72054	3202	154450	148933	5517
2100	78162	78997	-835	74275	74507	-232	152437	153504	-1067
2110	76982	80057	-3075	73154	75836	-2683	150135	155894	-5758
2120	75701	80532	-4831	71936	76478	-4541	147637	157010	-9373
2130	74344	80596	-6252	70647	76741	-6094	144991	157337	-12346
2140	72924	80240	-7316	69297	76543	-7246	142221	156782	-14562
2150	71459	79623	-8164	67905	76062	-8157	139364	155685	-16321
2160	69962	78785	-8823	66483	75358	-8875	136445	154143	-17698
2170	68443	77766	-9323	65039	74456	-9417	133482	152222	-18740
2180	66911	76615	-9704	63584	73416	-9832	130495	150031	-19536
2190	65374	75357	-9983	62123	72262	-10139	127496	147618	-20122
2200	63836	74016	-10179	60662	71019	-10357	124498	145034	-20536

Table 3
Demographic Indicators
World Population Projection No. 2070.B.M
Decline Below Replacement Fertility Level; Mortality Level: Medium

Year	1990	2000	2010	2020	2030	2040	2050	2060	2070	2080	2090
Birth Rate ‰	27.9	23.9	21.2	19.4	17.7	16.6	15.8	15.1	14.6	14.3	14.0
Death Rate ‰	11.0	9.4	8.7	8.4	8.9	10.1	11.0	11.7	12.5	13.1	13.5
Growth Rate %	1.69	1.45	1.25	1.10	0.87	0.65	0.48	0.34	0.21	0.12	0.05
Total Fertility Rate	3.400	3.037	2.702	2.490	2.356	2.267	2.206	2.163	2.130	2.105	2.085
GRR	1.684	1.480	1.324	1.217	1.150	1.107	1.076	1.054	1.038	1.026	1.016
NRR	1.5	1.4	1.3	1.2	1.1	1.1	1.1	1.0	1.0	1.0	1.0
IMR - Males	67.2	51.4	36.8	23.7	21.4	21.4	21.4	21.4	21.4	21.4	21.4
IMR - Females	62.8	46.2	29.6	16.9	14.8	14.8	14.8	14.8	14.8	14.8	14.8
IMR - Both Sexes	65.0	48.8	33.2	20.3	18.1	18.1	18.1	18.1	18.1	18.1	18.1
E(0) - Males	65.36	66.65	67.98	69.34	70.09	70.09	70.09	70.09	70.09	70.09	70.09
E(0) - Females	68.43	70.20	72.05	73.74	74.76	74.76	74.76	74.76	74.76	74.76	74.76
E(0) - Both Sexes	66.90	68.43	70.02	71.54	72.43	72.43	72.43	72.43	72.43	72.43	72.43

Year	2100	2110	2120	2130	2140	2150	2160	2170	2180	2190	2200
Birth Rate ‰	13.8	13.6	13.5	13.4	13.3	13.2	13.1	13.1	13.0	13.0	12.9
Death Rate ‰	13.9	14.1	14.3	14.5	14.6	14.7	14.8	14.9	15.0	15.0	15.1
Growth Rate %	-0.01	-0.05	-0.09	-0.11	-0.14	-0.15	-0.17	-0.18	-0.20	-0.20	-0.21
Total Fertility Rate	2.070	2.057	2.046	2.037	2.030	2.023	2.018	2.013	2.009	2.005	2.002
GRR	1.008	1.002	0.996	0.992	0.988	0.985	0.982	0.980	0.977	0.976	0.976
NRR	1.0	1.0	1.0	1.0	1.0	1.0	1.0	1.0	1.0	1.0	1.0
IMR - Males	21.4	21.4	21.4	21.4	21.4	21.4	21.4	21.4	21.4	21.4	21.4
IMR - Females	14.8	14.8	14.8	14.8	14.8	14.8	14.8	14.8	14.8	14.8	14.8
IMR - Both Sexes	18.1	18.1	18.1	18.1	18.1	18.1	18.1	18.1	18.1	18.1	18.1
E(0) - Males	70.09	70.09	70.09	70.09	70.09	70.09	70.09	70.09	70.09	70.09	70.09
E(0) - Females	74.76	74.76	74.76	74.76	74.76	74.76	74.76	74.76	74.76	74.76	74.76
E(0) - Both Sexes	72.43	72.43	72.43	72.43	72.43	72.43	72.43	72.43	72.43	72.43	72.43

Graph 1

Projected Total Population
World Population Projection No. 2070.B.M
Decline Below Replacement Fertility Level
Mortality Level: Medium

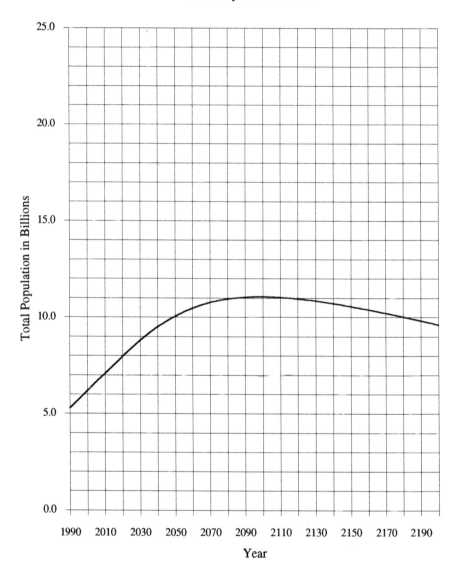

Graph 2

Components of Population Change
World Population Projection No. 2070.B.M
Decline Below Replacement Fertility Level
Mortality Level: Medium

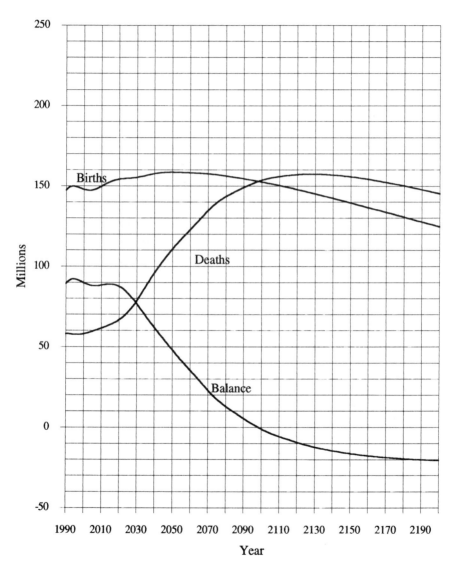

Graph 3

Age Structure of World Population 1990, 2050 and 2100

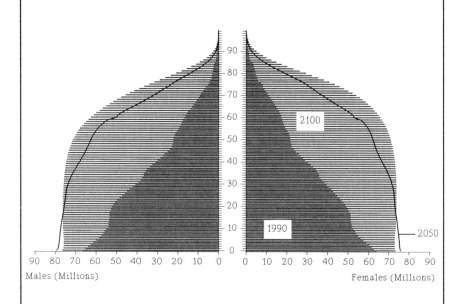

Population Projection No. 2070.B.M.

Decline below replacement fertility level
by the year: 2070
Form of fertility decline: Hyperbolic
Mortality level: Medium

Total population: 1990   5 275 Million
                                               2050 10 043 Million
                                               2100 11 062 Million

Table 1
Projected Total Population
World Population Projection No. 2070.B.L
Decline Below Replacement Fertility Level; Mortality Level: Low

- Millions -

Age Year	0-4	5-9	10-14	15-19	20-24	25-29	30-34	35-39	40-44	45-49	50-54	55-59	60-64	65-69	70-74	75+	Total
1990	625	563	528	519	490	436	380	342	282	230	214	186	160	123	87	108	5275
2000	688	666	609	555	519	508	479	425	367	328	265	210	185	150	115	126	6195
2010	703	682	675	659	600	546	509	497	466	409	347	301	233	172	136	166	7103
2020	745	720	694	677	668	651	592	537	498	481	444	379	310	252	176	205	8028
2030	760	753	739	716	689	670	661	642	581	522	477	451	400	323	239	295	8918
2040	772	761	755	749	734	710	682	662	649	626	558	491	432	386	312	401	9680
2050	781	774	767	758	750	743	727	701	670	645	624	588	506	420	337	500	10290
2060	782	778	776	771	761	752	743	734	714	683	644	606	565	503	394	555	10761
2070	781	778	777	775	771	764	754	742	730	715	686	641	583	519	440	648	11105
2080	777	776	776	775	772	768	763	755	741	723	701	671	622	549	455	703	11327
2090	771	770	772	772	771	768	764	759	750	735	712	679	636	575	485	739	11457
2100	763	763	766	767	767	766	763	758	751	739	721	691	645	581	495	778	11514
2110	753	754	758	760	761	760	759	756	750	739	721	694	653	591	503	796	11509
2120	743	744	748	751	753	753	753	751	746	737	720	694	654	594	509	808	11459
2130	731	733	738	741	743	745	745	744	740	732	717	692	653	594	509	816	11373
2140	719	721	726	730	733	735	736	735	732	725	711	687	650	592	509	817	11258
2150	706	709	714	718	721	724	725	726	723	716	703	681	644	588	506	816	11122
2160	693	696	701	706	709	712	714	715	713	707	695	673	637	583	502	812	10968
2170	679	683	688	693	697	700	702	703	702	696	685	664	629	576	497	805	10799
2180	666	669	675	680	684	687	690	691	690	685	674	654	621	568	490	796	10621
2190	652	656	661	666	670	674	677	679	678	673	663	644	611	560	483	786	10433
2200	638	642	648	653	657	661	664	666	665	661	651	633	601	551	476	775	10239

Table 2
Components of Population Change
World Population Projection No. 2070.B.L
Decline Below Replacement Fertility Level; Mortality Level: Low

Year	Males Births	Males Deaths - Thousands -	Males Balance	Females Births	Females Deaths - Thousands -	Females Balance	Total Births	Total Deaths - Thousands -	Total Balance
1990	75539	29422	46117	71783	28562	43221	147322	57985	89338
2000	75767	29636	46131	71999	26582	45417	147767	56218	91548
2010	76838	31460	45378	73017	26837	46179	149855	58297	91557
2020	79304	34028	45276	75360	28461	46899	154663	62489	92175
2030	80056	39457	40600	76075	33205	42870	156131	72661	83470
2040	81387	48611	32776	77340	42386	34954	158727	90997	67729
2050	82067	56576	25491	77986	50437	27549	160053	107014	53039
2060	82045	62938	19107	77965	56960	21005	160010	119897	40113
2070	81877	68985	12892	77806	63291	14514	159683	132277	27406
2080	81371	73626	7746	77325	68502	8823	158696	142127	16569
2090	80629	76617	4012	76619	71782	4837	157249	148400	8849
2100	79744	79080	664	75778	74484	1294	155522	153564	1958
2110	78704	80521	-1816	74790	76176	-1386	153495	156697	-3203
2120	77557	81260	-3704	73700	77065	-3365	151256	158325	-7069
2130	76326	81583	-5258	72530	77563	-5033	148855	159146	-10290
2140	75024	81464	-6440	71293	77597	-6304	146317	159061	-12744
2150	73671	81054	-7383	70007	77313	-7306	143678	158367	-14690
2160	72279	80414	-8135	68684	76797	-8113	140963	157211	-16248
2170	70857	79574	-8717	67333	76070	-8737	138190	155644	-17454
2180	69416	78588	-9172	65964	75188	-9224	135380	153776	-18396
2190	67963	77483	-9521	64583	74183	-9600	132546	151666	-19121
2200	66503	76284	-9780	63196	73077	-9881	129699	149361	-19662

Table 3
Demographic Indicators
World Population Projection No. 2070.B.L
Decline Below Replacement Fertility Level; Mortality Level: Low

Year	1990	2000	2010	2020	2030	2040	2050	2060	2070	2080	2090
Birth Rate ‰	27.9	23.9	21.1	19.3	17.5	16.4	15.6	14.9	14.4	14.0	13.7
Death Rate ‰	11.0	9.1	8.2	7.8	8.1	9.4	10.4	11.1	11.9	12.5	13.0
Growth Rate %	1.69	1.48	1.29	1.15	0.94	0.70	0.52	0.37	0.25	0.15	0.08
Total Fertility Rate	3.400	3.037	2.702	2.490	2.356	2.267	2.206	2.163	2.130	2.105	2.085
GRR	1.684	1.480	1.324	1.217	1.150	1.107	1.076	1.054	1.038	1.026	1.016
NRR	1.5	1.4	1.3	1.2	1.1	1.1	1.1	1.0	1.0	1.0	1.0
IMR - Males	67.2	49.5	34.0	21.0	18.2	18.2	18.2	18.2	18.2	18.2	18.2
IMR - Females	62.8	44.4	27.4	15.0	12.6	12.6	12.6	12.6	12.6	12.6	12.6
IMR - Both Sexes	65.0	47.0	30.7	18.0	15.4	15.4	15.4	15.4	15.4	15.4	15.4
E(0) - Males	65.36	67.19	69.03	70.84	72.06	72.06	72.06	72.06	72.06	72.06	72.06
E(0) - Females	68.43	70.71	73.00	75.08	76.51	76.51	76.51	76.51	76.51	76.51	76.51
E(0) - Both Sexes	66.90	68.95	71.02	72.96	74.28	74.28	74.28	74.28	74.28	74.28	74.28

Year	2100	2110	2120	2130	2140	2150	2160	2170	2180	2190	2200
Birth Rate ‰	13.5	13.3	13.2	13.1	13.0	12.9	12.9	12.8	12.7	12.7	12.7
Death Rate ‰	13.3	13.6	13.8	14.0	14.1	14.2	14.3	14.4	14.5	14.5	14.6
Growth Rate %	0.02	-0.03	-0.06	-0.09	-0.11	-0.13	-0.15	-0.16	-0.17	-0.18	-0.19
Total Fertility Rate	2.070	2.057	2.046	2.037	2.030	2.023	2.018	2.013	2.009	2.005	2.002
GRR	1.008	1.002	0.996	0.992	0.988	0.985	0.982	0.980	0.977	0.976	0.976
NRR	1.0	1.0	1.0	1.0	1.0	1.0	1.0	1.0	1.0	1.0	1.0
IMR - Males	18.2	18.2	18.2	18.2	18.2	18.2	18.2	18.2	18.2	18.2	18.2
IMR - Females	12.6	12.6	12.6	12.6	12.6	12.6	12.6	12.6	12.6	12.6	12.6
IMR - Both Sexes	15.4	15.4	15.4	15.4	15.4	15.4	15.4	15.4	15.4	15.4	15.4
E(0) - Males	72.06	72.06	72.06	72.06	72.06	72.06	72.06	72.06	72.06	72.06	72.06
E(0) - Females	76.51	76.51	76.51	76.51	76.51	76.51	76.51	76.51	76.51	76.51	76.51
E(0) - Both Sexes	74.28	74.28	74.28	74.28	74.28	74.28	74.28	74.28	74.28	74.28	74.28

Graph 1

Projected Total Population
World Population Projection No. 2070.B.L
Decline Below Replacement Fertility Level
Mortality Level: Low

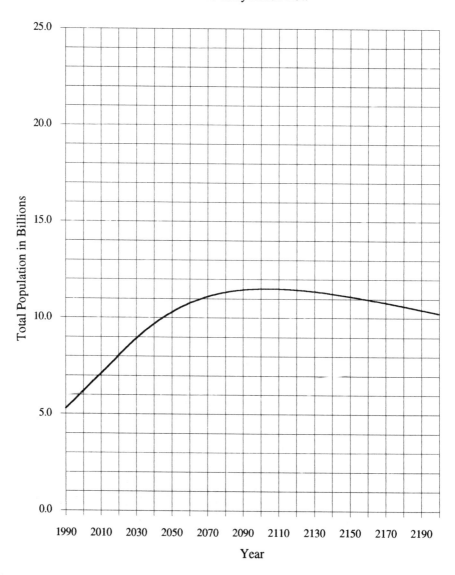

Graph 2

Components of Population Change
World Population Projection No. 2070.B.L
Decline Below Replacement Fertility Level
Mortality Level: Low

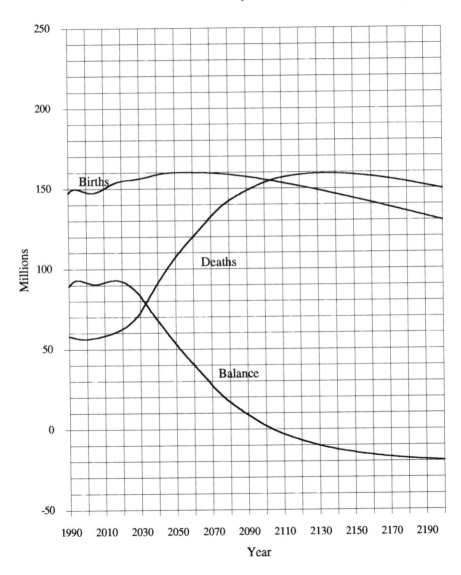

Graph 3

Age Structure of World Population 1990, 2050 and 2100

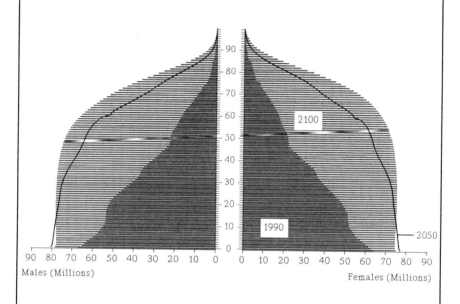

Population Projection No. 2070.B.L.

Decline below replacement fertility level
by the year: 2070
Form of fertility decline: Hyperbolic
Mortality level: Low

Total population:
1990 5 275 Million
2050 10 290 Million
2100 11 514 Million

Table 1
Projected Total Population
World Population Projection No. 2080.R.H
Decline to Replacement Fertility Level (2.13); Mortality Level: High
- Millions -

Age Year	0-4	5-9	10-14	15-19	20-24	25-29	30-34	35-39	40-44	45-49	50-54	55-59	60-64	65-69	70-74	75+	Total
1990	625	563	528	519	490	436	380	342	282	230	214	186	160	123	87	108	5275
2000	689	665	609	555	518	508	479	424	367	327	264	209	184	149	113	121	6182
2010	707	683	675	657	599	545	508	496	464	406	345	298	229	168	131	149	7059
2020	751	723	696	677	666	647	589	533	494	477	438	372	300	240	163	169	7934
2030	768	758	743	718	689	669	656	636	575	515	468	438	382	301	214	225	8754
2040	780	768	761	754	736	710	680	657	641	614	544	473	409	355	273	289	9444
2050	791	782	773	763	754	745	726	698	664	635	607	564	477	384	292	351	10006
2060	793	787	784	777	766	754	744	732	709	674	629	583	532	457	341	383	10446
2070	792	787	785	782	777	768	756	742	726	707	672	619	551	473	380	448	10766
2080	788	785	785	782	778	773	767	756	739	716	688	650	588	502	393	482	10972
2090	787	782	781	780	778	773	768	761	749	729	700	658	602	527	420	507	11102
2100	786	782	780	777	774	771	767	760	750	734	709	670	612	533	430	536	11173
2110	784	779	779	777	773	768	763	758	749	734	710	675	621	543	437	547	11199
2120	782	778	777	775	772	768	763	756	746	732	710	675	622	547	443	556	11200
2130	781	776	775	773	770	766	761	755	745	729	706	673	621	547	444	562	11185
2140	779	774	774	772	768	764	759	753	744	729	706	670	618	545	444	563	11162
2150	777	773	772	770	767	763	758	751	742	727	704	670	618	543	441	562	11138
2160	776	771	770	768	765	761	756	750	740	725	703	668	617	543	441	560	11114
2170	774	770	769	767	763	759	755	748	739	724	701	667	615	541	440	559	11091
2180	772	768	767	765	762	758	753	747	737	722	700	665	614	540	439	558	11067
2190	771	766	765	763	760	756	751	745	736	721	698	664	613	539	438	557	11044
2200	769	765	764	762	758	755	750	744	734	719	697	662	611	538	437	556	11020

Table 2
Components of Population Change
World Population Projection No. 2080.R.H
Decline to Replacement Fertility Level (2.13); Mortality Level: High

Year	Births	Males Deaths - Thousands -	Balance	Births	Females Deaths - Thousands -	Balance	Births	Total Deaths - Thousands -	Balance
1990	75539	29422	46117	71783	28562	43221	147322	57985	89338
2000	76387	31588	44799	72588	28259	44329	148975	59847	89128
2010	77887	34906	42981	74014	29600	44414	151901	64506	87395
2020	80523	38695	41829	76519	32067	44452	157042	70762	86280
2030	81478	45743	35730	77426	38149	39277	158904	83897	75007
2040	83017	53602	29415	78889	46403	32485	161906	100005	61900
2050	83799	60477	23322	79632	53618	26014	163431	114095	49336
2060	83820	66300	17520	79651	59671	19980	163471	125971	37499
2070	83674	72008	11665	79513	65902	13610	163186	137911	25275
2080	83234	76005	7228	79094	70557	8537	162328	146563	15765
2090	83274	78923	4352	79133	73771	5362	162407	152694	9713
2100	83031	81250	1781	78901	76490	2411	161932	157740	4192
2110	82851	82519	331	78730	78014	716	161581	160533	1048
2120	82697	83267	-570	78584	78923	-339	161281	162190	-909
2130	82507	83581	-1074	78404	79418	-1014	160911	162999	-2088
2140	82335	83528	-1193	78240	79461	-1221	160575	162989	-2414
2150	82162	83340	-1178	78076	79299	-1223	160238	162640	-2402
2160	81985	83138	-1153	77908	79090	-1182	159893	162228	-2335
2170	81812	82980	-1168	77743	78941	-1198	159555	161921	-2366
2180	81638	82800	-1162	77578	78775	-1197	159216	161575	-2359
2190	81464	82620	-1156	77413	78600	-1187	158877	161220	-2343
2200	81291	82449	-1157	77249	78438	-1190	158540	160887	-2347

Table 3
Demographic Indicators
World Population Projection No. 2080.R.H
Decline to Replacement Fertility Level (2.13); Mortality Level: High

Year	1990	2000	2010	2020	2030	2040	2050	2060	2070	2080	2090
Birth Rate ‰	27.9	24.1	21.5	19.8	18.2	17.1	16.3	15.6	15.2	14.8	14.6
Death Rate ‰	11.0	9.7	9.1	8.9	9.6	10.6	11.4	12.1	12.8	13.4	13.8
Growth Rate %	1.69	1.44	1.24	1.09	0.86	0.66	0.49	0.36	0.23	0.14	0.09
Total Fertility Rate	3.400	3.061	2.743	2.535	2.398	2.306	2.241	2.194	2.158	2.130	2.130
GRR	1.684	1.493	1.345	1.239	1.172	1.127	1.094	1.070	1.052	1.039	1.039
NRR	1.5	1.4	1.3	1.2	1.1	1.1	1.1	1.0	1.0	1.0	1.0
IMR - Males	67.2	53.4	39.5	26.3	24.6	24.6	24.6	24.6	24.6	24.6	24.6
IMR - Females	62.8	47.9	31.8	18.8	17.0	17.0	17.0	17.0	17.0	17.0	17.0
IMR - Both Sexes	65.0	50.6	35.7	22.5	20.8	20.8	20.8	20.8	20.8	20.8	20.8
E(0) - Males	65.36	66.12	67.01	67.99	68.39	68.39	68.39	68.39	68.39	68.39	68.39
E(0) - Females	68.43	69.71	71.16	72.53	73.25	73.25	73.25	73.25	73.25	73.25	73.25
E(0) - Both Sexes	66.90	67.91	69.08	70.26	70.82	70.82	70.82	70.82	70.82	70.82	70.82

Year	2100	2110	2120	2130	2140	2150	2160	2170	2180	2190	2200
Birth Rate ‰	14.5	14.4	14.4	14.4	14.4	14.4	14.4	14.4	14.4	14.4	14.4
Death Rate ‰	14.1	14.3	14.5	14.6	14.6	14.6	14.6	14.6	14.6	14.6	14.6
Growth Rate %	0.04	0.01	-0.01	-0.02	-0.02	-0.02	-0.02	-0.02	-0.02	-0.02	-0.02
Total Fertility Rate	2.130	2.130	2.130	2.130	2.130	2.130	2.130	2.130	2.130	2.130	2.130
GRR	1.039	1.039	1.039	1.039	1.039	1.039	1.039	1.039	1.039	1.039	1.039
NRR	1.0	1.0	1.0	1.0	1.0	1.0	1.0	1.0	1.0	1.0	1.0
IMR - Males	24.6	24.6	24.6	24.6	24.6	24.6	24.6	24.6	24.6	24.6	24.6
IMR - Females	17.0	17.0	17.0	17.0	17.0	17.0	17.0	17.0	17.0	17.0	17.0
IMR - Both Sexes	20.8	20.8	20.8	20.8	20.8	20.8	20.8	20.8	20.8	20.8	20.8
E(0) - Males	68.39	68.39	68.39	68.39	68.39	68.39	68.39	68.39	68.39	68.39	68.39
E(0) - Females	73.25	73.25	73.25	73.25	73.25	73.25	73.25	73.25	73.25	73.25	73.25
E(0) - Both Sexes	70.82	70.82	70.82	70.82	70.82	70.82	70.82	70.82	70.82	70.82	70.82

Graph 1

Projected Total Population
World Population Projection No. 2080.R.H
Decline to Replacement Fertility Level (2.13)
Mortality Level: High

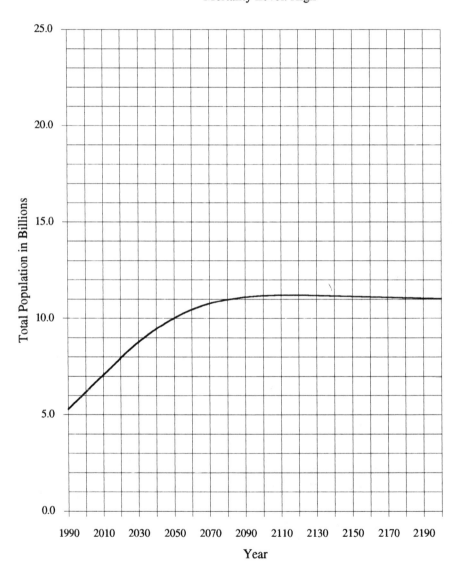

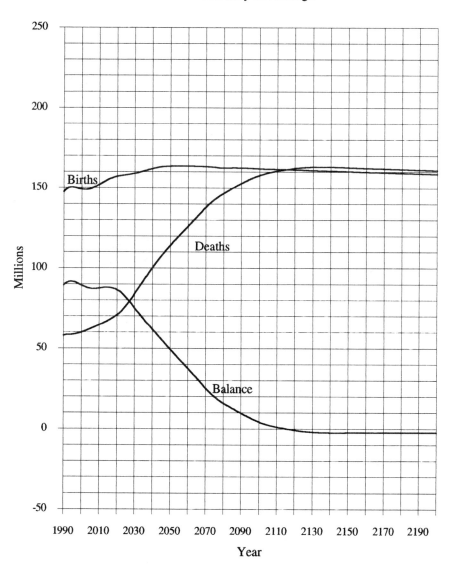

Graph 3

Age Structure of World Population 1990, 2050 and 2100

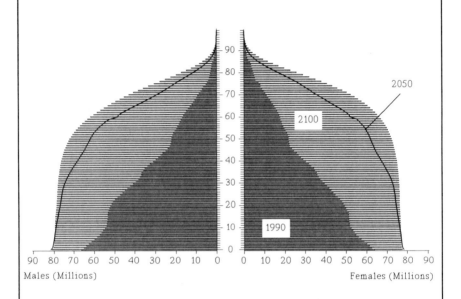

Population Projection No. 2080.R.H.

Target year for replacement fertility
level (TFR = 2.13):   2080
Form of fertility decline: Hyperbolic
Mortality level: High

Total population: 1990   5 275 Million
     2050   10 006 Million
     2100   11 173 Million

Table 1
Projected Total Population
World Population Projection No. 2080.R.M
Decline to Replacement Fertility Level (2.13); Mortality Level: Medium
- Millions -

Age Year	0-4	5-9	10-14	15-19	20-24	25-29	30-34	35-39	40-44	45-49	50-54	55-59	60-64	65-69	70-74	75+	Total
1990	625	563	528	519	490	436	380	342	282	230	214	186	160	123	87	108	5275
2000	691	666	609	555	519	508	479	424	367	327	264	209	185	149	114	124	6191
2010	710	686	677	659	600	545	508	496	465	408	346	299	231	170	133	157	7092
2020	755	727	700	681	669	649	590	535	496	479	441	375	305	246	169	186	8004
2030	774	764	748	723	694	673	660	639	578	518	472	444	391	312	226	257	8876
2040	789	776	768	760	743	716	686	663	647	620	551	482	421	370	292	339	9623
2050	802	792	783	772	762	753	734	705	672	643	617	576	491	401	314	417	10235
2060	805	799	795	788	777	764	753	742	719	684	641	598	550	480	366	459	10720
2070	806	801	798	795	789	780	768	753	738	719	686	636	571	498	410	537	11084
2080	803	800	799	796	792	787	780	769	752	731	704	668	611	530	426	581	11329
2090	805	799	797	796	793	788	783	775	764	745	717	679	627	557	456	613	11495
2100	804	800	798	795	791	788	784	777	767	752	729	693	639	565	468	649	11598
2110	804	799	798	796	792	787	781	777	768	753	732	699	649	577	477	665	11654
2120	804	799	798	795	792	788	783	775	766	753	732	700	652	582	484	678	11682
2130	804	800	798	795	791	787	783	777	767	752	730	700	652	583	486	687	11692
2140	804	799	798	795	792	787	782	776	767	753	732	698	650	583	486	690	11693
2150	804	799	798	795	792	787	782	776	766	752	731	700	652	582	485	690	11692
2160	804	799	798	795	792	787	782	776	767	752	731	699	651	583	486	689	11692
2170	804	799	798	795	792	787	782	776	767	753	731	699	651	582	486	689	11691
2180	804	799	798	795	792	787	782	776	766	752	731	699	651	582	486	689	11691
2190	804	799	798	795	791	787	782	776	766	752	731	699	651	582	486	689	11691
2200	804	799	798	795	791	787	782	776	766	752	731	699	651	582	486	689	11690

Table 2
Components of Population Change
World Population Projection No. 2080.R.M
Decline to Replacement Fertility Level (2.13); Mortality Level: Medium

Year	Males Births	Males Deaths - Thousands -	Males Balance	Females Births	Females Deaths - Thousands -	Females Balance	Total Births	Total Deaths - Thousands -	Total Balance
1990	75539	29422	46117	71783	28562	43221	147322	57985	89338
2000	76411	30644	45767	72611	27448	45162	149022	58092	90930
2010	77982	33256	44726	74104	28278	45825	152086	61535	90551
2020	80801	36491	44309	76782	30365	46418	157583	66856	90727
2030	81945	42848	39097	77870	35866	42004	159815	78714	81101
2040	83639	51371	32268	79479	44596	34884	163119	95966	67152
2050	84603	58795	25808	80396	52222	28173	164999	111017	53981
2060	84809	64928	19882	80592	58526	22065	165401	123454	41947
2070	84834	70969	13865	80615	64922	15693	165448	135890	29558
2080	84566	75499	9066	80360	70049	10311	164926	145548	19377
2090	84785	78719	6066	80568	73535	7034	165353	152253	13100
2100	84713	81399	3314	80500	76524	3976	165213	157923	7290
2110	84707	83013	1694	80494	78385	2110	165201	161398	3803
2120	84727	84013	714	80513	79527	986	165241	163540	1700
2130	84710	84580	129	80497	80259	237	165206	164840	367
2140	84710	84747	-37	80497	80522	-25	165207	165269	-62
2150	84709	84744	-35	80491	80543	-47	165288	165288	-82
2160	84704	84711	-7	80491	80498	-7	165195	165209	-13
2170	84702	84724	-22	80490	80508	-18	165192	165232	-40
2180	84699	84721	-22	80487	80513	-26	165186	165234	-48
2190	84696	84713	-17	80484	80500	-16	165180	165213	-33
2200	84694	84714	-21	80482	80502	-21	165175	165217	-42

Table 3
Demographic Indicators
World Population Projection No. 2080.R.M
Decline to Replacement Fertility Level (2.13); Mortality Level: Medium

Year	1990	2000	2010	2020	2030	2040	2050	2060	2070	2080	2090
Birth Rate ‰	27.9	24.1	21.4	19.7	18.0	17.0	16.1	15.4	14.9	14.6	14.4
Death Rate ‰	11.0	9.4	8.7	8.4	8.9	10.0	10.8	11.5	12.3	12.8	13.2
Growth Rate %	1.69	1.47	1.28	1.13	0.91	0.70	0.53	0.39	0.27	0.17	0.11
Total Fertility Rate	3.400	3.061	2.743	2.535	2.398	2.306	2.241	2.194	2.158	2.130	2.130
GRR	1.684	1.493	1.345	1.239	1.172	1.127	1.094	1.070	1.052	1.039	1.039
NRR	1.5	1.4	1.3	1.2	1.1	1.1	1.1	1.0	1.0	1.0	1.0
IMR - Males	67.2	51.4	36.8	23.7	21.4	21.4	21.4	21.4	21.4	21.4	21.4
IMR - Females	62.8	46.2	29.6	16.9	14.8	14.8	14.8	14.8	14.8	14.8	14.8
IMR - Both Sexes	65.0	48.8	33.2	20.3	18.1	18.1	18.1	18.1	18.1	18.1	18.1
E(0) - Males	65.36	66.65	67.98	69.34	70.09	70.09	70.09	70.09	70.09	70.09	70.09
E(0) - Females	68.43	70.20	72.05	73.74	74.76	74.76	74.76	74.76	74.76	74.76	74.76
E(0) - Both Sexes	66.90	68.43	70.02	71.54	72.43	72.43	72.43	72.43	72.43	72.43	72.43

Year	2100	2110	2120	2130	2140	2150	2160	2170	2180	2190	2200
Birth Rate ‰	14.2	14.2	14.1	14.1	14.1	14.1	14.1	14.1	14.1	14.1	14.1
Death Rate ‰	13.6	13.8	14.0	14.1	14.1	14.1	14.1	14.1	14.1	14.1	14.1
Growth Rate %	0.06	0.03	0.01	0.00	0.00	0.00	0.00	0.00	0.00	0.00	0.00
Total Fertility Rate	2.130	2.130	2.130	2.130	2.130	2.130	2.130	2.130	2.130	2.130	2.130
GRR	1.039	1.039	1.039	1.039	1.039	1.039	1.039	1.039	1.039	1.039	1.039
NRR	1.0	1.0	1.0	1.0	1.0	1.0	1.0	1.0	1.0	1.0	1.0
IMR - Males	21.4	21.4	21.4	21.4	21.4	21.4	21.4	21.4	21.4	21.4	21.4
IMR - Females	14.8	14.8	14.8	14.8	14.8	14.8	14.8	14.8	14.8	14.8	14.8
IMR - Both Sexes	18.1	18.1	18.1	18.1	18.1	18.1	18.1	18.1	18.1	18.1	18.1
E(0) - Males	70.09	70.09	70.09	70.09	70.09	70.09	70.09	70.09	70.09	70.09	70.09
E(0) - Females	74.76	74.76	74.76	74.76	74.76	74.76	74.76	74.76	74.76	74.76	74.76
E(0) - Both Sexes	72.43	72.43	72.43	72.43	72.43	72.43	72.43	72.43	72.43	72.43	72.43

Graph 1

Projected Total Population
World Population Projection No. 2080.R.M
Decline to Replacement Fertility Level (2.13)
Mortality Level: Medium

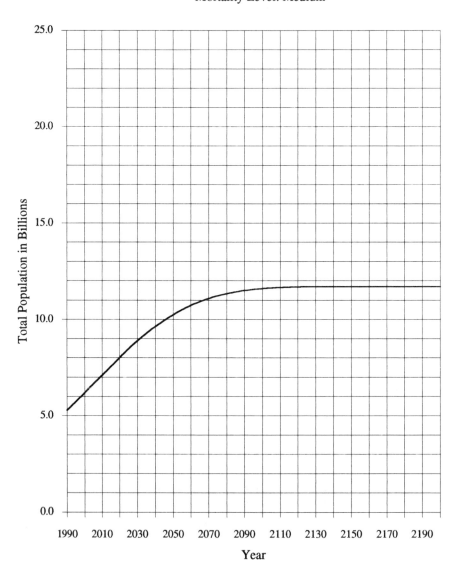

Graph 2

Components of Population Change
World Population Projection No. 2080.R.M
Decline to Replacement Fertility Level (2.13)
Mortality Level: Medium

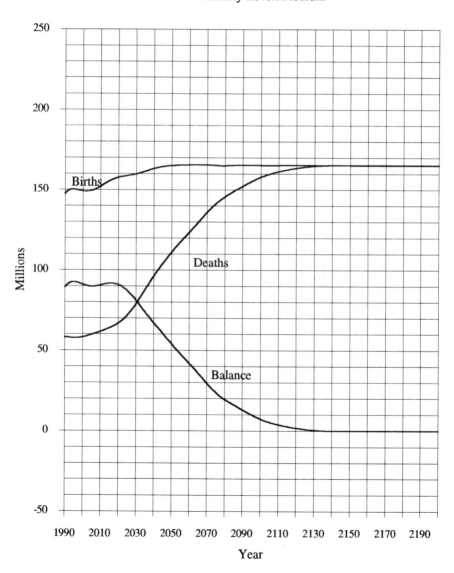

Graph 3

Age Structure of World Population 1990, 2050 and 2100

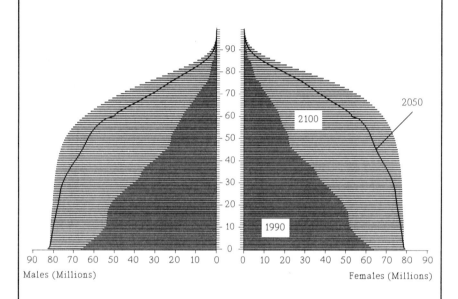

Population Projection No. 2080.R.M.

Target year for replacement fertility
level (TFR = 2.13):   2080
Form of fertility decline: Hyperbolic
Mortality level: Medium

Total population: 1990   5 275 Million
                                                 2050 10 235 Million
                                                 2100 11 598 Million

Table 1
Projected Total Population
World Population Projection No. 2080.R.L
Decline to Replacement Fertility Level (2.13); Mortality Level: Low

- Millions -

Age Year	0-4	5-9	10-14	15-19	20-24	25-29	30-34	35-39	40-44	45-49	50-54	55-59	60-64	65-69	70-74	75+	Total
1990	625	563	528	519	490	436	380	342	282	230	214	186	160	123	87	108	5275
2000	692	667	609	555	519	508	479	425	367	328	265	210	185	150	115	126	6199
2010	713	690	679	660	600	546	509	497	466	409	347	301	233	172	136	166	7125
2020	760	732	704	684	672	651	592	537	498	481	444	379	310	252	176	205	8077
2030	781	770	754	728	699	678	664	643	581	522	477	451	400	323	239	295	9005
2040	798	785	776	767	749	722	692	669	653	626	558	491	432	386	312	401	9816
2050	812	802	792	781	771	760	741	713	680	652	627	588	506	420	337	500	10484
2060	817	811	807	799	787	775	763	751	729	695	653	612	568	504	394	555	11019
2070	820	814	812	807	801	792	779	765	750	732	700	652	592	524	443	649	11432
2080	819	816	814	811	806	801	793	782	766	745	721	687	634	559	461	709	11723
2090	822	816	813	812	809	804	798	791	779	762	736	700	653	588	494	750	11927
2100	824	819	816	812	808	805	801	794	784	770	749	716	667	599	509	795	12068
2110	825	820	818	815	811	805	800	795	787	773	753	724	679	613	519	818	12156
2120	827	822	819	816	813	808	803	795	786	775	756	727	683	619	529	836	12213
2130	828	824	821	818	814	809	805	798	789	775	755	728	685	622	532	849	12252
2140	830	825	823	820	816	811	806	799	791	778	758	728	684	623	534	854	12280
2150	832	827	825	822	817	813	808	801	792	779	760	731	687	623	533	856	12304
2160	834	829	826	823	819	814	809	803	794	780	761	731	688	625	535	857	12330
2170	835	830	828	825	821	816	811	804	795	782	763	733	689	626	536	859	12355
2180	837	832	830	827	822	818	813	806	797	784	764	735	691	627	537	861	12381
2190	839	834	831	828	824	820	814	808	799	785	766	736	692	629	538	863	12406
2200	840	835	833	830	826	821	816	809	800	787	767	738	694	630	539	865	12432

Table 2
Components of Population Change
World Population Projection No. 2080.R.L
Decline to Replacement Fertility Level (2.13); Mortality Level: Low

Year	Births	Males Deaths - Thousands -	Balance	Births	Females Deaths - Thousands -	Balance	Births	Total Deaths - Thousands -	Balance
1990	75539	29422	46117	71783	28562	43221	147322	57985	89338
2000	76435	29688	46747	72634	26627	46007	149069	56315	92754
2010	78077	31536	46541	74194	26896	47298	152271	58432	93839
2020	81079	34107	46972	77047	28513	48534	158126	62620	95506
2030	82415	39557	42858	78316	33268	45048	160731	72825	87906
2040	84265	48758	35507	80074	42478	37597	164339	91236	73103
2050	85414	56802	28612	81166	50576	30590	166580	107378	59201
2060	85810	63316	22494	81542	57189	24353	167352	120505	46848
2070	86008	69651	16357	81731	63721	18010	167740	133372	34368
2080	85918	74767	11151	81645	69334	12311	167562	144101	23462
2090	86321	78345	7977	82029	73166	8863	168350	151510	16840
2100	86428	81377	5050	82130	76413	5717	168557	157790	10767
2110	86603	83383	3220	82296	78644	3652	168899	162027	6872
2120	86805	84660	2145	82488	80046	2442	169293	164706	4586
2130	86968	85496	1472	82643	81025	1618	169612	166521	3091
2140	87151	85903	1248	82817	81528	1289	169968	167431	2537
2150	87333	86098	1235	82990	81745	1245	170322	167843	2480
2160	87510	86241	1269	83158	81871	1287	170668	168112	2556
2170	87691	86429	1262	83330	82044	1287	171022	168473	2549
2180	87872	86612	1260	83502	82225	1277	171374	168838	2536
2190	88053	86783	1270	83674	82384	1290	171726	169167	2559
2200	88234	86966	1268	83846	82557	1289	172080	169523	2557

Table 3
Demographic Indicators
World Population Projection No. 2080.R.L
Decline to Replacement Fertility Level (2.13); Mortality Level: Low

Year	1990	2000	2010	2020	2030	2040	2050	2060	2070	2080	2090
Birth Rate ‰	27.9	24.0	21.4	19.6	17.8	16.7	15.9	15.2	14.7	14.3	14.1
Death Rate ‰	11.0	9.1	8.2	7.8	8.1	9.3	10.2	10.9	11.7	12.3	12.7
Growth Rate %	1.69	1.50	1.32	1.18	0.98	0.74	0.56	0.43	0.30	0.20	0.14
Total Fertility Rate	3.400	3.061	2.743	2.535	2.398	2.306	2.241	2.194	2.158	2.130	2.130
GRR	1.684	1.493	1.345	1.240	1.172	1.127	1.094	1.070	1.052	1.039	1.039
NRR	1.5	1.4	1.3	1.2	1.1	1.1	1.1	1.0	1.0	1.0	1.0
IMR - Males	67.2	49.5	34.0	21.0	18.2	18.2	18.2	18.2	18.2	18.2	18.2
IMR - Females	62.8	44.4	27.4	15.0	12.6	12.6	12.6	12.6	12.6	12.6	12.6
IMR - Both Sexes	65.0	47.0	30.7	18.0	15.4	15.4	15.4	15.4	15.4	15.4	15.4
E(0) - Males	65.36	67.19	69.03	70.84	72.06	72.06	72.06	72.06	72.06	72.06	72.06
E(0) - Females	68.43	70.71	73.00	75.08	76.51	76.51	76.51	76.51	76.51	76.51	76.51
E(0) - Both Sexes	66.90	68.95	71.02	72.96	74.28	74.28	74.28	74.28	74.28	74.28	74.28

Year	2100	2110	2120	2130	2140	2150	2160	2170	2180	2190	2200
Birth Rate ‰	14.0	13.9	13.9	13.8	13.8	13.8	13.8	13.8	13.8	13.8	13.8
Death Rate ‰	13.1	13.3	13.5	13.6	13.6	13.6	13.6	13.6	13.6	13.6	13.6
Growth Rate %	0.09	0.06	0.04	0.03	0.02	0.02	0.02	0.02	0.02	0.02	0.02
Total Fertility Rate	2.130	2.130	2.130	2.130	2.130	2.130	2.130	2.130	2.130	2.130	2.130
GRR	1.039	1.039	1.039	1.039	1.039	1.039	1.039	1.039	1.039	1.039	1.039
NRR	1.0	1.0	1.0	1.0	1.0	1.0	1.0	1.0	1.0	1.0	1.0
IMR - Males	18.2	18.2	18.2	18.2	18.2	18.2	18.2	18.2	18.2	18.2	18.2
IMR - Females	12.6	12.6	12.6	12.6	12.6	12.6	12.6	12.6	12.6	12.6	12.6
IMR - Both Sexes	15.4	15.4	15.4	15.4	15.4	15.4	15.4	15.4	15.4	15.4	15.4
E(0) - Males	72.06	72.06	72.06	72.06	72.06	72.06	72.06	72.06	72.06	72.06	72.06
E(0) - Females	76.51	76.51	76.51	76.51	76.51	76.51	76.51	76.51	76.51	76.51	76.51
E(0) - Both Sexes	74.28	74.28	74.28	74.28	74.28	74.28	74.28	74.28	74.28	74.28	74.28

Graph 1

Projected Total Population
World Population Projection No. 2080.R.L
Decline to Replacement Fertility Level (2.13)
Mortality Level: Low

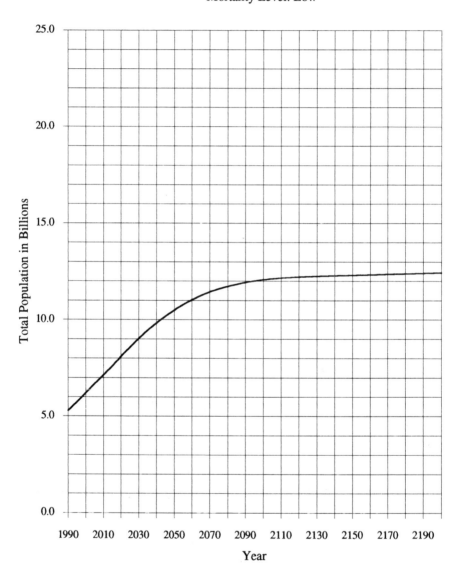

Graph 2

Components of Population Change
World Population Projection No. 2080.R.L
Decline to Replacement Fertility Level (2.13)
Mortality Level: Low

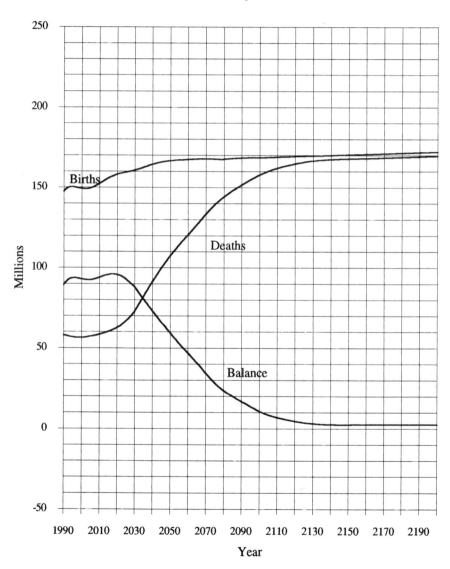

Graph 3

Age Structure of World Population 1990, 2050 and 2100

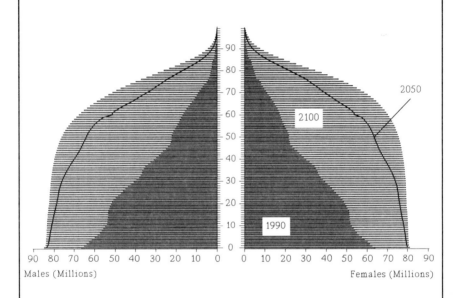

Population Projection No. 2080.R.L.

Target year for replacement fertility
level (TFR = 2.13):   2080
Form of fertility decline: Hyperbolic
Mortality level: Low

Total population: 1990 5 275 Million
                                        2050 10 484 Million
                                        2100 12 068 Million

Table 1
Projected Total Population
World Population Projection No. 2080.B.H
Decline Below Replacement Fertility Level; Mortality Level: High

Age Year	0-4	5-9	10-14	15-19	20-24	25-29	30-34	35-39	40-44	45-49	50-54	55-59	60-64	65-69	70-74	75+	Total
1990	625	563	528	519	490	436	380	342	282	230	214	186	160	123	87	108	5275
2000	689	665	609	555	518	508	479	424	367	327	264	209	184	149	113	121	6182
2010	707	683	675	657	599	545	508	496	464	406	345	298	229	168	131	149	7059
2020	751	723	696	677	666	647	589	533	494	477	438	372	300	240	163	169	7934
2030	768	758	743	718	689	669	656	636	575	515	468	438	382	301	214	225	8754
2040	780	768	761	754	736	710	680	657	641	614	544	473	409	355	273	289	9444
2050	791	782	773	763	754	745	726	698	664	635	607	564	477	384	292	351	10006
2060	793	787	784	777	766	754	744	732	709	674	629	583	532	457	341	383	10446
2070	792	787	785	782	777	768	756	742	726	707	672	619	551	473	380	448	10766
2080	788	785	785	782	778	773	767	756	739	716	688	650	588	502	393	482	10972
2090	781	779	781	780	778	773	768	761	749	729	700	658	602	527	420	507	11093
2100	772	772	774	775	774	771	767	760	750	734	709	670	612	533	430	536	11140
2110	762	762	765	767	767	766	763	758	749	734	710	675	621	543	437	547	11128
2120	750	751	755	758	758	758	757	753	746	732	710	675	622	547	443	556	11071
2130	738	739	743	747	748	749	748	745	739	727	706	673	621	547	444	562	10976
2140	724	726	731	735	737	738	738	736	731	720	700	668	618	545	444	563	10853
2150	710	712	718	722	724	726	727	726	721	711	692	661	613	541	441	562	10707
2160	695	698	704	708	711	713	715	714	710	700	683	653	606	536	437	559	10542
2170	680	683	689	694	697	700	701	701	698	689	672	644	598	529	433	553	10363
2180	665	668	674	679	683	686	688	688	685	677	661	633	589	522	427	547	10173
2190	650	653	659	664	668	671	674	674	672	664	649	622	579	513	420	539	9974
2200	635	638	644	649	653	657	659	660	658	651	636	610	568	504	413	531	9768

Table 2
Components of Population Change
World Population Projection No. 2080.B.H
Decline Below Replacement Fertility Level; Mortality Level: High

Year	Males Births	Males Deaths - Thousands -	Males Balance	Females Births	Females Deaths - Thousands -	Females Balance	Total Births	Total Deaths - Thousands -	Total Balance
1990	75539	29422	46117	71783	28562	43221	147322	57985	89338
2000	76387	31588	44799	72588	28259	44329	148975	59847	89128
2010	77887	34906	42981	74014	29600	44414	151901	64506	87395
2020	80523	38695	41829	76519	32067	44452	157042	70762	86280
2030	81478	45748	35730	77426	38149	39277	158904	83897	75007
2040	83017	53602	29415	78889	46403	32485	161906	100005	61900
2050	83799	60477	23322	79632	53618	26014	163431	114095	49336
2060	83820	66300	17520	79651	59671	19980	163471	125971	37499
2070	83674	72008	11665	79513	65902	13610	163186	137911	25275
2080	83139	76003	7136	79004	70556	8448	162143	146559	15584
2090	82339	78885	3454	78244	73746	4498	160583	152631	7952
2100	81372	81175	197	77325	76441	883	158696	157617	1080
2110	80226	82388	-2161	76237	77930	-1694	156463	160318	-3855
2120	78956	83057	-4100	75030	78790	-3761	153986	161847	-7861
2130	77589	83257	-5668	73731	79215	-5484	151320	162472	-11152
2140	76141	83015	-6874	72354	79143	-6788	148495	162158	-13663
2150	74633	82483	-7855	70921	78770	-7849	145554	161259	-15705
2160	73080	81708	-8628	69446	78138	-8692	142525	159846	-17320
2170	71494	80723	-9229	67939	77284	-9345	139433	158007	-18574
2180	69887	79585	-9698	66411	76268	-9857	136298	155853	-19555
2190	68267	78318	-10052	64871	75118	-10247	133138	153436	-20298
2200	66641	76954	-10313	63327	73862	-10535	129967	150815	-20848

Table 3
Demographic Indicators
World Population Projection No. 2080.B.H
Decline Below Replacement Fertility Level; Mortality Level: High

Year	1990	2000	2010	2020	2030	2040	2050	2060	2070	2080	2090
Birth Rate ‰	27.9	24.1	21.5	19.8	18.2	17.1	16.3	15.6	15.2	14.8	14.5
Death Rate ‰	11.0	9.7	9.1	8.9	9.6	10.6	11.4	12.1	12.8	13.4	13.8
Growth Rate %	1.69	1.44	1.24	1.09	0.86	0.66	0.49	0.36	0.23	0.14	0.07
Total Fertility Rate	3.400	3.061	2.743	2.535	2.398	2.306	2.241	2.194	2.158	2.130	2.108
GRR	1.684	1.493	1.345	1.239	1.172	1.127	1.094	1.070	1.052	1.038	1.027
NRR	1.5	1.4	1.3	1.2	1.1	1.1	1.1	1.0	1.0	1.0	1.0
IMR - Males	67.2	53.4	39.5	26.3	24.6	24.6	24.6	24.6	24.6	24.6	24.6
IMR - Females	62.8	47.9	31.8	18.8	17.0	17.0	17.0	17.0	17.0	17.0	17.0
IMR - Both Sexes	65.0	50.6	35.7	22.5	20.8	20.8	20.8	20.8	20.8	20.8	20.8
E(0) - Males	65.36	66.12	67.01	67.99	68.39	68.39	68.39	68.39	68.39	68.39	68.39
E(0) - Females	68.43	69.71	71.16	72.53	73.25	73.25	73.25	73.25	73.25	73.25	73.25
E(0) - Both Sexes	66.90	67.91	69.08	70.26	70.82	70.82	70.82	70.82	70.82	70.82	70.82

Year	2100	2110	2120	2130	2140	2150	2160	2170	2180	2190	2200
Birth Rate ‰	14.2	14.1	13.9	13.8	13.7	13.6	13.5	13.5	13.4	13.3	13.3
Death Rate ‰	14.1	14.4	14.6	14.8	14.9	15.1	15.2	15.2	15.3	15.4	15.4
Growth Rate %	0.01	-0.03	-0.07	-0.10	-0.13	-0.15	-0.16	-0.18	-0.19	-0.20	-0.21
Total Fertility Rate	2.090	2.076	2.064	2.053	2.045	2.037	2.031	2.025	2.020	2.016	2.012
GRR	1.018	1.011	1.005	1.000	0.995	0.992	0.988	0.986	0.983	0.981	0.981
NRR	1.0	1.0	1.0	1.0	1.0	1.0	1.0	1.0	1.0	1.0	1.0
IMR - Males	24.6	24.6	24.6	24.6	24.6	24.6	24.6	24.6	24.6	24.6	24.6
IMR - Females	17.0	17.0	17.0	17.0	17.0	17.0	17.0	17.0	17.0	17.0	17.0
IMR - Both Sexes	20.8	20.8	20.8	20.8	20.8	20.8	20.8	20.8	20.8	20.8	20.8
E(0) - Males	68.39	68.39	68.39	68.39	68.39	68.39	68.39	68.39	68.39	68.39	68.39
E(0) - Females	73.25	73.25	73.25	73.25	73.25	73.25	73.25	73.25	73.25	73.25	73.25
E(0) - Both Sexes	70.82	70.82	70.82	70.82	70.82	70.82	70.82	70.82	70.82	70.82	70.82

Graph 1

Projected Total Population
World Population Projection No. 2080.B.H
Decline Below Replacement Fertility Level
Mortality Level: High

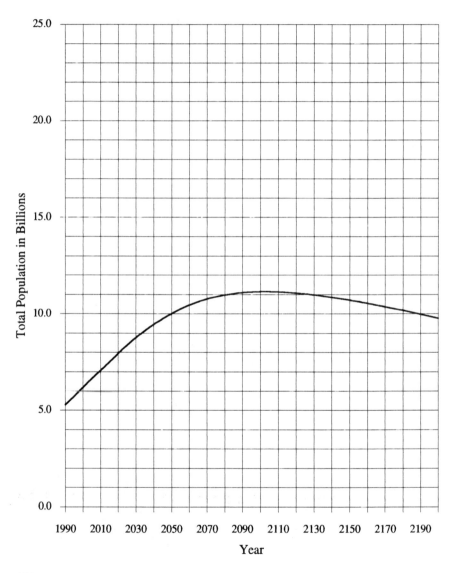

Graph 2

Components of Population Change
World Population Projection No. 2080.B.H
Decline Below Replacement Fertility Level
Mortality Level: High

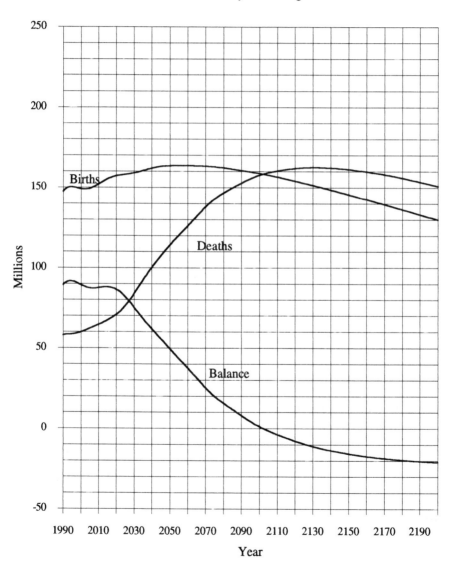

Graph 3

Age Structure of World Population 1990, 2050 and 2100

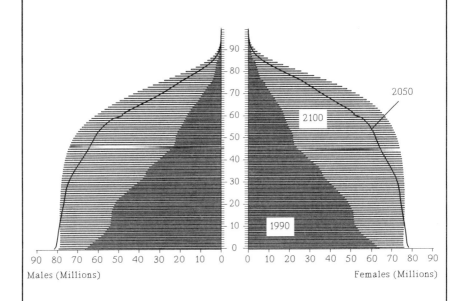

Population Projection No. 2080.B.H.

Decline below replacement fertility level
by the year:　　　　　　　　　　　　　　　2080
Form of fertility decline:　　　　　　　　　　Hyperbolic
Mortality level:　　　　　　　　　　　　　　High

Total population:　　　　　　　　　　　　　1990　5 275 Million
　　　　　　　　　　　　　　　　　　　　　2050　10 006 Million
　　　　　　　　　　　　　　　　　　　　　2100　11 140 Million

Table 1
Projected Total Population
World Population Projection No. 2080.B.M
Decline Below Replacement Fertility Level; Mortality Level: Medium

- Millions -

Age Year	0-4	5-9	10-14	15-19	20-24	25-29	30-34	35-39	40-44	45-49	50-54	55-59	60-64	65-69	70-74	75+	Total
1990	625	563	528	519	490	436	380	342	282	230	214	186	160	123	87	108	5275
2000	691	666	609	555	519	508	479	424	367	327	264	209	185	149	114	124	6191
2010	710	686	677	659	600	545	508	496	465	408	346	299	231	170	133	157	7092
2020	755	727	700	681	669	649	590	535	496	479	441	375	305	246	169	186	8004
2030	774	764	748	723	694	673	660	639	578	518	472	444	391	312	226	257	8876
2040	789	776	768	760	743	716	686	663	647	620	551	482	421	370	292	339	9623
2050	802	792	783	772	762	753	734	705	672	643	617	576	491	401	314	417	10235
2060	805	799	795	788	777	764	753	742	719	684	641	598	550	480	366	459	10720
2070	806	801	798	795	789	780	768	753	738	719	686	636	571	498	410	537	11084
2080	803	800	799	796	792	787	780	769	752	731	704	668	611	530	426	581	11329
2090	798	796	797	796	793	788	783	775	764	745	717	679	627	557	456	613	11485
2100	791	790	792	792	791	788	784	777	767	752	729	693	639	565	468	649	11565
2110	782	782	784	786	785	784	781	777	768	753	732	699	649	577	477	665	11580
2120	771	772	776	778	778	778	776	773	766	753	732	700	652	582	484	678	11548
2130	760	761	765	768	769	770	769	766	760	749	730	700	652	583	486	687	11477
2140	747	749	754	757	759	760	760	759	754	743	725	696	650	583	486	690	11374
2150	734	737	742	745	748	750	750	749	745	736	719	691	646	580	485	690	11246
2160	721	723	729	733	736	738	739	739	735	727	711	684	640	575	482	687	11098
2170	707	710	715	720	723	725	727	727	724	716	701	675	633	569	477	682	10933
2180	693	696	701	706	710	712	715	715	712	705	691	666	625	562	472	676	10756
2190	678	681	687	692	696	699	701	702	700	693	680	655	615	554	466	668	10569
2200	663	667	673	678	682	685	688	689	687	681	668	644	605	546	459	659	10373

Table 2
Components of Population Change
World Population Projection No. 2080.B.M
Decline Below Replacement Fertility Level; Mortality Level: Medium

Year	Males Births	Males Deaths - Thousands -	Males Balance	Females Births	Females Deaths - Thousands -	Females Balance	Total Births	Total Deaths - Thousands -	Total Balance
1990	75539	29422	46117	71783	28562	43221	147322	57985	89338
2000	76411	30644	45767	72611	27448	45162	149022	58092	90930
2010	77982	33256	44726	74104	28278	45825	152086	61535	90551
2020	80801	36491	44309	76782	30365	46418	157583	66856	90727
2030	81945	42848	39097	77870	35866	42004	159815	78714	81101
2040	83639	51371	32268	79479	44596	34884	163119	95966	67152
2050	84603	58795	25808	80396	52222	28173	164999	111017	53981
2060	84809	64928	19882	80592	58526	22065	165401	123454	41947
2070	84834	70969	13865	80615	64922	15693	165448	135890	29558
2080	84469	75497	8972	80268	70048	10221	164738	145545	19193
2090	83833	78685	5147	79663	73513	6151	163496	152198	11298
2100	83020	81332	1688	78892	76481	2410	161912	157814	4098
2110	82024	82896	-873	77945	78310	-366	159968	161207	-1238
2120	80894	83825	-2931	76871	79409	-2537	157766	163234	-5468
2130	79660	84291	-4631	75699	80078	-4379	155359	164369	-9010
2140	78337	84286	-5949	74441	80237	-5796	152777	164523	-11746
2150	76946	83973	-7027	73119	80068	-6948	150065	164041	-13976
2160	75503	83396	-7893	71748	79630	-7882	147251	163026	-15776
2170	74019	82597	-8578	70338	78956	-8618	144357	161553	-17196
2180	72506	81631	-9125	68900	78106	-9206	141407	159737	-18331
2190	70974	80525	-9551	67444	77111	-9667	138418	157636	-19218
2200	69429	79307	-9879	65976	75998	-10023	135404	155306	-19901

Table 3
Demographic Indicators
World Population Projection No. 2080.B.M
Decline Below Replacement Fertility Level; Mortality Level: Medium

Year	1990	2000	2010	2020	2030	2040	2050	2060	2070	2080	2090
Birth Rate ‰	27.9	24.1	21.4	19.7	18.0	17.0	16.1	15.4	14.9	14.5	14.2
Death Rate ‰	11.0	9.4	8.7	8.4	8.9	10.0	10.8	11.5	12.3	12.8	13.3
Growth Rate %	1.69	1.47	1.28	1.13	0.91	0.70	0.53	0.39	0.27	0.17	0.10
Total Fertility Rate	3.400	3.061	2.743	2.535	2.398	2.306	2.241	2.194	2.158	2.130	2.108
GRR	1.684	1.493	1.345	1.239	1.172	1.127	1.094	1.070	1.052	1.038	1.027
NRR	1.5	1.4	1.3	1.2	1.1	1.1	1.1	1.0	1.0	1.0	1.0
IMR - Males	67.2	51.4	36.8	23.7	21.4	21.4	21.4	21.4	21.4	21.4	21.4
IMR - Females	62.8	46.2	29.6	16.9	14.8	14.8	14.8	14.8	14.8	14.8	14.8
IMR - Both Sexes	65.0	48.8	33.2	20.3	18.1	18.1	18.1	18.1	18.1	18.1	18.1
E(0) - Males	65.36	66.65	67.98	69.34	70.09	70.09	70.09	70.09	70.09	70.09	70.09
E(0) - Females	68.43	70.20	72.05	73.74	74.76	74.76	74.76	74.76	74.76	74.76	74.76
E(0) - Both Sexes	66.90	68.43	70.02	71.54	72.43	72.43	72.43	72.43	72.43	72.43	72.43

Year	2100	2110	2120	2130	2140	2150	2160	2170	2180	2190	2200
Birth Rate ‰	14.0	13.8	13.7	13.5	13.4	13.3	13.3	13.2	13.1	13.1	13.1
Death Rate ‰	13.6	13.9	14.1	14.3	14.5	14.6	14.7	14.8	14.9	14.9	15.0
Growth Rate %	0.04	-0.01	-0.05	-0.08	-0.10	-0.12	-0.14	-0.16	-0.17	-0.18	-0.19
Total Fertility Rate	2.090	2.076	2.064	2.053	2.045	2.037	2.031	2.025	2.020	2.016	2.012
GRR	1.018	1.011	1.005	1.000	0.995	0.992	0.989	0.986	0.983	0.981	0.981
NRR	1.0	1.0	1.0	1.0	1.0	1.0	1.0	1.0	1.0	1.0	1.0
IMR - Males	21.4	21.4	21.4	21.4	21.4	21.4	21.4	21.4	21.4	21.4	21.4
IMR - Females	14.8	14.8	14.8	14.8	14.8	14.8	14.8	14.8	14.8	14.8	14.8
IMR - Both Sexes	18.1	18.1	18.1	18.1	18.1	18.1	18.1	18.1	18.1	18.1	18.1
E(0) - Males	70.09	70.09	70.09	70.09	70.09	70.09	70.09	70.09	70.09	70.09	70.09
E(0) - Females	74.76	74.76	74.76	74.76	74.76	74.76	74.76	74.76	74.76	74.76	74.76
E(0) - Both Sexes	72.43	72.43	72.43	72.43	72.43	72.43	72.43	72.43	72.43	72.43	72.43

Graph 1

Projected Total Population
World Population Projection No. 2080.B.M
Decline Below Replacement Fertility Level
Mortality Level: Medium

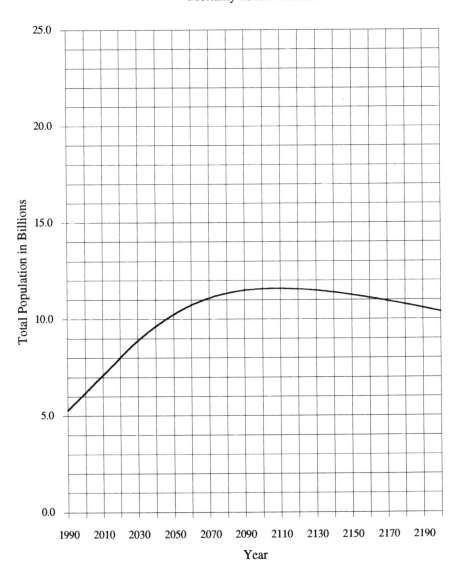

Graph 2

Components of Population Change
World Population Projection No. 2080.B.M
Decline Below Replacement Fertility Level
Mortality Level: Medium

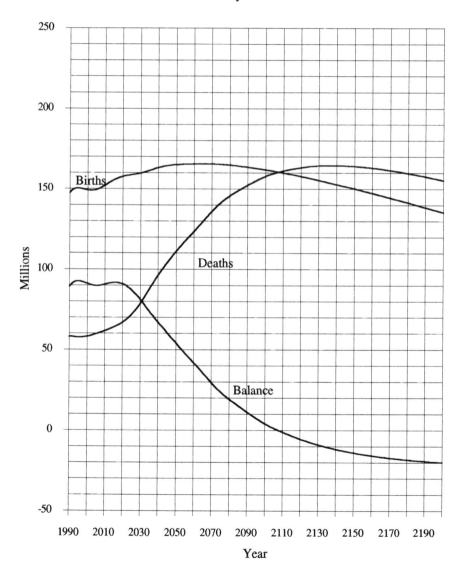

Graph 3

Age Structure of World Population 1990, 2050 and 2100

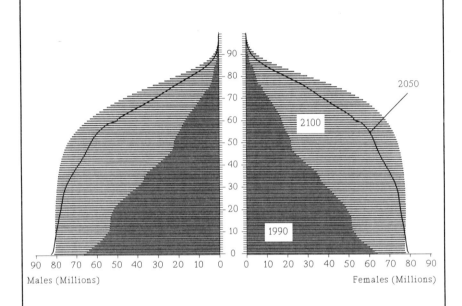

Population Projection No. 2080.B.M.

Decline below replacement fertility level by the year:	2080
Form of fertility decline:	Hyperbolic
Mortality level:	Medium
Total population:	1990 5 275 Million
	2050 10 235 Million
	2100 11 565 Million

Table 1
Projected Total Population
World Population Projection No. 2080.B.L
Decline Below Replacement Fertility Level; Mortality Level: Low
- Millions -

Age Year	0-4	5-9	10-14	15-19	20-24	25-29	30-34	35-39	40-44	45-49	50-54	55-59	60-64	65-69	70-74	75+	Total
1990	625	563	528	519	490	436	380	342	282	230	214	186	160	123	87	108	5275
2000	692	667	609	555	519	508	479	425	367	328	265	210	185	150	115	126	6199
2010	713	690	679	660	600	546	509	497	466	409	347	301	233	172	136	166	7125
2020	760	732	704	684	672	651	592	537	498	481	444	379	310	252	176	205	8077
2030	781	770	754	728	699	678	664	643	581	522	477	451	400	323	239	295	9005
2040	798	785	776	767	749	722	692	669	653	626	558	491	432	386	312	401	9816
2050	812	802	792	781	771	760	741	713	680	652	627	588	506	420	337	500	10484
2060	817	811	807	799	787	775	763	751	729	695	653	612	568	504	394	555	11019
2070	820	814	812	807	801	792	779	765	750	732	700	652	592	524	443	649	11432
2080	819	816	814	811	806	801	793	782	766	745	721	687	634	559	461	709	11723
2090	815	813	813	812	809	804	798	791	779	762	736	700	653	588	494	750	11918
2100	809	808	810	810	808	805	801	794	784	770	749	716	667	599	509	795	12033
2110	802	802	804	805	804	803	800	795	787	773	753	724	679	613	519	818	12080
2120	793	794	797	798	799	798	796	793	786	775	756	727	683	619	529	836	12076
2130	783	784	788	790	791	791	791	788	782	772	755	728	685	622	532	849	12031
2140	772	773	778	781	782	783	783	782	777	768	752	725	684	623	534	854	11950
2150	760	762	767	770	772	774	775	774	770	762	746	721	681	621	533	856	11843
2160	747	750	755	759	761	763	765	764	761	754	740	715	676	617	531	855	11714
2170	734	737	742	747	750	752	754	754	751	745	731	708	670	612	527	851	11566
2180	721	724	729	734	737	740	742	743	741	735	722	699	663	606	522	845	11403
2190	707	711	716	721	725	728	730	731	729	724	712	690	654	599	516	837	11229
2200	694	697	703	708	711	715	717	719	717	712	701	680	645	591	510	828	11046

Table 2
Components of Population Change
World Population Projection No. 2080.B.L
Decline Below Replacement Fertility Level; Mortality Level: Low

Year	Males Births	Males Deaths - Thousands -	Males Balance	Females Births	Females Deaths - Thousands -	Females Balance	Total Births	Total Deaths - Thousands -	Total Balance
1990	75539	29422	46117	71783	28562	43221	147322	57985	89338
2000	76435	29688	46747	72634	26627	46007	149069	56315	92754
2010	78077	31536	46541	74194	26896	47298	152271	58432	93839
2020	81079	34107	46972	77047	28513	48534	158126	62620	95506
2030	82415	39557	42858	78316	33268	45048	160731	72825	87906
2040	84265	48758	35507	80074	42478	37597	164339	91236	73103
2050	85414	56802	28612	81166	50576	30590	166580	107378	59201
2060	85810	63316	22494	81542	57189	24353	167352	120505	46848
2070	86008	69651	16357	81731	63721	18010	167740	133372	34368
2080	85820	74765	11055	81552	69333	12219	167371	144098	23274
2090	85352	78316	7036	81107	73147	7961	166459	151462	14997
2100	84701	81320	3381	80489	76375	4113	165189	157695	7494
2110	83860	83281	579	79689	78579	1110	163549	161860	1688
2120	82878	84496	-1619	78756	79943	-1187	161634	164439	-2805
2130	81784	85243	-3459	77717	80866	-3150	159501	166109	-6608
2140	80594	85498	-4905	76585	81279	-4693	157179	166777	-9598
2150	79328	85416	-6088	75383	81326	-5943	154712	166742	-12031
2160	78003	85058	-7055	74124	81098	-6974	152127	166156	-14029
2170	76630	84461	-7831	72819	80618	-7799	149450	165079	-15630
2180	75221	83682	-8460	71480	79947	-8467	146702	163629	-16927
2190	73785	82750	-8965	70116	79120	-9005	143901	161870	-17969
2200	72330	81694	-9364	68733	78164	-9431	141062	159857	-18795

Table 3
Demographic Indicators
World Population Projection No. 2080.B.L
Decline Below Replacement Fertility Level; Mortality Level: Low

Year	1990	2000	2010	2020	2030	2040	2050	2060	2070	2080	2090
Birth Rate ‰	27.9	24.0	21.4	19.6	17.8	16.7	15.9	15.2	14.7	14.3	14.0
Death Rate ‰	11.0	9.1	8.2	7.8	8.1	9.3	10.2	10.9	11.7	12.3	12.7
Growth Rate %	1.69	1.50	1.32	1.18	0.98	0.74	0.56	0.43	0.30	0.20	0.13
Total Fertility Rate	3.400	3.061	2.743	2.535	2.398	2.306	2.241	2.194	2.158	2.130	2.108
GRR	1.684	1.493	1.345	1.240	1.172	1.127	1.094	1.070	1.052	1.038	1.027
NRR	1.5	1.4	1.3	1.2	1.1	1.1	1.1	1.0	1.0	1.0	1.0
IMR - Males	67.2	49.5	34.0	21.0	18.2	18.2	18.2	18.2	18.2	18.2	18.2
IMR - Females	62.8	44.4	27.4	15.0	12.6	12.6	12.6	12.6	12.6	12.6	12.6
IMR - Both Sexes	65.0	47.0	30.7	18.0	15.4	15.4	15.4	15.4	15.4	15.4	15.4
E(0) - Males	65.36	67.19	69.03	70.84	72.06	72.06	72.06	72.06	72.06	72.06	72.06
E(0) - Females	68.43	70.71	73.00	75.08	76.51	76.51	76.51	76.51	76.51	76.51	76.51
E(0) - Both Sexes	66.90	68.95	71.02	72.96	74.28	74.28	74.28	74.28	74.28	74.28	74.28

Year	2100	2110	2120	2130	2140	2150	2160	2170	2180	2190	2200
Birth Rate ‰	13.7	13.5	13.4	13.3	13.2	13.1	13.0	12.9	12.9	12.8	12.8
Death Rate ‰	13.1	13.4	13.6	13.8	14.0	14.1	14.2	14.3	14.3	14.4	14.5
Growth Rate %	0.06	0.01	-0.02	-0.05	-0.08	-0.10	-0.12	-0.14	-0.15	-0.16	-0.17
Total Fertility Rate	2.090	2.076	2.064	2.053	2.045	2.037	2.031	2.025	2.020	2.016	2.012
GRR	1.018	1.011	1.005	1.000	0.996	0.992	0.989	0.986	0.983	0.981	0.981
NRR	1.0	1.0	1.0	1.0	1.0	1.0	1.0	1.0	1.0	1.0	1.0
IMR - Males	18.2	18.2	18.2	18.2	18.2	18.2	18.2	18.2	18.2	18.2	18.2
IMR - Females	12.6	12.6	12.6	12.6	12.6	12.6	12.6	12.6	12.6	12.6	12.6
IMR - Both Sexes	15.4	15.4	15.4	15.4	15.4	15.4	15.4	15.4	15.4	15.4	15.4
E(0) - Males	72.06	72.06	72.06	72.06	72.06	72.06	72.06	72.06	72.06	72.06	72.06
E(0) - Females	76.51	76.51	76.51	76.51	76.51	76.51	76.51	76.51	76.51	76.51	76.51
E(0) - Both Sexes	74.28	74.28	74.28	74.28	74.28	74.28	74.28	74.28	74.28	74.28	74.28

Graph 1

Projected Total Population
World Population Projection No. 2080.B.L
Decline Below Replacement Fertility Level
Mortality Level: Low

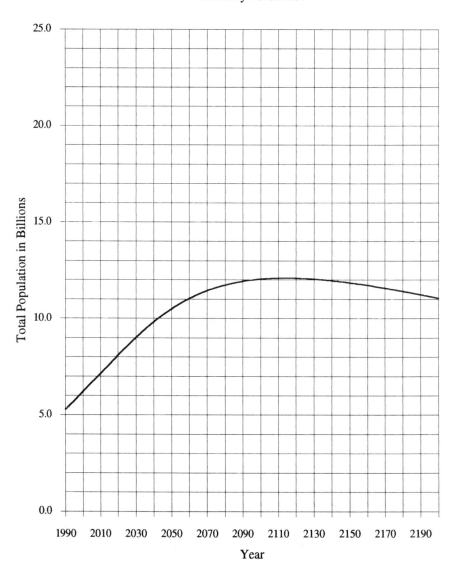

Graph 2

Components of Population Change
World Population Projection No. 2080.B.L
Decline Below Replacement Fertility Level
Mortality Level: Low

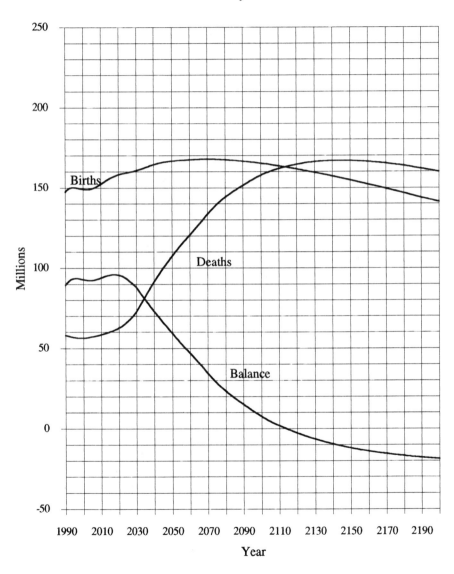

Graph 3

Age Structure of World Population 1990, 2050 and 2100

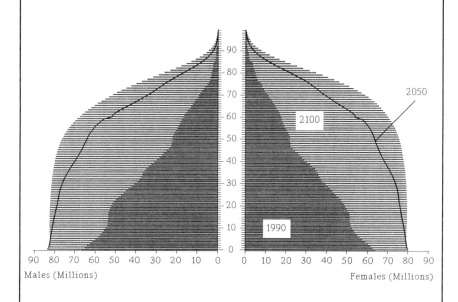

Males (Millions) Females (Millions)

Population Projection No. 2080.B.L.

Decline below replacement fertility level
by the year: 2080
Form of fertility decline: Hyperbolic
Mortality level: Low

Total population: 1990 5 275 Million
2050 10 484 Million
2100 12 033 Million